Women, Art, Freedom: Artists and Street Politics in Iran

PAMELA KARIMI

WOMEN ART FREEDOM

ARTISTS AND STREET POLITICS IN IRAN

LEUVEN UNIVERSITY PRESS

This book will be made open access within three years of publication thanks to Path to Open, a program developed in partnership between JSTOR, the American Council of Learned Societies (ACLS), University of Michigan Press, and The University of North Carolina Press to bring about equitable access and impact for the entire scholarly community, including authors, researchers, libraries, and university presses around the world. Learn more at https://about.jstor.org/path-to-open/

The publication of this book was made possible through the generous support of the Persian Heritage Foundation.

Minderbroedersstraat 4, B-3000 Leuven / Louvain (Belgium)

ISBN 978 94 6270 418 3
eISBN 978 94 6166 563 8 (ePDF)
eISBN 978 94 6166 587 4 (ePUB)
https://doi.org/10.11116/9789461665638
D/2024/1869/31
NUR: 652, 640

Design and typesetting: Stéphane de Schrevel
Cover design: Daniel Benneworth-Gray
Cover images: Mohammad Parvizi, Mahsa Masoudi, Pantea Mehdinia, et al., *Call me by My Name* (mixed media installation), December 2023 – April 2024. Risheh 29 Gallery, Tehran, Iran. Courtesy of Mohammad Parvizi and the Deyhim Foundation. Photograph by Vida Mousavian.

To Iranian artists:

Resolute. Resilient. Relentless

Contents

Introduction

The Woman, Life, Freedom quasi revolution stands apart from any other uprising or political movement in the history of Iran, distinguished not only by its feminist perspective and the remarkable courage of the youth but also by the unprecedented volume of visual imagery and art it has produced.[1] The desire to document some of the most striking artistic manifestations of the uprising was the driving force behind my decision to write this book, but to fully understand the significance of the movement's art, it is essential to recognize the event that set it in motion—the tragic death of Jina Mahsa Amini, a twenty-two-year-old Iranian Kurdish woman, on September 16, 2022, in a hospital in Tehran.[2] Amini had been arrested by the Guidance Patrol, Iran's "morality police," for the alleged crime of not wearing the hijab according to government standards. While the authorities claimed that she suffered a heart attack and fell into a coma at a police station, eyewitnesses, including fellow detainees, reported that she was severely beaten and died as a result of police brutality.[3] Her death sparked widespread protests across Iran and later globally, united around the rallying cry of "Woman, Life, Freedom." The phrase comes from the Kurdish "Jin, Jiyan, Azadi," and is rooted in decades of activism by transregional Kurdish feminist groups associated with the Kurdistan Workers' Party (PKK).[4] Linking womanhood (*jin*) with *jiyan*, representing the right to life, and *azadi*, symbolizing the quest for freedom, the movement challenges traditional gender roles and misogyny, fighting the idea that "woman is weak; extremely incapacitated and dangerous," as Abdullah Öcalan, a founding member of the PKK, put it in a speech in 1988.[5] While there is no direct political connection between the uprising in

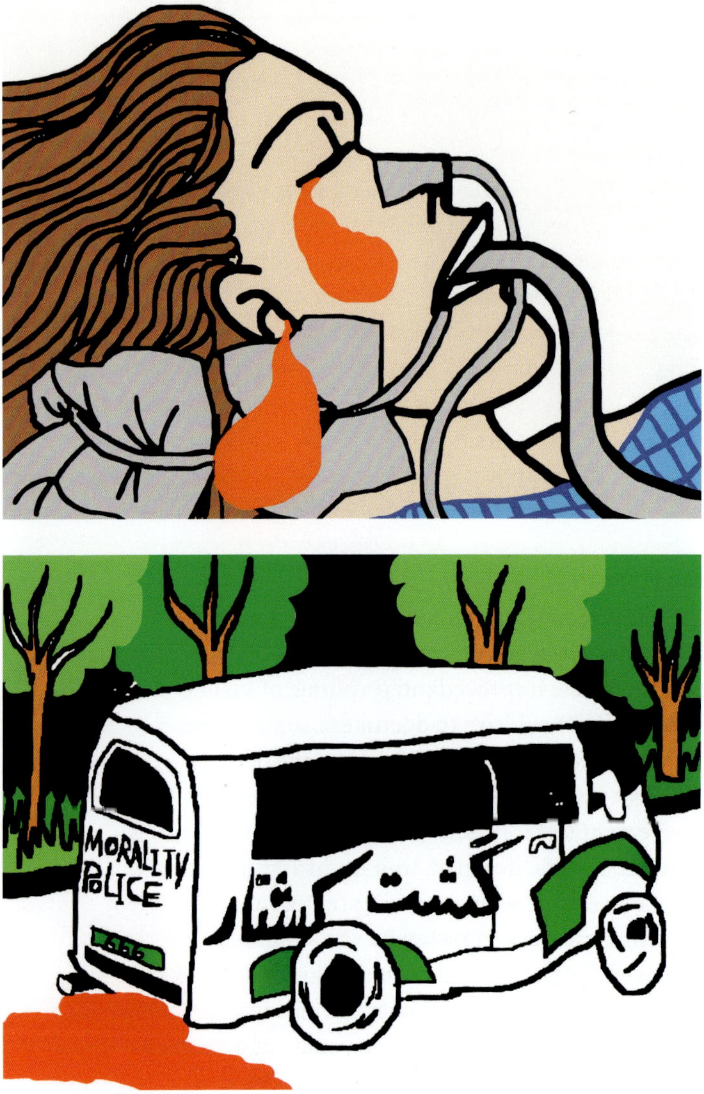

FIG. 1 Niknaz Khlouzadeh, two consecutive snapshots from *The Epic of Mahasa*, 2022. Courtesy of the artist.

Iran and these movements, Amini's Kurdish background makes the slogan an apt representation of the struggle in Iran.

The world's first encounter with Amini was a shocking photograph, taken by the journalist Niloofar Hamedi, that showed her comatose and hooked up to a ventilator—her punishment for showing some hair through a loosely worn scarf. The image would be seen by millions as they browsed through news sites and social media feeds.

A week after the image's publication, Hamedi was sent to prison. Despite this clear warning shot from the government, artists began reproducing the image in stylized reiterations, at times coupling the portrait of Amini with mourning songs or counterrevolutionary music. One example is *The Epic of Mahsa* by Brussels-based artist Niknaz Khalouzadeh (b. 1997), who honed her skills in animation during her high school years in Iran before moving to Belgium to study painting. Released nine days after Amini's death, Khalouzadeh's video quickly went viral, amassing over three million views overnight and emerging as one of the most impactful and striking early artistic pieces related to Amini's death. Curiously, Khalouzadeh crafted this video entirely on her iPhone, utilizing basic illustration and video-making apps, Folioscope and InShot. Each element was meticulously hand-drawn using these applications, yet the entire project was completed in just three days. A punchy musical piece from Khuzestan adds to the overall impact of the work. The video begins by displaying Amini's name on the screen, swiftly transitioning to an artistic representation of the morality police van: instead of the usual "Gasht-e Ershad" (Guidance Patrol), the van is labeled "Death Patrol," a rhyming play on words substituting *koshtar* ("killing" in Persian) for *ershad*. Subsequent scenes artfully cycle through various striking images—a stylized portrait of Amini on her deathbed, a tulip flower (representing martyrdom in Iran), a trembling iPhone displaying Amini's image—followed by a powerful visual of young women casting their headscarves into a fire. The focus then shifts to the phrase "Woman, Life, Freedom," presented in both Persian and English. The video concludes with a poignant message: "Mahsa Amini, your name become[s] the code [word]." FIG. 1.

In the days after Amini's murder, unrest erupted all over Iran, particularly in the Kurdish region where she came from. Many of the protests were remarkable, bordering on performance: unveiled women confronted state authorities FIG. 2, young girls danced and twirled headscarves, activists set fire to government billboards, residents joined in nighttime chants from apartment windows, college students dismantled dividers between gender-segregated dining areas. Taking action involved considerable personal risk. If not killed by beatings, bullets, or the "noncombat" paintballs that can be fatal when discharged at close range, protesters could be captured and, once identified, faced suspension from official positions, imprisonment, and even execution.

More than any texts or reasoned arguments, it was the universal language of art that potently conveyed the essence of this unfolding uprising. Alongside the portraits and works inspired by the victims and the street protests that verged on performance art,

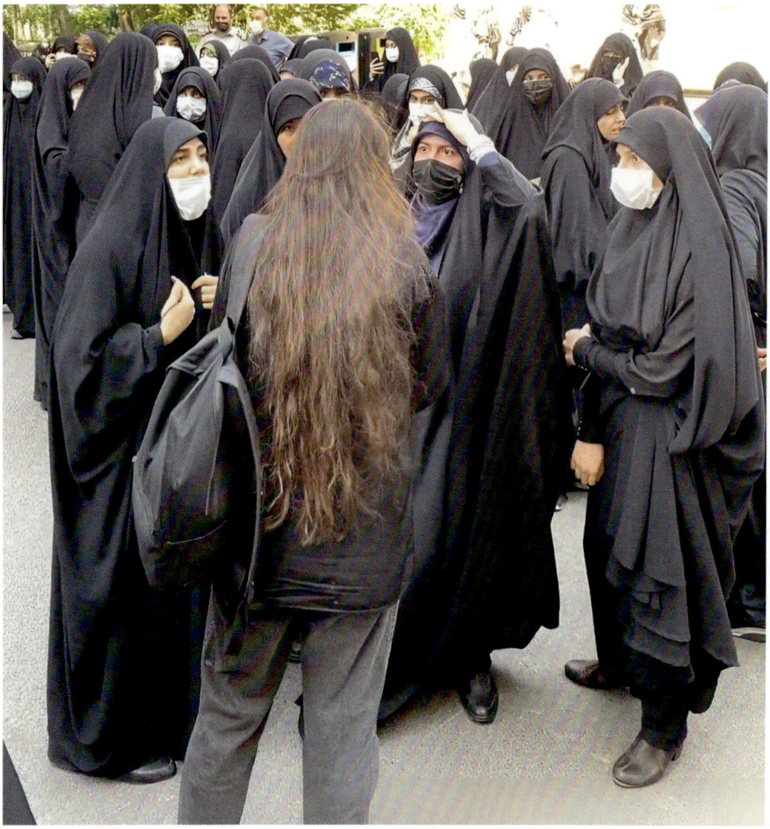

FIG. 2 A student's encounter with authorities at Al-Zahra University captured on September 21, 2022. Photograph courtesy of Instagram/@1500tasvir.

performative acts conducted in homes were widely shared across social media platforms. Live streamed on smartphones, the act of women from diverse cultures chopping their hair in solidarity with Iranian women gained traction, drawing in celebrities like Juliette Binoche and Marion Cotillard. A show of defiance against compulsory veiling in Iran, the act of hair-cutting harks back to a Persian tradition of women trimming their locks in mourning. And the symbolic performance not only permeated digital screens but made its presence felt in unexpected physical locations. In Heidelberg in October 2023, not long after completing the initial draft of this book, I came across a lamppost bearing a Woman, Life, Freedom sticker that showed a woman defiantly holding aloft the hair she had just shorn off, against the backdrop of an orange sun, perhaps intended to denote hope. This unexpected discovery reminded me of the enduring power and emotional resonance of visual arts in the narrative of the uprising. Long after the sparks of the quasi revolution have cooled, these visuals persist—on street furniture and café corners, on university information boards and anonymous city streets around the world—as silent yet compelling testaments to the enduring power of art and imagery over words and discourse FIG. 3.

While the art of the Woman, Life, Freedom movement is mainly associated with images shared globally, this book focuses on the specific contributions of professional artists in Iran, providing a distinct perspective on the artistic response to events before, during, and after the uprising. Its primary concern is not to analyze artworks that were widely distributed on social media—a task already undertaken and likely to be explored further by historians of media and social media—but rather to highlight the deep-rooted, often unseen artistic programming and practices that were inspired by, or significantly influenced, the movement on the ground in Iran. What emerges are the largely untold narratives of professional artists who actively contributed to the uprising's performative and visual lexicon, not in the privacy and safety of their studios, but in public places. Through interviews with artists, curators, students, and art professors involved in the quasi revolution, I examine the

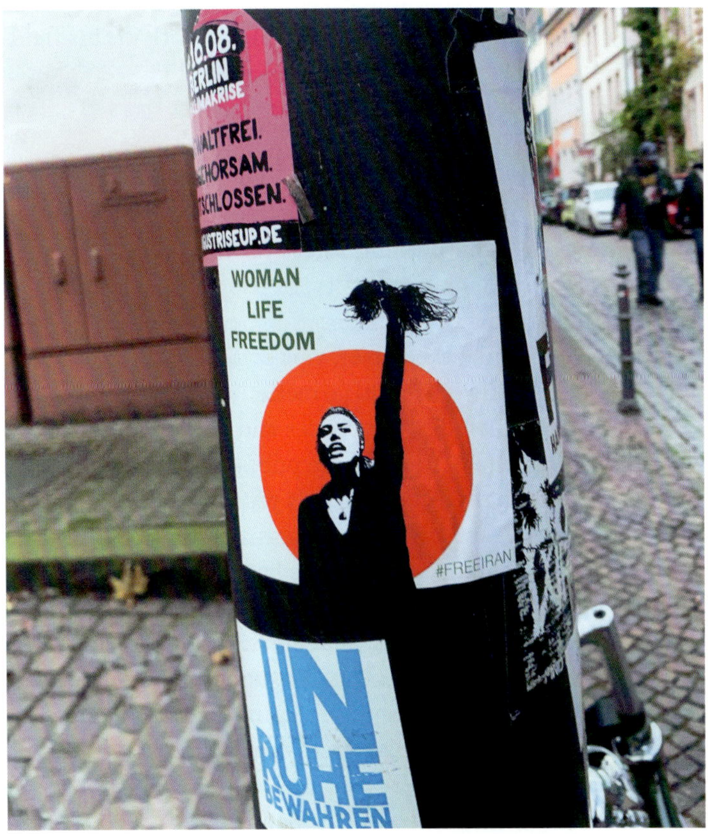

FIG. 3 Sticker reading "Woman, Life, Freedom" spotted in the historic district of Heidelberg, Germany, October 2023. Photograph by the author.

transformative power of artistic vision in shaping the protests that surged through the streets of Iranian cities. This shift of focus—from the interpretation of the art of the uprising to the personal stories of the artists themselves—casts light on how artistic creativity can inform the various strains of civil disobedience that are the essential elements of political action. Above all, by examining the role of rigorous preparation in professions like sculpting, installing, designing, performing, poetry jamming, painting, and "film-dancing," I reveal in the book how these artistic techniques can articulate a unique kind of street occupation, a demonstration of resistance, that stands apart from other random and organized acts of protest by nonartists.

While unique in its approach, this book aligns with the broader goal of documenting activist art practices associated with the Woman, Life, Freedom uprising, thereby adding to the expanding corpus of work in this field. Numerous initiatives, both inside and outside Iran, have focused on cataloging the images and artworks inspired by the movement. In what follows, I will provide an overview of these existing documentation efforts and then set out a detailed exposition of my own approach and methodology, showing how my perspective and techniques of documentation both differ from and enhance the existing body of work in this field.

THE MANY WAYS OF DOCUMENTING AN UPRISING

The events of the Woman, Life, Freedom uprising were recorded with unprecedented intensity, as people from all walks of life filmed critical moments of confrontation between state authorities and protesters. From the outset, this evidence of the regime's mistreatment of its citizens was meticulously documented by various collectives, including art circles and academic institutions both inside and outside Iran. Made public on websites, social media, or in printed journals and books, this process of documentation was at the same time an act of resistance and a revolutionary gesture grounded in the belief that past uprisings had not been systematically documented, leaving gaps in the collective memory of those events.

In the previous political uprisings of 2009, 2017, 2019, and 2021, ordinary individuals took it upon themselves to record their own experiences rather than relying on professionals or outsiders. As the authorities attempted to control the narrative by blocking or interrupting satellite broadcasts, Iranians turned to platforms like X (formerly Twitter), Facebook, and YouTube to share images and videos, effectively giving shape to Iran's citizen journalism. This democratization of documentation led to a massive influx of footage accessible in almost real time, but while these videos were widely disseminated and shared, many proved to be impermanent records: YouTube videos can be deleted; photos shared on social media platforms may vanish. Social media accounts filled with protest images may be voluntarily closed by their owners, for fear of being identified by the regime, or else forcefully shut down by state authorities. Many records of the 2009 Green Movement have disappeared from the vast internet landscape. They are kept alive in some form, however, by the work of the historians, journalists, and anthropologists who have reflected on those events. A prime example is Negar Mottahedeh's book *Hashtag Solidarity and the Transformation of Online Life*, which examines materials and ideas that appeared on ephemeral social media platforms. Specifically, she explores how social media posts and blogs replaced traditional reporting by major news outlets like CNN, which were felt to have inadequately covered the protests against the election results—a sentiment that became known by the hashtag #CNNfail alongside #iranelection, according to Mottahedeh.[6] Though not always extensively captured in visual documentation, the crucial concepts of the uprising are preserved—saved from complete erasure—through textual explanations and historical analysis by scholars like Mottahedeh. But rather than being merely of scholarly interest, these concepts are invaluable for their role in inspiring the creative methods of protest that hold particular significance for artist researchers. In this book, I will explore these research-oriented facets in depth when they are pertinent to a specific art project.

Like Mottahedeh's approach, my work is predominantly text-based and scholarly in nature, yet it also embraces the approach to documenting the art of the uprising, capturing artworks not yet highlighted by other initiatives that have emerged since the movement's inception. The contents of these initiatives vary widely: some are developed with well-defined critical objectives and descriptions, while others primarily serve as repositories for images. Since it is not feasible to provide a comprehensive survey of all these endeavors, many of which are still ongoing, I will provide instead a selective overview of these undertakings.

Founded in 2013, Kaarnamaa (a portmanteau derived from the fusion of the words for "work" and "presentation") brands itself as a thinktank with the mission of fostering discussions around the visual arts and culture of Iran. With a core team of independent artists, writers, and editors based in Tehran, London, and New York, it operates primarily in Persian, in both spoken and written forms, through online platforms such as Google Meet, YouTube, and Instagram. Kaarnamaa's initiatives are organized into three interrelated sections: a journal, *Karnameh* (meaning "transcript"); an oral history archive, featuring stories of prominent art practitioners in Iran in their own words; and educational courses and public information sessions. Most of Kaarnamaa's revenue comes from its online classes. It also thrives on collaboration with various research, educational, and artistic organizations, among them the Charsou Art and Cultural Institute, the Iran Heritage Foundation, the Tandem Institute, Rayan School, and the Tanbafi Group.

Karnameh: Journal of Art Criticism and History, established in 2014, lies at the heart of Kaarnamaa's activities, offering a platform for analytical, research-oriented, and critical articles, mainly translated content from English resources. In the fall of 2022, the journal shifted focus, devoting several special issues to the Woman, Life, Freedom uprising in Iran.[7] It pledged to be "a witness to history [...] for the sake of those who have witnessed both terrifying and hopeful chapters of Iran's history and have experienced them firsthand." As artists, the editorial team wrote, it was "their duty not only to echo and comprehend the movement but also to immortalize it"—to "amplify the movement's voice."[8] Conventionally, every issue of the journal features a section called "Faramatn" ("beyond the text") featuring images and artworks. In the fall issue, this section shaped the entirety of the publication, presenting significant images from key moments of the uprising collected by the editorial team, who are primarily from the generation of Iranians born in the 1980s (known as *daheh shastiha*). Working around the clock, the editors undertook this task themselves because they felt that local and international news media platforms were not capable of doing it. For them, images taken directly from social media accounts or MP4 files or pictures sent from smartphones played "the same role offered by the professional images taken by highly acclaimed photographers and photojournalists during the 1979 revolution, such as Abbas, Kaveh Golshan, and Maryam Zandi."[9] At the dawn of the Woman, Life, Freedom movement in fall 2022, Faramatn formed "a record of this visual experience, seemingly endless, of the revolution that Iranians have lived through with their flesh and blood and felt in the marrow of their bones." What mattered was not the refinement of the images but their power to move: "while a low-quality image of a teenager falling amidst incomprehensible voices and the terrified presence of people played on our screens, our real bodies perspired, and our hands froze, becoming numb."[10]

The accompanying notes indicate how the editorial team understands this collection, which is categorized into three sets of images: "Woman," defined as the main victim of the last four decades and the movement's greatest hero; "Life," which ironically tells a gripping narrative of death; and, finally, the epicenter of the movement, "Freedom," with images and ideas that underscore a rejection of the system of oppression and censorship—an openness to crossing boundaries and unveiling hair that dances loose in the wind. The volume also features statements by activist artists. Seeing the Woman, Life, Freedom uprising as a form of collaborative effort, the editorial team takes pride in this spirit of collectivity, which is reflected not just in the diversity of resources in the journal but also in the design of the pages, with their layering of images.

Images of the uprising were disseminated in such numbers and at such speed that it created an almost simultaneous, overlapping visual experience. Constantly changing, images came and went, were forgotten, then resurfaced—at times they did not seem to cohere at all, as the data moved on the swiftly evolving social media feeds.[11] This continuous cycle of the appearance and disappearance of imagery provoked recurring meditations on the significance of the unfolding events while instigating an embodied transmission that registered activism—and the violence meted out in response to it—at the level of sensation.[12] According to philosopher Jacques Rancière, images become "sensible" (or *feelable*) when they are consumed in an engaged way, rather than passively perceived.[13] In the absence of a plethora of revolutionary dialogues propagated through organized political factions, revolutionary goals manifested as constantly circulating images and feelings.

Similarly, the use of the artistic technique of montage on the pages of *Karnameh* indicates a desire to capture the spirit of the revolt on the ground, skillfully weaving together images that at first glance may seem unconnected. For example, a series of striking images of artists defying authority is presented as a collage on a wall: one group is shown without veils in public spaces, another performs revolutionary songs and music at art college campuses, while others reenact the agony of those who have been tortured and killed. Connecting them all is graffiti declaring "Bodies are signs and meanings." The diverse and dynamic facets of the movement are effectively portrayed on a single page FIG. 4.

Art, Culture, Action is another collective that coalesced at the start of the Woman, Life, Freedom uprising, bringing together prominent Iranian artists, writers, and art professionals in and outside Iran.[14] The group campaigns for the inalienable right of artists and writers to freely express themselves using various means, publishing statements to raise awareness, calls for collective action, collecting and archiving censored documents and works, supporting

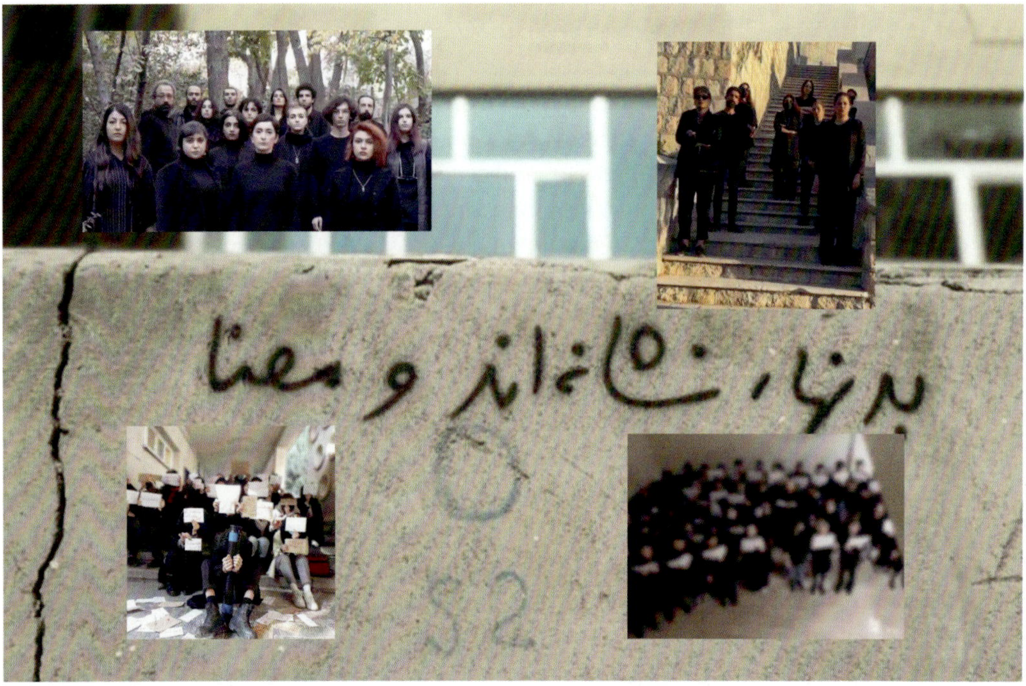

FIG. 4 Editorial feature from Kaarnamaa. A page excerpted from *Karnameh: Journal of Art Criticism and History*, vol. 6, no. 3 (Fall 2022). Courtesy of Kaarnamaa.

victims of censorship, and organizing discussions about the challenges facing the artistic community.[15] Apart from its activist endeavors, often undertaken in collaboration with projects such as Pen America's Artists at Risk Connection, the collective generates manifestos and texts of various kinds that have surfaced since the onset of the uprising.

Notebooks before the Fall (*Daftarha-ye Pisha Soghoot* in Persian, *Les Cahiers d'avant la Chute* in French) is a special printed supplement to the trilingual *Journal of Thought and Literature* from Naakojaa Press in Paris, which is known for its commitment to publishing Persian literature free from censorship or constraints. The intention of the supplements, as the editorial team elaborates, is

> to record history. To tell the stories of women and men who no longer conform to [...] oppression [...] with fists clenched in anger, they stand firm and fight against tyranny without necessarily knowing the outcome of their path. But haven't we always said that it is the journey that matters, not the destination?
> The necessity of the *Notebooks before the Fall* became clear to us when no print magazine, over these years, had followed the

> uprisings of the people of Iran in '99, '09, '17, '19, and '21. [...] The most important communication tools of the 2022 revolution are social networks and foreign televisions, none of which leave [...] the possibility for a discerning thought that can sometimes differ from the conventional narrative of the movement. Publishing the *Notebooks before the Fall* is a clear necessity for us on the path to freedom.[16]

The unfolding uprising was meticulously documented through *Notebooks*'s daily log. On Wednesday, September 28, 2022, for example, we read: "A woman, identified as Donya Raad, shared a photo of herself and a friend having breakfast at a traditional café, notably without wearing hijabs. Following this, she was detained by the police. The incident dominated conversations throughout the day, drawing widespread attention and concern." On October 16, the focus is on how "the defiant act of Elnaz Rekabi, the celebrated Iranian rock climber, who competed without her hijab during the Asian Championships, has become the talk of the nation, earning her waves of admiration and support." The narrative for November 22 captures a significant declaration: "The House of Cinema made a public statement asserting that any further summoning and detention of its members would result in a strike and a cessation of all collaboration with state television. In a related development, filmmaker Sahar Mosayebi openly removed her scarf, signaling solidarity and defiance."[17]

In addition to the daily logs, the *Notebooks* brim with critiques on topics ranging from the dynamics of the uprising to the intersections of feminism and Islam, and from the ideals of freedom and democracy to personal memoirs and vignettes crafted by artists. The journal features the satirical art of celebrated cartoonists such as Mana Nayestani and provides vivid imagery of the protests, complete with detailed captions, though the photographs themselves are often unattributed (for fear of repercussions). Covers depict important fallen figures or moments in the movement, mostly animated by Hassan Nozadian, who began his journey of illustration activism with a portrait of Sepideh Rashnu, a published poet, a graphic designer, and a graduate student in painting at Al-Zahra University in Tehran—who was detained in July 2022 for not wearing her headscarf in the state-approved manner.[18] Rashnu's resistance to the hijab escalated into a physical altercation on a public bus with a conservative woman, who was advocating for Iran's compulsory hijab law.[19] This incident was recorded on a smartphone and subsequently gained widespread attention on social media. In retaliation, the

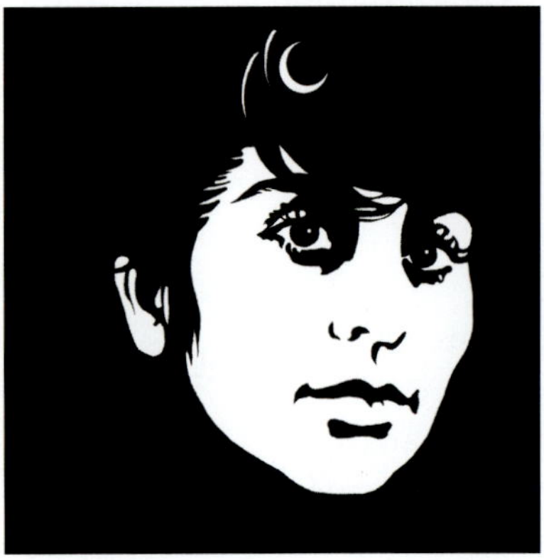

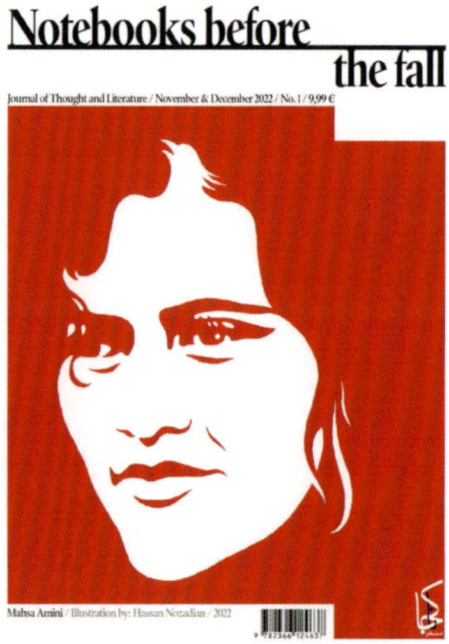

FIG. 5 (L) Hassan Nozadian, *Portrait of Sepideh Rashnu*, 2022. Courtesy of the artist.
FIG. 6 (R) Hassan Nozadian, *Portrait of Jina Mahsa Amini* featured in the first issue of *Notebooks before the Fall*, a special supplement to *The Journal of Thought and Literature*, published by Naakojaa Press, 2022. Courtesy of the artist.

regime forced her to confess her "mistake" on television—a ritual of humiliation that ignited a wave of widespread indignation. Initially released on bail, Rashnu later received a suspended sentence.[20] Nozadian had illustrated his portrait of Rashnu, shrouded in darkness and mystery, well before the unconscious Amini drew increased attention to the brutal enforcement of Iran's religious dress code FIG. 5. Nozadian's portrait of Amini—finished at the moment her death was announced—features an elongated forehead with a phoenix at the hairline, symbolizing her rebirth FIG. 6. This was the image chosen for the cover of the first issue of the *Notebooks before the Fall*. Taken together, the series of supplements reflects an unwavering commitment to bearing witness to the events of the Woman, Life, Freedom uprising and to documenting its intellectual underpinnings, driven by a sense of protest and the firm belief that this information could be valuable to others, now or in the future.[21]

Another collaborative effort in this area is Woman, Life, Freedom: An Archive of Defiance, a digital platform curated by Shahrzad Mojab and Afsaneh Hojabri under the auspices of the University of Toronto.[22] While still evolving, the archive already encompasses an impressive array of images, from drawings and sketches to recordings of performances, dance sequences, and pivotal moments of protest. The impetus behind its creation is the desire to preserve a collective history and memory: "We did not want to just provide links," Mojab and Hojabri write, "We wanted to have the originals of the artworks so that history would remember them."[23]

Social media platforms abound, with groups such as @womanlifefreedom.art, @womanlifefreedomNYC, @woman.revolution, @blackfishvoice1, @1500Tasvir, @unche.studio, @iranianwomenofgraphicdesign, @zanzendegiazadi.story, @iranprisonatlas, @modakheleh, @Iranianpopart, and @khiabantribune, to name a few. Predominantly on Instagram, these channels capture creative responses to the uprising in Iran and among the broader Iranian diaspora. While some maintain a strict focus on art, others combine art with protest imagery to create a potent visual dialogue. Certain groups explore how art might be actively deployed to bring about social change. Modakheleh ("intervention"), for example, describes itself on Telegram as:

> a collective research project about art; here, we intend to think about art together within a broader perspective, while also understanding the possibilities and limitations that our current situation has imposed on us, and to devise strategies for changing these circumstances. The aim of this project is to reconsider the meaning of art and the role it can play in society. We live in a time where numerous crises threaten our lives. We feel a profound dissatisfaction with various aspects of our lives; from work and career, relationships, the homes we live in, to the environment, our cities, and government. Art provides a means through which we can discuss our dissatisfactions and hopes and creatively find solutions to face these crises. We are not here to discuss the history of world art. We want to think together about art and the opportunities it presents for social change, specifically in Iran, about what shapes our understanding of social art and how this understanding impacts [...] the current situation.[24]

Another presence on Telegram, the mysterious Manjanigh ("catapult") group, circulates street art and posters originating from various Iranian cities. Telegram also paves the way for podcast platforms that veer away from visuals, zeroing in on voices intertwined with the uprising. The Bimarz ("without borders") podcasts on Telegram, for example, examine the nuances of gender disparities and street life in Iran as recounted by anonymous citizens. They describe harrowing encounters with the morality police and reveal the internal family dynamics that influence women's experiences in public spaces. For instance, daughters in conservative families may be harshly punished for shedding the traditional chador, but more liberal families will also impose restrictions, driven by the fear that the woman might attract the attention of the morality police and—in their eyes—bring dishonor to the household. These stories illuminate the complex ways the boundaries between the public and private spheres are navigated and policed by various actors, offering a unique lens through which to examine the politics that govern public life in Iran. Through these personal accounts, we see how societal and familial pressures, often reinforced by the country's conservative laws, increasingly leave women vulnerable and sidelined.[25]

There has also been an upsurge of scholarly articles and books documenting aspects of the uprising. Notably, the anthology compiled by Malu Halasa, *Woman Life Freedom: Voices and Art from the Women's Protests in Iran*, showcases a collection of essays, art, and photography from renowned and emerging Iranian diaspora artists, as well as anonymous voices in Iran. A text by the cartoonist Mana Neyestani highlights the crucial role of art as a lifeline in suffocating political climates, while a photo essay by Shiva Khademi illustrates the defiant fashion statements of young Iranian women, a precursor to the larger shifts happening on the streets of Tehran. Also featured is the work of the anonymous Iran-based collective Khiaban Tribune, which, since its inception in 2017, has been posting political graffiti seen on the streets of Iran on its Instagram and Twitter/X platforms. The group identifies itself as a "democratic, anti-capitalist campaign" made up of "socialist youth primarily engaged in defending the rights of political prisoners, workers, immigrants, [ethnic and] religious minorities, women, and the LGBTQ+ community."[26] The campaign "primarily centered on the rebellious essence of graffiti in its true setting—the street—over its digital portrayal."[27] However, as the initiative progressed, Khiaban Tribune recognized the significance of digitally documenting street graffiti. This archival effort is vital for giving voice to the suppressed narratives that unfold over time. It also helps preserve this "underground history" for future generations.[28] In documenting the graffiti, the group's posts have been pivotal in giving it an afterlife following its inevitable erasure by the authorities.[29]

Archiving the collective memory is a central theme across various platforms discussed above. While some utilize websites, others prefer the medium of Instagram. Though these platforms might be in competition, they all speak of a remarkable increase in collecting and archiving during and after the Woman, Life, Freedom uprising. Is this perhaps a therapeutic process? Or a form of political activism or resistance? Might Iranians be reacting to years of unspoken oppression, police brutality, and state harassment? While the motivations might be varied or hard to pin down, the undeniable result is a powerful and unprecedented movement toward documentation and preservation.

While the study throughout this book is thematically underpinned by visuals from protests and the voices of the masses, the spotlight remains firmly on the narratives of artists who interact with the streets and public spaces of Iran. Transcending mere art analysis, the book probes deeper into the indispensable role played by artists in the uprising, clarifying the general nature and the essence of their political engagement. As I will show, art inside Iran serves as a vibrant canvas, continually evolving and resonating with both its creators and its audiences. Through its depiction in the media, and its ripple effect on later works, every piece of art not only offers insights into the country's society and politics but also contributes to the continual reshaping of the cultural landscape of Iran.

POLITICAL ART, ACTIVIST ART, AND REVOLUTIONARY ART

Iran remains a politically volatile country, with the potential for revolt always simmering below the surface. While artists do not have the same power to shape public policy as political agents, they have been among the most active voices calling for fundamental change. The terms "political," "activist," and "revolutionary," as applied to art, may seem to generate similar results, but I want to differentiate them here. In doing so, I am inspired by art historian Lucy Lippard's distinction between the terms "political" and "activist" in Western, and particularly American, art. Lippard associates political art with an occasional or sporadic engagement with social issues, usually reflected through ironic critique. By contrast, activist art, which only fully crystallized as a coherent set of practices in the 1960s, is a more instrumental hybrid cultural expression, with one foot firmly planted in the revolutionary practices of the Situationists and the other in the spirit of "the street." While political art may approach social issues with a degree of detachment and irony, activist art embodies the politics of participation and is driven by a desire for direct engagement and tangible change. Understanding these distinctions helps clarify the diverse ways art can intersect with social and political landscapes.[30]

While the terms of political and activist art can be applied to Iran, the Iranian context entails additional categories of oppositional art. In previous writings, I have proposed categorizations that expand beyond Lippard's binary framework. Terms such as "unofficial art" (*honar-e gheyr-e rasmi*), "art that challenges" (*honar-e konesh gara*), and "protest art" (*honar-e e'terazi*) are frequently used by Iranian artists, each representing gradations of political or activist engagement—from political to subtly political, from purely activist to somewhat activist, depending on the specific context and circumstances in which these art forms are created.

Iran also introduces a third distinct dimension to the Lippard dynamic: revolutionary art. Here, revolution is not an abstract concept: the numerous mass uprisings that have followed in the wake of the Iranian Revolution of 1979 have been revolutionary acts, even if they have had limited success in achieving significant transformations. In the context of Iran, revolutionary art transcends mere engagement with the population in public spaces. It entails extraordinary acts of sacrifice, the threat of physical harm, the loss of employment, the risk of imprisonment—even execution.

The events that unfolded during the Woman, Life, Freedom uprising and its aftermath represented a convergence of all the approaches outlined above. The more cautious art experts adhered to the conventional approach of opposition, essentially maintaining the status quo of political discourse. Others adopted a more direct stance, actively participating in street protests, issuing public statements, and openly supporting victims of police brutality during the peaceful demonstrations. But a distinct group of individuals went further, presenting their artworks with an audacity seldom seen in antiestablishment art after the 1979 revolution. Many would pay a severe price for expressing their criticism in such a bold and vivid manner.

During the height of the uprising, many galleries chose not to display art. Tehran's O Gallery was initially targeted—its door splashed with red paint—for opening a prescheduled exhibition FIG. 7.[31] However, it went on to embrace a new direction, with an exhibition of collaborative art that effectively transformed the gallery into a vivid reflection of the streetscape itself.[32] This collaborative journey began on January 5, 2023, when five artists met gallery director Orkideh Darroudi to discuss their roles and artistic perspectives and the

FIG. 7 The entrance of O Gallery defaced with a blood-red color in November 2022. Courtesy of Mojtaba Amini.

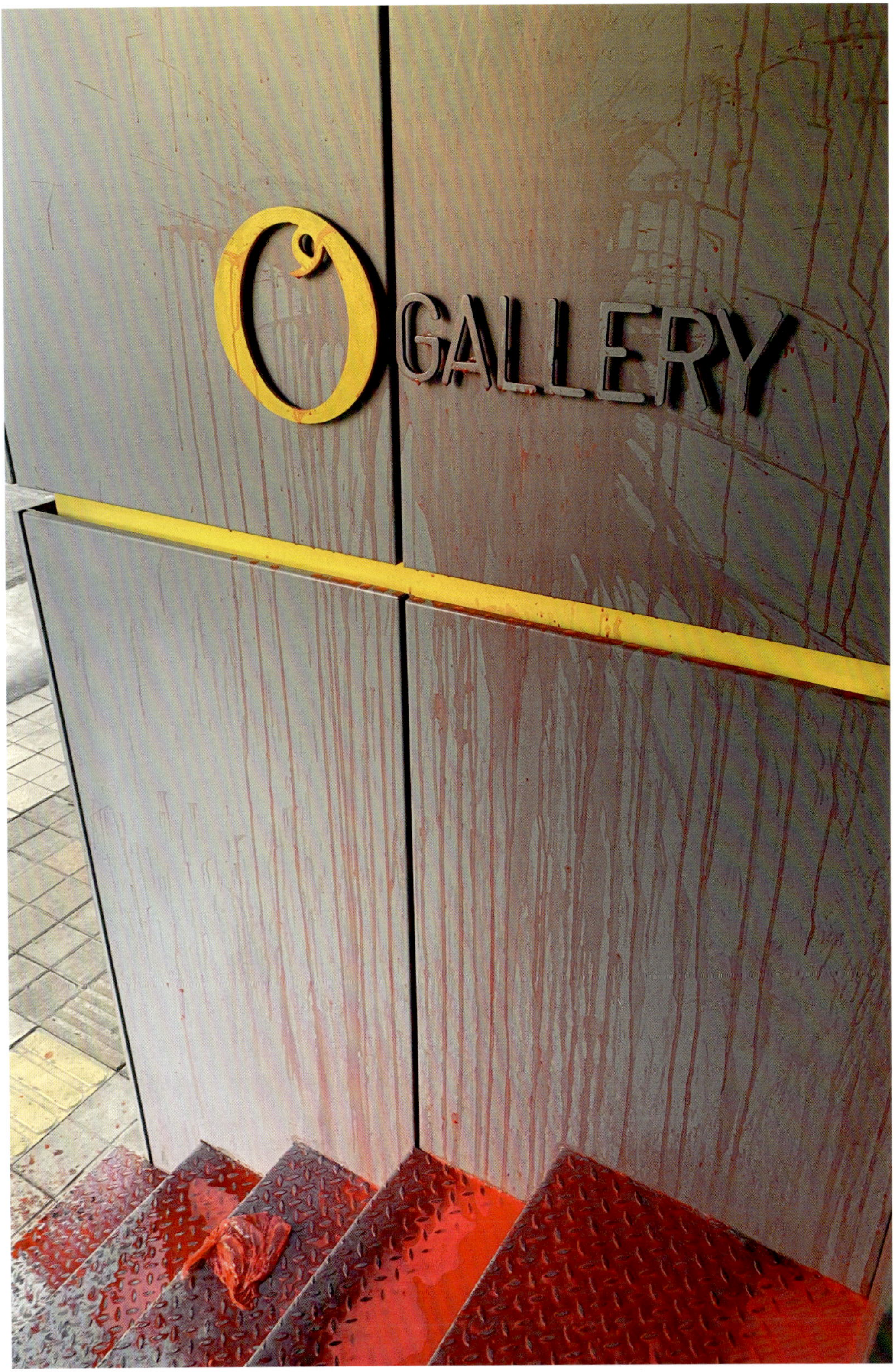
GALLERY

intended audience. By January 10, more artists had joined the group. From January 24, the team held numerous brainstorming sessions, culminating in the decision to name their collective endeavor *Joint* (*mafsal* in Persian) on February 13.

The exhibition, which opened soon after, on February 24, included diverse projects, some of them politically charged. One notable feature was the artists' reinterpretation of parts of a painting by the highly political New York–based Iranian artist Nicky (Nikzad Nodjoumi, b. 1942) depicting a besuited man with a seemingly distorted head fallen from his chair. This image was creatively reimagined in various forms, including small, unsettling drawings of limbless bodies and caricature-like versions.

However, the primary objective was not necessarily to create political art. As one prominent artist who participated in *Joint* noted, many projects were not directly related to protest themes.[33] Instead, the focus was on redefining the gallery's role during politically turbulent times, when art often faces scrutiny for either being too fanciful or too closely tied to capital. O Gallery's decision to transform the gallery into a public space, giving artists the freedom to explore and reinterpret ideas, was arguably one of the best possible outcomes during the peak of the political turmoil. In the subsequent period, the art exhibited in galleries has become more cautious, largely due to the stringent oversight from the regime.

If galleries cross the lines defined by the authorities, they risk losing their official status. However, art that is created independently—whether it is temporarily installed on the streets, displayed as graffiti, or presented on social media platforms under pseudonyms—typically exhibits a more daring character. The examples showcased in this book mostly fall into the latter category of independent works, but I will also feature the convoluted stories of artworks that have required the permission of the authorities to be displayed in official gallery platforms.

To grasp how Iranian artists navigate public spaces, it is essential to examine the material conditions shaping these appearances: the dynamics of street interaction and the politics and regulations dictating the structure and function of these spaces. In the following section, I will focus on street politics in Iran, a term that encompasses not only the implementation of regulations but also the ways individual citizens—including creative agents and professional artists—have consistently challenged these street rules through everyday acts of disobedience.

ARTISTS AND STREET POLITICS

Published in 2022, after a long wait for approval from the Ministry of Culture and Islamic Guidance (hereafter MCIG), *Khiaban-e Vali Asr: Revayathay-e Gheyr-e Dastani* (Vali Asr Street: Nonfiction Stories from Tehran) explores the political dynamics of one of the main routes in the capital through a collection of critical personal narratives.[34] Each contributing author focuses on a particular aspect of the street they perceive as flawed, bringing their unique perspective from diverse disciplines such as architecture and anthropology. One advocates for the urgent creation of "pause spaces" on Vali Asr, arguing that a sense of belonging is absent in areas that are designed merely as pathways leading from one destination to the next.[35] Another discusses the authorities' constant redevelopment and repurposing of spots that are perceived as welcoming or are popular with young people. These revitalizations are understood to have been carried out under the guise of renewal but in effect are a deliberate strategy to wipe out collective memories.[36] A third contributor confesses that, for her, the street no longer holds remnants of the past, making her feel more alienated here than she did when she was living abroad.[37] While all the authors adopt a subtle tone, they collectively hint at the intricate interplay between the street and politics—a realm where invisible powers dictate the public lives of citizens, stripping away their dreams and disregarding their desire to cling to certain places as anchors to better times.

But does the population passively accept the street politics imposed from above? In his 1997 book, *Street Politics: Poor People's Movement in Iran*, sociologist Asef Bayat describes the struggle of the disenfranchised to make their voices heard in the public domain during the revolutionary years of the late 1970s and early 1980s.[38] He argues that for marginalized groups who lack formal channels to express their grievances—such as squatters, the unemployed, street traders, beggars, prostitutes, and housewives—streets serve as vital platforms for communal expression. Bayat's analysis aligns with the concept, introduced in Michel de Certeau's *Practice of Everyday Life*, of a society with a dual structure, split between the dominant system, which relies on "strategies" to maintain control, and the users within that system, who employ "tactics" to disrupt existing structures. Strategies entail power calculations within defined temporal and spatial frameworks, while tactics typically lack a distinct space or comprehensive plan, instead relying on mobility and on exploiting openings in the surveillance of the dominant powers to gradually infiltrate the space of others.[39]

Along the same lines, Bayat explains that the "tactics" of marginalized social groups have typically evolved without access to institutional support or definitive leadership. In Iran, as he points out, urban areas are increasingly subject to state control, with the authorities expecting passive adherence to the rules and regulations defining their use. But when people actively choose instead to engage with public spaces—to use them for participatory purposes—they become critical sites for expressing dissent and furthering social and political discourse. This kind of active engagement underscores the political essence of such tactics, pushing back against the state's attempts to dictate the terms of use of public space.

But there are other kinds of street politics, beyond those discussed by Bayat. What if the aim of "tactical" interventions is not to claim a space and time to gain control or capital, as seen in the case of illegal street vendors? What if the "tactic" is employed solely as a theatrical action? What if intervening with the system is a repetitive act of performance, serving as an elegant and clever means to express grievances? What if the modes of engagement are not spontaneous but rather deliberately crafted by expert artist citizens? What if we view street activities not as organic, evolving phenomena but as calculated efforts to challenge and subvert the state rules governing street dynamics? What if we think of "tactics" as counterstrategies?

While Bayat and others have acknowledged the roles of banned sidewalk book retailers, underground video cassette vendors, street musicians, and amateur graffiti artists in their studies of street politics,[40] there has been markedly little discussion of the prominent artists who leverage the dynamic nature of city streets, transforming them from mere pathways into vibrant channels of expression. My aim here is to redress this imbalance and to shed light on the significant contribution of this segment of society to the broader landscape of street politics in Iran. In the absence of major initiatives to make the country's urban spaces safer and more appealing, artists have developed projects that alter the flow or ambiance of a street, even if only for brief periods, using artistic props or even their own bodies—an approach that distinguishes their work from more traditional, stationary forms of artistic expression. Artists who adopt a mobile approach are often identified by the specific objectives they aim to achieve. As these artworks traverse the city, engaging with key symbolic locations, they subtly confront and challenge existing power structures and social representations, making a significant statement about public space, collective purpose, and communal identity, themes that resonate regardless of the diverse forms these mobile art pieces may take.

In this book, I will demonstrate that artistic interventions in street settings can be categorized into two distinct types. First, there are tactical works that align with protest and activism, often occurring at the crescendo of an uprising. These are bold, direct, and highly visible forms of expression. Second, there are strategic and subtler yet equally impactful artistic engagements with street politics, which might take place before or after periods of active protest; they may also unfold in spaces that serve as natural extensions of the street, such as private galleries featuring open yards and gardens, which are accessible to the public at no cost. These interventions, whether overtly protest oriented or more understated and perhaps even concealed, targeting a limited audience, are the culmination of years of dedication and effort by artists. Both approaches reflect the depth and diversity of artistic responses to the sociopolitical landscape.

In contrast to the dispersed layout typical of North American suburbs, most Iranian streets have a compact, centralized urban design, a characteristic shared with many older, historically rich parts of the world. Streets in Iran, especially in large cities like Tehran, function as vital socioeconomic veins, enabling the flow of traffic and providing access to individually owned buildings. Iran's streets are hubs of diverse activities, ranging from the daily hustle of commerce to the more charged atmosphere of political protests. Their multifaceted nature makes them a significant backdrop for various forms of public engagement, but at the same time they are embedded with power structures that prevent a broad segment of the population from freely expressing themselves.

The streets in Iran present considerable limitations for women. In the early days of the revolution, the mandatory hijab was subject to debate and its wearing was required only in governmental institutions. However, on August 9, 1983, that requirement was extended to all public spaces and to all women in Iran, regardless of their citizenship or religious beliefs.[41] The Islamic Revolution Committee (or Komiteh, an abbreviation of the Persian term Komiteha-ye Enqelab-e Eslami) began to monitor the hijab as well as people's activities on the streets. Penalties for nonadherence could include flogging and even imprisonment. With Mahmoud Ahmadinejad's inauguration as president of the Islamic Republic in 2005, the Komiteh was rebranded as the Gasht-e Ershad (Guidance Patrol). Functioning as a specialized patrol unit within the Law Enforcement Command of the Islamic Republic of Iran, the Gasht-e Ershad is tasked with monitoring the behavior of both men and women. Its primary focus, however, is on enforcing the dress codes that require women to wear loose-fitting clothing to cloak their bodies and, more specifically, to cover their hair. Monitoring the behavior of men mostly comes down to issues such as warning them about the length of their hair or regulating their interactions with women.[42] The intensity of these patrols has varied under different presidential administrations: since August 2021, with the beginning of the tenure of the conservative Ebrahim Raisi, the rules have been more strictly enforced.

But street politics in Iran, as shaped by the regime, goes beyond controlling women or monitoring public behavior. In the 1990s, there was a significant push by "reformists" to decentralize government by establishing city councils and local authorities to address district- or neighborhood-related issues. Yet, rather than being autonomous, these local entities have come to represent a form of electoral authoritarianism, as demonstrated by Kian Tajbakhsh's book *Creating Local Democracy in Iran: State Building and the Politics of Decentralization*, which draws on two decades of research. Indeed, Tajbakhsh reveals that, contrary to initial appearances, local authorities such as city councils actually undermine democratic processes and reinforce the Islamist regime.[43]

Nazanin Shahrokni's *Women in Place: The Politics of Gender Segregation in Iran* examines the attempts of Islamic Republic reformists to increase public spaces for women, with initiatives such as women-only parks. Shahrokni argues that while these spaces ostensibly expand women's access to public areas, providing what is referred to as freedom within "proper boundaries," they also enforce further regulations on women's bodies and behavior.[44] Far from enhancing women's freedom in public, the parks ensure their constant surveillance by guards.

Prime examples of scholarly research that elucidates the complexities of street politics in the Islamic Republic of Iran, these two books illustrate how the efforts of the reformists, while appearing on the surface to push for greater democracy and freedom, ultimately reinforce the top-down ideology of the regime. They also explain why participants in the Woman, Life, Freedom protests not only resist radical approaches to controlling the streets but also express disillusionment with reformist policies, choosing to take matters into their own hands.

For artists in Iran, the challenges extend beyond the general restrictions faced by ordinary citizens. To show any artwork in public, they must navigate a complex web of bureaucratic permissions, obtaining approvals from local municipalities, traffic organizations, and the MCIG. Moreover, if the artwork is to be displayed in historic areas, additional permissions from heritage organizations are required. In Iran, pragmatic issues—for example, potential traffic disruption caused by art installations—are frequently compounded by ideological constraints, making the pursuit of street politics particularly challenging for artists, especially women artists. This is why it is so crucial to study and document the art that unfolds in the streets and public spaces of Iran, regardless of whether this art is mobile or stationary, created with or without official permission, overtly political in nature or subtly so.[45] Such documentation is vital not only because of the risks artists take—whether they are operating at the height of an uprising, in the years leading up to it, or in its aftermath—but also because of the ingenious counterstrategies and diverse mediums they employ in their work. It is this quality perhaps, this frequently risky nature, that has made street art a form of activism and even a way of life in Iran.

ART AND LIFE

The title of this book, *Women, Art, Freedom*, substituting "art" for "life," pays homage to the spirit of the 2022 uprising, but it also captures the politically conscious approach to art that developed in Iran in the decades leading up to it. The renowned theater director Peter Brook, who contributed to the Shiraz Arts Festivals during the twilight of the Pahlavi monarchy, regarded art, and theater and performance especially, as a medium for authentically depicting the intricacies and dynamism of human existence. Many Iranian artists identify with this belief. Postrevolutionary Iranian experimental theater groups like Av, for example, use their performances as therapeutic tools—emotional escape valves—providing both actors and audiences with momentary relief from the routinized violence of sociopolitical conditions. Art and life are indeed intricately intertwined in performance art and theatrical disciplines in Iran.[46]

In more recent years, there has been a shift in the field of visual arts education in Iran, with the rising popularity of privately-run alternative schools where artists can learn about art history in the context of politics. Previously, however, at least up to the mid-2000s, art education was largely informed by formalist principles, and in particular by the teaching methods of the avant-garde Bauhaus school in Germany (1917–1933). Many of the older artists I interviewed for this book acknowledged the emphasis on formalist approaches, which I believe can be traced to the years leading up to the 1979 revolution. Art historian Fereshteh Daftari has used the term "apolitical formalism" to describe the style of many prominent prerevolutionary Iranian painters such as Nasser Assar, Manoucher Yektai, Leyly Matine-Daftary, or Freydoun Ave. By focusing their creative efforts on certain formal aspects—the abstract division of space, the extreme simplification of forms, the vibrancy and freshness of color, the flattening of space—these artists were able to steer clear of overtly political themes.[47] The Bauhaus model, which emphasizes abstract thinking and the use of corporal senses in art making, offered a similarly neutral path after the Iranian Revolution of 1979, when discussion of political art, barring regime propaganda, was restricted.

After the revolution, Iranian visual arts departments incorporated practices that were abstract and sense oriented, aimed at enhancing students' perception, creativity, and material understanding.[48] The methodologies and writings of the Swiss artist Johannes Itten were an essential part of the Iranian curriculum; he had developed the basic course (*Vorkurs*) at the Bauhaus and was an adherent of Mazdaznan, a philosophy with ties to the ancient Persian religion of Zoroastrianism. In Itten's classes, students engaged with various textures while blindfolded, to intensify their sense of touch, creating distinctive montages of textures with structures and effects that were considered groundbreaking at the time.[49] The emphasis on direct physical experience would play a central role in postrevolutionary art education in Iran, even if the Islamicized academic environment was unable to accommodate all aspects of the experimentation that was fundamental to the Bauhaus approach. Diverting the focus from politically sensitive discussions, these practices encouraged students to immerse themselves in the exploration of color and form, prioritizing the experiential and aesthetic aspects of art over its potential connotative meanings.

One natural outcome of this educational focus is the prominence of the living and breathing body in many of the projects discussed in this book. I must, however, highlight the contrast between the emphasis on bodily senses in art and art that celebrates the body itself. After the 1979 Iranian Revolution, many Iranian diasporic artists used depictions of women's bodies to comment on the subjugation and marginalization of Iranian women under the Islamic regime. Shirin Neshat has referred to how her renowned *Women of Allah* series

> question[s] how female bodies have continuously been used as a form of battlefield for various authorities' political and religious ideologies [. . .] How throughout time, like during

> the reign of Reza Shah, women were forced to unveil, and then they were forced to veil during the Iranian Revolution. [...] And how in fact women are the first [...] who are immediately impacted by any change of governance in Iran and how [this dynamic] still exists today. [T]he 'Women of Allah' series [...] fit[s] into this wider conversation about how the representation of women is always a signifier for, or reflection of, the kind of government that rules the country.[50]

As I will show in this book, within Iran itself, the exploration of these themes has evolved differently, due to censorship and restrictions on women's bold use of their bodies in art. The resulting feminist art often diverges from or even opposes the work of better-known artists like Neshat.

As noted, in recent decades there has been a notable trend among Iranian artists to engage more actively with socio-political issues and incorporate these themes into their artworks. So, in exploring the intricate relationship between contemporary art and life, it is essential to emphasize not just the physical body's central role in art making but also the agency embodied within it. The agency of the artist manifests itself as a form of *intellectual inquiry*—as an ongoing process, rather than a final product displayed in galleries and museums. In late December 2022, artist Jinoos Taghizadeh issued a manifesto that scrutinized and challenged the role of art and artists within the Woman, Life, Freedom uprising, asking: "Can artists authentically create during an uprising, or are they relegated to mere propaganda-like producers?" The essential points of her text are reproduced below.

> [...] generally speaking, discussions about art's role in echoing resistance often lead to a prevalent perception: the artist is seen as a mere instrument, expected to conform to demands and fulfill obligations assigned by others. In this sense, the artist's scope and boundaries are externally defined, relegating them to the role of a mere executor tasked with visualizing others' perspectives. Deviation or failure in this prescribed role often subjects the artist to criticism and scorn.
>
> When discussing art during times of protest, revolution, and sociopolitical movements, what form should this art take? Are we referring to art that visually conveys the movement's message, or perhaps art that translates these themes into something eye-catching? Does discussing art

in the context of resistance mean focusing on revolutionary posters and anthems?

[...]

Is the creation of a tangible 'art object' or 'art commodity' a prerequisite for something to be considered art?

[...]

In the realm of protest art, what is the role of aesthetics, and is it appropriate to apply traditional aesthetic criteria to evaluate such art? [...] Where does protest art find its most appropriate home: in traditional venues like museums and galleries, or in public spaces such as streets, social media, and news platforms? When protest art is showcased in any artistic setting, is it seeking legitimacy or validation? In protest art, how important is the anonymity of the artist? Does revealing their identity suggest personal gain from the movement or a genuine contribution to the cause?

[...]

Is it incumbent upon artists to channel their credibility into their artwork, or should they engage in protests and activism on a par with others? [...] Furthermore, should artists with celebrity status leverage their media presence to elevate the voices of protesters, or does this cross into the realm of self-promotion?

[...]

How do we distinguish between mere showmanship and genuine efforts to garner international solidarity for an uprising?

[...]

Can artists authentically create during an uprising, or are they relegated to mere propaganda-like producers? Ideally, shouldn't art evolve through multiple levels of insight and imagination over time? Is it realistic to expect artists to produce work

> rapidly that is both in harmony with a movement and deeply impactful?
>
> [...]
>
> I hold numerous other questions and likely you do as well. Often, the act of posing questions may be more apt and thought-provoking than seeking concrete answers. Isn't this, after all, the essence of an artist's role—to provoke and stimulate questions in the minds of others?[51]

Challenging the notion that artists are merely tools for executing the visions of others, Taghizadeh's manifesto delves into the nature and purpose of art during times of political upheaval. While she questions the limits of artistic expression, the manifesto does not conclude with pessimism, but realistically considers the potential of artists to create meaningful art even if it is postponed: "Ideally, shouldn't art evolve through multiple levels of insight and imagination over time?" Above all, Taghizadeh emphasizes the value of intellectual inquiry over definitive answers, suggesting that nurturing curiosity is central to the role of the artist in turbulent times. In alignment with Taghizadeh's perspective on art as a process and intellectual inquiry, I view the artist's role as an ongoing endeavor, a pursuit of knowledge that transcends any specific time or place. It is an evolving process that can expand, adapt, and serve as a foundational pillar for future artistic or even social movements.

In this book, I explore the distinctive role played by artists in the Woman, Life, Freedom movement. But rather than trying to build a comprehensive repository of artworks from the uprising—a task that has been meticulously undertaken by art collectives in and outside the country—my intention is to amplify the voices of the artists themselves, to grant them agency, moving away from traditional top-down art historical perspectives. While it is impossible to do justice to every voice and creative mind involved, I hope that the selected stories and trajectories in this book will serve to illuminate the movement as a whole.

WHY DOES THE ART OF WOMAN, LIFE, FREEDOM MATTER?

Not all individuals featured in this book have consistently advocated for feminism or women's rights throughout their careers. Similarly, not every artwork presented directly addresses women's or gender issues. A few pieces are included for containing visual elements that emerged during protests, such as blood stains. Nevertheless, this volume's main goal is to encourage a debate about feminist or pro-women art in Iran and the relevance of that art not only to contemporary injustices in the country but also to the inequalities rooted in interpretations of feminism in the context of the Islamic communities and the Middle East. Art history, often bound by Eurocentric perspectives, historically tended to exclude Middle Eastern women's visual production or relegate it to categories like craft and domestic production.[52] Later, in the context of postcolonial discourse, art created by women or pro-women art from Islamic regions was often anticipated to represent a way of life that was perceived as being simultaneously rooted in traditional cultures and capable of operating independently within that specific ethnic context. This perspective, stemming from feminism among faithful Muslims or postcolonial activists and academics, asserted that in order to enjoy equality and justice, women do not have to look or act like white, Western women: indeed, the life they live cannot appear as a hollow copy of Western women's aspirations and Western feminists.[53] What happened during the Woman, Life, Freedom uprising, then, caught many people around the world off guard. Explaining the situation was at times a challenge. For example, some university professors and administrators hesitated to engage in conversations or to display images of Iranian women publicly setting fire to their veils, as they were concerned about showing disrespect toward veiled individuals and practicing Muslims in their communities.

The Woman, Life, Freedom uprising has fundamentally shifted our perspective, providing a more nuanced and intricate understanding of feminism and feminist art not just in Iran and the Islamic world but outside the Western canon more generally. Investigating how Iranian artists embrace and engage with this women's rights movement, regardless of their gender or sexual orientation, is especially pertinent for contemporary women artists of color. It is a means to grapple with—and redress—the oversimplified interpretations prevalent in art historical literature, which often stem from colonial legacies separate from those affecting white feminist women and white feminist art.

In a statement released in late September 2022, the philosopher Slavoj Žižek portrayed the Woman, Life, Freedom uprising as a global wake-up call, in light of the resurgence of religious fundamentalism in many developed countries:

> What goes on now in Iran [...] combines different struggles (against women's oppression, against religious fundamentalism, for political freedom against state terror) into an organic unity. [...] *Zan, Zendegi, Azadi* [Woman, Life, Freedom] is very different from MeToo in Western countries: it mobilizes millions of ordinary women, and it is directly linked to the struggle of all, men included [...] Women and men are together in it, the enemy is religious fundamentalism supported by state terror. [...] [T]he oppression of women is not a special case, it is the moment in which the oppression that permeates the entire society is most visible. The protesters who are not Kurds also see it clearly that the oppression of Kurds puts limits on their own freedom: solidarity with Kurds is the only way towards freedom in Iran. [...] What goes on now in Iran is thus not a thing of the past, it is something that awaits us in the developed Western world where political violence, religious fundamentalism and oppression of women are growing daily. We in the West have no right to treat Iran as a country which just has to catch up with the West. We in the West have to learn from Iran, we will soon need a similar movement in the US, in Poland, in Russia, and in many other countries. Whatever the immediate result of the protests, the crucial thing is to keep the movement alive, to organize social networks which, even if state oppression will temporarily win, will continue its underground work and lay the foundation for a new explosion. It is not enough just to express sympathy or solidarity with Iranian protesters: they are not out there, far from us, part of a different exotic culture. All the babble about cultural specificities (often used by reactionary forces to justify religious and ethnic oppression) is now meaningless: we can immediately see that the Iranian struggle is the struggle of us all.[54]

Žižek's declaration not only encapsulates the core of Iran's uprising but also elucidates how the "feminist" message of this movement differs from traditional conceptions of women's rights vis-à-vis men. I consider his view a starting point for discussing the role of feminism and religion in writing about the art of the Woman, Life, Freedom uprising. A key insight I wish to emphasize in this book is the inherently *parafeminist* nature of the art produced for or in response to the Woman, Life, Freedom movement in Iran. While primarily centered on women's liberation, feminism, and gender matters, this art extends its reach to broader societal issues. The term "parafeminist," which I adopt from art historian Amelia Jones, suggests that principles emerging from feminist discourse are instrumental in addressing and resolving broader societal challenges. Jones explains the concept as follows:

> [The] most important legacy of feminism is a broader articulation of a *politics of positionality* [...] Positionality [here] [...] is indicative of the way in which we continue to 'identify' ourselves and others in relation to perceived and complexly interwoven identifications. [...] [P]arafeminism, with this politics of positionality, understands 'gender' as a question rather than an answer—and a question that percolates through other subjective and social identifications—sexual orientation, race, ethnicity, nationality, and so on, which can never be fixed but always take meaning in relation to each other.[55]

In addition to Jones, numerous other writers in the field of feminist art history have stressed that feminism should not merely seek to "add [...] to the existing narratives of a discipline that (re)articulates masculinist knowledge and power," but rather should revisit and reconstruct art history from a feminist perspective.[56] It is in this context that Griselda Pollock, for instance, prefers the term "feminist interventions in art history" over "feminist art history."[57]

Questions surrounding methodology constantly resurfaced while I engaged with this project. Many of the art experts I spoke to seemed to be keener to highlight or mention only women artists who contributed to the movement; others questioned male artists' approaches. In the end, I chose to engage in dialogues with a diverse range of artists whose work revolved around the themes of the Woman, Life, Freedom movement, not excluding men who advocate for women's rights through art.

While this book mostly explores women-related topics, it also sensitively examines the ways a multiplicity of gender identities intersect with the visual language and performative aspects of this movement. In my study of men's art, where relevant, I have highlighted their perspectives on feminism and skillful representations of the nuances of masculinity, which they themselves describe as being more subtle and gentle than the rigid definitions promoted by the Islamic Republic. This exploration provides insight into their understanding of gender dynamics and challenges traditional perceptions of masculinity in the context of Iranian society. When questioned about the significance of the feminist or pro-women theme of the Woman, Life, Freedom uprising, all the artists featured in this book identified themselves as feminists. However, some observed that while the concept of feminism is understood in theory, its practical implementation is often lacking, even among those who profess to support women's causes. I was told that a common misconception, prevalent even among those who are more educated and more openminded about women's issues, is that any initiative organized exclusively by women is inherently feminist or contributes to women's freedom in society. Many artists critiqued this viewpoint, noting that rather than truly advancing equality, such gender-based segregation underscores the distance—physical, social, psychological—that separates the sexes. In my discussions with various artists, both women and men, I came to understand that, without explicitly naming it, they were all advocating not only for "parafeminism" or "feminist interventions" but also for what is commonly referred to in the social sciences and humanities as the "femme episteme," a concept that represents a type of feminism or feminist knowledge that rejects a rigid gender binary, recognizing that individuals can exist anywhere along the gender spectrum.[58]

Echoing Kimberlé Crenshaw's late 1980s theory of *intersectionality*, which posits that individual identities are complex, formed by the dynamics of power structures, my discussions with women artists from smaller cities shed light on the nuanced class- and ethnic-influenced gender experiences in Iran.[59] Some women artists advocating feminist viewpoints face greater challenges due to less economically-privileged backgrounds, conservative religious environments, or family beliefs. The intensity and risks of artistic activism vary significantly. For instance, a lesser-known female artist performing unveiled in the streets of the religious city of Mashhad faces a far greater risk of being apprehended and punished than a well-known male artist creating a monument for the Woman, Life, Freedom movement in a well-to-do neighborhood in northern Tehran. As I will highlight in this book, it is crucial not to homogenize these endeavors, or to see one as more effective or powerful than the other, but rather to recognize the distinct levels of activism and political significance each project embodies on its own terms.

A particularly enlightening aspect of my exploration into the "feminist dimensions" of the movement came from my interactions with a number of devout Muslim women artists who expressed solidarity with those who choose not to wear the hijab while remaining deeply faithful to their own beliefs. Engaging with these women broadened my perspective, moving it beyond the standard postcolonial narrative that advocates for the preservation and autonomy of Muslim practices and beliefs, free from the influence of white Euro-American feminist discourse. The devout women I conversed with showed little interest in the issue of veiling or the preservation of Islamic values for society as a whole. Instead, they showed how through their art and activism they are vigorously involved in challenging the patriarchal power systems that sustain gender disparities within the Islamic Republic. Through these conversations, I learned to move beyond the simplistic binary of veiling being either good or bad. Instead, I began to explore how ethical and just feminist stances are formed, positioned, and practiced in Iran.[60]

In *Living a Feminist Life*, Sara Ahmed remarks that "to become a feminist is to stay a student."[61] Beyond presenting the various artists who have contributed to the Woman, Life, Freedom uprising, this study is also my attempt to understand what feminist art (and, by extension, feminism) means in contemporary Iran. Rather than focusing on the extensive literature about feminism in Iran or spotlighting mainstream debates of women's rights activists or Amnesty International records on the suppression of Iranian women's rights (a task already accomplished by other scholars), I have chosen to stay attuned to simpler feminist art practices as they unfold on the streets of Iran, in keeping with Ahmed's idea that "staying closer to the everyday makes feminist theory more accessible."[62] Viewing feminism through the lens of daily artistic practices has allowed me to unravel an important aspect of a discourse that can sometimes feel distant and alienating when approached from a purely theoretical, legal, or political perspective. Following in Ahmed's footsteps, I strive to "keep my words" close to the world of my protagonists, by "showing how feminist theory" is what they do when they live their lives "in a feminist way."[63]

Noushin Ahmadi Khorasani, an Iranian women's rights activist, has likewise stressed the significance of tackling women's issues within the context of Iranians' everyday realities. She notes: "[I]f we base our movements within [...] 'the latest global feminist standards' (not considering 'the conscious and unconscious gender norms of society' and based on internal standards) [...] we can certainly weaken the women's movement and ultimately undermine the whole society."[64] She goes on to say, "[F]or example, if we create a particular feminist identity within the Mahsa movement and form a group campaign [...] against women who accept 'hijab' as a personal belief [...], we are actually replacing patriarchal hegemony with feminist hegemony and exacerbating conflicts."[65] Consequently, examining the daily practices of Iranian artists provides a more valuable and nuanced understanding than attempting to interpret Iranian activist art solely through the lens of a "global feminist standard."

Art in Iran is not only influenced by but also sometimes reinforces the patriarchal structures of the commercial markets and official institutions it operates within. The uprising and its aftermath have exposed and challenged these structures, highlighting the need for further critiques. Like the artists themselves, who come from a variety of backgrounds, the art produced during the uprising spans a wide spectrum, from the immediate and pressing concerns of women's rights and access to public spaces in the Islamic Republic to more intricate inquiries into culture, religion, power structures, ethics, history, memory, the rights of ethnic and minority groups, and resistance. Recognizing that the uprising is ongoing and evolving, my primary objective is not to present its art as a fait accompli but to deeply engage with its form and the circumstances and debates surrounding its production.

The art emerging from the Woman, Life, Freedom uprising is significant as it offers insights into various facets of contemporary art on a global scale, not just within Iranian communities. The approach I have adopted in narrating the story of this art movement aims to illuminate its diverse aspects. This, in turn, can broaden the horizons of contemporary art criticism and theory worldwide.

ORGANIZATION OF THE BOOK

This book is structured around key themes that in my view define the art of the Woman, Life, Freedom movement. Some of these themes emerged briefly during the peak of the protests; others have been long-standing elements of Iranian art, pre-dating the 2022 uprising, but gaining greater clarity and significance as the events unfolded. Rather than more traditional "chapters" or "sections," I have organized these thematic elements into "acts," each representing a distinct performative quality. While some acts trace their roots back years, necessitating additional context and historical framing, others represent novel approaches. In each case, the book aims to highlight the work of artists who are primarily engaged with street and public space, offering a fresh perspective on this critical yet inadequately studied facet of the movement. When structuring this study, I gave priority to themes that were more prominent during the protests and more likely to be recognizable to readers. Some might question why the section on anonymous artists and opaque art is not immediately followed by an exploration of camouflaged poetry performances. The reason is straightforward: there are themes that are significantly more familiar to a global audience. Some may also observe overlaps between the themes. It is a valid observation: certain art projects featured in one act could easily fit into another. However, in arranging the case studies, I emphasized the aspects of each project that resonated most with the theme of the respective act. As an author, I have exercised some creative license in this process. After all, this book seeks to narrate stories that are still unfolding—nothing is definitive, as the movement remains ongoing, with speculations permeating the atmosphere.

In preparing this book, I engaged in extensive interviews with artists, spending hours exploring everything from their formative influences, including their educational and personal backgrounds, to their works leading up to and during the peak of the movement and after. We discussed specific examples of their art, reflecting on how each piece contributed to the uprising, whether directly or subtly. Some of the artists featured in this book have chosen to remain anonymous, driven by concerns that extend beyond the fear of arrest and interrogation. Others have openly shared their experiences, undeterred by potential repercussions from the state or from conservative relatives, friends, or employers. Through this engagement, I came to intimately understand the courage of the artists. Their passion and frustrations were palpable in their voices.

There is an inherent boldness in art that allows it to transcend boundaries and obstacles. Compared to codified disciplines such as law, its possibilities are boundless. With this in mind, *Women, Art, Freedom* aims to capture just a fraction of the myriad ways that Iranian artists have found to intervene, to challenge, and to question the status quo. In highlighting their innovative and impactful approaches to art and activism, it is my hope that this book will serve as a catalyst for further exploration into the relationship between art and street politics in Iran. ■

Act One

PARADING THE BODY ON SIDEWALKS

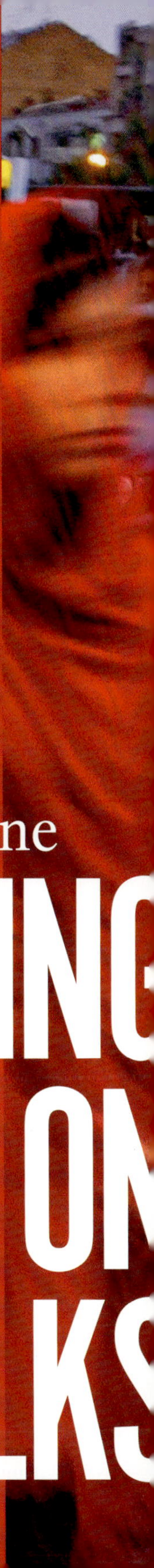

During the peak of the Woman, Life, Freedom uprising, booksellers in Tehran reported a surge in the popularity of certain titles.[1] Among them, Hannah Arendt's *The Human Condition* garnered interest for its emphasis on civil society as a "space of appearance" that can always be made anew "wherever men are together in the manner of speech and action"[2]—that is, wherever people gather with common goals and interests—an idea that paralleled the approaches of the artists and activists who strategically asserted their presence on the streets of Iran.[3] For Judith Butler, writing about the relevance of Arendt's ideas to an earlier wave of protest, the Occupy Movement, this space of appearance "is not only an architectural given" but a dynamic locus activated and animated by collective action.[4] "No one body establishes the space of appearance," Butler concludes; rather, the "performative exercise" takes place "only between bodies, in a space that constitutes the gap between my own body and another's."[5] Throughout the Woman, Life, Freedom protests, these sentiments were frequently echoed in discussions involving academics and intellectuals as well as artists. Notably, sociologist Bayat referred to Iranian women's resistance to the restrictions imposed upon them as the "art of presence" (*honar-e hozur*).[6] Taking his cue from Arendt, he defined this art as the ability of women to "make themselves [...] seen, felt, and realized."[7] Aligned with Bayat's insights, my goal in this "act" is to explore the historical *appearances* of female artists, and especially their guerrilla-style forays into public spaces and streets, a less examined facet of protest art in Iran.

For over thirty years, Iranian women artists have engaged in public art activism, creating moments of rupture in everyday life without declaring an overt political stance. Using methods such as painting graffiti, playful wandering, or occupying empty urban spaces, they have challenged conventions entangled with decades of subordination and exclusion and asserted their right to the city. Their performances bear resemblances to acts of protest, which similarly arise in response to institutional oppression and constitute a civil action both in their inception and implementation. But, before delving into examples of these art forms, it is essential to understand how women's public lives have evolved—and the perception of their bodies has changed—from the 1990s on.

REFORMING THE LIVES AND ARTS OF WOMEN

Suppressed for many years after the revolution, conversations around women's issues gradually surfaced in the less restrictive atmosphere that followed the end of the Iran–Iraq War in 1988. Between 1992 and 2000, the magazine *Payam-e Zan* (Women's message), which espoused conservative Islamist views, conducted nearly one hundred interviews with prominent women, such as parliamentary deputies and government officials, who were all aligned with the government of the Islamic Republic.[8] These interviews provided insights into the lives and perspectives of women holding leadership roles who were evidently aligned with and supportive of the regime.[9] Beyond ideological rhetoric, concrete legal measures were implemented to improve the status of women in Iran. For instance, in 1992, the High Council of the Cultural Revolution introduced employment policies aimed at enhancing opportunities for women. While upholding traditional family values and retaining restrictions on select professions deemed inconsistent with Islamic tenets, these policies also sought to promote women's involvement in the workforce and address their specific concerns.[10] During this period, more open discussions about ordinary female citizens were likewise set within the framework of Islam as defined by the regime, and spearheaded by a group of women linked to the political elite—among them, Azam Taleqani, Faezeh Hashemi, Ma'sumeh Ebtekar, Monireh Gorji, and Shahla Sherkat. Although scholars, such as Shahrzad Mojab and Ziba Mir-Hosseini, would later use the term "Islamic feminists" to refer to such active women, some critics, such as Valentine Moghadam, dispute the label, believing that feminism is constrained by this Islamic context.[11] The term is also rejected by some of those whom it is meant to designate, such as Shahla Sherkat, whose participation and involvement with the revolutionary elite was motivated more by political pragmatism. Nevertheless, the pragmatic approach of "Islamic feminism" permeated all other areas during that period, as reflected in the publications of the era.

Dailies and periodicals directed by the so-called progovernment Islamic feminists—*Zan* (Woman), *Zanan* (Women), *Zan-e Rooz* (Women of today) and *Farzaneh* (Prudent)—published incisive analyses of women's participation in public life, a theme particularly relevant to this book. A notable example, from earlier in the decade, is a 1994 summer issue of *Zan-e Rooz*, which focuses on young women who come to Tehran to study and the challenges they face in accessing public spaces independently, without the oversight of a male guardian. The cover features veiled women walking across a bare, tiled platform, signifying the infinite scale of the capital. They are heading toward imposing concrete buildings, with a large "no entry" sign looming on the distant horizon like a setting sun—a warning of the perils of autonomy and freedom of women in the capital FIG. 8. The bold headline in the lower left corner of the cover reads, "Girls on their own, university students, under what roof?" At first sight, this might seem to be a call for greater freedom. But the accompanying image simultaneously implies that women require supervision—specifically, state-provided guardianship and shelter—when they are away from home. This dual messaging encapsulates the essence of government-run feminist publications of the time. Ostensibly forward-looking, appearing to advocate for women's liberation from spatial restrictions, they simultaneously call for state regulation of these "unsupervised" women.

This nuanced dynamic—of new freedoms colliding with old constraints—becomes particularly poignant in the realm of the arts

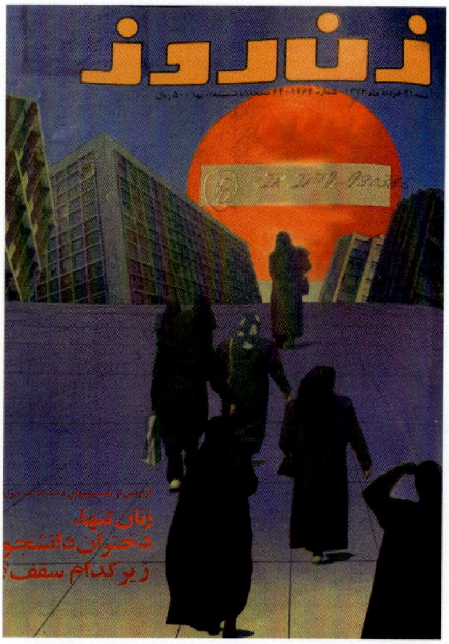

FIG. 8 Cover of *Zan-e Rooz Magazine* from 1994. Courtesy of the Firestone Library, Princeton University.

in 1990s Iran, where we find echoes of the same complex interplay of progressiveness and conservatism in mediums that are heavily regulated, such as cinema. Films would reflect the limits placed on women's rights, but instead of pointing the finger directly at the theocratic regime, directors tactfully shifted the blame onto certain character types or deep-rooted traditions predating the revolution. A prime example is Tahmineh Milani's critically acclaimed *Two Women*, from 1999, which follows a pair of architecture students as they grapple with the cultural traditions that hinder their personal and professional growth. While both women faced significant challenges, their stories took divergent paths as they navigated the complex landscape of a patriarchal society. One woman managed to overcome the obstacles in her way and achieve success, while the other found herself constrained and ultimately oppressed by the very same systemic barriers. "There are unspoken rules that govern our country, and one such example is the gender roles of men and women. [...] These unwritten laws are deeply ingrained in our society," Milani said in an interview with film critic Saeed Zeydabadi-Nejad.[12] But she also indicated that the title of the film symbolized the two life paths available to a single woman in postrevolutionary Iran, and her potential to succeed (against all the odds, one might add) in her career. The message went down well at the Fajr Film Festival, Iran's premier government-sponsored film event, where *Two Women* was lauded for its thoughtful and subtle examination of women's roles and was awarded Best Screenplay.

Other films of the time explored the societal constraints on women's agency, capacity, and mobility in more abstract ways. For instance, Marziyeh Meshkini's *The Day I Became a Woman* (2001) uses the black chador as a metaphor to depict the difficulties that women face in challenging traditional boundaries: in one scene, the protagonist, Ahu, stands out from other women in a race as she struggles to keep her chador in place. As film critic Michelle Langford observes, the film does not challenge veiling but rather shows it as a space for conciliation.[13] Indeed, despite the chador's impracticality, *The Day I Became a Woman* suggests that it does not prevent women from renegotiating their mobility in the public sphere. At the same time, it also inadvertently implies that women still need the veil—in conservative areas, the chador—when taking part in physical activities such as a cycle race.

Regardless of one's perspective on the legitimacy of the feminist goals pursued by the regime's elite, which became increasingly pervasive in all spheres of life and cultural expression that needed permission from the government, the movement sparked a surge of secular and nonideological initiatives aimed at empowering women. Not long after the emergence of the "Islamic feminist" movement, secular figures like lawyers Mehrangiz Kar and Shirin Ebadi, along with writer and publisher Shahla Lahiji, intensified their activism.[14] Having previously worked more discreetly, they began to campaign openly for changes to laws and regulations discriminating against women.

Concrete reforms under the presidency of Muhammed Khatami (1997–2005) included the removal of restrictions on the courses women could study at university, greater access to contraception, and the limitation of men's right to divorce upon payment of compensation. There was an upsurge in women's advocacy and women-led NGOs and informal initiatives, with public debate fomented by an increasingly active women's press.[15] *Hoghough-e Zanan* (Women's rights), *Negah-e Zanan* (Women's perspective), and *Jens-e Dovvom* (Second sex) were among the titles that ventured beyond the limits prescribed by the government elites, for example by translating key articles by prominent Western feminists.[16]

This same period also saw a flourishing of unofficial and informal art in various genres and unconventional spaces. In contrast to official art, which depends on authorization from government bodies like the MCIG, these artworks had a more liberal stance. Intertwined with the urban landscape, with a street-based presence and ephemeral nature, they emerged as guerrilla interventions—precursors to the art associated with the Woman, Life, Freedom uprising. Initially, they adopted common cultural themes and symbols from public rituals and presentations of religious groups and systems within the Islamic Republic. But as the examples discussed below illustrate, the interventions of women artists in public spaces became progressively more audacious over two decades.

WOMEN'S BODIES AND STREET ART

In the early 2000s, Tehran experienced an extraordinary construction boom. New high-rises transformed the urban landscape, but at the same time the rapid development created leftover urban spaces, such as vacant lots and suspended construction sites, that women artists in the capital began to occupy for their art. This movement mirrored similar trends in postindustrial American landscapes (recall the projects of Gordon Matta-Clark, for example), with the difference that the leftover spaces were a temporary product of real-estate speculation rather than the residue of long-term economic decline. Artist Bita Fayyazi took part in a series of projects in which artists transformed abandoned and deteriorating buildings (*kolangi*) into art installations.[17] Often these *kolangis* were old residential complexes, awaiting demolition to make way for more profitable high-rises. In another piece of collaborative public art, Fayyazi installed 150 terra-cotta dogs by the side of a road (flattened and crushed, the sculptures looked like roadkill) and then buried them in a mass grave at a site designated for a future high-rise—a powerful statement on the speed of urbanization in Iran and its associated political dynamics.[18] Later, Fayyazi found a unique way to bring her art to a broad cross section of Tehran society, beyond the elite audience for gallery exhibitions. Displayed in a mobile van that stopped every forty-five minutes, her sculptures were encountered by a diverse group—passersby, schoolchildren, motorists, shopkeepers, road sweepers, and tramps.[19]

Neda Razavipour, collaborating with several other artists, took advantage of logistic problems that caused temporary halts in construction projects, focusing her artistic efforts on empty window frames in these unfinished structures.[20] Razavipour also envisioned a project that gathered sanitary workers on the concrete slabs of one of the tallest of Tehran's new towers, a structure unrivaled in height since the 1979 revolution. This initiative reflected a creative use of urban spaces in transition, blending art with the city's evolving architectural landscape.

While the works of Fayyazi and Razavipour did not overtly challenge the authorities or directly critique the role of women in public spaces, their engagement in urban art projects that scrutinized facets of Tehran's development represents a significant shift by artists, especially women artists: the move beyond the secure confines of their studios to leave a mark on public discourse.

As mentioned, under President Khatami's reformist government, there were several years of relative openness when progressive forces were able to build momentum: women challenged Iran's gender laws more intensely, and writers and journalists voiced societal grievances more openly. But these initiatives would be met by fierce opposition from Khatami's hard-line successor, Mahmoud Ahmadinejad (in office 2005–2013). Farideh Shahsavarani was one of the artists who responded to the further erosion of basic human rights, particularly freedom of expression, under the new regime. Her immersive exhibit in the deserted *Ettela'at* newspaper building in 2006 enveloped visitors in a space densely layered with newspaper pages, accompanied by the ambient sounds of typewriters and sirens, paying tribute to journalists who had been detained. The installation was short-lived: set up without official authorization, it remained in place for only seven days.[21]

The One Million Signatures Campaign, launched in 2006, was a bold and direct attempt by Iranian women to change the laws that discriminated against them.[22] Internationally, it received wide recognition. At home, many of the feminists and activists involved in the endeavor were attacked and jailed. The following two years were tumultuous. As the hard-liners tightened their grip on power, there was increasing suppression, and many young people left the country in search of a brighter future. In 2009, the general sense of despair and frustration found an outlet in the Green Movement, which rejected the official results of an election that installed Ahmadinejad for a second term of office. The uprising profoundly influenced the creative output of many visual artists, particularly women, among them Mehraneh "Chupan" Atashi (hereafter Chupan).[23]

Chupan, born in 1980, studied photography at Tehran University of Art under the mentorship of Bahman Jalalai, a distinguished documentarian and artistic photographer. Growing up during a period of intense upheaval—marked notably by the "chain murders," a decade-long campaign of killings and disappearances targeting dissident intellectuals[24]—Chupan's interest in societal issues was sparked early. Inspired by the renowned photojournalist Kaveh Golestan, they explored the areas around Tehran City Theater and Daneshjoo Park, engaging deeply with the lives of the marginalized individuals, including homeless prostitutes and transgender people, they encountered there. After graduating in 1998, Chupan worked briefly as a photojournalist before taking up independent artistic photography.[25]

Their breakthrough series in 2004 focused on the *zurkhaneh*, a traditional men's sport practicing a blend of wrestling, calisthenics, strength training, and spirituality. Women are forbidden from participating in this world—it is even rumored that the presence of a woman, the mere fact of her breathing, would taint the atmosphere of the *zurkhaneh*. Despite this, Chupan was captivated by the sport. With the support of some open-minded athletes, they placed a large mirror in the central pit of the compound and captured the athletes reflected in it, positioning themself as the photographer within the frame. At first glance, their project appears to be a straightforward celebration of an ancient sport in Iran. However, there is a deeper layer to Chupan's work that transcends the documentation of a traditional way of life. Through their simple presence at the *zurkhaneh*, they made a powerful statement about female agency.

At the time, Chupan was unaware of the work of American photographer Collier Schorr, who, two years before, had delved into the world of amateur American wrestlers, revealing the raw emotions of vulnerability, struggle, and pain inherent in the seemingly macho sport.[26] But whereas Schorr sought to reflect a wide range of male emotions, including a romantic aspect to the sport, Chupan's objectives were more complex.[27] Their photography challenged gender norms, making a woman the active protagonist and the men the passive subjects of the camera lens—a reversal that also provided a fresh perspective on power dynamics in Iranian society.[28] By positioning themself as the central character in a traditionally male-dominated space, Chupan transformed the role of the woman photographer: no longer an invisible, bodiless presence (*bi-tan*), they were now the pivotal figure in the scene, adopting the role of an observer gazing upon men.

While this series garnered considerable attention, it was frequently perceived through an exoticizing lens. Instead of engaging with the critical themes of gender and power relations that Chupan sought to highlight, many viewers, particularly outside Iran, appeared to be more intrigued by the visual novelty of the veiled female body positioned within a male-dominated environment.[29] Despite such misinterpretations, this practice of self-portraiture, which Chupan refers to as *khod negareh*, would become a hallmark of their work, serving as a catalyst for their activism FIG. 9.

Chupan's subsequent project, *Tehran's Self-Portrait* (2008–2010), started as a response to the rapid urban development that was changing the face of the capital, erasing personal and collective memories. The series of evocative self-portraits set against the parts of the city still untouched by modernization present Chupan as a living embodiment of Tehran's history and spirit, emphasizing the role of the photographer not just as an observer but as an active participant and commentator in the social narrative. Here, Chupan used a Holga 120 camera with a pinhole aperture rather than a lens, a choice of equipment that lent a unique, unpredictable quality to the photographs. Captured with an extensive depth of field, the images were characterized by a dreamlike, vintage aesthetic, reflecting the transient and nostalgic nature of Chupan's personal and urban exploration, as well as their desire to reconnect with their roots and safeguard their identity. In each image, Chupan displays a different emotion, ranging from happiness to anger and sadness. Their work drew inspiration from renowned photographers who placed themselves in front of urban settings, such as Cindy Sherman or Diane Arbus. They also took their cue from Eugène Atget, who captured the changing face of Paris over an extended period.

When the Green Movement erupted in 2009, Chupan took to the streets, this time with throngs of protesters as the backdrop

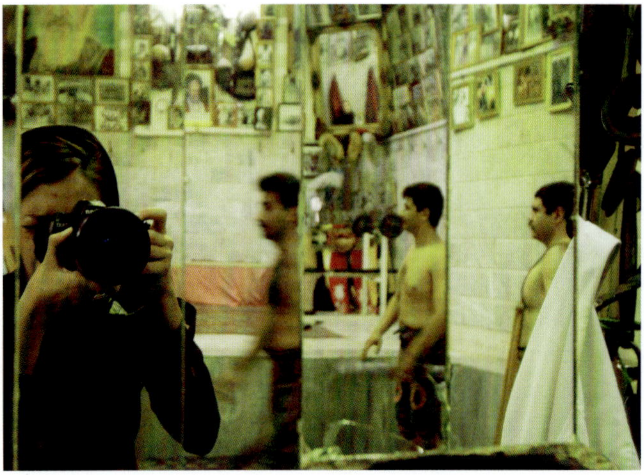

FIG. 9 Chupan Mehraneh Atashi, *Bodiless, I (zourkhaneh)*, 2004, Tehran. Courtesy of the artist.

to the photographs FIG. 10. We see Chupan actively participating in the protests—both the photographer and the photographed—but also their discomfort as a female subject confronting the shock of being exposed in space and on the photographic image.[30] Chupan's use of exaggerated facial expressions, red hue lighting, and flawed compositions convey both a sense of unease and the impermanence that shapes the relationship of their body to a suffocating urban environment.[31]

This activism did not go unnoticed. Following the religious month of Ashura of that year, Chupan was arrested and spent forty-eight days in the notorious Evin Prison, where they were brutally beaten and interrogated about their motives and their self-perception. A change of direction in their work was proposed: from documenting the fight for freedom to photographing flowers. Chupan's captors described in intricate detail a tender pink rose, adorned with a single glistening droplet, set against a green background—a "poetic image" that Chupan saw as an affront, a metaphorical death sentence echoing the Iranian custom of using flowers as a symbolic replacement for a deceased woman's image at funerals, where displaying women's faces is often deemed inappropriate. The parallel highlighted not only the stifling of their artistic expression but also the deeper societal constraints on the representation and visibility of women.

Strong and outspoken during their time in prison, Chupan was consumed by a sense of disorientation and confusion upon their release. Before their arrest, they had been working on an exhibition; now they were unsure how to proceed. The authorities had returned Chupan's negatives—after first ensuring they were no longer usable (the only ones to be preserved had been hidden

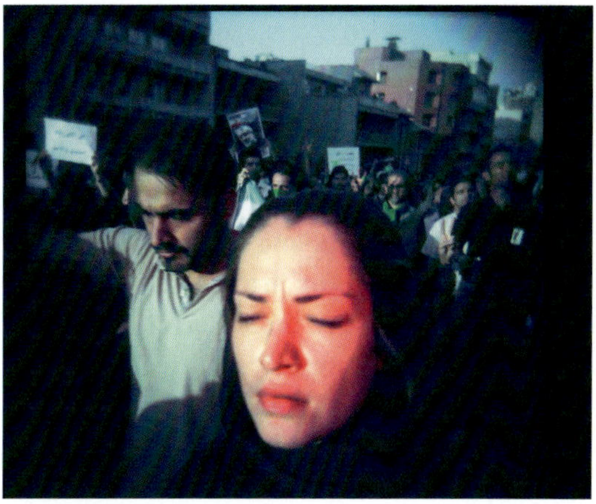

FIG. 10 Chupan Mehraneh Atashi, a photograph from *Tehran's Self-Portrait* series, 2009, Tehran. Courtesy of the artist.

away in Chupan's grandmother's house). It was during this difficult period, amid the general chaos, that the idea of exploring the theme of flowers began to take root—but not in the way the authorities had envisaged. Encouraged by renowned artists such as Rozita Sharafjahan, Homayoun Sirizi, Mehdi Navid, and Barbad Golshiri, Chupan delved into the deeper symbolism and significance of plants, spending countless hours meticulously capturing the wildflowers that flourish in the desert terrain bordering the highways in Tehran, in places people seldom visit FIG. 11. An exhibition of the work was arranged, but when a reporter from the *New York Times* got wind of it, the gallerist got cold feet, fearful of the negative publicity that could arise from associating with a recently released prisoner.[32] Unceremoniously canceled, the project would be resurrected years later, when Chupan was in exile (see Act Four).

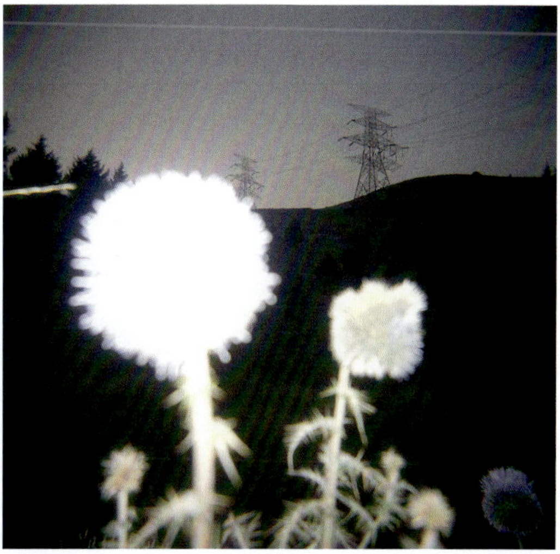

FIG. 11 Chupan Mehraneh Atashi. Photograph of wildflowers on a Tehran roadside (from *Unmediated Nature* series), 2010, Tehran. Courtesy of the artist.

As the Green Movement subsided, women's artistic engagement with the streets continued in a quiet yet persistent manner. One notable exponent of performance art during these years was Tehran Carnival, a group of six women born in the early 1980s—Ayda Alizadeh, Mahtabeh Alizade, Elnaz Ezzati, Elmira Yousefi, Elmira Mahnia, and Sepideh Zamani—who worked together from 2009 to 2014. The primary goal of the collective was simple: to derive joy and improve their emotional well-being through their art. They did not make overtly political statements; rather, their works were personal expressions of anti-institutional sentiment and private amusement, taking playful forms such as a papier-mâché shark in a plastic cube, or a yellow cardboard car and gigantic binoculars. And they often chose unconventional spaces for their installations, placing them in visible and remote locations where they might go noticed or unnoticed by the general public.

Iranian art traditionally shies away from the use of humor, especially in relation to political matters. But the group's approach subtly undermined this tendency, using humor and absurdity as creative tools, in line with Mikhail Bakhtin's concept of the carnivalesque. Crafting ephemeral moments of joy and levity within a cultural landscape that often lacks such expressions, Tehran Carnival created a nuanced, nonconfrontational reflection on the spaces they could inhabit as artists and women in Tehran.[33]

While Tehran Carnival mostly maintained a discreet profile in the capital, another group of women emphatically asserted their presence through a performance in Tehran's busy Ferdowsi Square. In July 2011, seventy-four women clad in red gathered in the place

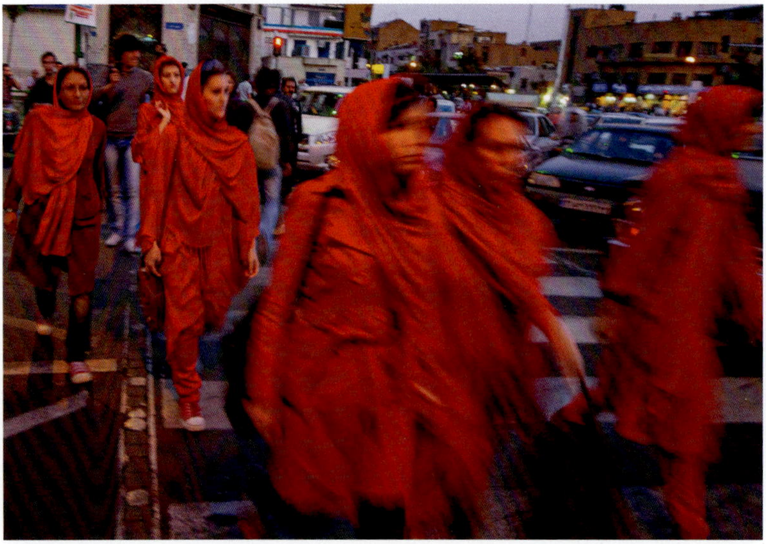

FIG. 12 Mohammad Hosseini et al., *Women in Red*, 2011, Ferdowsi Square, Tehran. Photograph by Saeed Kiaee.

where a local legend, the mysterious Yaqut, or Lady in Red, had stood in the 1960s and 1970s, apparently waiting for someone who never showed up. Curated by Mohammad Hosseini, and repeated daily from July to September, this act of remembrance evoked a narrative of love and longing that was once brightly woven into the collective memory of the city. While the government at first tried to claim the event was a film shoot, Hosseini insisted on its true intent: it was performance art—a work that transformed public space into a stage of homage to the city's more vibrant past, and an act of defiance against the repression imposed in the wake of the Green Movement FIG. 12.

The collective yearning to reconnect with a past that is both cherished and contested was made clear when more volunteers, propelled by social media, swiftly joined the performance. These women performed in different ways: some stood still in silent tribute; others distributed the red roses that symbolized Yaqut's legacy and the attempt to reignite the flame of love in a city more often overshadowed by darker emotions. The performances were interrupted by the authorities and drew mixed reactions from passersby, ranging from curiosity to intimidation, from appreciation to disdain. Embodying both visibility and silence, the women encountered the paradox of empowerment and vulnerability in their act of public artistry.[34]

Women navigating public spaces in Tehran have to constantly negotiate a landscape of scrutiny and control—of societal and moral judgment. Consequently, many choose to be subtle and discreet in their artistic expressions, finding creative avenues to be both seen and unseen, present and absent. In this context, the *Women in Red* performance appears all the more audacious, with its deliberate quest for high visibility, for direct engagement with the public in one of Tehran's busiest spots. A fragile yet powerful assertion of memory, love, and women's voices in the urban heart of Tehran, the project exemplifies the importance of the presence of the body in political activism, as described by Butler, drawing inspiration from Arendt. When an artist's body serves as a medium for their artistic project to manifest as "political action," it must "appear to others in ways [it] cannot know, and in this way, [the] body [of the artist] is established by perspectives that [it] cannot inhabit, but that, surely, inhibits [it]." In other words, "it is not the case that the body only establishes [its] own perspective; it is also what displaces that perspective and makes that displacement into a necessity."[35]

The significance of *Women in Red* lies in its site-specific nature. Rather than overtly conveying political themes, it links to a place in the teeming heart of the city where a somewhat enigmatic historical

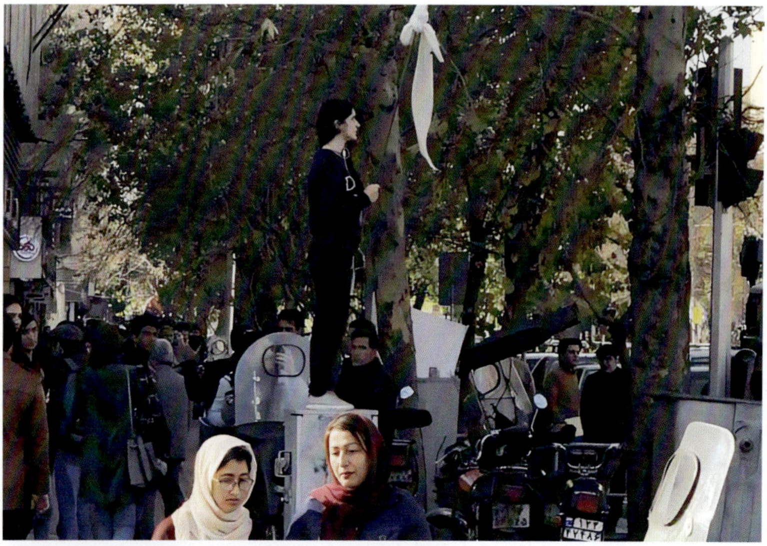

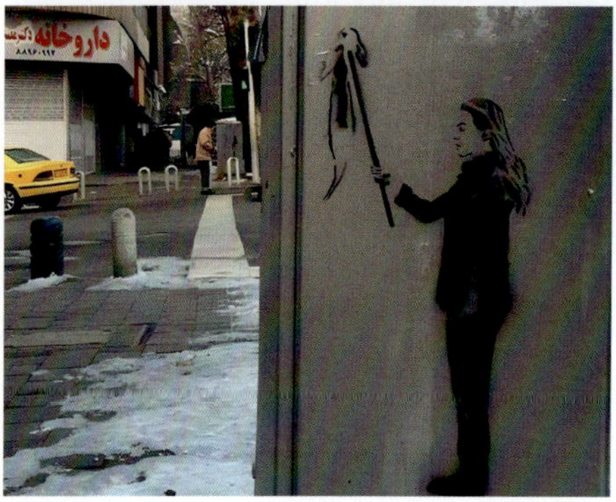

FIG. 13 Image capturing an anti-compulsory hijab protest scene on Enqhelab (Revolution) Street, Tehran, in 2017. Courtesy of an anonymous photographer and modified by an anonymous artist in Tehran. Image also appears in a number of media outlets, including https://www.platformspace.net/
FIG. 14 Street art commemorating the moment on a utility box in Tehran in 2019. Courtesy of a photographer in Tehran who wishes to remain anonymous. Image also appears in a number of media outlets, including https://amwaj.media/

figure displayed an expression of feminine love. *Women in Red* can thus be seen as a precursor to even bolder acts of public bodily expression on the streets of Tehran.

In 2014, journalist Masih Alinejad, who has lived in exile since 2009, set up the Facebook group "My Stealthy Freedom" to encourage Iranian women to share photos of themselves without a hijab, despite the personal risks involved.[36] Hundreds of women, both in Iran and abroad, participated in the movement, and it drew international attention. A few years later, in December 2017, the activist Vida Movahed became an icon for protests against mandatory veiling when she stood on a utility box in Tehran and waved her hijab tied to a stick. She was jailed for her act of defiance, as were many other women, but the movement to end mandatory veiling continued to build momentum in Iran FIGS. 13–14.[37]

In parallel to these events, artists in Tehran used impromptu public performances and, at times, covert tactics to disrupt the usual patterns of urban life and to reclaim for women—even if only temporarily—the streets and spaces that are normally controlled by the authorities. In 2015, Jinoos Taghizadeh attached a GoPro camera to her forehead to record a series of visits to politically significant sites in the capital—a risky undertaking, as filming in public without official permission is prohibited. The resulting work is a three-hour-long video drawing inspiration from William Shakespeare's *Titus Andronicus*, set in ancient Rome, but with universal themes of killing and revenge. Mirroring the five acts of Shakespeare's tragedy, Taghizadeh's video visits five locations in Tehran, each associated with violence against its citizens, including Evin political prison and the notorious Lot 41 at Behesht Zahra Cemetery, where political activists lie in unmarked graves FIG. 15.[38] Remarkably, Taghizadeh's presence in the video is felt not visually but through her voice. In this work, she is an observer rather than a subject, shifting the focus between the sound of herself reading Shakespeare's text and brief glimpses of the locations, creating a mental map that challenges official narratives and exposes the violence that lurks beneath their ostensibly calm surface.[39] In the video, the artist's body mostly eludes our view—we occasionally see her shadow. On the street, however, as she was navigating politically sensitive areas, her body would have fearlessly conveyed the bold themes. Taghizadeh's street intervention—her "parading" of her body—is a paradoxical act, simultaneously positioning her as a target for the police and concealing her from the scrutiny of viewers of her art. This form of intervention carries a feminist essence, challenging the *scopophilic* and *voyeuristic* elements often found in video art and film where the protagonist is female.[40]

The examples described above all pre-date the Woman, Life, Freedom uprising. They illustrate how many Iranian artists, and particularly women, have engaged over the years in street based interventions in which they have tactically employed their bodies to draw attention to the injustices of street politics. In doing so, these artists have also—whether intentionally or not—expanded the

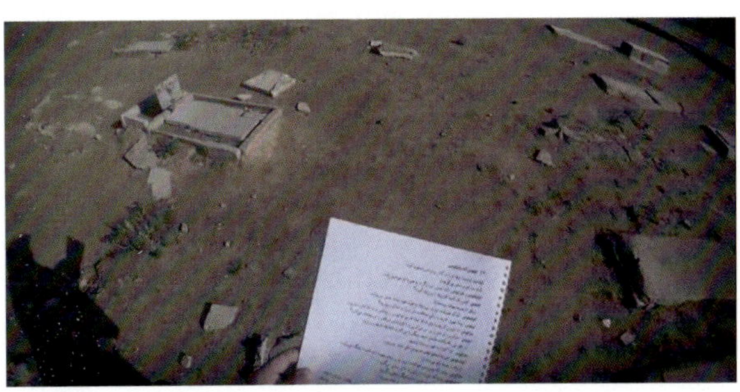

FIG. 15 Jinoos Taghizadeh presents *Titus Andronicus*, 2015, capturing moments of reading and walking in Behesht Zahra Cemetery, Tehran. Video courtesy of the artist.

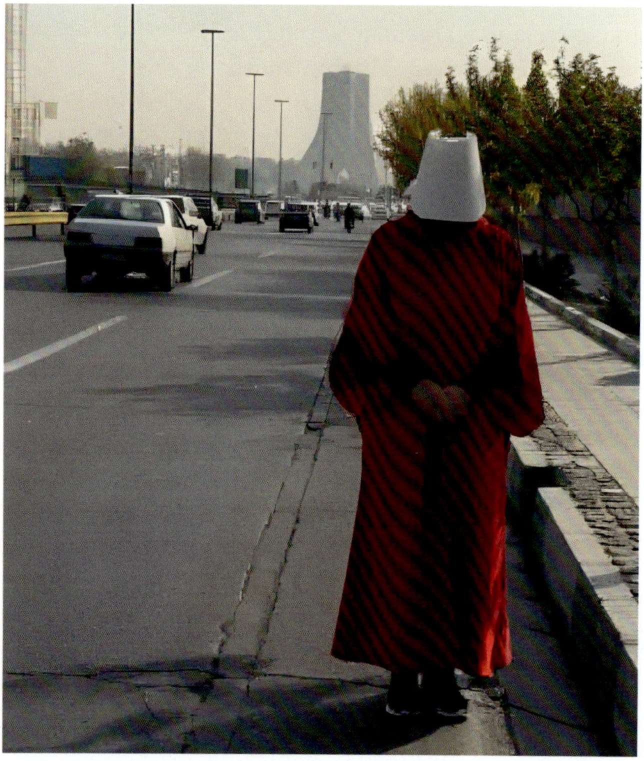

FIG. 16 An unidentified woman, dressed in a costume evocative of the 2017 TV series *The Handmaid's Tale*, stands on a bustling street corner with Azadi (Shahyad) Tower in the backdrop. The image has been featured in various media outlets, including *Iranwire*. Captured and modified by anonymous artists in Tehran.

impact of the feminist movement beyond its usual confines, reaching a wider "space of appearance."[41]

In the following discussion, I will focus on how women artists paraded their bodies on streets during and after the peak of the uprising, in the face of heightened surveillance. There was a marked increase in the number of women who ventured into Iranian cities without the obligatory trench coat and veil, defying the ever-vigilant gaze of the CCTV cameras.[42] Others went further. In late November 2022, an unidentified woman stood on the main road leading to Azadi Tower in Tehran, dressed in a costume from the TV adaptation of Margaret Atwood's dystopian *The Handmaid's Tale* (1985)—an allusion to the frequent comparisons between the Islamic Republic and the fictional Gilead, a repressive society where women are considered property of the state FIG. 16.[43] Other "handmaids," dressed in long red cloaks, surfaced in other places around the capital. Their interventions show the capacity of Iranian protesters to replicate without duplicating—"to repeat without copying, to embed difference in similarity, to be at once both *self* and *other*."[44] Taking on the role of a fictional character while maintaining anonymity (by concealing their face with a bonnet) was undoubtedly a bold act of bodily expression, particularly during the height of the protests.

However, an even greater bravery was displayed by the artists who openly performed on the streets without disguising or masking their true identity.

THE ARTIST ASSERTS HER PRESENCE

Born in 1986, Zohreh Solati exemplifies the courage and spirit of a bold street artist in Tehran, especially in the months following the height of the uprising. Solati's early life was shaped by the strict religious beliefs of her relatives, dominated by patriarchal figures. Any deviation from orthodox norms was met with stern disapproval. Imagine, then, the response of her religious relatives when, at college, and majoring in figurative painting, she began studying anatomy through the re-creation of nude figures from Western masterpieces. Solati was forced into marriage at the age of just eighteen—a bond or binding it would take years of legal battles to dissolve. During her numerous court appearances, Solati was disheartened to realize that she was often perceived as the primary problem, even by women working within the judicial system.

Life in the aftermath of divorce was another ordeal. In more traditional Iranian contexts, there is a stigma attached to divorce, particularly for women, and Solati was urged to keep the end of her marriage secret. After the divorce, she was often excluded from extended family gatherings, reinforcing her sense of isolation—of a diminished existence. What changed her situation was, ironically, the outbreak of the COVID-19 pandemic. With the whole world "self-isolating," Solati found solace in introspection. She turned the lens on herself, capturing myriad images across various settings, making herself the center of her artistic narrative. Alongside this profound journey inward, she also went out into hospitals, to comfort COVID-19 patients and document their struggles. The distance between Solati and her estranged relatives increased further, as she could not risk infecting the older members of the family.

When the Woman, Life, Freedom movement began, Solati stepped up her activism, publicly discarding her veil in contravention of both societal norms and the wishes of her family. In some parts of Tehran, such as Ferdowsi Square, this was an act that invited severe harassment and potential arrest. In June 2023, she translated her "daily acts of defiance" into an art project. Donning a costume made of interconnected square mirrors, she showcased herself across the city, receiving varied reactions depending on the area's demographics FIG. 17. In the upscale Shariati Street, for example,

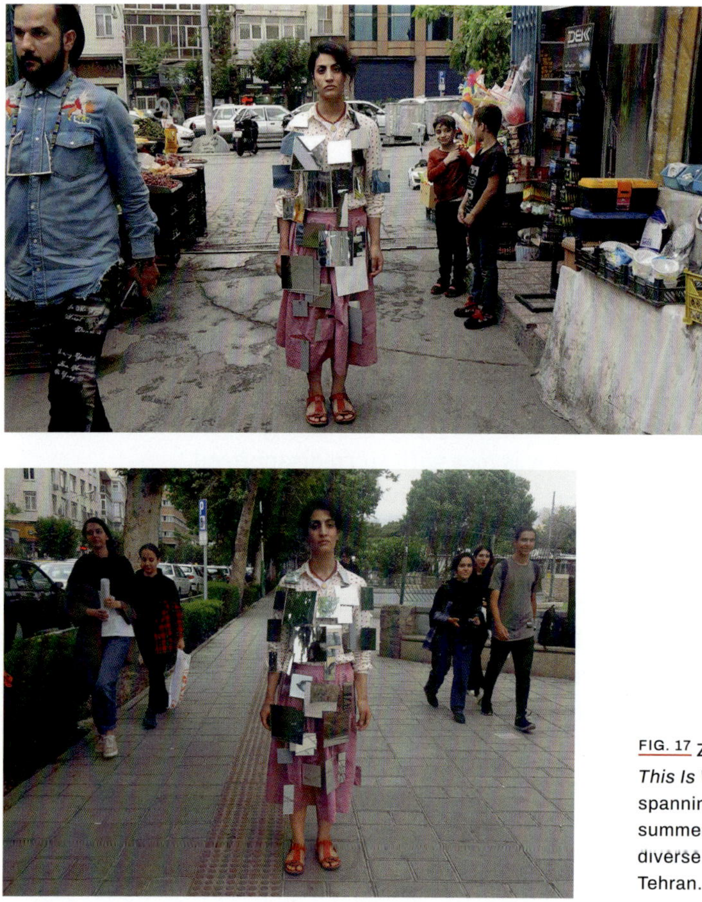

FIG. 17 Zohreh Solati unveils *This Is Who I Am*, a series spanning winter 2022 to summer 2023, exhibited across diverse neighborhoods of Tehran. Courtesy of the artist.

accolades flowed her way. Some passing cars honked in appreciation; outside the Tehran Museum of Contemporary Art people voiced their admiration for her bravery, while many captured her presence, likely for sharing on social media.

In Tehransar, a neighborhood where many of the inhabitants have family ties to Sepah (the Islamic Revolutionary Guard Corps), people were unsurprisingly less welcoming. Many threw disapproving glances. Some hurried away, anxious they might be captured in the backdrop of photos or videos of her performance. Others warned her, in hushed or assertive tones, that she should make herself scarce, as the police were on their way.

Yet, alongside its traditionally conservative population, Tehransar is also home to a younger Iranian demographic, drawn there by its relatively low cost of living. According to Solati, some of these young women dress even more daringly than their counterparts in more affluent areas of the capital. They move around confidently without hijabs, maintaining their assertive demeanor when they are looked at—their blouses may be low-cut, or reveal their belly buttons—and they are not shy about opting for cosmetic alterations or vibrant hair colors. Solati recalls that these young women showered her with admiration, pledging to relay her actions to platforms like *Iran International TV*, *Man O To*, *Radio Farda*, or *BBC Persian*. Yet what Solati remembers most is that she stood still through it all, overwhelmed by a feeling of perspiring, not so much because the day was warm, but because of the intensity of the reactions—some of them confrontational, menacing even.

Solati's performances did not go unnoticed by the authorities, who saw them as a threat, fearing they would inspire other young women, and summoned her to account for her actions. Facing intense pressure to erase her boundary-pushing images, she stood firm, defending her art. When I asked her about how art bolsters her activism, Solati stressed its unparalleled potency. Art, she said, "provides a nuance that direct mediums, like writing, sometimes lack. It allows interpretations, offering a unique kind of empowerment."[45] For Solati, the inherently ambiguous language of art makes it a more feasible vehicle for activism than written commentary on cultural and societal problems, especially in a context like Iran. She drew a parallel with the famous Iranian poet Forough Farrokhzad, musing that Farrokhzaad might have faced less criticism in 1960s Iran if she had been a visual artist. Concluding our conversation, Solati acknowledged her apprehension about the future but affirmed her unwavering commitment to activism through her art, knowing fully well there is no turning back.

If performance provided a suitable platform for Solati in the public spaces of the capital during the uprising, it also proved to be an effective medium for another artist living in a more traditional and religious city, whose work extended for the first time beyond the confines of her studio, finding its way onto the streets.

THE CRY OF THE BODY

Nasrin Shahbeigy was born in 1993 in Zahedan, in the province of Sistan and Baluchestan. She initially gravitated toward athletic training—a strong swimmer, she had been introduced to swimming at an early age by her father, who disguised her as a boy so she could practice at the pool at his workplace. Growing up near the Baluchi communities, she was also captivated by their resilience and their art, especially the traditional ceramics of the Kal Pouregan region, which are crafted collaboratively: men prepare the clay while women

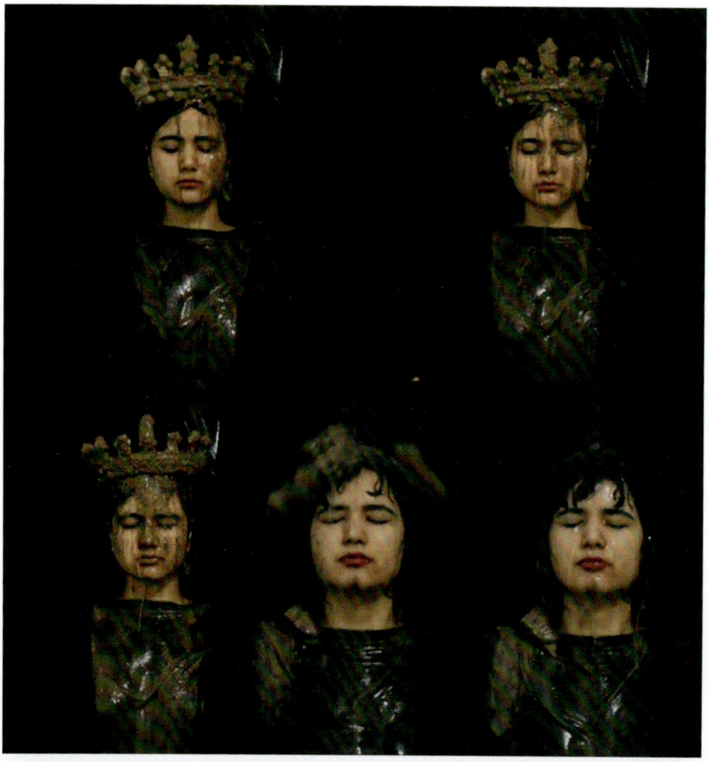

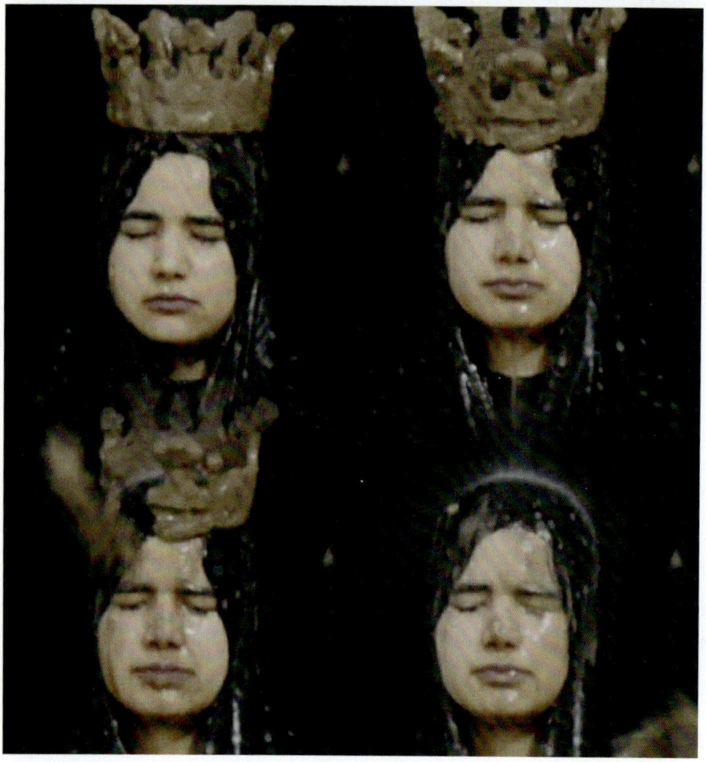

FIGS. 18A–B Nasrin Shahbeigy presents *Khodkavi* or *Finding Self*, a video installation created for the 11th National Ceramic Biennial of Iran, held in Tehran from October to November 2020. The top image featuring the unveiled artist was rejected by the biennale, while the bottom image was reproduced and exhibited during the event. Courtesy of the artist.

shape the pots manually, without wheels, and decorate them with distinctive, historic patterns. This fascination led Shahbeigy to pivot her studies from athletics to ceramics, eventually earning an MFA from the University of Tabriz, but she would find a way to combine her love for both disciplines. For the 2020 Ceramics Biennial in Tehran, she crafted a video that showed her taking a shower with an unfired clay crown on her head: the crown slowly dissolved to clay under the running water, leaving just her hair. The video was rejected on the grounds that her hair was visible. Undeterred, she reshot wearing a chador, feeling this version spoke even more powerfully to the situation of women in the Islamic Republic, underscoring the disconnect between their "official" elevated status and their underlying powerlessness FIGS. 18A–B.

Profoundly affected by the tragic death of Amini—which she referred to as the "martyrdom of Mahsa"[46]—Shahbeigy told me she had shaved her head, emphasizing the significance of such an act for someone her age, still living at her parents' home in Mashhad. "At one point, I felt willing to risk my life during the protests, if it meant paving the way for a just society for Iranian women," she confided.[47] By December 2022, she was channeling her grief into art, and specifically performance art, aiming to inspire thoughts of change in the public places of Mashhad. She began physically rolling her body along the ground on streets, sidewalks, parks, pedestrian bridges, graveyards, and other busy areas in and around the city. More precisely, she playfully rolled her body across public spaces, an act that might seem innocuous when done by a young child on a park lawn or soft surface, but is decidedly unusual behavior for an adult, especially an adult woman. Engaging in this act of rolling for extended periods, repeatedly on a daily or weekly basis, she marked herself an unconventional figure in her religious city, where the morality police stringently monitor the hijab and enforce public modesty. "I was met with astonishment," she said.[48] Some responded by blasting their car horns, but she remained engrossed in her performances. Continuing to roll, Shahbeigy felt a profound connection to her surroundings, akin to the spiritual experience of a Sufi practicing the *sama'*: "The streets—the entirety of the outside world—felt like they belonged to me" (Figs. 19a–b).[49] Interestingly, this way of describing her artwork resonates with the experience of protesters during the Arab Spring. During his winter 2012 visit to Homs in Syria, the French American writer Jonathan Littell noticed that the nightly protests against the regime's assaults resembled and were influenced by traditional Sufi celebrations. But rather than just reflecting those traditions, the rebels' actions imbued them with new meaning. "The demonstration is a *dhikr*," one local explained,

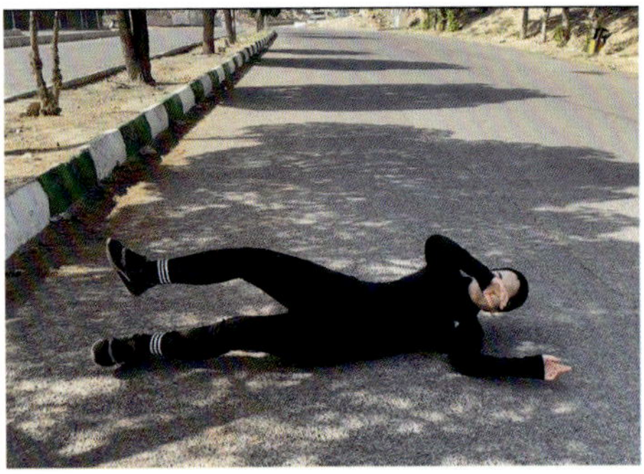
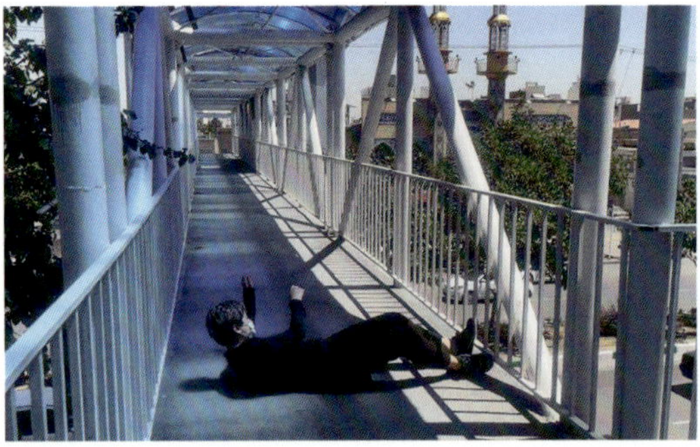

FIG. 19A–B Nasrin Shahbeigy, *The Cry of the Body*, performed in multiple locations across Mashhad and showcased in video format at Persbook's 12th Annual of Contemporary Art in fall 2023. Courtesy of the artist.

likening it to the Sufi practice of praise through song, chanting, and rhythmic movement, yet reimagined as a secular revolutionary ritual.[50] While Shahbeigy's rolling performances do not intentionally evoke an Islamic (specifically Sufi) tradition, they illustrate how a sensation of those old practices could be captured—albeit in a way that diverged entirely from their original form—in the context of the Woman, Life, Freedom movement.

Shahbeigy initially intended to perform in her everyday attire or even her nightgown, reflecting her deep spiritual connection to her art. But her desire to reach art professionals as well as an everyday audience caused her to reconsider. For the recordings of her performances, she was unveiled and wore a modest black shirt and pants—an outfit she thought would be better received at professional art venues, competitions, or biennales. When I asked about who was behind the camera, doing the filming, she surprised me by saying that it was her parents. Despite their religious convictions, they were intrigued by her displays. Initially, they perceived them as playful pranks, but as they continued to observe and film her relentless drive to revisit locations and refine her craft, they gained deeper insights into her intentions. They came to realize that her performances were not designed just to entertain or to display her athletic prowess: they were, more profoundly, an attempt to reclaim urban spaces that women are barred from accessing freely. On one level, involving her parents was a way to bridge the generation gap within her own family, but it also suggested to Shahbeigy that if she could connect with her parents in this manner, she could reach countless others. If activism is often lacking in creativity, Shahbeigy said, then art can fill the void: "To get people's attention, protesters should be prepared to go beyond the ordinary, introducing elements of the unexpected."[51] As Shahbeigy exemplifies through her art, these need not be extreme acts. Rather, the gestures can be subtle, yet remarkable. A direct engagement with the street, sensing its aroma, feeling its texture, connecting with it through every sinew and fiber of the body, can become a profound form of dissent.

In the US, artists of color have often used their own bodies as a medium to address issues of subjugation and racism in neighborhoods that are inhospitable to Black lives, especially those from underprivileged communities. A striking example of this is William Pope.L's *eRacism* project, begun in the late 1970s, which extended to over forty endurance-based performances called "crawls." In the 1991 *Tompkins Square Crawl*, for instance, Pope.L donned a business suit and crawled along the sidewalk holding a potted flower. The choice to crawl, rather than walk, while handling a delicate object, powerfully symbolized the challenges faced by a Black man in occupying street space: the effort is not only strenuous and exhausting, it also often requires the safeguarding of the precious, fragile aspects of his life.

Shahbeigy was unaware of Pope.L's crawls, though her own performances represent an analogous solution to a similar challenge. When access to a space is restricted, an effective form of protest is to assert ownership over it, embracing it in its entirety—in its complexities, imperfections, beauty, and all. In Iran, women face severe punishment for not adhering to hijab regulations, let alone engaging in acts like Shahbeigy's. In this context, her rolling practices stand out as particularly potent, performed at risk to her own freedom and life. Above all, we see how nonverbal actions of this kind are effective models for conveying feminist messages. As feminist art historian Pollock writes,

> art is itself a form of thought, a thinking through making. We do not impose words on it, but allow a passage from what is thought through varied forms of artistic practice into the wider debates by which we can [also] understand feminism as more than a series of local disturbances caused by uppity women in this field or that.[52]

While the practices highlighted in this section are aimed at gaining visibility, other artistic interventions are carried out incognito. On the surface, this approach might appear to provide greater protection for the artist, and call for less courage, but it can paradoxically lead to significant challenges, as I will explain in the following "act". ■

Act Two

HIDING IN PLAIN SIGHT

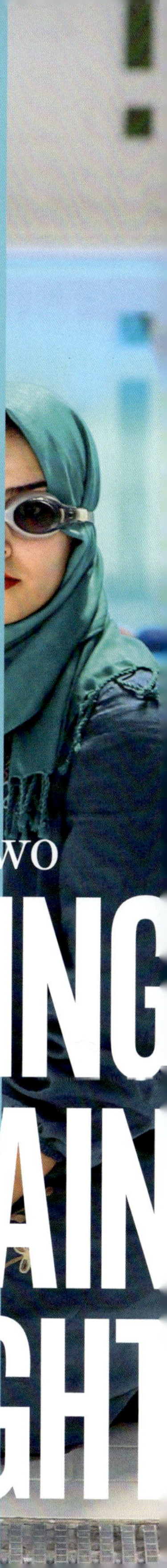

The strategies of anonymity, inconspicuousness, and obscurity are not new to the recent uprising, but have been deployed for many years by graffiti artists who inscribe city walls with their political art. Though their stylized signatures are famous, Black Hand, Ada, Blind, Nafir, and many more have managed to keep their identities secret. Taking their cue from graffiti artists, many artists turned to "anonymous" expression as the Woman, Life, Freedom protests gathered strength. In early October 2022, in response to an attack on demonstrators in Tehran's Sharif University, two unnamed women artists tied red nooses to trees in Daneshjoo Park. Though the installations were quickly removed by the police, pictures of them continued to surface online. Artists canceled public performances that would have had to have been vetted by the Ministry of Culture and Islamic Guidance: "At this crucial historical juncture, we denounce the word 'guidance' and its incompatible juxtaposition with the word 'culture'; any work that requires permission from the MCIG will be barred from now on," a prominent artist and musician wrote on his social media platform.[1] Art students abandoned their classes and their professors supported them with public statements (and later paid a heavy price for their support, as their contracts were suspended or terminated; see Act Nine).[2] Instead of participating in regular recitals, music majors at Tehran's University of Art performed protest songs in the corridors—the accompanying footage blurs their faces or only shows their tapping feet—and issued a statement condemning acts of violence against students. Other art colleges followed suit. Students at University of Tehran covered their faces with written slogans as they sat behind an unveiled female student who bent forward, her long hair hiding her face and her wrists tied to a poster tube—a pose evoking the turturous hours of the Baluchi dancer and activist, Khodanoor Lojei, who was allegedly handcuffed to a flagpole by the security forces and left in the scorching heat, without water, but with a glass of water in front of him, out of reach FIG. 20.[3] Lojei was later murdered during the Zahedan massacre, or Bloody Friday, which occurred on September 30, 2022, when protesters gathered and chanted in front of a police station near the Great Mosalla of Zahedan, Iran. This led to a violent crackdown resulting in numerous casualties.[4]

In November 2022, a group of high-profile theater directors and actors posted a powerful video on Instagram: it shows them walking into a public park, as onto a stage, and standing in silent solidarity with the protests, the women unveiled. FIG. 4 [TOP LEFT IMAGE] The first two to appear in the clip, actor Soheila Golestani and director Hamid Pourazari, were arrested and jailed soon after. Their performance, however, would be repeated by another group of people, who walked to the same location and took up the same pose before the camera, except that, this time, their faces were covered with stained bandages, like the acid attack victims of Islamic extremists. In December 2022, following the execution of Mohsen Shekari and Majidreza Rahnavard—who were convicted of "enmity against God," having been accused (without verification) of injuring or killing members of the militia—a series of anonymous artists in balaclavas formed a long line in a park with nooses around their necks.[5]

Anonymity, however, is not adopted solely for protection, which it does not guarantee in any case. The comedian Zeynab Mousavi, who was behind the anonymous satirical Instagram account of "Empress Kuzcooo," for example, was identified by the cyber police and was released on bail following 25 days in solitary

FIG. 20 Students protesting at the University of Tehran's Faculty of Fine Arts adopt poses reminiscent of that of Khodadad Logei. Image courtesy of a private Instagram account. The photographer and modifier of the image prefer to remain anonymous.

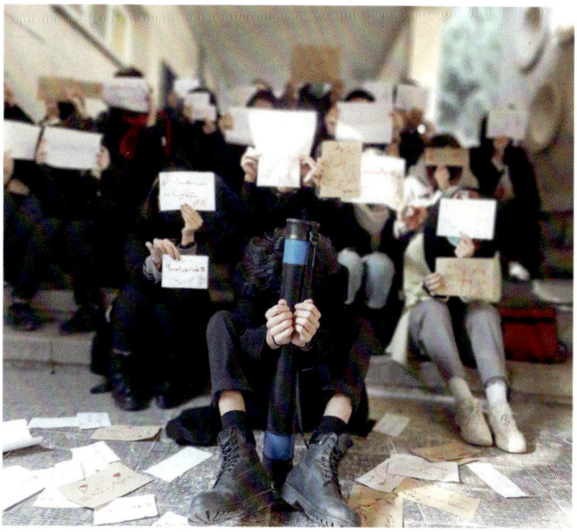

confinement and later received a two-year sentence for charges that were not disclosed FIG. 21.[6] Despite her lawyer challenging and subsequently changing the charges, the fact that she faced punishment and interrogation by the Iranian regime underscores that anonymity does not always guarantee protection for activist artists. Many creative agents now choose anonymity, removing themselves from the story, to amplify the political message in their work. In part, this is a reaction to the fact that global art institutions have tended to focus on the biographies and works of celebrity Iranian artists in the diaspora, reinforcing an orientalist gaze. In the early 1990s, the art world was fascinated by a series of staged self-portraits of a veiled, gun-toting Shirin Neshat with Persian feminist verses written across her body—a stance that aimed to capture the "rebellious silence" of Iranian women forced into Islamic dress codes. Thirty years later, when the Neue Nationalgalerie in Berlin put up a banner with one of those self-portraits, *Unveiling* (1993), overlaid with the mantra "Woman, Life, Freedom," there was a backlash among Iranian artists, who objected to the use of an image of a seemingly passive veiled woman to represent the feminist ideals that Iranians were fighting, even dying for.[7]

The activist art of this quasi revolution seemed to gain in impact when it was made by anonymous or little-known artists. There was a greater freedom both for the viewer, with no assertive author to set limits on their imagination, and for the artist, who was able to jettison the propagandistic visual language of the Islamic Republic—the kind of language that Walter Benjamin famously termed the "aestheticization of politics."[8] Instead, art entered the realm of the political in informal, tangible, and profound ways, becoming part of everyday life without the support of powerful agents, big names, auctions, galleries, or museums.[9]

THE PRICE OF ANONYMITY

Those who choose to be anonymous risk losing the chance to flourish as artists. Not only are they unable to participate in the art market, but many institutions, wary of reprisals from the regime, cut off ties with them. One Iranian artist who has suffered this fate is Meysam All-of-The (a moniker that resonates and rhymes with his real surname), who uses the Instagram handle @all-of-the.

Born in 1993 to a Kurdish family in Sanandaj, Meysam describes himself as politically engaged from an early age. He dubs his initial style "critical design" (*design-e enteghadi*), conveying both his training in graphic design and his critique of the Islamic Republic's oppressive power structures, including those that curtail women's rights and their access to public spaces.[10] These biases divided his own family, with his younger sister succumbing to societal norms and Meysam, a self-proclaimed feminist, moving to Tehran to forge an independent life and career. In the capital, his talent was swiftly recognized and he collaborated with top designers and artists, especially at Tehran's University of Art, and produced compelling book covers for major publishers. But as the morality police ratcheted up their persecution of women under the new president, Ebrahim Raisi (installed August 2021), his designs began to take on a more dissenting tone. In September 2022, devastated by news of the deaths of young girls at the hands of the authorities, Meysam channeled his emotions into his art, juxtaposing protest images with various forms of typography, calligraphy, and *nagh-ghashi-khat* (a type of calligraphic painting)—the words ingeniously framed to fit Instagram's square format. This turn to what Meysam calls "protest design" reflects his belief that, throughout Iran's history, written words, calligraphy, and poetry have been a more potent means of voicing grievances than the visual arts, especially for the common people. In one particular post, the Persian word for veil or hijab is shown four times. The topmost iteration is bold and rendered in a deep red, distinctly spelling out "hijab." But each time the word is repeated, it loses color and weight and the diacritics are altered, bringing about a subtle transformation from hijab to *hobab*, which translates to "bubble" in Persian FIG. 21.

Meysam's layered calligraphic compositions during the uprising intertwined bold typewriter typography with delicate calligraphic writing, primarily featuring the phrase "Woman, Life, Freedom." The written form gave him the agility to respond quickly

FIG. 21 Instagram image by Meysam All-of-The depicting the transformation of the word "hijab" into "hobab," meaning "bubble." Courtesy of the artist.

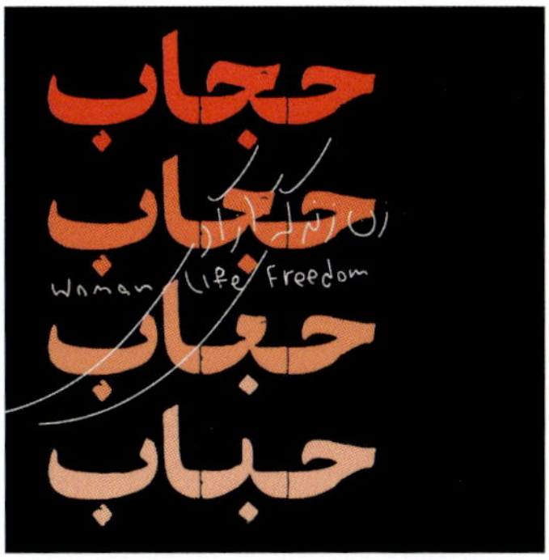

FIG. 22 Meysam All-of-The's anarchist reinterpretation of the title "The Art University," cleverly designed to replace the letter *n* in the word for "art" (honar) with "no" (*na* in Persian). Courtesy of the artist.

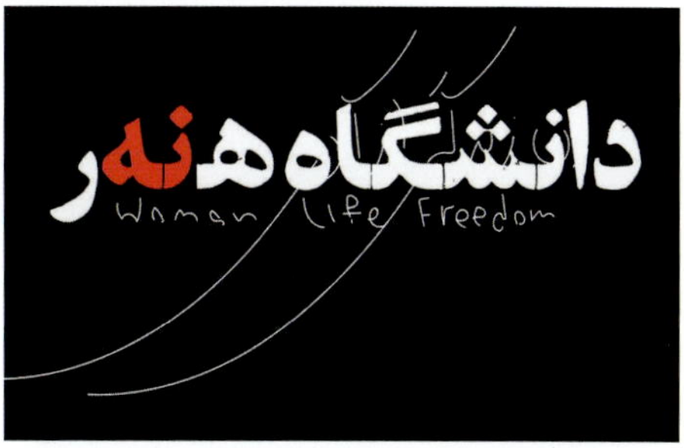

to unfolding events. The resistance of the University of Tehran's Faculty of Fine Arts, for example, was recorded in a piece in which the letter *n* in the word for "art" (*honar*) is cleverly designed to signify "no" (*na* in Persian) FIG. 22.

Meysam would be arrested twice during the uprising. Twice, while he was in custody his popular Instagram account was deleted by friends who were concerned for his safety. Twice, Meysam rebooted the account, altering aspects of its design to reflect his feelings after his release. Yet his activism has had long-term consequences. Once a celebrated multi-award-winning designer, he is now shunned by former collaborators and struggles financially in Tehran. Despite the setbacks, Meysam remains unwavering in his beliefs. While his Kurdish heritage brings particular challenges in Iran, he focuses on a larger goal, not aligned with any political faction, but emphasizing women's freedom as a foundation for a more just society.[11] Months after the peak of the uprising, he still dedicates himself solely to the Woman, Life, Freedom movement and to his anonymous online activism.

The desire to be part of a larger collective, just as much as the need to safeguard against identification, explains why many video creators chose anonymity.[12] Writing about the videos that were disseminated by the general public during the Arab Spring, Rabih Mroué suggests they are not just individual expressions but a shared asset, and that the very act of uploading them signifies a renunciation of personal ownership and identity that resonates with the overarching revolutionary spirit.[13] Rather than celebrating the work of a particular expert or photojournalist, the widespread practice of circulating these videos without reference to the original creator reinforces their collective nature. The same could be said of the art made by nameless contributors to the Woman, Life, Freedom uprising. In analyzing the experience of Meysam All-of-The, I hope to have shown how professional artists are exposed to particular challenges that the general populace might not encounter. While anonymity might align with collective ideals, it does not shield an individual from the Islamic Republic's security apparatus. Meysam's story underscores a grim reality: even under the cloak of anonymity, artists are not safe.

Anonymity is not confined to art within Iran's borders but is sometimes embraced by artists elsewhere in response to the unique dynamics of diasporic Iranian culture and its politicization within certain communities and groups. In the following case study, I will illuminate this aspect through the example of a diasporic Iranian artist who sought anonymity, particularly during the height of the Woman, Life, Freedom uprising.

ANONYMOUS IN THE LAND OF THE FREE

In summer 2023, a male US-based illustrator whose work I follow told me that he had chosen to remain nameless to avoid being associated with any specific political group or faction within the Iranian diaspora. He does not feel compelled to promote his work widely or to seek fame in the comic book realm; rather, his artistic endeavors serve primarily as a form of therapy.

On Instagram, he documents the Woman, Life, Freedom movement under the handle @1401comic. On his social media platforms, he goes by the pseudonym Parviz Bina. Outside the digital sphere, his identity remains a mystery, as does his actual location in the US. He also remains elusive about his artistic background, a choice consistent with his anonymous persona.[14] Bina consented to a Zoom interview with me on the condition of anonymity, asking for the camera to be disabled during our conversation. Though fluent in Persian, he expressed a preference for communicating in English. Born in 1984, he spent his early childhood in Tehran and remembers the final stages of the Iran–Iraq War, particularly the missile attacks on the city by Saddam Hussein's forces. He also has vivid memories of the street life of Tehran, which have stayed with him over the years.

Profoundly affected by the brutality of the clashes between protesters and the authorities at the peak of the Woman, Life, Freedom uprising, Bina found a source of solace—and a means of articulating his deep-seated pain and turmoil—in the visual imagery of comics. He told me that he hoped others might find the same kind of therapeutic outlet in his work, but seemed uncomfortable with my mention of Marjane Satrapi's *Persepolis*, saying that he wanted his comics to be more than a convenient means for outsiders to learn about Iran. To maintain an authentic connection to his roots, he chose to write his narrative in Persian. Rather than give an amusing form to the story of an uprising met with brutal violence, the point, for him, was to craft a work that resonated with Iranians and the diasporic community, offering them a mirror of their own experiences and struggles.

Steering clear of the geopolitical reverberations of the Woman, Life, Freedom uprising, Bina centers his narrative around five characters representing different degrees of religious and secular perspectives—a microcosm of Iranian society. Mehdi hails from a traditionally conservative religious household. A former member of the Basij, a paramilitary volunteer militia, he comes from a family with a history of *shahids*, or martyrs. Mehdi's journey in the narrative involves a profound awakening as he confronts the systemic oppression exercised by the regime. Then there is Saba, a medical doctor and the epitome of education and independence, who is forced by circumstances to make the difficult decision to abandon her medical career. Afshin, an alumnus of the prestigious Sharif University, comes to the crossroads of emigration but chooses to remain in Iran, testifying to his commitment to (or perhaps simply hope for) change. On the surface, Asal, a vivacious partygoer from an affluent, liberal family, has a carefree lifestyle, but she bears the scars of betrayal by the regime. Finally, the youngest character, Negin, personifies the bold and indomitable energy of the younger generation—a demographic at the forefront of the demonstrations, bravely facing up to the authoritarian forces in the urban heart of Iran.

Though from different walks of life, these characters become friends, drawn together by their shared aspiration for freedom of expression and a democratic society. United, they present the collective face of defiance, challenging the government's authoritarian rule. Individually, each stands for a distinct strand of resistance.

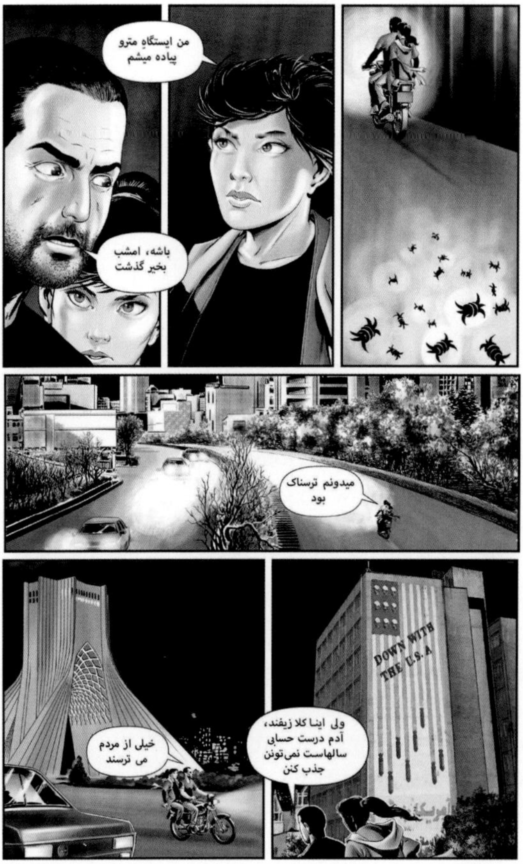

FIG. 23 Parviz Bina (pseudonym), a page from the comic book *Woman, Life, Freedom*, 2023. Courtesy of the artist.

Weaving together a chronicle of rebellion and solidarity, Bina's narrative reflects his desire for neutrality. In our conversation, he described how the tensions that have arisen in the wake of the uprising have reinforced his decision to remain anonymous. He is determined to avoid scrutiny from various generations of Iranians in the diaspora who would form opinions about him based on his age, his depth of knowledge about Iran, or his views on the country's past and present. In Iran, he observed, disagreement is often perceived as a personal affront—a sentiment that is further amplified on social media. In the diaspora, anonymity allows an artist to escape unwanted political associations FIG. 23.

As literary historian Amy Malek notes, the 2022 protests in support of the Woman, Life, Freedom uprising made clear the divisions within the diaspora, with the overwhelming sense of solidarity with the movement being marred by internal conflicts among different groups of overseas Iranians. Malek adds that the resulting mistrust and polarization, made worse by the proliferation of disinformation on social media, raises questions about the capacity of the diaspora to contribute to meaningful change in Iran—a concern also shared by individuals like Bina.[15]

The previous two stories relate to professional artists who have chosen for various reasons to remain anonymous. Now I want to shed light on a different kind of art that is "hidden in plain sight." This concealed form of art holds great significance both for the artists and their immediate audiences, though the artists' names often remain undisclosed, and their works frequently remain unseen by the wider world. In this context, I will explore a facet of art that is often overlooked in Middle Eastern and Iranian art history—prison art.

ART BEHIND BARS

Prison art has notably evolved with the Woman, Life, Freedom movement, adopting an innovative, abstract, and opaque style of performance. Within the walls of the political wards, hidden from the public eye and, mostly, the surveillance of the prison guards, it has allowed young detainees to create a space they can call their own. Before shedding light on this art, and on what makes it different, I will first explore the longer tradition of prison art in the years before the uprising. In all the examples discussed below, the significance of the prison space is evident; it mirrors, with a much-heightened intensity, the public spaces of Iran, where citizens are constantly surveilled by the morality police.

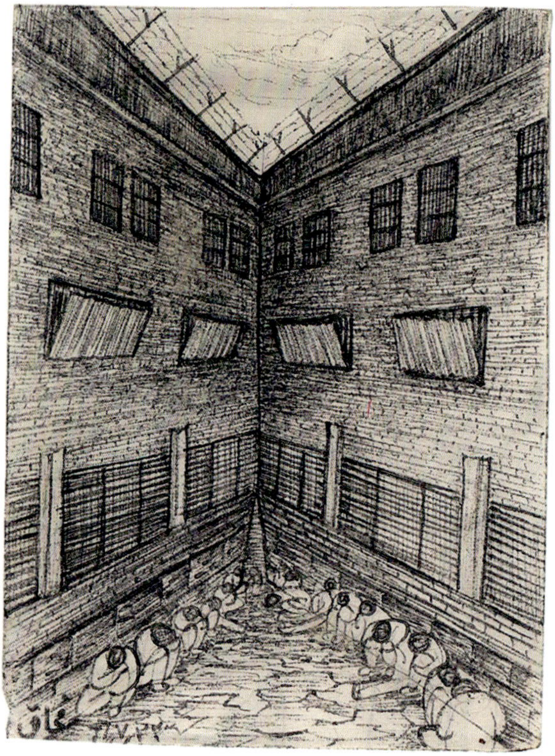

FIG. 24 Soudabeh Ardavan's small-scale drawing, created during her time of incarceration, portrays different wards and open spaces within Evin Prison in Tehran, all merged into a single image, giving the impression of one unified building. Courtesy of the artist.

In the decade following the establishment of the Islamic Republic, the regime detained and killed thousands of political activists, notably in a series of mass executions conducted in secret over a period of a couple of months in 1988. Thousands of activists, particularly on the left, were imprisoned for extended periods. Among them was Soudabeh Ardavan, an architecture student who was sent to Evin Prison in 1981, at the age of twenty-three, and remained there until 1989. Her crime was participating in an antigovernment demonstration. Using improvised materials—flower petals and tea for paint, toothpicks and human hair for brushes—Ardavan crafted intricately detailed artworks that vividly capture the mood and atmosphere of life in the political wards and interrogation corridors FIG. 24.[16] To reduce the risk of her artwork being discovered and destroyed by the guards, Ardavan made necessarily small-scale drawings and stashed them in ingenious hiding places, including, Ardavan says, under the plastic cushion of a paddle hairbrush.[17]

While Ardavan was professionally trained in painting, her fellow inmates used different methods to create art within the confines of the prison, turning to embroidery, jewelry making, and, occasionally, crafting small sculptures as their primary forms of artistic expression. One prominent figure in this regard is Monireh

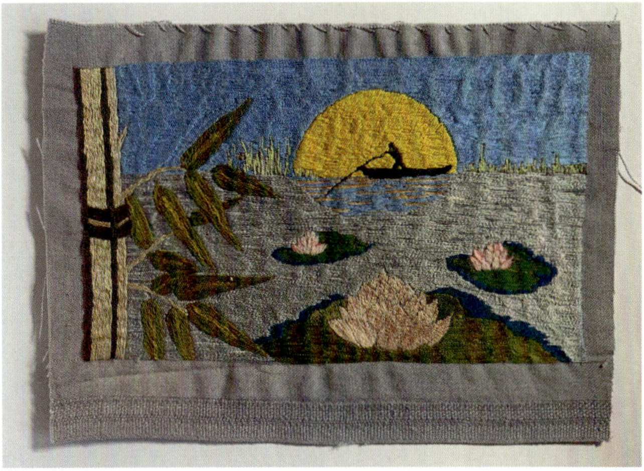

FIG. 25 Monireh Baradaran, *Embroidery*, 1987, Evin Prison, Tehran. Courtesy of the artist.

Baradaran, who survived nine years in prison, from 1981 to 1990, enduring spells of solitary confinement as well as longer periods in communal cells, where she was held either with fellow political detainees or with a more diverse prison population, including addicts. In both solitary and communal detention, Baradaran and her fellow inmates in Evin engaged in creating art using the limited resources at their disposal: from date pits or small stones to scraps of paper that were smuggled into inmates' cells, hidden in diapers or clothing, on the rare occasions they were allowed to have physical contact with their children.[18] Towels or unused socks were repurposed, cleaned, and shredded into threads for use in embroidery or other textile-based art forms.[19]

In one piece, Baradaran devised an intricate embroidery depicting a boatman, oar in hand, navigating a serene lake. This scene, likely set at dawn, features a bright yellow sun in the background. There are waterlilies in the foreground, and a bamboo tree gracefully enters the frame, adding depth and tranquility to the composition FIG. 25.

Baradaran shared with me that she sewed this piece in a solitary cell, while still in shock at the killings of her young cellmates. She was anxious to hide her work from the guards, as having a thread and needle was forbidden, and crafts were not allowed in solitary confinement. The flowers symbolize the youth and purity of her executed cellmates, a poignant reminder of innocence lost. The sun, for her, invariably embodies the truth, while the figure on the boat signifies the survivors who stayed behind to testify their experiences. Baradaran also spoke of the nuances of her embroidery, pointing out how she manipulated her needle to mimic the texture of water, and carefully shaded the areas around the waterlilies to reflect a murkier, shadowy effect.[20] I was profoundly moved—to the point of tears—to hear her describe in affectionate detail a piece that had been created under such harrowing conditions. Baradaran's work can be said to embody the quality of human resilience, but this resilience, she makes clear, was not driven by the need to prove anything to others; rather, it was essential for her own survival. "To survive as a human, one must create," she says. "Without creation, we perish."[21] In her memoir, she refers to some verses by twentieth-century Russian poet Vladimir Mayakovsky to sum up the struggle to be creative when you are denied the basic means of self-expression: "In this life it's not difficult to die. To make life is more difficult by far."[22] Baradaran was able to study Mayakovsky's *How to Make a Verse* in Evin, after gaining access to a clandestine, handwritten copy smuggled in from another facility where there was a library. She also helped transcribe further copies to circulate among her fellow inmates, an effort that required heightened vigilance, both to ensure not a single word was missed, and to avoid attracting the attention of the guards.[23] Living in Germany since her release, Baradaran was one of the cocurators (along with prominent artist Parastou Forouhar) of a 2012 exhibition in Frankfurt that showcased the resourcefulness and creativity of political prisoners and exiles in 1980s Iran. Held at the Anne Frank Educational Center, the exhibition was titled *My Name is Hope*.[24]

In recent years, a strong interest in theater has emerged among political prisoners, at times with the complicity of guards who are no longer adhering strictly to the ideologies of the regime.[25] Plays were performed in Evin's political ward as early as 2012, a period marked by a relative easing of conditions, as a series of construction projects gave prisoners access to additional space and open-air areas.[26] But in 2012 Evin also housed a remarkable prisoner, Nazanin Deyhimi (1988–2017), known for her translation of plays from English and German into Persian. During her three-month stay, she convinced some of her fellow inmates to stage her adaptation of Ariel Dorfman's *Death and the Maiden* (1990), a play that highlights themes of justice, revenge, and the elusive nature of truth. The "maiden" is Paulina Salas, a former political prisoner scarred by rape. When Salas's husband unknowingly brings her rapist home, she holds him hostage under gunpoint, wanting to force him to confess his wrongdoing. Her husband initially supports her, but then starts to question the validity of her story. As the narrative unfolds, the dynamics between the two men and the sole female victim become increasingly complex and intense, leading to an ambiguous ending

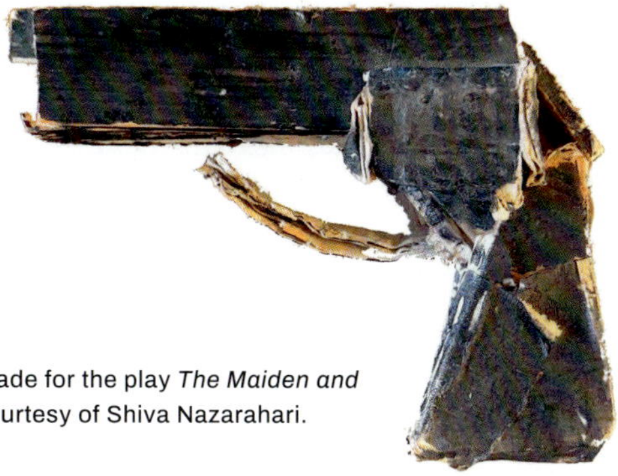

FIG. 26 Shiva Nazarahari, Wooden gun made for the play *The Maiden and the Death*, 2012, Evin Prison, Tehran. Courtesy of Shiva Nazarahari.

that leaves the audience pondering the reality of the events and the lasting effects of trauma.

Deyhimi unfortunately died very young, due to complications from asthma, but her outpouring of energy into the staging of the play, and her striving for a high degree of professionalism, is described by one of the participants, the women's rights activist Shiva Nazarahari.[27] The extensive rehearsals involved physical movements and screaming in the gym—techniques Deyhimi had experienced in her previous work with theater groups. For the performance itself, bedside lamps were borrowed from inmates' cells and arranged around the gym, where they were operated by a backstage team. Interlocking plastic exercise mats were transformed into makeshift steps, mimicking a theater's raked seating for the thirty members of the audience. Flower boxes added a domestic touch to the scene, complemented by props like a styrofoam recorder and a wooden gun crafted in the prison workshop FIG. 26. Relatives of Deyhimi provided a CD of Franz Schubert's String Quartet No. 14 in D minor, *Death and the Maiden*, based on a sixteenth-century personification of Death as a seducer of young women, which was played for a short time on a stereo under the watchful eye of the prison guards.[28]

Despite the difficulties involved in putting on the play, the actors' performances were compelling, making a deep impression on the audience. One notable cast member was Bahareh Hedayat, a women's rights activist and prominent force behind the One Million Signatures campaign, who was then serving a nine-and-a-half-year sentence for "antistate propaganda."[29] She would be imprisoned again during the height of the Woman, Life, Freedom protests, but her bold letter addressing the aims of the movement was smuggled out of Evin and subsequently translated into English and widely circulated (I will return to this letter in Act Eight).[30]

Among those sitting in the audience was Nasrin Sotoudeh, one of the most resolute voices in the women's movement in Iran, a lawyer who represents imprisoned activists and who has herself endured years of incarceration. Years later, she would describe how she admired the play not only for its professional delivery but also, most importantly, for its significant theme.[31] The play can indeed be interpreted as a reflection of the plight of political prisoners in Iran: the security forces' systematic use of rape and sexual assault as a means of punishing or silencing those detained during the 2022 Amini protests is detailed in a report that was released by Amnesty International in the summer of 2023.[32]

While the decision to perform *Death and the Maiden* at Evin seems a profoundly political choice, the staging of the play was also, as Nazarahari has described it, "a form of collective care" (*mor-aghebat-e jam'i*), promoting a spirit of collaboration, solidarity, and resolve among young people who had been—and still are today—incarcerated simply for holding democratic views that diverge from the government's stance.

Some 150 artists have reportedly been detained and imprisoned since the beginning of the Woman, Life, Freedom uprising.[33] According to data collected by the Art, Culture, Action group, these artists are from all kinds of backgrounds, notably music, theater, and cinema.[34] Being in prison has not stopped them from practicing their art, but while traditional theater remains feasible, recent performances in Evin have evolved into something more abstract and opaque. Tehran-based multimedia artist Homayoun Sirizi, who maintains close ties with the friends of a few young detainees, has described the increasing importance in prisons of a unique form of theater, often referred to as *Teatr-e haghighat* or *Teatr-e zendegi* (Truth Theater or Life Theater), that he finds even more intriguing than the art performed on the streets.[35] Here, the routine and restrictive environment of prison becomes a stage for artistic invention. Interactions with guards, for example, might inspire a quietly whispered rap song. At mealtimes, in the prison refectories, rather than engaging in mundane conversation, the inmates might use poetic and coded language to reimagine their situation or to mock the lives of their guards.[36] Particularly in the women's wards, the bodies of the inmates have been turned into canvases for artistic expression. Imprisoned tattoo artists use ordinary markers to create their designs and these "tattoos" then become part of impromptu performances when the inmates are able to interact, whether at mealtimes, yard time, or other activities throughout the day.

The performance-based art forms observed in prison environments today are quite different from the prison art of the 1980s, which was typically small-scale, made with improvised materials such as bread or date pits, and concealed from the guards with great ingenuity. Today's prisoners have subtly integrated art into their daily lives. Rather than having to find a physical place to hide it, they are able to conceal it with covert language, hushed, rhyming expressions, and bodily gestures. Anonymity in art manifests in various forms, but its embodiment in the political wards of prisons is particularly sophisticated, providing a vital means of sustaining the spirit of the inmates.

But anonymity in art goes beyond merely concealing the artwork or hiding the name or the presence of the artists; it also encompasses the depiction of bodies in a way that leaves them nameless, without distinct identity. This trait notably marked the artistic expressions that surfaced in the years leading up to the uprising, capturing a sense of opaqueness.

OPAQUE BODIES

The Woman, Life, Freedom uprising has challenged many entrenched perceptions about women. However, in Iran, there is still a very fine line between the Islamic Republic's legal regulation of women's dress codes and behaviors and the broader societal expectation that women will remain subtle, polite, and opaque. Often this means that citizens and communities follow the societal norms, irrespective of whether they are politically aligned with the regime. Artist Sara Sasani challenges this state of acceptance through her photography, addressing the subtler yet all-pervasive aspects of these norms.

Born in 1985 into a female-dominated household, Sasani naturally gravitated toward contemplating the intricacies of women's lives, first studying photojournalism and then majoring in sociology for her master's. After graduation, she collaborated with prominent news agencies, for example *Mehr*, with journals such as *Cinema and Culture*, and with newspapers including *Hamshahri* and *Etemad*. While all these outlets operate under a governmental umbrella, the newspapers in particular offer a perspective that is relatively progressive. Even so, Sasani soon found that she did not have a free hand and there were obscurely defined limits to what could be openly discussed or photographed. In the Islamic Republic, she emphasizes, it is not just about what is explicitly prohibited; there are myriad subjects that, although not labeled illegal, are subtly deemed unworthy of mention or coverage.[37]

Sasani's background in sociology, and her association with the more liberal media, allowed her to discern the nuanced boundaries she had to navigate. During her master's studies, she delved into the history of feminism, discovering the multifaceted nature of feminist

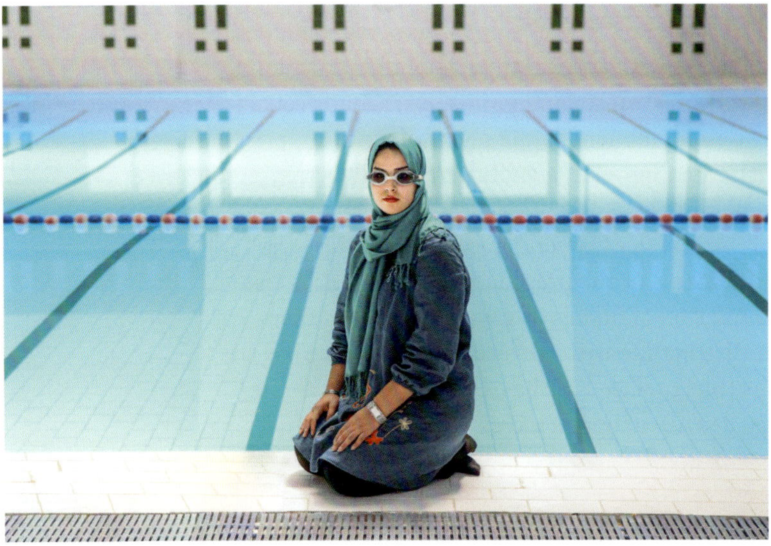

FIG. 27 A swimming champion dressed in official Islamic attire—including a trench coat, trousers, and headscarf—paired with swimming goggles. Sara Sasani, from the series *We Are Born Too Late*, 2019, Tehran. Courtesy of the artist.

thought. While the approach of some early feminists seemed to her too black and white, authors like Julia Kristeva resonated for their nuanced perspectives. As Sasani understood it, distinct from the earlier stages of the feminist movement, which Kristeva criticized for oversimplifying womanhood, Kristeva's third-wave feminist ideas focused on exploring a diverse array of identities, which notably includes a spectrum of sexual identities. While some critics raise concerns about the viability of feminist agency within Kristeva's framework, her ideas offer a flexible and nuanced approach to identity, difference, and ethics.[38] This knack for navigating nuanced terrains, Sasani observes, has always been particularly relevant to both her professional experience within media and her encounters with feminism.

In an assignment for the Tehran municipality's monthly bulletin, Sasani was tasked with making a portrait of Tehran's female athletes, focusing in particular on a successful swimming team. Arriving at the stadium where they practiced, she found herself confronted with a major challenge: how could she photograph them in their swimsuits? The newspaper suggested a workaround, which was to do a group portrait of the team outside the pool area, clad in full Islamic attire, holding a banner celebrating their achievements. Sasani complied with the guidelines, but her artistic instincts took her back to the pool the next day. Taking advantage of her sister's position at the stadium, she persuaded the athletes to take part in a more creative photo shoot. One image captures a swimming champion clad in official Islamic attire—trench coat, trousers, and headscarf—intriguingly paired with swimming goggles FIG. 27. Sasani clicked the shutter just as the athlete posed in front of an emptied pool. The photograph is disconcerting at first—how could she possibly swim in that attire?—yet, as the scene settles, one detects a subtle, playful humor woven into its composition.

Sasani is also fascinated by the roles of women in Iranian professions traditionally dominated by men. While there are no specific laws barring women from these careers, there are also no regulations mandating equal pay or access to benefits like insurance. Jobs such as being a DJ or a barista fall into this category. While women can undertake this work without facing overt discrimination or public shaming, they have to operate without the protections typically afforded to male workers. What is striking for Sasani is the ignorance or indifference of society toward these women, who often go unnoticed even by those who avail themselves of their services. Despite their groundbreaking presence in typically male-dominated fields, their contributions also remain largely uncelebrated and unreported by the media.[39]

After observing these women, Sasani was inspired to capture their essence through art photography, in a series titled *We Are Born*

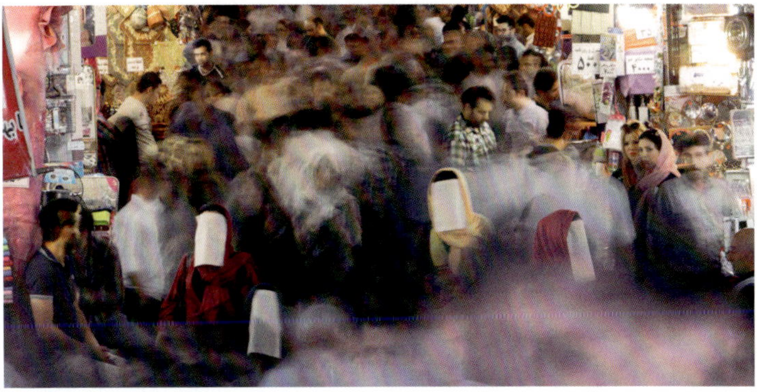

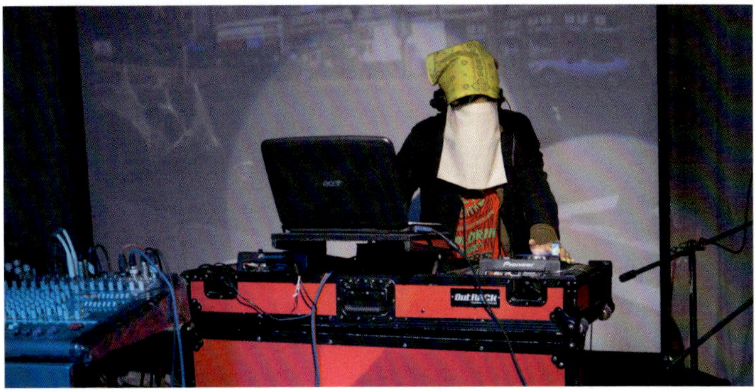

FIG. 28 Anonymous women wearing white masks in the old Tehran Bazar. Sara Sasani, from the series *We Are Born Too Late*, 2014. Courtesy of the artist. FIG. 29 Masked female DJ in Tehran. Sara Sasani, from the series *We Are Born Too Late*, 2014. Courtesy of the artist.

Too Late. Here, the subjects remain faceless, veiled under white sheets that render them anonymous. While they are central in the compositions, their identities and roles remain enigmatic. Adding to the irony, bystanders in the photos seem oblivious to their presence. The women exist in a poignant duality: both present and invisible. In a striking photograph taken in Tehran Bazaar, Sasani positioned herself at an elevated vantage point, gazing down on the bustling crowd. Using a tripod and a slow shutter speed, she directed her sheet-covered subjects to remain still, a technique that rendered them in sharp focus, while the surrounding crowd blurred into a hazy motion. The image captures the paradox of Iran's "invisible" women: in a society where women often go unnoticed, here they stand out boldly, even though their faces remain obscured by white sheets of paper, and it is the rest of the world that fades into obscurity FIG. 28.

The same series also engages directly with the female workers who are actually "invisible" in society—for example, a female DJ in Tehran, who is depicted in her professional setting, with her face and identity entirely concealed FIG. 29.

Sasani saw how women bore the brunt of the economic fallout from the pandemic.[40] Legal and societal norms in Iran perceive men as the primary breadwinners, so when cuts needed to be made to company and institutional budgets, women were usually laid off more quickly than their male counterparts. Relegated to domestic roles, many found themselves confined to their homes for extended periods during the lockdown, their enthusiasm for their professions dwindling in line with their job prospects. In this context, Sasani crafted a series inspired by the compound word *roozmarregi*. In Persian, the term refers to everyday mundane tasks. However, when read without certain vowel markers over the *m*, the word sounds like "Death of the Day," which became the evocative title of this collection. These pieces vividly capture the sense of despair and stagnation during that time, with a recurring theme of women partly submerged in piles of dirt, as if buried alive. In the two-part photograph featured here, the women are faceless and anonymous, their facelessness representing their perceived value FIG. 30. Alongside the photographs, the series includes video components and a soundtrack in which women narrate their experiences of the COVID-19 lockdown. Some are somber in tone, expressing a sense of the emptiness of life and thoughts of suicide, while others provide a glimmer of hope amid the darkness.

Sasani's photographs offer profound insights into women's roles in Iranian society. In our conversations, she reiterated that she is concerned with capturing more nuanced and complex realities.

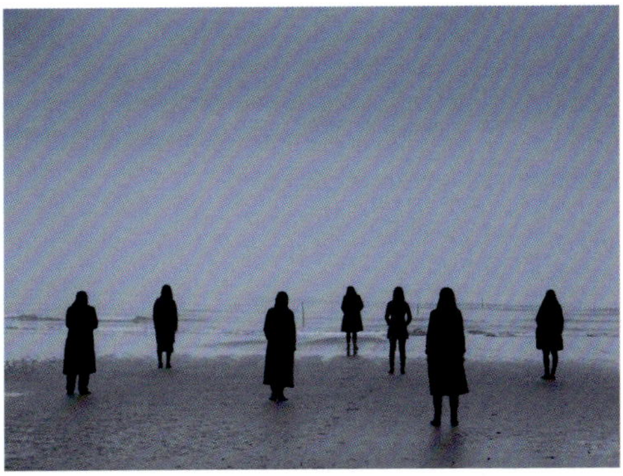

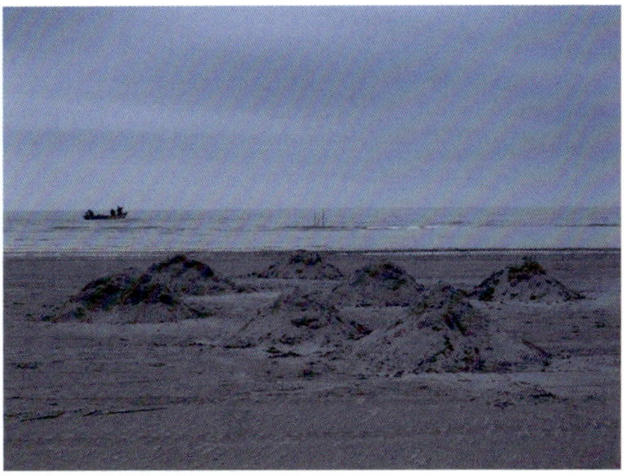

FIG. 30 Staged photographs and video stills, presented in two parts. Sara Sasani, from the *Death of the Day* series, 2020–2021, Caspian Sea Shore. Courtesy of the artist.

As she points out, life in Iran is not always clear-cut: women often have to navigate the gray areas between the rules, and their rights are violated in ways that are often more insidious and subtle than the overt actions of the morality police or the imposing of the mandatory hijab.[41] Despite the grim atmosphere of the *Death of the Day* series, Sasani's interpretation suggests there is a certain ambiguity to the images. They do not directly associate women with death, nor do they depict women as victims. In figure 30, the fact that the women are shown facing the sea could be seen as a symbol of potential escape from their predicament.

Reflecting on the Woman, Life, Freedom movement, Sasani confesses she was astounded by the visual richness of the uprising, which she credits with having brought about a pictorial revolution.[42] For over forty years, the government had aggressively promoted its portrayal of the hijabi woman. Now that dominant image of Iranian womanhood had been supplanted.[43] Women's hair, previously concealed, had become a potent visual symbol of defiance and change in a country traditionally inclined toward poetic expression and language. Sasani interpreted this shift from words to images as a counterresponse to the government's persistent emphasis on religious texts, revolutionary propaganda, and poetry (with the supreme leader himself being a poet).[44]

While opaqueness is a bold aspect of women's appearance in Sasani's art, for a slightly older generation it assumes a more abstract form. As I noted in the introduction to this volume, the Bauhaus educational approach, which prioritizes direct experience over intellectual mediation as the foundation of artistic creation, was a central aspect of the training of many Iranian artists educated before the 2000s. Here, a focus on form, texture, and abstraction tended to overshadow any engagement with the theory or history of art, and to push aside any hints of social issues. When these issues did surface, they were expressed through the language of abstraction, using textures and forms rather than a conceptual or narrative-based approach. In this context, I would like to present an alternative perspective on "anonymity" rooted in the distillation of ideas and entities into abstract forms and textures—a strand of Iranian art exemplified by the work of Shaya Shahrestani. Though replete with social and political themes, particularly concerning women's bodies, Shahrestani's art is a testament to her generation's educational influences and their subtle approach to addressing culturally complex or politically charged issues.

Born in 1972, Shahrestani studied classical guitar from the age of thirteen, showing enough promise to be recommended by her private tutors for prestigious global conservatoires. However, the untimely passing of her father, which forced her to stay in the country with her mother, combined with the subdued state of music in Iran during the 1980s, led her to shift her focus to the visual arts. Enrolling at a Tehran art college in 1990, Shahrestani immersed herself in the world of painting, experimenting with forms, shapes, and abstraction. Her style evolved as she trained under renowned painters, eventually embracing mixed media and using raw wooden materials as her canvas—a transition that gave her entry into respected art circles, with her works featured in Tehran painting biennales.

Shahrestani's artistic expression took a significant turn as she began to incorporate plastofoam into her paintings, creating rough textures reminiscent of the fragmented surfaces of old and decaying plastered walls: the impact on the urban fabric of Tehran of the Iran–Iraq War, which lingered for a long time after the protracted conflict finally came to an end, deeply influenced Shahrestani's work. These large abstract sculptures became a language through which she communicated the pain and discomfort of everyday life—a nonverbal narrative of resilience and survival. However, the expense of producing the large sculptures, and their apparent lack of relatability, would lead Shahrestani to turn back two-dimensional art, this time to drawings characterized by twisted and gnarled figurative elements that subtly conveyed the emotional landscape of women in Iran.[45] Shahrestani's art reflected, and continues to reflect, her experiences under the Islamic Republic, starting with the 1979 revolution—a life journey that encompasses war, interrogation, and harassment. But more than just her personal story, it also reflects the broader sociopolitical atmosphere of Iran.

Shahrestani's art may call to mind works by Lucian Freud or Jenny Saville, but she firmly believes that her art is quintessentially Iranian, embodying the essence of her homeland even though it may not overtly display traditional Iranian symbols or themes. Regarding her influences, Shahrestani expresses her admiration for the German artist Käthe Kollwitz, whose works are filled with expressions of pain and struggle that resonate with the sociopolitical challenges faced in Iran. For Shahrestani, this shared life experience is more profound than visual influences from artists like Saville or Freud.[46]

In the wake of the Woman, Life, Freedom movement, Shahrestani produced a series of large-scale drawings of distorted female figures, *The Witness* (2023), which captures the essence of living through tumultuous times. The drawings were displayed at Tehran's Iranshahr Gallery using "accent lighting," a technique that created a dramatic and immersive experience for the viewer, perfectly accentuating the twisted, tortured textures in her work, depicting bodies seemingly distorted by violence or surgery FIG. 31. Shahrestani perceives the female body as a central theme, not only in the protests but also in the experience of public conflict and street violence. Her work also reflects a collective sense of bodily shame and vulnerability, particularly among women, under the oppressive gaze of authority: paintings with motifs like hands covering eyes serve as a testament to this pervasive sense of intimidation. Among the various forms of anonymity and obscurity I have discussed in this "act", I believe Shahrestani's work offers a distinctive reaction to the circumstances following the 2022 uprising. It encapsulates the characteristics and uncertainties not only of women today but also of the multiple generations who have experienced life under the Islamic Republic. Although they might appear as figures marked by defeat, I perceive them as a potent confrontation by an artist with her genuine emotions, reflecting not just on a particular uprising but on a whole life marked by fear and the intimidation and marginalization of women.

Anonymity and opaqueness in art typically emerge through subtle artistic methods, whereas bold, feminine protest props aim for a more conspicuous impact, even when used by anonymous protesters. Moving forward, my focus will shift from the creators of art to the protest props themselves and their inherent power. Rather than attributing agency solely to the artists and creators behind protest art, I will explore the significance, agency, and influence of the protest props. ■

FIG. 31 Shaya Shahrestani, *The Witness*, oil pastel and pencil on canvas, lit by accenting light, 2023, Iranshahr Gallery, Tehran. Courtesy of the artist.

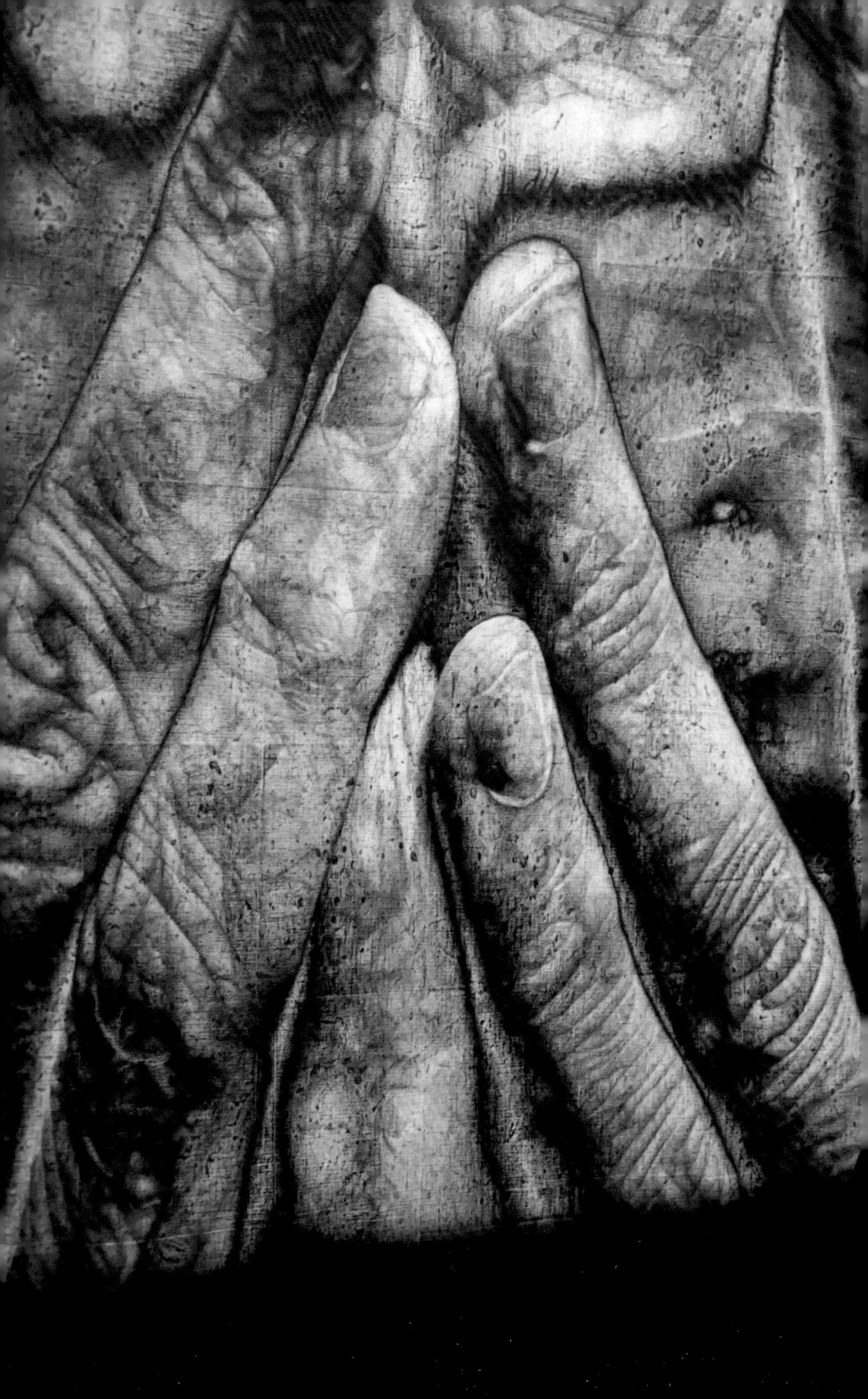

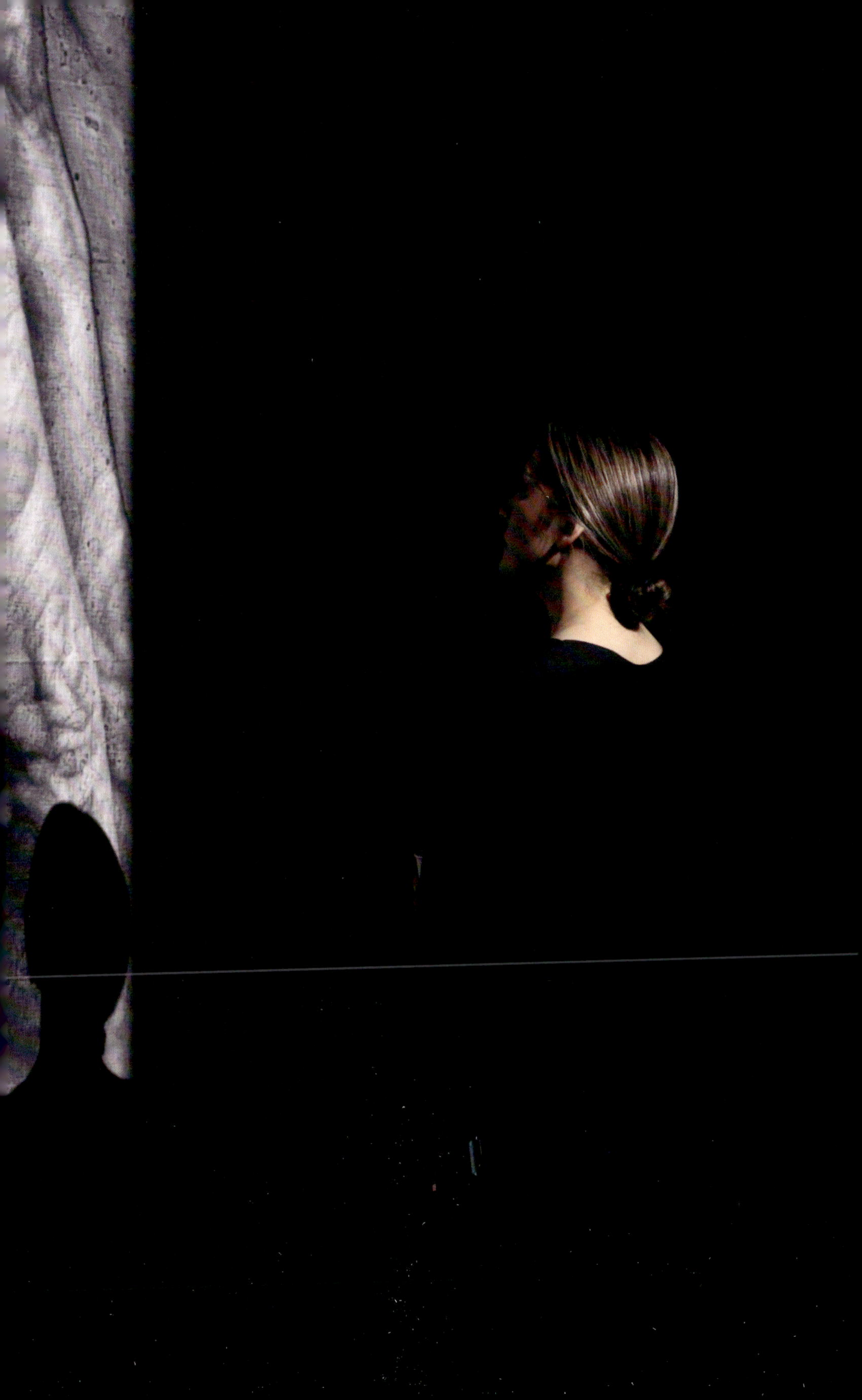

Act Three

STAGING CITYWIDE PROTEST PROPS

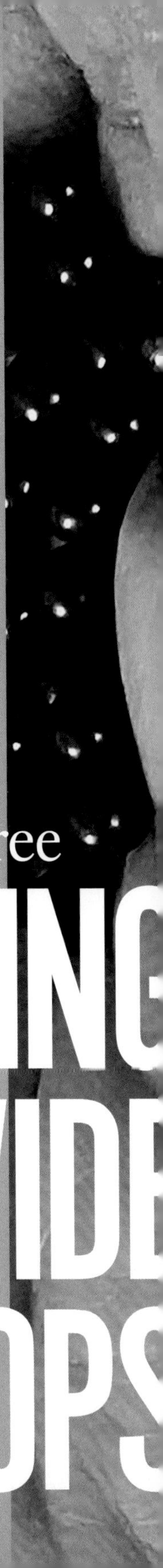

Headscarves have been a powerful symbol of protest in Iran ever since October 2017, when Vida Movahed stood on top of a utility box on busy Enghelab Street, waving her white headscarf on a stick FIG 13. In the wake of that iconic demonstration, women have expressed their rejection of the mandatory hijab by deploying their headscarves in various creative ways: removing them, twirling them, setting them on fire, casting them into the wind, or brandishing them on sticks, Movahed-style.[1] Women's hair, too, has become a compelling, shape-shifting emblem of protest: whether chopped or cropped or flowing in the wind, whether painted or crafted from synthetic materials for specific protests. In essence, women's hair, the hijab, and even certain items of clothing have taken on such significance as tools of dissent that even the subtlest references to them continue to

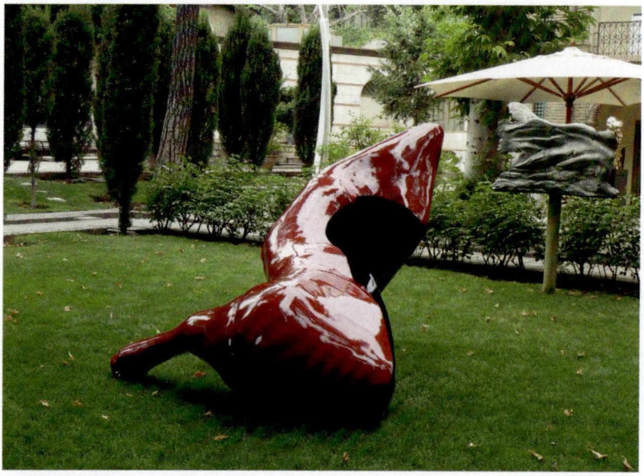

FIG. 32 Nastaran Safaie, *Red Shoe*, presented at the Society for Calligraphers Gardens, Sculpture Expo, Tehran, 2010. Courtesy of the artist.

attract scrutiny, long after the peak of the uprising. The reason for their symbolic power lies in the dilemma that has confronted Iranian women for more than four decades now. As artist Nastaran Safaie puts it, Iranian women

> must reconcile societal expectations to maintain a refined appearance with the overwhelming pressure to satisfy various external parties, ranging from the morality police to casual passersby. This includes the scrutiny of other women, who may pass judgment if they fall short of established dress codes or behavioral norms.[2]

Safaie drew attention to the challenges women face with a daring monumental sculpture, a distorted glossy red high heel, three meters long and one meter high FIG. 32. Exhibited at the 2010 Sculpture Expo in Tehran, this work was one of the first to portray both the beauty and the pain behind the clothing of women in Iran.

The following year, in 2011, a collective of young female artists placed an installation of large red roses made from rice bags on a grassy knoll between Hemmat and Sheikh Fazlollah Noori highways, on a site that was rumored to be owned by the Islamic Revolutionary Guard Corps. Tehran Carnival's installation, *Urban Green House*, was quickly removed by the authorities: perhaps it

FIG. 33 Tehran Carnival, *Urban Green House*, 2011, Sheikh Fazlollah Nouri Freeway, Tehran. Courtesy of Tehran Carnival.

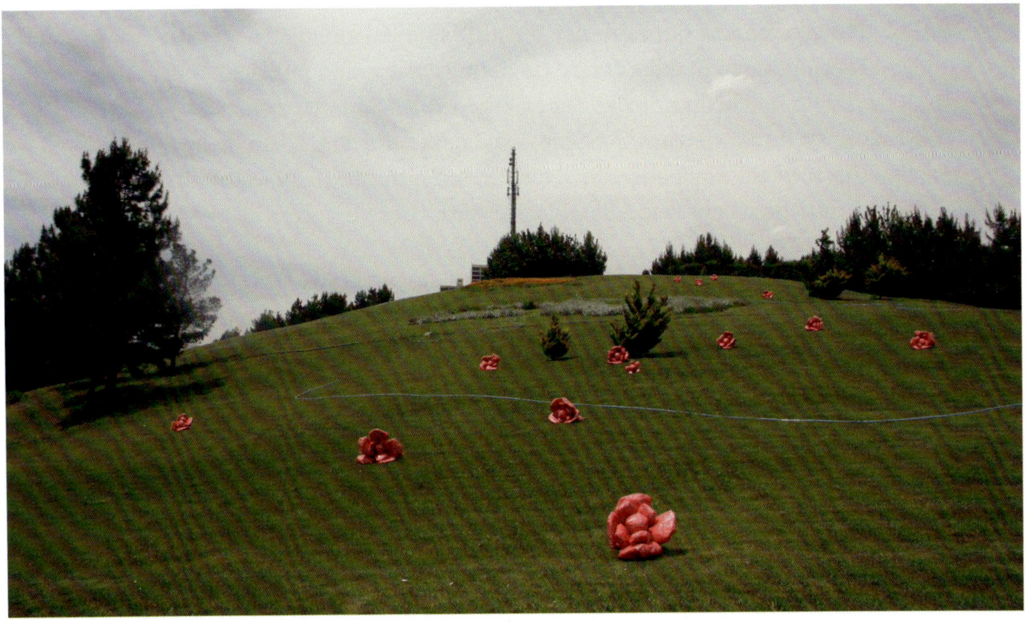

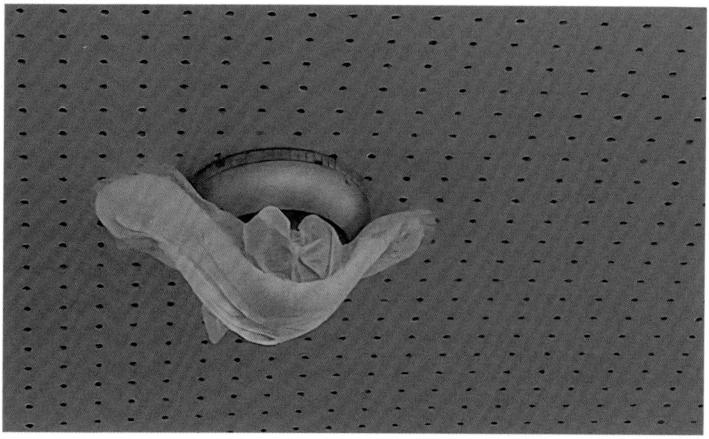

FIG. 34 A security camera shielded with sanitary protection in a Tehran metro train, captured in November 2022. The photographer and modifier of the photo wish to remain anonymous.

disrupted the formal use of the urban environment, or perhaps it was just too provocative—red flowers, with their implied reference to women's reproductive organs, can project all kinds of images in the mind's eye FIG. 33.

What if we view Safaie's public sculpture and Tehran Carnival's urban display not merely as art objects but as tools of street protest, precursors of the objects that appeared on the streets of Iran at the height of the Woman, Life, Freedom uprising? Some of these objects were infused with the same sense of ambivalence, both celebrating the female condition and conveying the discomfort attached to it. In November 2022, after security forces opened fire on commuters in a Tehran metro station, activists retaliated by covering CCTV cameras inside metro trains with layers of menstrual pads, thwarting the authorities' attempts at surveillance FIG. 34. Displayed alongside some of these blinded cameras were the names of Iranian political dissidents who had been imprisoned or killed since September 2022. Viewed from a distance, the coverings looked like flowers. Even if the use of adhesive sanitary pads allowed the cameras to be disabled more quickly, installing them was a daring act, with those involved risking arrest or even execution.[3]

Other materials traditionally associated with femininity were incorporated into artworks briefly displayed in public settings. One notable example is a mantel appliquéd with swan's wings intricately created from women's hair by the artist Mansooreh Bagharaee (b. 1978), FIG. 35. In her statement, she notes:

> Courage manifests in various forms, and brave individuals nurture their courage through a distinct source of strength. For some, it is the conviction in their beliefs, for others, it is physical might [...] Women find their bravery through their hair

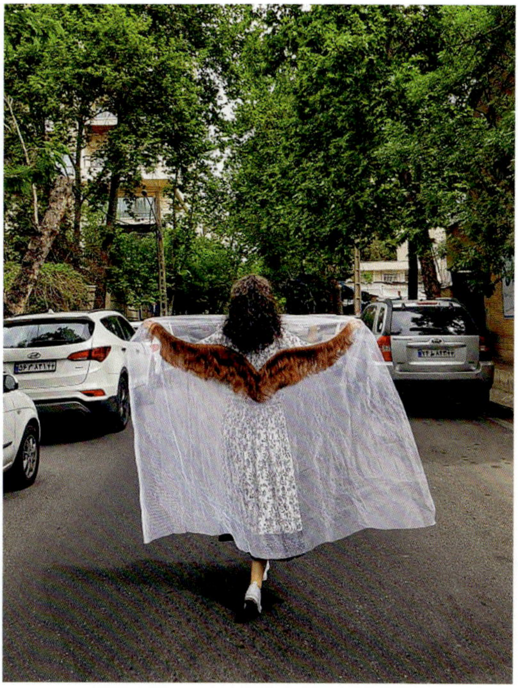

FIG. 35 Mansooreh Bagharaee, *Wings to Fly*, October 2023, Tehran. Courtesy of the artist.

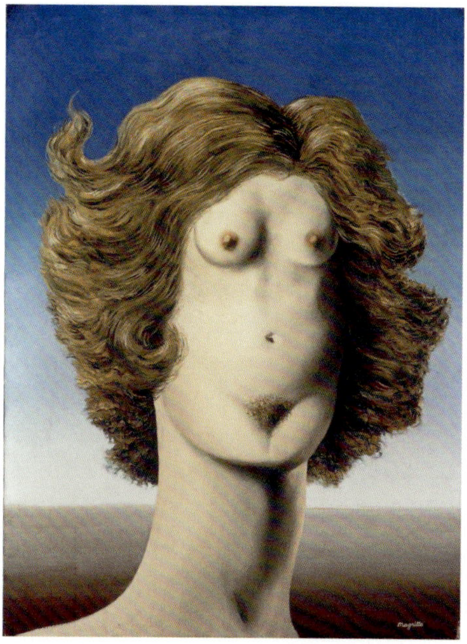

FIG. 36 René Magritte, *Le viol* (Rape), 1934, oil on canvas, 73 × 54 cm. Courtesy of Banque d'Images, ADAGP / Art Resource, NY. © ARS, NY.

> and in their pursuit of freedom. This very hair, once mandated to be concealed in public spaces, has transformed into a symbol of their liberation and empowerment. They are now embracing this newfound expression on the streets, displaying their 'wings' with pride. It is akin to a young bird embarking on its earliest flight, full of hope and determination.[4]

In her textile art, Bagharaee employs a technique similar to that used by toupee makers, painstakingly sewing individual strands of hair into a fine mesh of organza.[5] Akin to the flowerlike configurations of sanitary pads covering CCTV cameras on trains, this art evokes multiple associations—not only wings but also men's mustaches and pubic hair. It also calls to mind the Surrealists' symbolic use of hair. In René Magritte's *Rape* (*Le viol*, 1934), for instance, a woman's face, typically the first thing about her to be noticed, is transformed into a sexual object—replaced with a nude torso and pelvis—in an implicit commentary on the male gaze FIG. 36. Likewise, the mantel's meaning is ambiguous: it is uncertain whether it symbolizes the artist's aspiration to soar, an adherence to male-dictated norms, or a radical celebration of womanhood through the depiction of pubic hair. This ambiguity enriches the piece, making it a profound statement that simultaneously celebrates and critiques the fraught struggle over hair, often dominated by male perspectives. Bagharaee acknowledged that although it was not her initial intention, a common interpretation of her work has emerged.[6] Many observers perceive a certain ambiguity surrounding the mantle; it is designed to represent a wing, yet it also resembles a mustache; while meant to symbolize freedom, it unintentionally reflects the constraints and clichés of a male-dominated society, perhaps the very foundation from which the wearer of the mantle attempts to free herself. Bagharaee expressed fascination with these varied interpretations, emphasizing that art should evoke diverse emotions and interpretations to avoid becoming static and preachy.[7] Indeed, Bagharaee's protest art stands in stark contrast to propaganda art, which seeks to impose a singular narrative and stifle alternative perspectives. While propaganda art aims to manipulate and confine the viewer's thoughts, Bagharaee's work invites a multiplicity of interpretations, encouraging the audience to engage with the artwork on their own terms and draw their own conclusions. The nuanced complexity in Bagharaee's artwork also underscores the significance of protest props, highlighting their ability to elicit diverse interpretations from a wide audience, transcending the exclusive domains of art connoisseurs and museum spaces.

FIG. 37 Oslo, January 17, 2017. Thousands Join the Women's March Norway, one of 670 global protests on the day after the inauguration of US President Donald Trump. Photograph by Ryan Rodrick Beiler. Alamy Live News. Courtesy of Alamy Stock Photo.

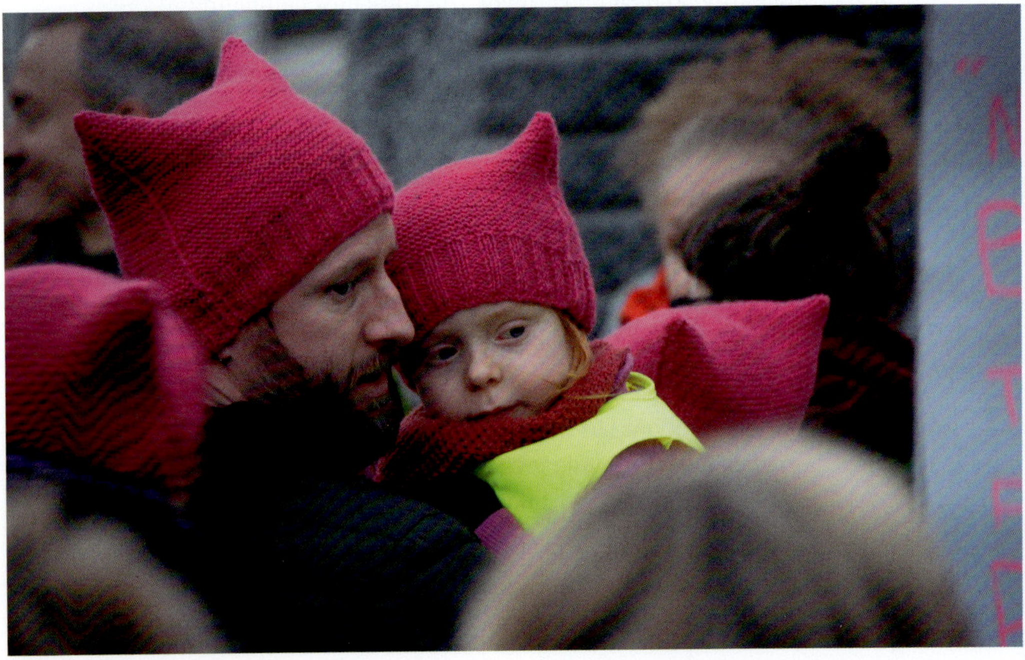

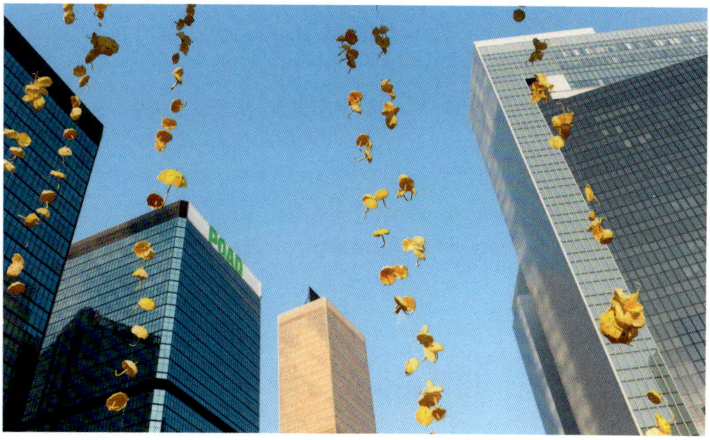

FIG. 38 Strings of paper umbrellas hang from a bridge in front of the government offices at Tamar Admiralty during the Hong Kong protests, October 12, 2014. Courtesy of Alamy Stock Photo.

Protest props, such as the one created by Bagharaee, can be compared to the sea of pink Pussyhats in the 2017 Women's Marches, which were crafted—knitted, crocheted, sewn together with fabric—using patterns available on the Pussyhat Project website FIG. 37. Conceived by Krista Suh and Jayna Zweiman, the project initially aimed to distribute one million hats at the US march in Washington, DC. What started as an expression of protest against the elevation of self-avowed "pussy-grabber" Donald Trump to the highest office in the US would become a global symbol of solidarity and political activism.[8]

This was neither the first nor the last instance in which thousands embraced props of a similar and unified character. Looking back to 2014, thousands of Hong Kong protesters who advocated for electoral transparency used umbrellas to defend against the police force's use of pepper spray and tear gas to deter protesters. The movement later became known as "Umbrella Revolution" or "Umbrella Movement," indicating the protesters' commitment to nonviolent advocacy for democratic reforms.[9] The protesters made the umbrella a lasting symbol of the movement's resilience and quest for fair elections FIG. 38.

In the challenging climate of the 2022 uprising in Iran, protesters employed various objects, notably those symbolizing women's issues, like hair and sanitary pads, albeit with less visibility than seen in movements like the Pussyhat Project or the Umbrella Revolution. Nevertheless, at a time when traditional text-based means of protest, such as giving speeches or distributing written pamphlets, have become increasingly difficult to implement due to the absence of political parties and the lack of institutional support, the use of protest props is transforming activism on the streets of Iran, merging politics and dissent into an art form. In transferring the agency from the artist or protester to the political art object or prop, this practice effectively blurs the line between art and activism, making it difficult to distinguish between the two. In this "act", I will present case studies that exemplify this convergence, often referred to as "artivism," a term that underscores the dual roles that artists and activists have assumed since the series of intense—and brutally repressed—antigovernment protests that marked the end of 2019.

POLITICAL ART OBJECTS OR PLAYFUL PROTEST PROPS?

The uprising at the end of 2019—later referred to as "Bloody November"—is seen by some as one of the most turbulent periods of civil unrest in Iran since the 1979 revolution. Focusing on the rights of workers and the impoverished, the protest movement was embraced by numerous artists who saw their work as a means to bring social inequities to the forefront of the public consciousness.

Erfan Ghiasi (b. 1989) is a multimedia artist who earned his MFA from Louisiana State University before returning to Iran in 2019. Motivated by a strong sense of social responsibility, Ghiasi uses the means of intervention and disruption to "generate a moment of error and deviation from existing conditions" to challenge the status quo.[10] Ghiasi chose to bring his interactive art to an important location, Kargar (literally, "Workers") Street, near Laleh Park and the Tehran Museum of Contemporary Art. Here, at a popular gathering spot for chess enthusiasts, he set up an asymmetrical chess game of his own devising. The white side of the chessboard featured a complete set of sixteen pieces in the traditional style: one king, one queen, two rooks, two bishops, two knights, and eight pawns, all meticulously crafted.

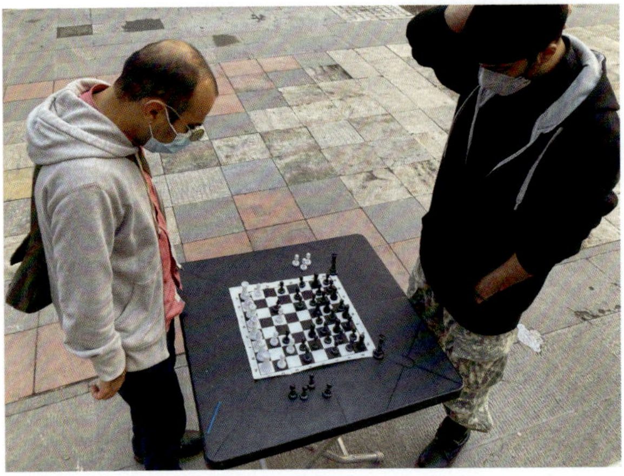

FIG. 39 Erfan Ghiasi, *Asymmetrical Warfare*, 2020, performed at the Laleh (Farah) Park, Tehran. Courtesy of the artist.

On the opposing side, every single one of the black chess pieces was a pawn, but there was a greater number of them. The game invited players and passersby alike to ponder whether these "lesser" pieces could triumph in such a lopsided battle FIG. 39. How could ordinary workers—symbolized by the pawns—defeat the more powerful figures of authority? Transcending the realms of mental exercise and entertainment, Ghiasi's chess game served as a metaphor for the struggle for greater social equality.

If using chess as a protest prop proved an effective way to highlight workers' rights, then various other games, with their accompanying pieces, have served as powerful tools for women artists who have taken bold discussions about women and gender issues onto the streets of Iran. Shaghayegh Kamyar (b. 1986) is well known within the artist community for her active participation in the 2022 protests, especially in police-dominated areas like Keshavarz Boulevard. Her street interventions are rarely recorded, as she has always focused on the immediate impact of her work, prioritizing its activist aspect over its artistic element. Occasionally, she will use her smart phone to capture elements of her work for personal remembrance, like the sound of spray paint during a graffiti session, but when asked about other photographs or footage, she explains that her artistic acts during the uprising were meant for the moment, not for publication in art history books or gallery exhibitions. Some of her projects are so perilous that none of her artist friends are willing to accompany her, leaving no one to document her actions. Kamyar acknowledges that she herself is fearful, but emphasizes the need for sacrifice at critical historical moments: "If we want a different Iran, we have to work for it," she says.[11]

Other artists design their performances with the express intention of photographing or filming them, regardless of whether they have a live audience. In such cases, the documentation becomes more than a mere record; it transforms into the actual space where the performance lives, with the events that it represents existing solely within the framework of the photograph or recorded footage. Thus, rather than directly reflecting reality, photographic (and, to a lesser extent, video) documentation often acts as a stand-in for the real world.[12] In contrast, what Kamyar accomplishes on the streets of Tehran during the intense moments of protest is an embodiment of pure activism. These acts are not performed for the sake of documentation or to be perceived as a version of reality: they *are* reality in its rawest form. The absence of documentation serves as a testament to their authenticity.

Unlike many artists who use their bodies as a medium (recall the works of Solati and Shahbeigy featured in the previous act), Kamyar often employs props in her appropriations of childhood games, tensions of daily life, or historical art performances.[13] As I will explore further in the following "act", the idea is not merely to replicate the past but to engage in an active dialogue with it. Kaymar's choice of props—such as darts or ropes or board game components—may on the surface seem playful, emphasizing a dynamic exchange with her audience, but frequently the work hints at deeper, darker underlying themes. A notable example is *Dart!* (2014), where participants were invited to throw darts at a target filled with a bloodlike substance. The interactive installation delves into the realities of human relations and the impact of unwanted disturbance and abuse. Inspired by a quote from the Austrian poet Erich Fried, "The boys throw stones at the frogs in jest. The frogs die in earnest," the game viscerally conveys the harmful consequences of ostensibly innocent actions.[14]

In another gamelike art project, *Tug of War* (2013), Kamkar confronted the challenges faced by Iranian women in a society. In this action, performed at Mah-e Mehr Gallery, the players—typically a man and a woman—engaged in a "tug-of-war" using a rope crafted from women's hair. Positioned on opposite sides of a circle, they attempted to pull each other over the line into their territory FIG. 40. The piece represents the struggle of women living under the constraints of religious norms and the discrimination they face in daily life. Above all, it is a metaphor for the ongoing war between civilians and the state over women's hair. While this project was realized nearly a decade before to the Woman, Life, Freedom uprising, it aptly fits the theme of the protests.

Kamyar's oeuvre also includes pieces that engage more directly with street politics. *Un-monopoly* (2019) is her response to the controversial development plans for University of Tehran, which envisage the displacement of a large portion of the existing population. For this theme, Kamyar designed a board game that is a reimagined version of Monopoly, with the twist that players are encouraged to assert their rights and resist property speculation. Challenging the original game's narrative of promoting wealth accumulation, it focuses on the themes of fair resource distribution and opposition to government policies that favor a select few.

Each project, in its own unique way, serves as a medium for Kamyar to explore societal norms and to highlight ongoing change and conflict. For her, the significance of games lies in the fact that they:

> possess an inherent quality that sets them apart from other art forms: their interactive nature enables direct engagement with

> the audience, transforming them from passive spectators to active participants. By granting players the decision-making power, games foster a deeper connection and immersion in the artistic experience. This involvement not only enhances their enjoyment but also allows for a more profound understanding and appreciation of the artistic intent. In societies where freedom of expression is suppressed, games can provide an avenue for personal and social expression. By creating games that convey critical messages or explore controversial themes, individuals can challenge societal norms and raise awareness without direct confrontation.[15]

Another of Kamyar's urban projects responded to the arrest in July 2022 of Sepideh Rashnu after she was filmed arguing with a woman on a bus over the mandatory hijab. Beaten and forced to give a confession on state TV, Rashnu was barred from her studies at Al-Zahra University and has since been handed another sentence for, among other "crimes," publishing "obscene images on social media."[16] In solidarity with Rashnu and fellow artists Anisha Asadollahi and Keivan Motamedi, who have also endured detention and interrogation, Kamyar chose to re-create Francis Alÿs's renowned *Green Line* project (2014), in which the Belgian artist walked a twenty-four-kilometer

FIG. 40 Shaghayegh Kamyar, *Tug of War*, 2013, Mah-e Mehr Gallery, Tehran. Courtesy of the artist.

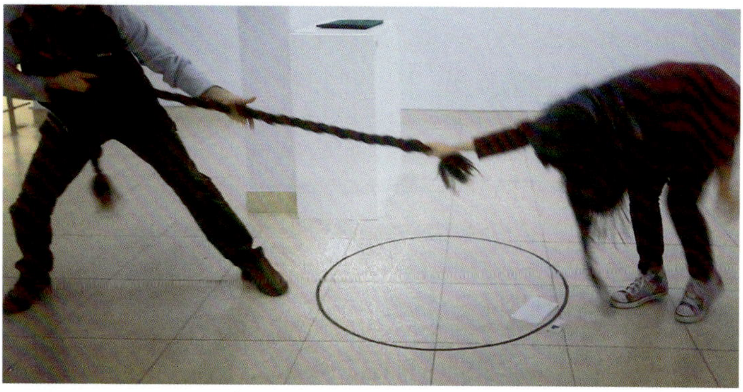

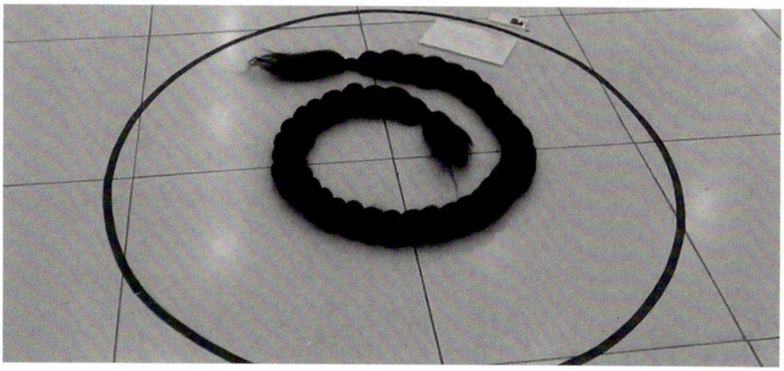

portion of the pre-1967 border or demarcation line that runs through Jerusalem, dribbling a trail of green paint behind him—an action that was at once poetic and political, making a significant statement on religious and geographical divisions.

The Green Line was itself a reprisal of an action performed by Alÿs in São Paulo in 1995 with blue paint. In her adaptation, titled *In Praise of Francis Alÿs*, Kamyar carried a can of red paint placed discreetly inside a punctured shopping bag, seemingly leaving a trail of blood behind her. The path she chose to walk led from Enghelab Square to Azadi Square, a favored location for state-sponsored demonstrations and parades. Rather than delineating politically charged geographical borders between countries, as Alÿs's work did, Kamyar's action focused on the internal tensions and contradictions within Iran. In this context, the protest props—the bloodstains on the pavement—evolved into *indexical signs*. Analogous to how smoke indicates the presence of fire, a bloodstain functions as an index of the protester.

Kamyar's artistic appropriation can be seen not just as a dialogue but as a deliberate and strategic engagement—a "mind game"—with prominent figures in the art world, not only artists from more democratic nations advocating for justice globally but also those living under oppressive regimes who face imprisonment, interrogation, and torture for championing democratic ideals.[17] Her approach intertwines these diverse narratives and creates a complex and thoughtful commentary on the global quest for more equal and just societies.

The work of another Belgian artist, Edith Dekyndt, provided the inspiration for an action outside the hospital on Keshavarz Boulevard where Amini passed away. Dekyndt's 2014 video project *Ombre Indigène* continuously loops a captivating image of what seems to be black hair flowing in the wind atop a flagpole. Translating this idea to the context of Tehran, Kamyar carried a flag fashioned from black hair as a symbol of protest and remembrance and installed other hair flags in various locations, including traffic poles FIG. 41.

Over the following months, Keshavarz Boulevard would be the site of brutal clashes with the police, who intentionally targeted the eyes of protesters with paintballs. In a moving gesture of solidarity, Kamyar stood on the sidewalk and gave away white balloons on which she had drawn eyeballs, and she engaged passersby in conversations about the protesters' injuries. Along with the balloons, she handed out small black ball-shaped candies reminiscent of the sight-destroying paintballs—five hundred of them in all, representing the number of eye injuries documented by a human rights website FIG. 42.[18] In this way, the act of giving was intertwined with a powerful message about the human cost of the demonstrations.

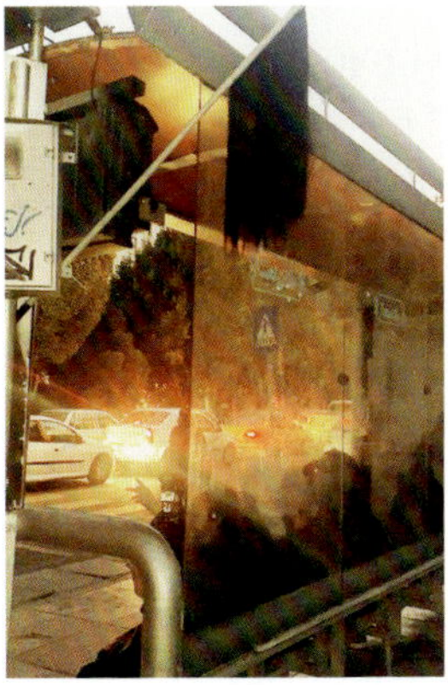

FIG. 41 Shaghayegh Kamyar's synthetic hair flag installation, erected at a bustling city corner during the fall 2022 protests. Courtesy of the artist.

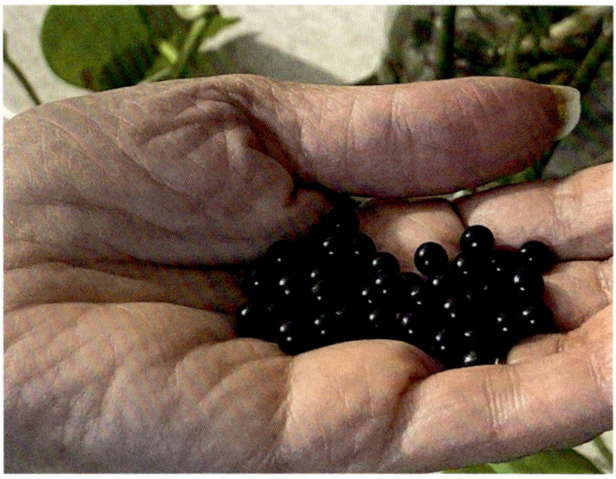

FIG. 42 Shaghayegh Kamyar's participatory activist art project involved distributing candy resembling paintballs, which caused five hundred eye injuries to protesters during fall 2022. Courtesy of the artist.

KNOTTING AND UNKNOTTING SOCIAL DILEMMAS

Another artist, Mojdeh Atrak (b. 1983), came to participatory art on the city streets by a different route during the uprising, after making the leap from studio work and an interactive installation in a gallery setting. Atrak's upbringing was immersed in the arts, with painting and drawing forming the fabric of her everyday life—her parents and siblings are artists. After graduating from college with a degree in a field outside the visual arts, she returned to the artistic roots planted by her family, finding her unique voice in a style reminiscent of her childhood drawing and scribbling practices. She began with an intense focus on doodling ropes, exploring their aesthetic appeal, utilitarian function, and the complex emotions they evoked. Ropes, whether woven from natural or synthetic fibers, have a textured complexity and a duality of purpose: they are indispensable for mundane tasks such as securing possessions, yet they have a darker significance in Iran, where they are used by the regime to hang both political dissidents and convicted criminals. The term for knot, *gereh*, likewise captures a spectrum of concepts, from the tangible—*gereh* functions as a unit of measurement—to the metaphorical, being used, like the English term "knotty," to describe intractable problems. As seen in the craft of carpet weaving, the tying and untying of knots secures and embellishes: in Persian, this same idea is used to encapsulate life's conundrums and the twists of fate.

The symbolic significance of knotting and unknotting has also found its way into certain folkloric traditions. For example, during Sizdah Bedar, or "Nature's Day," held on the thirteenth day of the

Nowruz (Persian New Year), young women seeking marriage tie seven knots in fresh green leaves while whispering a poem that expresses their hopes for their future partner. Here, the act of knotting has the potential to bring bad luck if the fragile leaves are broken.[19] While this tradition is thought to be rooted in ancient Zoroastrian beliefs, there are others that are mostly linked to Shiite Islam. One of these is tying a votive (*dakhil bastaan*) in a place considered to be sacred, such as the shrine of a great figure, in anticipation of the healing of the sick or the fulfillment of a wish.

After years of dedication in the studio, Atrak was ready for a public exhibition of her expansive drawings of knots, meticulously inked onto paper and silk, and laden with rich interpretations. However, in a twist that mirrored the entanglements depicted in her art, a legal dispute between the gallery and its landlord resulted in Atrak's artworks being impounded soon after the opening. Friends and acquaintances began to whisper, some half-joking, others superstitious, that the knot's symbolism had manifested itself as a curse. So, in 2021, Atrak embarked on a "cleansing" endeavor, using these commentaries as a conceptual backdrop for another work, titled *Not Knots Anymore*, in which she crafted 1,400 meters of rope into an immense mound of knots and then invited the public to a different gallery, not just to view but to actively unravel this woven mass. The response was remarkably eager, and within two hours the artist and the participants had transformed the knotted hill into straightened lengths of rope, an act Atrak found profoundly exciting FIG. 43.

The knot project assumed a new form of expression during the Woman, Life, Freedom uprising, when Atrak was invited by artist and curator Neda Darzi to participate in Persbook's 12th Annual of Contemporary Art. Atrak took the concept to the streets, creating another intricate knot out of a long rope and touring it through various cities, starting with the capital FIG. 44. Titled *From One Hand*

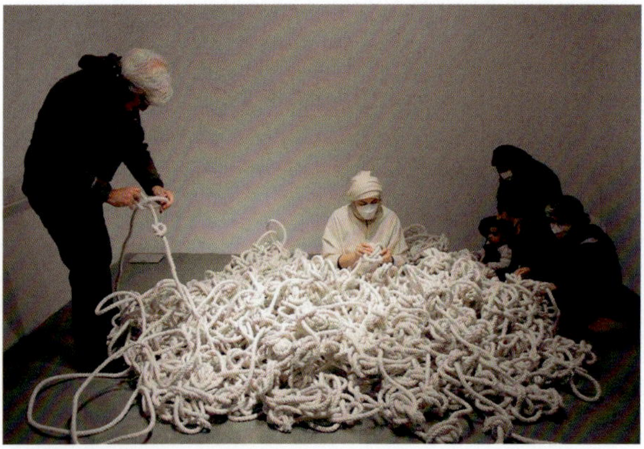

FIG. 43 Mojdeh Atrak, *Not Knots Anymore*, participatory art project at the Soo Contemporary, a gallery setting in Tehran, 2021. Courtesy of the artist.

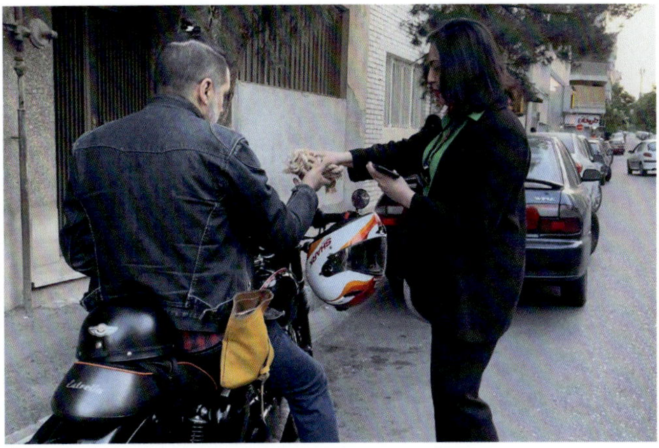

FIG. 44 Mojdeh Atrak, *Hand to Hand*, 2023, Tehran. Courtesy of the artist.

to the Next or *Hand to Hand*—phrases akin to the English idiom "passing the baton"—the project resonated with people on the streets, who quickly grasped its artistic essence; after helping untie the knot, they would often part with the words, *In dard-e moshtarak joda joda darman nemishavad* ("This shared pain cannot be resolved alone," meaning we must unite in addressing our nation's challenges), a phrase also chanted by protesters, painted as graffiti, and turned into songs during the uprising.

Transcending metaphor, Atrak's effort became a performative act of unity. A project that began with a stroke of bad luck evolved into a collaborative movement, serving as a symbol of good fortune and an inspiring reminder of the power of collective action.

CONFESSIONS OF A VENDOR ARTIST

Hamed Safaie (b. 1976), a multimedia artist and film director, grew up steeped in the world of women's fashions, defined by the daily routine of his seamstress mother taking the measurements of the women who visited their home. Another childhood memory is of flipping through black-market issues of the sewing magazine *BurdaStyle*, which allowed his mother to stay abreast of the latest fashions even after the revolution. Being raised in a predominantly female environment fostered a deep connection with women's lives, to the extent that, as an adult, Safaie became profoundly empathetic toward women. This empathy naturally evolved into a strong advocacy for enhancing women's rights in Iran. For Safaie, participating in the Woman, Life, Freedom movement was a natural progression; it aligned seamlessly with his values.[20]

After studying cinema at Tehran's University of Art, Safaie was hired to edit and direct episodes of *Asr-e Jadid*, a talent competition on Iranian state TV. Launched under President Hassan Rouhani's administration, the show aimed not just to provide entertainment but to integrate underground music and performance groups into the mainstream, where they could be overseen by the government. Safaie often found his job challenging and intimidating. Working in the basement of a government building surrounded by surveillance cameras, he was constantly under pressure to ensure everyone adhered to strict guidelines. What he found most distasteful of all was the expectation that he would edit footage to remove any scenes of interaction between the sexes—any hint that boundaries had been crossed. The final straw came in July 2022, when he was instructed to manipulate scenes of young men and women practicing an Asian martial art to make it seem as if they were training separately rather than competing together. Safaie decided to resign from his job, a decision that coincided with the arrest of Sepideh Rashnu and several other artists, which enraged the artistic community.

Though Safaie's colleagues and even his boss begged him to reconsider, he firmly declined their requests. Adopting a look that would make him unemployable in a government setting, he pierced his ears and various parts of his face and started to wear nail polish. He returned to his roots: when he was young, his leftist father had encouraged him to earn for himself the money he needed to pay for the things he wanted—be it new clothes or subscriptions to periodicals.[21] Drawing inspiration from these formative lessons in self-sufficiency and entrepreneurship, Safaie became a *dastforush*, or street vendor, setting up his stall at a popular spot for street vendors in northern Tehran FIG. 45.

At the time of the uprising, many of Safaie's friends assumed that his role as a street vendor was an artistic performance, a subtle act of rebellion against the regime. However, Safaie insists that his transition into vending was a straightforward, honest engagement in the trading of goods, with no underlying artistic motives.[22] His merchandise included nostalgic images from past decades—for example, scenes from the iconic 1969 Woodstock concert (a time of another youth revolution), or posters of classic films and detective shows. His customer base consisted mainly of women. In the first few days, Safaie had to reacquaint himself with the skills of street vending, emphasizing the need for assertiveness—any hint of hesitation could put customers off. This understanding was crucial, since sales of the images now constituted his sole source of income.

The uprising began just a few weeks into this new chapter of Safaie's life. As the unrest intensified, his stall became a refuge amid

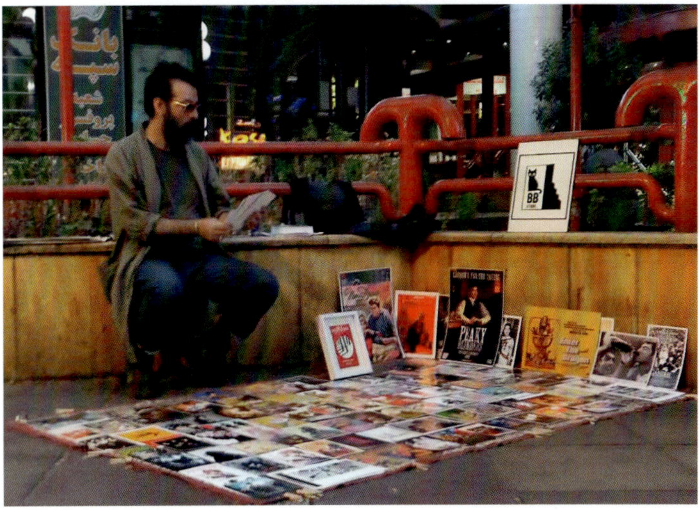

FIG. 45 Hamed Safaie as vendor in Tehran. Courtesy of the artist.

the chaos. Safaie handed out free hydrogen peroxide pills for first aid and gave shelter to panicking demonstrators. He recounted how the police fired indiscriminately: after each shooting incident, he would pick up the scattered bullets or paintball casings, amassing a significant collection over time. Like his stall (i.e., a protest prop), these would serve as protest props. Occasionally, in a display of dark humor, he would offer the spent shells to passersby as souvenirs of the uprising's tumultuous days, but he eventually gave a large part of his cache to a nearby jewelry vendor, who made necklaces out of the ammunition. Thus, Safaie's protest props were repurposed and disseminated—passed from hand to hand—and the remnants of conflict were transformed into symbols of resilience.

Safaie's engagement with the uprising in Tehran was multifaceted, a blending of selling art, conducting therapy sessions, and engaging in actions using protest props. It seemed to be art, yet not quite; it looked like activism, but not entirely. The combination of its outward simplicity and underlying complexity made it challenging for others to fully grasp the situation, regardless of how close they were to the artist. Aside from the friends who speculated that it was an artistic performance, a form of "artivism," there were those who questioned why someone with a well-paid stable job would give it up and turn to what they perceived as a lowly trade.

As the uprising gained momentum, Safaie drew on his insider knowledge of *Asr-e Jadid*, using his Instagram account to spread the word about Shervin Hajipour, the artist responsible for the song "Baraye," meaning "for" in Persian. The song, inspired by the use of the word on Twitter/X to convey people's motivations for participating in the protests, garnered widespread recognition, ultimately winning the prestigious Grammy Award in the Best Song for Social Change category. Safaie disclosed that although Hajipour had taken part in the state-sponsored TV show, he was never one to conform. His opposition to the system was apparent in his performances, his clothing style, and his overall demeanor. This post quickly went viral, and people became increasingly interested in Safaie, even visiting his stall in northern Tehran to express their admiration and support. Passing cars would honk horns in acknowledgment, and passersby would shout out, calling him a "real man" for his decision to quit his government job.[23] Some even stopped to inquire if he would sell pictures of Nika Shahkarami or Sarina Esmailzadeh, the young girls who had died under suspicious circumstances after taking part in the protests. However, Safaie refused to do so, adamant that he would not turn the memory of these lost lives into mere commodities in an "amusement shop."[24] Safaie, instead, posted statements on social media expressing solidarity with the youth involved in the uprising, openly signing off with *dastforoosh* (vendor).

For Marxist philosophers such as Theodor Adorno and György Lukács, the "very Idea [...] of 'stating something' is irrelevant to art [...] art may forgo the right to make definite pronouncements." For them, a work of art could only become an important source of knowledge "when taken as a totality, i.e., through all its mediations, not through the artist's intentions."[25] In the same vein, one could say that the art of Safaie, as an artist who also operates as a vendor, becomes meaningful when it is viewed in its entirety. In his case, the significant relationships and connections he formed with his audience and customers made his business a catalyst for the production of "knowledge" at an important historical juncture. The approach to business as an art form embodies a complex interplay of creativity, strategy, and presentation that goes beyond the artist's intentions or the tangible characteristics of the goods for sale. One could argue that the principles of interaction apply to all forms of art, especially when performed in public places. However, they are particularly apposite to Safaie's role as a vendor artist. His retail allowed him to interact with passersby in a practical way, engaging their interest in buying his products. Simultaneously, his reputation as an artist meant that passersby engaged with him at a conceptual level, appreciating his work without necessarily participating in the commercial aspect. Above all, Safaie engaged in the protest as a healer, with his "art" creating a safe zone for those in danger. These multiple roles of vendor, artist, and guardian augment the level of engagement and the "totality" of his art.

Safaie's role as a vendor—the cornerstone of the "artivist" aspect of his work—also highlights a distinctive method by which Iranians have historically engaged with heavily monitored street and public spaces, claiming these areas as their own. In *Street Politics: Poor People's Movement in Iran*, Bayat describes how street selling became a form of political expression shortly after the 1979 revolution, when politically aware but unemployed graduates and students, seeking opportunities in the midst of the chaos, set themselves up as vendors. Like Safaie, they gravitated toward more prosperous locations and prime spots near major public parks and universities. These vendors mostly displayed books, newspapers, music cassettes, and tapes of political speeches, though some expanded their offerings to include sandwiches, hot tea, and soft drinks. The more determined among them built permanent structures, using metal and wood, and even tapped into nearby power lines for electricity. In the evenings, vendors interacted with shoppers and passersby, creating a lively atmosphere lit with colorful lamps and accompanied by music and a heavy dose of politics. As Bayat elucidates, this unique blend of commerce and community engagement became a defining characteristic of the city's postrevolutionary street life.[26]

Although Safaie does not explicitly relate his work to the revolutionary practices of the past, it is likely that his approach was influenced by years of observing similar activities on the city's streets. Even in the late 1990s and early 2000s—during Khatami's presidency, a period marked by the granting of relative freedoms to citizens—one could easily notice the reemergence of numerous street vendors selling books from the prerevolutionary era, many of them officially banned, or *Jeld Sefid* books, distributed by leftist groups who removed the titles and cover images for safety. More than just a personal form of protest, Safaie's decision to engage in street vending following Sepideh Rashnu's arrest suggests a continuation of a revolutionary tradition where vending (an activity involving commodities that can be indirectly read as protest props) serves not just as a commercial activity but also as a medium for political expression.

It is important to consider the implications of the reclaiming, appropriation, resurgence, adaptation, and circulation of bold, revolutionary styles. While the art of the Woman, Life, Freedom uprising does not directly continue the legacy of the 1979 Iranian Revolution or leftist movements, the overlaps, whether deliberate or coincidental, are crucial. In the next "act", I will delve into the enduring impact of revolutionary movements in Iran, looking at how their themes, goals, and iconic imagery have become ingrained in the collective memory, setting the stage for the work of artists across the decades, particularly in the context of the Woman, Life, Freedom uprising. ■

Act Four

RECLAIMING OLD THEMES FOR NEW PROTEST ARTS

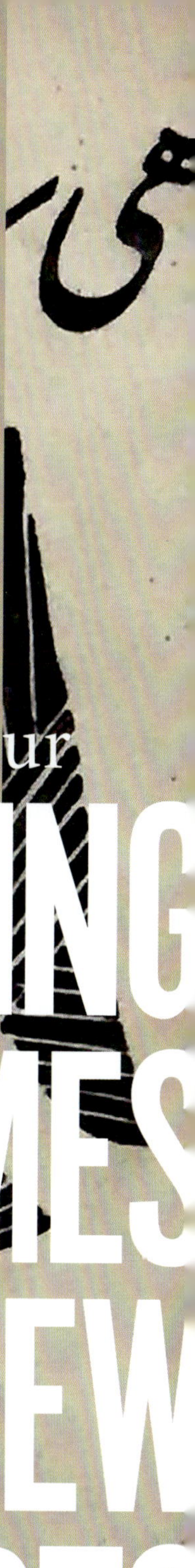

A recurring phenomenon, in almost all forms of uprising around the world, is the creation of potent new symbols out of the blending of established rituals and systems with contemporary means of communication. This is true both historically, for example with the Paris Commune,[1] and with revolutions much closer to us in time, such as the Arab Spring, when ancient cultural rituals were transformed into secular revolutionary acts through the use of modern media tools.[2] From this perspective, revolutionary movements could be seen, not so much as a rupture with the past but as a revival of older modes of coexistence that resist the dominance of the state. In his writings, Mohammed A. Bamyeh highlights a revolutionary insight, or "anarchist gnosis," that he equates with the lifestyle and actions of a self-governing community existing mainly beyond the influence of the state.[3] Similarly, Ayman El-Desouky talks of the Egyptian practice of *amara*, which represents collective memory in everyday life.[4]

This section of the book aims to explore how established themes of protest art have been reclaimed and reworked in the iconic imagery of the 2022 uprising in Iran. While I acknowledge that Iranian revolutionary images have been adopted by global neoliberal markets, I must clarify that this topic, which pertains more to the international perception of the situation in Iran, is not my focus here. Instead, my primary emphasis is on the domestic context and the more recent protest arts.

Parallels have been drawn between the Woman, Life, Freedom uprising and the Constitutional Revolution of 1905–1911, sparked in part by the human trafficking of two hundred and fifty girls in northeastern

Iran, who were kidnapped and sold by the provincial government in lieu of taxes. *The Story of the Daughters of Quchan: Gender and National Memory in Iranian History*, by Harvard professor Afsaneh Najmabadi, published in 1998 and later translated into Persian, describes the significance of the episode and the role played by newspapers in fueling calls for social justice.[5] Social media commentators and media experts have also pointed out similarities between images of the recent movement and photographs from the International Women's Day demonstrations in Tehran on March 8, 1979, shortly after the revolution that overthrew Mohammad Reza Shah.[6] The protest, involving men and women, was in part a celebration of the beginning of a new era, but it was, above all, a response to Ruhollah Khomeini's decree imposing Islamic dress code on women—the mirror image of another autocratic edict, forcing all women to unveil, that had been issued by Reza Shah (Mohammad Reza Shah's father) in 1936 and lasted till his ousting in 1941. The 1979 protest had the effect of temporarily delaying the enforcement of the mandatory hijab, which only became the subject of an Islamic Punishment Law in 1983. The points of connection with Iranian women's long-standing struggle and activism also go beyond the visual realm: "The Song of Equality" (*Sorood-e barabari*), a poem written by a group of feminist activists in 1999,[7] would be adapted into a revolutionary song for the Woman, Life, Freedom protests.[8]

Aside from feminist themes, the recent protests have also referenced leftist and communist motifs from Iran's revolutionary past, the 1968 student uprising in France, and decolonial movements globally. As I will demonstrate, some artists deliberately engage with these themes—notably to reinforce the connection between the uprising and the low-waged workers' movement of 2019—while others draw on these influences more indirectly. Nahid Siamdoust has ascribed this form of reclaiming heavily ideological themes to "Iran's post-ideological generations," who "draw from multiple ideological histories without bowing to any, instead highlighting their universal demands for freedom from their position as dissident[s]."[9]

When a historical image comes to stand as a source of inspiration for a present event, we must consider "the reality not of the past, but of present meanings and of changing discursive systems," writes John Tagg in his classic *The Burden of Representation*.[10] In what follows, I will explore how past revolutionary themes have been reclaimed—given present meaning—using unique artistic techniques including appropriation, adaptation, and direct borrowing. These methods go beyond mere influences; they exemplify distinct stylistic approaches to art.

SUBVERSIVE APPROPRIATION

Appropriation in art is the deliberate borrowing, copying, and alteration of existing images and ready-made objects. As cultural critic Julie Sanders argues, appropriation is different from the better-known technique of adaptation, which maintains a close connection with its source material. Film versions of great works of literature, for example, mostly remain faithful to the original, even if they might give the story a twist to appeal to new audiences. In contrast, as Sanders relates, appropriation often involves a noticeable departure from the original, leading to an entirely new creation. Furthermore, the original source is not always referenced as explicitly as it would be in an adaptation.[11] Unlike "influence," which obscures authorship and agency, "appropriation" confidently locates both in the person of the maker.[12]

From medieval times to the modern period, powerful rulers and art patrons in Iran have appropriated artistic elements from ancient Persian empires to construct a distinctive identity for themselves.[13] The appropriation of images and calligraphic writings was essential to the making of books and albums. Under the Timurids (1370–1507), for example, royal albums containing specimens by earlier master calligraphers, all affixed with strips of paper, were reformatted: the fragmentary sheets were bound into new folios and retouched or illuminated in unison to produce a seamless effect—a sign of historical consciousness that was clearly expressed visually before it was articulated in writing.[14]

Appropriation took on a renewed significance in the early 1960s, with the rise of Saqqakhaneh, an art movement that looked to local vernacular cultures for inspiration (at a time when global Pop art was in the ascendant). Artists like Siah Armajani, Massoud Arabshahi, and Parviz Tanavoli incorporated found objects—old suit jackets, traditional crochet pieces, and obsolete vessels, respectively—into their calligraphic pieces and oil paintings, with wide-ranging intentions, from boldly evoking past events to augmenting the medium for further sensory engagement and poking fun at outdated customs. While the 1979 Iranian Revolution and Iran–Iraq War (1980–1988) put an end to the pioneering movement, techniques of appropriation would find a new home in the political propaganda posters and murals that emerged after the relatively dormant 1980s.

In postrevolutionary Iran, artists with a stance critical of the regime have necessarily had to be subtle, whether they work in the visual arts, theater, or film. Rather than submit to the censorship apparatus of the MCIG (which fulfills the same function in the arts as the "morality police" does in wider society), they co-opt an

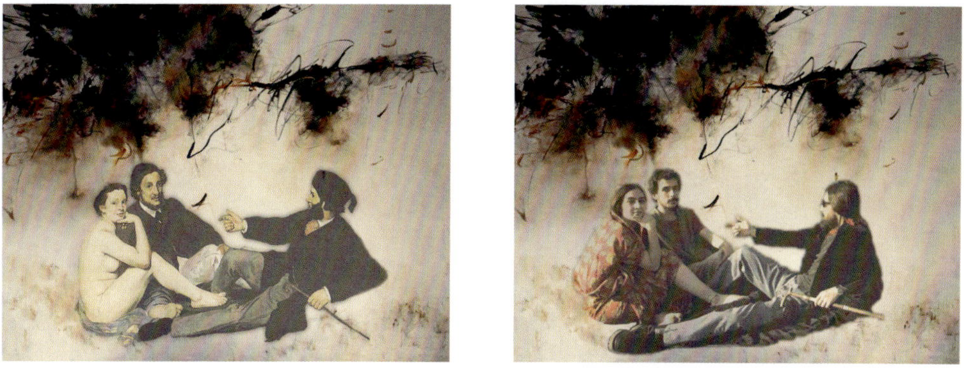

FIG. 46 Two modified snapshots from Farideh Lashaie's video *Le Temps Perdu*, created between 2007 and 2012. The pieces combine painting (oil and graphite on canvas) with projected animated photographic images and sound. Courtesy of the Farjam Collection.

indirect language or employ allegorical methods to express disobedience. Without speaking overtly about oppression, artists use metaphor or "subversive appropriation,"[15] distancing effects, parody, and pastiche to interrogate the regime's foundational ideologies and totalizing beliefs. The work of artist Farideh Lashai exemplifies some of these techniques. Her *Le Temps Perdu*, in particular, blends oil painting and video to express the interplay of gender themes across different eras and cultures.[16] The piece is based on Édouard Manet's *Le Déjeuner sur l'herbe*, which was in turn inspired by a print by Raphael. Manet's painting deftly accentuates the nuances of the relations between the sexes, a subject as delicate and contentious in late nineteenth-century France as it is in contemporary Iran. In Lashai's video interpretation, as Manet's image gradually fades, the indistinct figures transform into depictions of Iranian youth: two men and a woman who is described as "badly veiled"—a term for women who adhere only loosely to the hijab rules. Lashai's approach is subtle and indirect, using art historical themes to hint at deeper meanings and societal critiques, creating layers of interpretation while maintaining obliqueness FIG. 46.[17]

Pastiche allows for a further critical deviation from the weight of the provenance or authorship of the original work of art. Here, the genre of video art has been particularly effective in rendering the category of "expert" producer obsolete: in place of the "author," it offers a platform for the proliferation of remixes—a term applicable to altered or distorted video works as well as to popular music. Lashai's *El Amal* (2011) is a four-minute remix of her signature-style abstract painting accompanied by dissenting content from artists before her: a projection of the notorious "globe scene" from Charlie Chaplin's *The Great Dictator* (1940) and a clip of Egyptian national

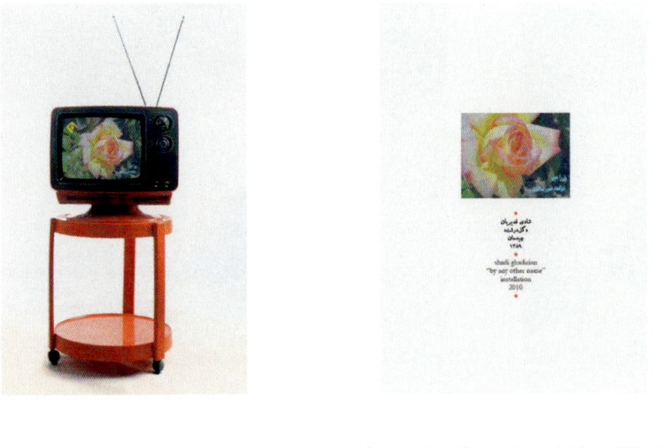

FIG. 47 Spread from *Only the Morning Bird Treasures the Flower Garden*, 2019, featuring the work of Shadi Ghadirian. Image courtesy of Chupan Mehraneh Atashi.

icon Umm Kulthum singing "Al Amal" (Hope, 1971)—one a parody of Hitler's evil yearning to conquer the world, the other an expression of forgiveness, perseverance, and hope for a better future. The incongruous juxtaposition of the familiar audiovisuals confers new meanings on the appropriated historical material.[18]

An intriguing facet of "subversive appropriation" is the way artists humorously repurpose and reapply signs and symbols originating within the regime itself. This can be seen in the work of Chupan (discussed in Act One), who was prompted to delve into the sociopolitical symbolism of flowers in Iran after their prison interrogator suggested that flowers would be a more "poetic" focus for their work than the critical themes of gender and power relations they had explored up to then. After leaving Iran in 2012, Chupan made the role of flowers in the work of Iran-based artists the subject of a book and accompanying exhibition, both titled *Only the Morning Bird Treasures the Flower Garden* (in Persian: *Ghadr-e majmoo'eh gol morgheh sahar danad o bas*).[19] The words are taken from a verse by Hafez, which continues: "Not everyone who reads a page understands its meanings."[20] Following Hafez's wisdom, the publication invites readers to ponder the sociopolitical associations of something as seemingly innocent as a flower.[21]

The images of the artworks in the book are accompanied by brief narratives in which the artists explain the inspiration behind them. For instance, Shadi Ghadirian's staged photograph of a small red television on a typical 1980s Iranian TV stand is paired with a note about how Iranian state TV often displayed images of flowers that filled the screen and were accompanied by music FIG. 47. Substituting the image of a simple flower, a single rose, for images of the people actually producing the music was a means of censorship—a strategy to distract viewers. On a more personal level,

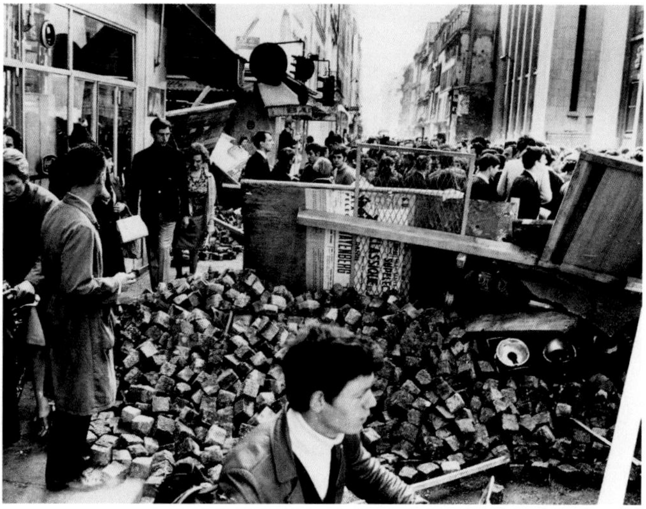

FIG. 48 Student revolt, 1968. Barricade made from paving stones and streetlights in rue des Saint-Pères on the Left Bank in Paris, France, May 1968. GRANGER—Historical Picture Archive. Courtesy of Alamy Stock Photo.

Ghadirian recalls that as a child in the early 1980s, whenever the TV showed images of war or missing people, her mother would switch to the channel displaying a rose to shield her from the violence, saying, "Look Shadi, here is a flower, just like the one you drew yesterday." In Chupan's book, Ghadirian's artwork titled *Gol Dorosht* (meaning "larger-than-life flower," but also "kitsch" or "empty proclamation" in popular parlance), encapsulates the role of flowers in post-revolutionary Iran: as tools for whitewashing reality, distracting from harsh truths, and enforcing simplicity and emptiness in public perception.

Chupan's "flower" project not only reflects their personal experiences with street politics but also addresses themes that are deeply embedded in the nation's collective imagination and memory and are continually claimed and reclaimed in culture, state media, posters, poetry, and prose.

In discussing subversive appropriation—a "strategy of concealment well suited to an era of censorship"[22]—it is also important to highlight the subtle and indirect influences Iranian artists have absorbed from global revolutionary movements. In the summer of 2016, Tehran-based artist Homayoun Sirizi and Moscow-based Natalya Nusinova curated an exhibition at Moscow's Triumph Gallery titled *Tehran: Capital in Capital Letters*. Several of the works in the show reflected on the 2009 Green Movement. One piece, by Mojtaba Amini, alluded directly to the uprising in May 1968 in Paris, when students tore up the paving stones on the streets and used them to build barricades FIG. 48. Amini's installation consisted of stones he had collected from the streets of Tehran, knowing they had been used to fight the police during the Green Movement.[23] In

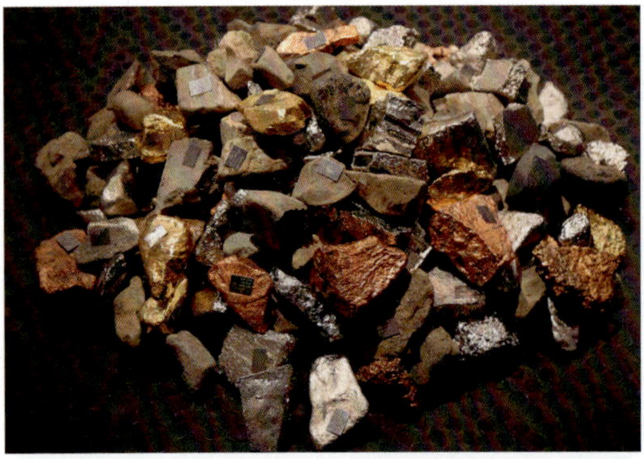

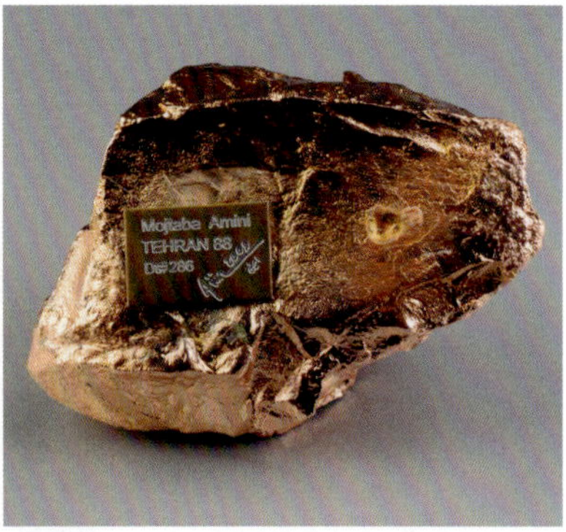

FIG. 49 Mojtaba Amini, *Tehran: Capital in Capital Letters*, exhibited at Moscow's Triumph Gallery, 2016. Courtesy of cocurator Homayoun Sirizi.

the Moscow piece, each of these stones was covered in precious gold leaf and fitted with a small plaque inscribed "Mojtaba Amini Tehran 88," marking the year it was gathered (2009 is 1388 in the Persian calendar) FIG. 49. Amini's work adapts a concept from a different sociopolitical movement; it also incorporates actual stones—found objects from the streets of Tehran—into its composition. The twofold appropriation adds an intriguing layer to the work. However, similar to other political artworks before the recent uprising, its political tone and expression remain subtle

BOLD EXCHANGES

While the incorporation of older themes has long been a feature of Iranian art, such acts of borrowing became markedly more direct and forceful with the Woman, Life, Freedom uprising. Compare two posters by graphic designer Pedram Harby FIGS. 50–51. The one on the left, created for the Woman, Life, Freedom protests, shortly after the demise of Jina Mahsa Amini, is animated by a female mouth shouting grievances. Appearing next to a #MahsaAmini hashtag, and between the confidently rendered words *Zan* (woman) and *Zendegi, Azadi* (life, freedom), the work seems bold in relation to his 2013 poster design for Azadeh Ganjeh's *Unpermitted Whispers, a* thirty-five-minute play that was staged four times a night, not in a theater, but in taxis that traveled the streets of downtown Tehran. For each performance, three actors were picked up and dropped off in sequence. The roles they played were inspired by iconic women in Shakespeare's plays, now transposed to contemporary Iran. The intense love, madness, and despair of Ophelia, for instance, were

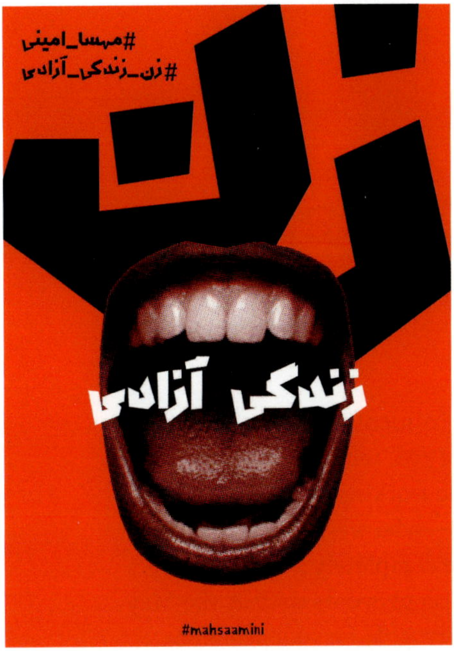

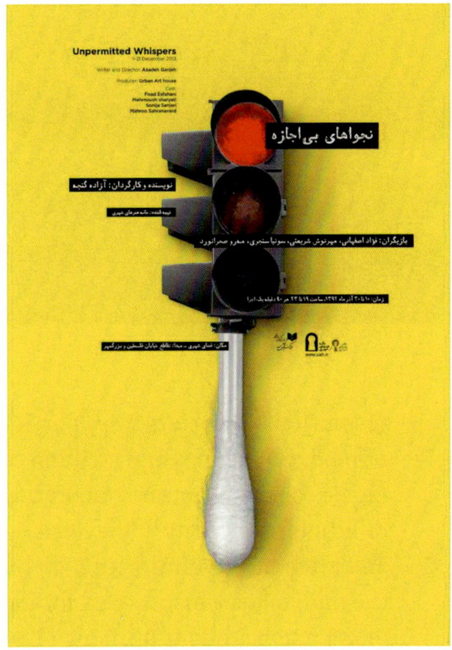

FIGS. 50–51 Left: Pedram Harby, *Woman, Life, Freedom*, 2022. Courtesy of the artist. Right: Poster for the play *Unpermitted Whispers*, directed by Azadeh Ganjeh in 2013, designed by Pedram Harby. Courtesy of Azadeh Ganjeh.

funneled into the character of a woman who spoke of conflicts between ordinary Iranians and the police. Despite the play's political tone, Harby's poster remains understated: the ensemble of a red traffic light affixed to a Q-tip stands for the threat of being blocked and unheard.[24]

The choice of the colors in Harby's Woman, Life, Freedom poster also alludes to revolutionary themes found in both of the factions—Islamist and leftist—that helped bring down the Shah's regime in 1979, as seen, for example, in an Islamist poster from the early revolutionary period, now housed at the University of Chicago Library FIG. 52. This poster features a powerful visual composition where the *shahada*, the Islamic declaration of faith stating "There is no god but God," is ingeniously integrated into the silhouette of protesters with raised fists. The use of stark, contrasting colors projects a sense of urgency and solidarity. The superposition of the *shahada* over the raised fists is an artistic choice that aligns the demonstrators' actions with religious righteousness and underscores the Islamic dimension of their revolutionary zeal.[25]

Posters from the revolutionary period of the 1970s and early 1980s were in sync with the prevailing visual culture of global revolutionary movements of the twentieth century.[26] Soviet

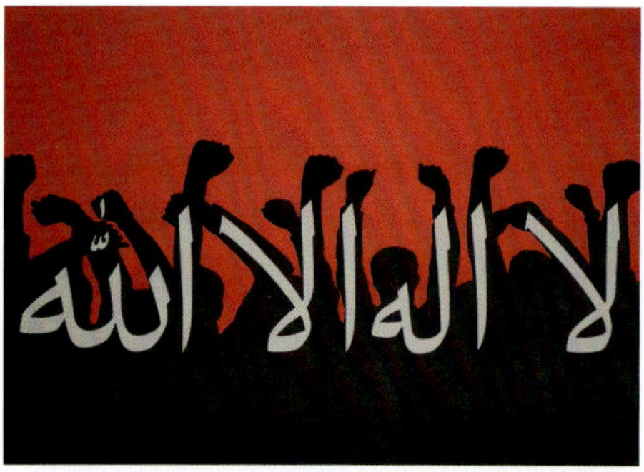

FIG. 52 Silhouette of crowd with *shahada*, ca. 1970s–1980s. Middle Eastern Posters Collection. Box 4, Poster 188. Courtesy of the University of Chicago Library Collection.

revolutionary posters were particularly influential, with their use of bold, flat shapes and striking colors of red, white, and black to tackle themes from the celebration of the working classes to visions of utopian harmony.[27] The leftist groups—who were active before and after the revolution of 1979 but were completely suppressed by the mid-1980s—also looked for inspiration to events such as the May 1968 French student uprising FIG. 53, the struggle for independence from colonial rule in Algeria and Latin America, and the Palestinian resistance movement. This bold visual language permeated the Iranian scene through not only the posters and printed materials produced by political factions such as Peykar but also professional art circles in universities, and especially through Group 57, a collective of professors and students based at the Fine Arts College at the University of Tehran. Group 57 took its name from the year of the revolution in the Iranian calendar (1357). Originally formed for a workshop and exhibition at the university (for which we have photographic documentation, thanks to Maryam Zandi), the group would become renowned for posters that critiqued the shah, the US, imperialism, and social inequalities.[28] Its style was bold, deploying the daring colors, clear text, symbolic imagery, and ease of reproducibility characteristic of international radical posters. And its impact was particularly enduring, as many of its student members went on to become teachers themselves.

THE ARTIST'S LENS ON REVOLUTIONARY ARCHIVES

Unintentionally marooned in Australia during the height of the Woman, Life, Freedom uprising, Tehran-based artist Homayoun Sirizi channeled his desire for participation into researching the roots and connotations of the iconography of the movement, and especially of the works animating the walls of Tehran. He looked at

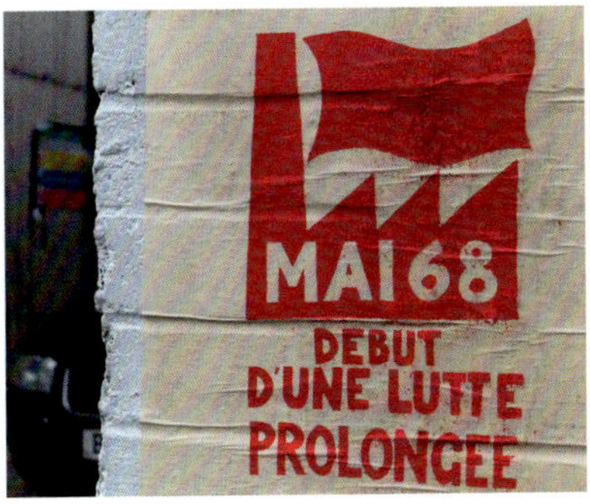

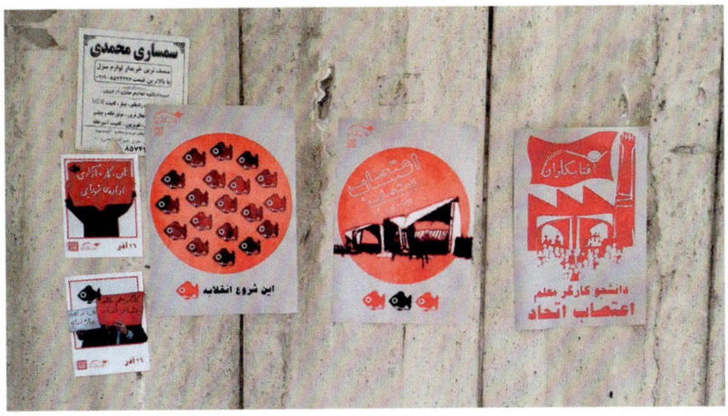

FIG. 53 A reproduction of the iconic French May 1968 revolutionary poster spotted in Brighton, UK. Photograph taken by Adrian Turner. Courtesy of Alamy Stock Photo.

FIG. 54 Composite image: original photograph of posters on a wall in Tehran, incorporating elements from other revolutionary materials. Courtesy of Telegram/@Manjanighcollective.

the posters created by various underground activists, notably the Aftabkaran Group, which stands for the rights of all marginalized groups, including women and the impoverished. Long before Woman, Life, Freedom, this group was creating graffiti and illustrated slogans to call attention to issues like poverty and economic mismanagement. Their activism intensified in 2019, a year marked by the protests of low-waged workers and culminating—as mentioned in the previous act—in the brutal government crackdown of "Bloody November," in which some 1,500 protesters lost their lives. Reflecting their leftist views, the Aftabkaran Group's Woman, Life, Freedom posters often replaced the word "life" with "community." Other times, the words "women" and "life" were also replaced by "bread" and "work": Bread, Work, Freedom FIG. 55).

In his research, Sirizi explored the visual and thematic aspects of the Aftabkaran Group's grassroots activism, which mirrors the historical and ongoing struggles within Iran. A key discovery was the importance to the group of the iconography of the 1968 student uprisings in France: intriguingly, this influence is not drawn directly

FIG. 55 Graffiti by Aftabkaran. Courtesy of Telegram/@Manjanighcollective.

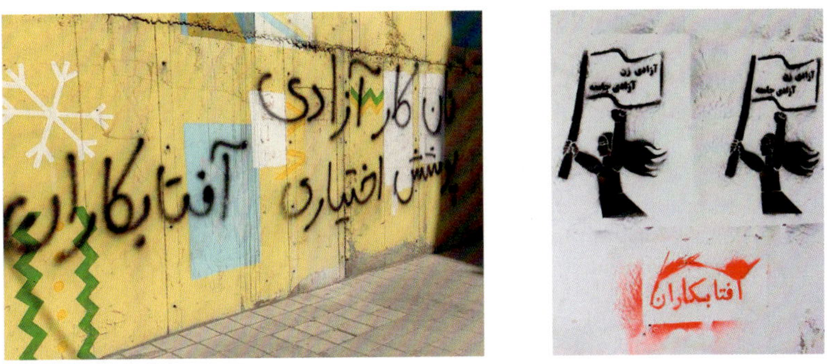

from the original French sources, but rather is mediated by the works shown in the Group 57 exhibition at the University of Tehran, which were themselves derived from the French visual materials. It is this incorporation of iconographic elements from Group 57 and other 1960s revolutionary groups that distinguishes the posters that bear the signature "Aftabkaran" FIGS. 54–55.

As described by Sirizi, the imagery in these posters encompasses a range of powerful symbols echoing posters from the 1968 French student uprising. Solitary raised fists emerge from immense crowds, symbolizing unity and resistance; men and women march in solidarity, carrying an oversized flower that serves as a symbol akin to a flag. There are factory silhouettes and, more starkly visceral, bloody handprints set against a plain white backdrop.

One of the most curious aspects of the posters are the little red or black fishes that evoke Farshid Mesghali's cover design for the celebrated children's book *The Little Black Fish*, first published in 1967 and banned in prerevolutionary Iran FIG. 56. Written by social activist and teacher Samad Behrangi, the book tells the story of an extraordinary black fish that yearns to leave a small pond for the vastness of the ocean—an allegory of the desire of young people to expand their horizons beyond the limits placed on them by society. Behrangi's works, with their message that individuals have the power to change their circumstances through their own efforts, resonated with leftist groups of his time, and in particular with the Organization of Iranian People's Fedai Guerrillas. The influence of these ideologies and Behrangi's narrative style is evident in the Aftabkaran Group's posters, which reflect a blend of political allegory and a call

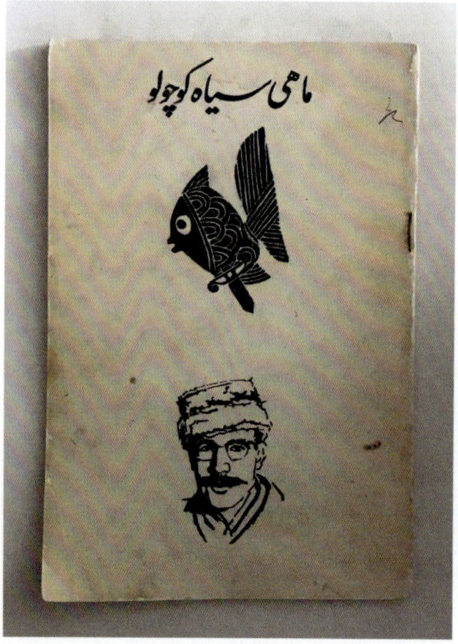

FIG. 56 Cover design by Farshid Mesghali for Samad Behrangi's *The Little Black Fish*, ca. 1967. Courtesy of Homayoun Sirizi.

for individual initiative and change. The replicating of Farshid Mesghali's fish also alludes to a method of appropriation in art that relies heavily on the reproduction of the whole or a part of a work by another artist.[29] In the realm of imitation and citation that constitutes pastiche, the political posters of Aftabkaran empty the signifiers of their original historical meanings.

In his exploration of prerevolutionary imagery, Sirizi also came across the work of photojournalist David Burnett, who spent forty-four days in Iran during the 1979 revolution and captured some of its most iconic moments, from the shah's departure to Khomeini's return. Sirizi was particularly taken with the striking images that juxtaposed bullets and flowers. During a period of intense upheaval, red flowers were inserted into the barrels of guns taken from the shah's defeated army by militia members and civilians alike. These flowers emerged as emblems of peace and unity, prominently displayed at demonstrations.

In response to this work, Sirizi created a series of evocative art pieces using aged wooden frames. One side of the frames shows images of red flowers, historical symbols of peace. On the opposite side, the white canvas is marked by bullet-like impressions, creating a floral pattern. This side is timeless, perhaps referring to the bodies recently punctured by paintballs. The duality of the pieces is further emphasized by the thick red threads that emerge at the points where the bullet marks or flowers appear, making it seem as if the frames themselves were bleeding, and symbolizing the intertwining of violence and peace. Regarding this collection, I am unable to provide an image. Nevertheless, I echo Sirizi's description of the series, which characterizes it as follows:

> Many may not know that some years before the events in 57 [1979], revolutionaries in Portugal had blended flowers and bullets to such an extent that they took the name 'Carnation Revolution' for themselves.
> As I searched for photos of these 'carnations' [in Iran], I saw the faces of 57 [1979] children, men, and women with idealistic expressions that always seemed distant and strange to me. I never imagined that these very faces could be seen again on the streets: the images of women holding flowers in one hand, a symbol of victory in the other, and their hair flowing like a flag in the breeze of freedom.
> [...] In [1979], a slogan was chanted among the people and directed at the Iranian army, asking, 'Tell the Iranian army, was the answer to flowers bullets?' This slogan could still be heard forty-four years after that photo, which David Burnett

took during his forty-four days in Iran, but this time it was heard from the lips of women who were placing flowers, not inside gun barrels, as they had done before, but into the empty eye sockets where bullets had previously struck.[30]

The juxtaposition of old and new—the interplay between archival photos and recent revolutionary movements—vividly illustrates how enduring themes persist in the creations of contemporary artists. Sirizi's work is defined by his unique interest in leftist imagery, driven by his advocacy for the rights of the marginalized in society. However, other artists explore symbols that are less culturally specific, such as the universal icon of blood.

AN UNFADING CRIMSON

In the wake of the Iranian Revolution, the government would often dye the water in public fountains red to remind the population of the sacrifices that had been made and to urge the nation to stand tall. This practice—a trusted weapon in the state's arsenal of propaganda—is still prevalent in Tehran's Behesht Zahra Cemetery, particularly in the section dedicated to the martyrs of the Iran–Iraq War FIG. 57. But the very act of coloring fountains, of evoking the crimson hue of bloodshed, has been repurposed by artists and activists, who have transformed it into a powerful assertion of resistance against government oppression.

During the Woman, Life, Freedom uprising, fountains in cultural hotspots of the capital were transformed by unidentified activists into vivid red symbols, the waters tainted with paint to resemble blood. Fine arts majors at Tehran's University

FIG. 57 Jinoos Taghizadeh, Behesht Zahra, Tehran. Courtesy of the artist.

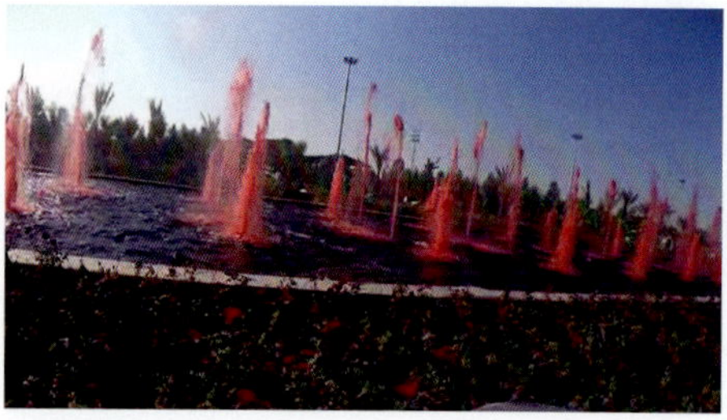

FIG. 58 Tehran's University of Art. On October 10, 2022, fine arts majors participated in the mass choreography of the word "blood" (*khoon*) on the quad. Courtesy of Instagram/@1500tasvir. Image modified by anonymous artist in Tehran.

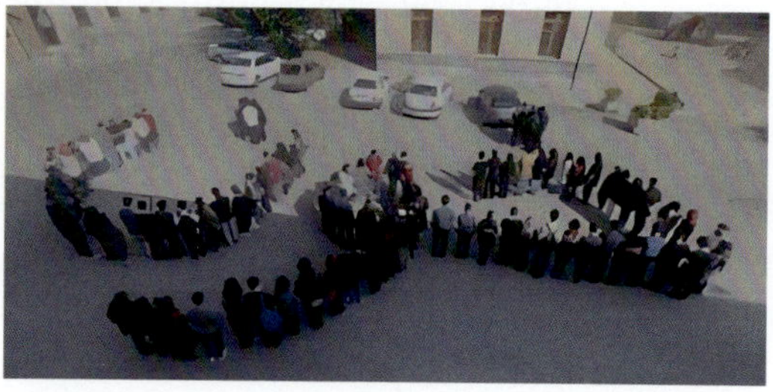

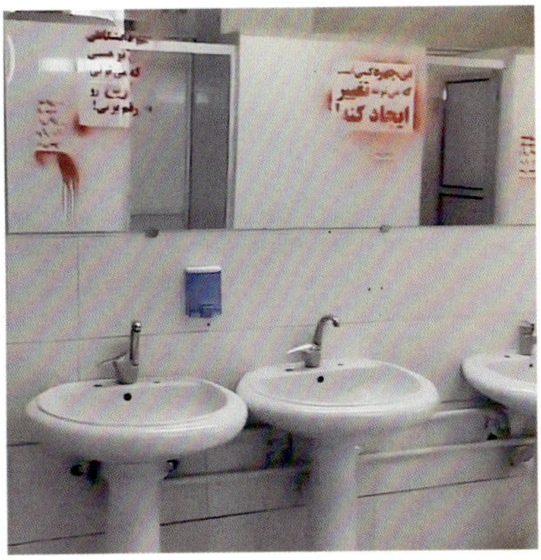

FIG. 59 Tehran's University of Art. On October 30, 2022, bathroom mirrors were stained with red stencils spelling out: "This is the face of someone who can make a change." Courtesy of Instagram/@blackfishvoice1. Image modified by anonymous artist in Tehran.

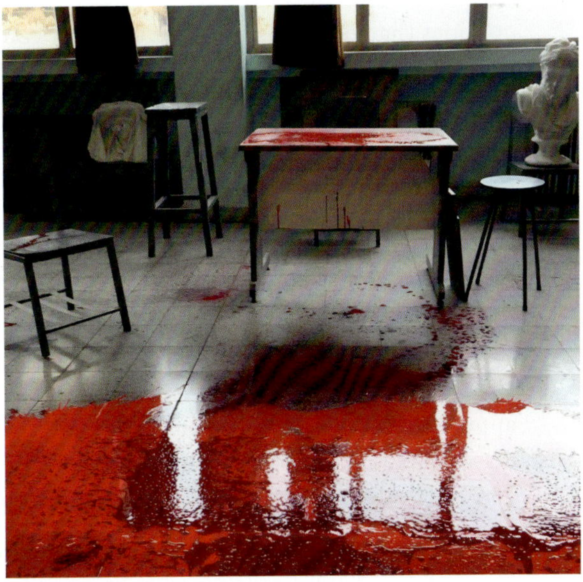

FIG. 60 Blood in a University of Tehran's Faculty of Fine Arts art studio, November 12, 2022. Photographer unknown. Courtesy of Instagram/@blackfishvoice1. Image modified by anonymous artist in Tehran.

of Art participated in the mass choreography of the word "blood" (*khoon*) on the quad.[31] Bathroom mirrors were stained with the red stenciled words: "This is the face of someone who can make a change."[32] FIGS. 58–59.

The doorways of art theory classrooms at Al-Zahra University were splattered with bloodlike colors, as were the studio floors of the University of Tehran's School of Fine Arts. FIG. 60.[33] As mentioned in the introduction, certain galleries were also targeted—shamed for attempting to go on with business as usual FIG. 7. Even the larger-than-life murals of the ayatollahs were not spared, but were drenched in symbolic red, while the streets bore witness to the brutal reality of the bloodshed—to the shooting or beating of young people by the police or undercover Basij militias.

Rather than being unexpected, the recurrence of the theme of blood in the Woman, Life, Freedom uprising was a development that had been foreshadowed for months, if not years, in Iran's political and activist art—for example, in Shaghayegh Kamyar's adaptation of Francis Alÿs's *Green Line* project, discussed in Act Three. This raised a question for state authorities: were the visually potent acts of bloodstaining the work of activists, or did artists also have a hand in their making? One artist, Amir Varasteh, refutes any personal involvement in the defacement of public spaces, but confides that such acts were hot topics of conversation in many artistic communities.

Born just a year before the Iranian Revolution of 1979, Varasteh initially studied traditional crafts but soon developed a passion for public art. In this respect, even after graduate studies in art theory at an Asian university, he considers himself largely self-taught, building on the practical experience he gained at the Tehran municipality's Beautification Bureau. While Varasteh found inspiration in the intersection of art and its environmental context, over time he saw the realm of public art become increasingly entangled with the government's corrupt economic practices.[34] Seeking an alternative approach that would allow for the creative evolution and broader dissemination of public art, Varasteh defined his own distinctive genre of "presentation art" to confront and challenge prevailing power structures, whether they manifest as neoliberal, exploitative, or dictatorial.[35]

Varasteh's most captivating project in this vein is *Neoliberalism's Walkway* (*Gozar-e Neoliberalism*), an installation designed for the 2019 Paeez Barg (Autumn Leaves) art festival, curated by Fereshteh Zamani. Celebrating the fall season, this annual event is held in the historic center of government in Tehran, in an area known for its architecturally significant buildings. Varasteh chose as the site of his installation a grand foreign ministry building designed in the 1930s by the renowned Armenian Iranian architect Gabriel Guevrekian. The fluted columns of the building closely mimic those found in Persepolis, while the façade is adorned with sculpted figures of bulls and other mythical creatures. In front of this façade, Varasteh laid out a sixty-meter-long "red carpet" made entirely of leaves and skillfully orchestrated a scenario where high-ranking officials, including the then foreign minister, Mohammad Javad Zarif, walked on his red carpet FIG. 61. At the beginning of the walk, Zarif was handed a wireless headset that

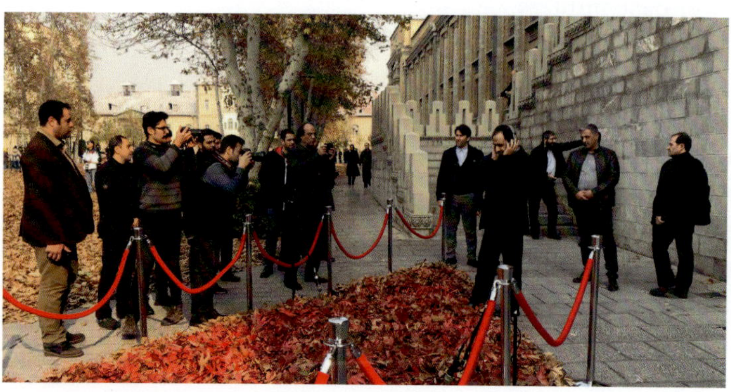

FIG. 61 Amir Varasteh, *Red Carpet*, 2019, Tehran. Courtesy of the artist.

played a soundtrack that was an integral component of the installation, adding layers to the experience. The minister might have assumed that he would be hearing something akin to natural sounds, perhaps reflecting the autumnal theme, like the crunch of leaves underfoot. What he heard instead was the sound of people's cries in his ears, which got louder the further he walked, symbolizing the escalating grievances of the population against the authorities.

The color red resurfaced in another of Varasteh's poignant "art presentations," titled *Civilizing Mission*. In May 2022, just three months before the start of the Woman, Life, Freedom uprising and the death of Jina Mahsa Amini, Varasteh took several white sheets smeared with blood-red paint to the House of the Artists (Khaneh Honarmandan), established during the relatively liberal Khatami presidency. Timing his display for a Saturday, when the institution was closed, Varasteh began washing the sheets in large basins: as the water mingled with the paint, the blood-red stains were gradually diluted and the fabric took on a uniform pink hue. Varasteh then hung the sheets from a rope he had set up in front of the building. Performed by a male artist, this act of laundering—traditionally a task associated with women—was a powerful statement in itself, symbolizing how male artists were actively participating in the movement against gender apartheid in Iran. At the same time, it was a subtle yet poignant critique of pinkwashing, a propaganda tactic that manipulatively uses LGBTQIA+ rights to foster a progressive international image, while obscuring the ongoing apartheid policies that suppress other groups FIG. 62.[36]

Varasteh has frequently been questioned about his potential involvement in acts like staining Tehran's fountains red or splashing red paint on the doors of institutions that have not shown solidarity with the movement. He has consistently denied all these allegations. However, the recurring themes of pink and red in his artwork are unmistakable, subtly hinting at his underlying messages. In analyzing Varasteh's body of work, particularly his use of crimson red or his sarcastic take on pinkwashing, all presented in public places, I perceive a link between past artistic expressions and those that emerged during and after the Woman, Life, Freedom uprising.

In November 2023, an impactful image of Zohreh Solati (an artist profiled in Act One), was relayed to me. Part of a collaborative project discussed further in Act Five, the piece seems to metaphorically depict a scene where a woman's body, enveloped in blood, stretches across an entire highway FIG. 63. The use of crimson red as a tool of protest is a powerful example of the reinterpretation of a revolutionary symbol. Whereas the government dyed fountains red to commemorate the martyrs of the revolution and the Iran–Iraq

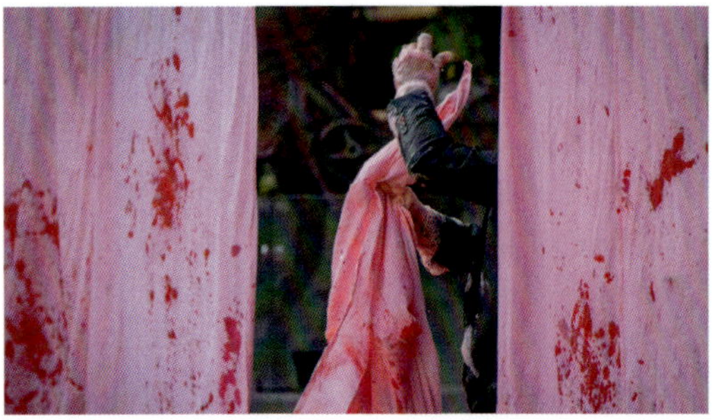

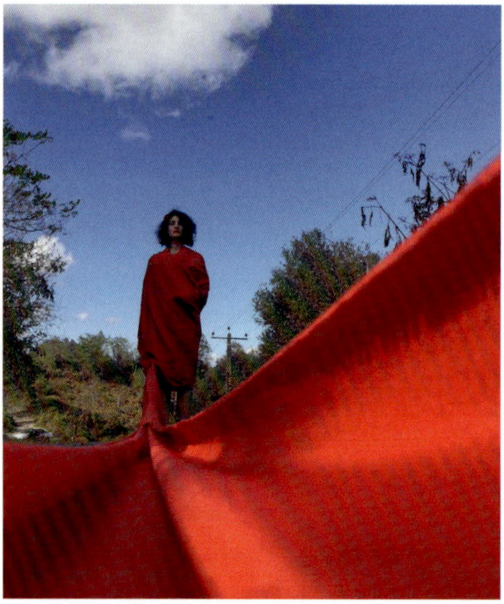

FIG. 62 Amir Varsteh, *Civilizing Mission*, 2022, Tehran. Photograph by Mohammad Talebi. Courtesy of the artist.
FIG. 63 Zohreh Solati, performance at the Siahkal Forest for Persbook's 12th Annual of Contemporary Art, November 2023. Photograph by Ensieh Saleh Nia. Courtesy of Neda Darzi.

War, the same hue is used by artists today to pay tribute to those who have perished fighting against the regime's unjust policies. The iconic crimson red resurfaces in various forms, becoming a striking gown worn by a bold, unveiled female artist, marking the walls of university classrooms, and serving as a critique of the government's treatment of the poor and working class, among other interpretations. I have traced the evolution of this emblematic red because I want to show how traditional themes are repurposed to inspire new forms of protest. As these themes morph and acquire new meanings, the narrative continues to evolve.

During the height of the uprising, the appropriations went beyond historical revolutionary icons to encompass cartoons and other images that found their way onto the streets of Iranian cities after being taken from the World Wide Web. On January 7, 2023, the French satirical weekly *Charlie Hebdo* marked the eighth anniversary of the deadly extremist attack on its Paris offices by publishing cartoons of Iran's supreme leader, Ayatollah Ali Khamenei. The French ambassador was summoned and rebuked over the "insulting and indecent" cartoons. *Charlie Hebdo* itself was hit by a cyberattack, assumed to have been orchestrated by the regime.[37] But the very next day, *Charlie Hebdo*'s depiction of the supreme leader, showing him with a turban made of nooses, appeared on a banner hung from a large commercial billboard over Tehran's busy Hemmat expressway FIG. 64. The banner featured the head of Khamenei next to a raised fist and phrases such as: "Water the tree of the revolution with my

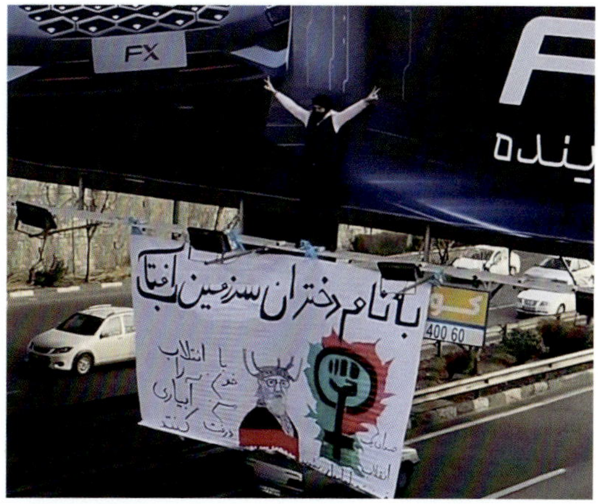

FIG. 64 A woman installs a protest banner below a billboard on Tehran's Hemmat expressway, January 2023. Courtesy of Instagram/@masih-alinejad.

blood." The video that circulated on social media showed a poised young woman in a mask who stood for a moment after she had installed the banner, balanced on top of a flimsy metal structure, her arms outstretched and making the "V" sign for victory. One commentator wrote:

> Just how daring do you have to be to walk along that flimsy gantry without being scared you will fall to your death on the busy road below? How brave do you have to be to stand next to a highly insulting representation of the supreme leader for long enough to become a likely target for a bullet from a roving police car? How courageous do you have to be to stand there long enough for the footage to go viral, potentially exposing yourself to identification and arrest? Just how brave can you be?[38]

The reproduction in Iran of cartoons from *Charlie Hebdo*, which is known for its contentious stance on Islam, reflects the boldness with which imagery from global protest movements circulated during the Woman, Life, Freedom uprising. This instance is a striking example of *parody*, a form of appropriation that involves humorous imitation or satire of a subject by mimicking its form. While the use of this technique, particularly for sensitive political topics, is evident in the work of Iranian artists in the diaspora, it has rarely been applied in such a public manner.[39] The installation of the banner over a busy freeway also highlights the strategic use of the female body in protest art and activist art, an aspect that is central to the book's next "act", which explores how artists reclaim and appropriate street protests using their own physical presence, instead of relying on iconic images that appear in other people's works. ■

Act Five

REENACTING STREET BATTLES

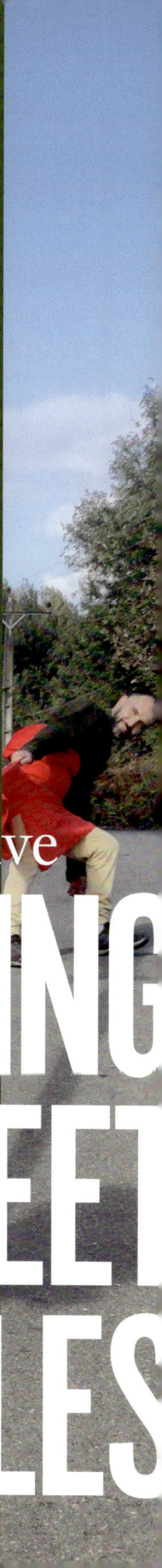

Earlier in this book, I explored examples of reenactment as acts of solidarity with the Woman, Life, Freedom uprising. When Iranian women chopped off their hair, turning a traditional act of mourning into an angry gesture of protest, women around the world followed suit, hacking their own hair and sharing the footage on social media platforms. I also described a particular stance—seated on the ground, body bent forward, head bowed, hands tied around a pole—that mimicked the posture of the Baluchi activist Khodanoor Lojei, who was restrained in this way and left to die, without water, in the blistering heat.[1] This stance was replicated in protests on university campuses, beginning in Tabriz and Sanandaj, then spread to other locations—not just in Iran but around the world FIG. 65.[2] In November 2022, a group of activists dressed in black handcuffed themselves to Chris Burden's *Urban Light* installation outside the Los Angeles County Museum of Art.[3] They were not only paying tribute to Lojei but also marking the fortieth day of mourning after the massacre at Zahedan, when security forces opened fire on Woman, Life, Freedom protesters, killing close to one hundred people.

The reenactment or reprisal of past events can also offer contemporary audiences a new perspective that enhances their understanding of history.[4] One example is Jeremy Deller's *Battle of Orgreave* (2001), which shed light on the painful process of deindustrialization that Britain went through in the 1980s. The Conservative government, led by Margaret Thatcher, was intent on curbing the power of trade unions and shutting down unprofitable sectors of the economy. The striking miners, in turn, were desperate to stave off the closure of the pits and preserve a way of life that had defined their community for generations. With a cast of one thousand people, including two hundred former miners who had taken part in the original event in 1984, Deller restaged a clash between the workers and the police that had "the quality of a war scene rather than a labor conflict."[5]

Iran has a long tradition of reenactment in the form of the *ta'ziyeh*, or passion plays, which commemorate the martyrdom of the Prophet Muhammad's grandson, Imam Hussein, at the Battle of Karbala in 680 AD. Performed during the month of Muharram, especially on Ashura, the plays involve elaborate costumes, poetry recitations, music, and dramatic portrayals of the battle's events. But today's reenactments depart significantly from these traditional practices. Rather than mere reproductions of past events, they are bold, site-specific performances in public spaces, often imbued with political intent. In essence, it could be argued that religious reenactment has given way to a secular form of reenactment, which nevertheless, like the original passion play, serves as a means of remembrance and resistance against tyranny.

Unlike simple acts of replication, reenactments demand action through a living and breathing body that puts itself in a place where an important event has unfolded; they necessitate practice and rehearsal to effectively mimic and exaggerate the actions on which they are based. It is this specific connection to real events that gives the reenactments a much greater political charge than the bodily

FIG. 65 Reenactment of Khodadad Lojei's pose by university students at the campus quad at Kurdistan University in Sanandaj, Kurdistan region, Iran. Photographer unknown. Courtesy of Instagram/@blackfishvoice1. Image modified by anonymous artist in Tehran.

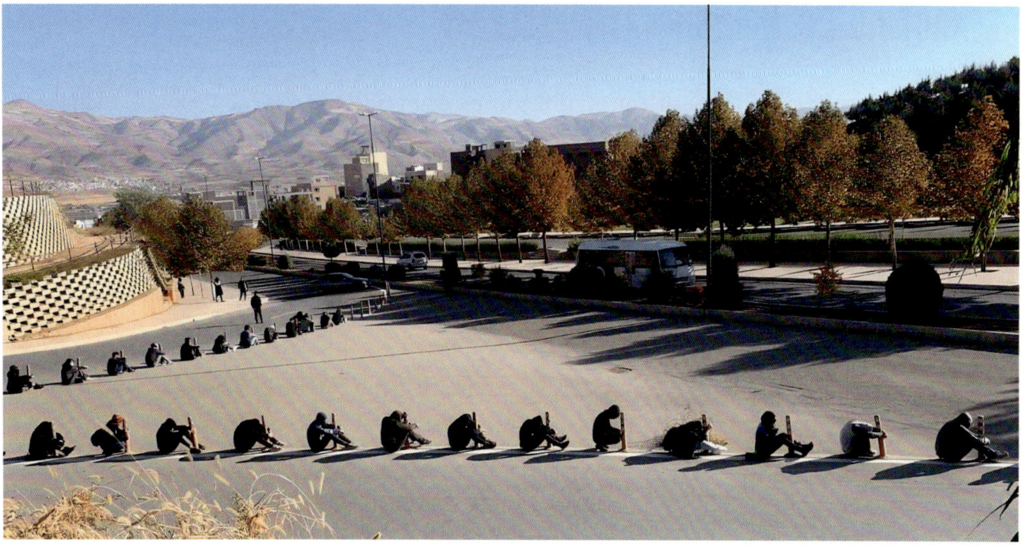

performances presented in Act One. By restaging actions that are seen as politically sensitive—which people generally are not allowed to refer to, much less mock—they offer an upfront critique of the socio-political landscape in Iran and a direct challenge to the authorities.

Tanin Torabi's *Until...* is a compelling blend of artistic representation and live protest that captured in real time the unfolding uprising in the fall and winter of 2022, recording the movements of the actors reenacting these events in a distinct and provocative cinematic style. To fully understand this art project, it is crucial to grasp Torabi's background, with her roots in choreography and her development into a seasoned screen dancer and creator of filmdance—a burgeoning genre in filmmaking. Much of Torabi's previous work has involved reenacting everyday life on Tehran's streets. Harmoniously melding multiple art forms, her performance style challenges the conventional boundaries between reality and performance, between life and art. "If Art and Truth Cannot Coexist, Let Art Perish" is the maxim echoed across her social media platforms.[6] Torabi's oeuvre provokes complex inquiries about deviating from the norm. What occurs when we envision a body acting and moving outside normative behaviors? What kinds of reactions does such a body elicit? How do bystanders perceive this nonconforming presence, and how does this divergence integrate into everyday life? Could this serve as a precursor to the nonnormative behaviors observed at the height of the uprising? These questions form the core of the two films by Torabi that I will discuss before shifting focus to her reenactments of actual protest activities.

REENACTING THE NONNORMATIVE SELF

Torabi was born in 1992 into a religious minority family. Growing up, she was immersed in a world of music and dance, influenced by her mother, who had received professional dance training prior to the revolution. However, as a member of a persecuted religious minority, she led a sheltered existence, with learning primarily taking place within the confines of her home. She did go to college to study English literature, but was expelled after a year: the regime systematically denies her community's access to higher education. Torabi then pursued sociology at an underground institution.[7] At the same time, she devoted countless hours to honing her ballet skills under the guidance of both a private dance instructor and the dancers in the YouTube videos that she diligently studied and emulated. After spending an entire summer in ballet training in Armenia, she was able to begin giving private dance classes herself. Over time, the classes she taught at her family home evolved into a haven for many; interaction with her students imparted a distinctive lifestyle and outlook. The income from the classes also allowed Torabi to go abroad to study in a unique graduate program in contemporary dance performance at the University of Limerick in Ireland. Combining her passion for dance with the craft of filmmaking, she was charting a path less explored by Iranian arts professionals. Her master's project, *Derive* (or *Gozar* in Persian), made in the summer of 2017, features a dancer (Torabi herself) gracefully moving through the bustling Tajrish bazaar in Tehran, performing dance movements that are forbidden for women in Iran and capturing the responses of passersby.[8] The piece represents an audacious claim by a single woman to the urban spaces of Iran—an unapologetic occupation of the streets of the city.

Torabi takes center stage in *Derive*, dancing to original music composed by Faran Fahimi, with the performance filmed by Milad Sanaei. We see her gracefully navigating various spaces, weaving around bystanders in an unhurried dance. While some onlookers react with surprise, others remain indifferent. As the narrative progresses, her movements become increasingly unconventional, epitomized in a scene where she boldly pushes against the current of passersby. Charting a path through the bazaar's intricate pathways required meticulous planning, for which Torabi enlisted the help of an architect friend FIG. 66.

The challenges posed by the setting were not merely physical. Tehran's traditional bazaars are not just simple marketplaces but sites of strategic importance, economically and politically. As political economist and historian Arang Keshavarzian points out, Tehran's bazaars might not have the architectural elegance of the grand bazaars in Istanbul or Isfahan, but their regional economic influence is unparalleled, as they serve as the base for vast trading companies that distribute imports across the country and collate exports.[9] Historically, traditional bazaars like the Tajrish have also been pivotal in shaping revolutionary events. The merchants, steeped in tradition and patriarchy, may choose to shutter their establishments, disrupting the economy, or to throw their weight behind their preferred political figures, supporting their agendas.

A further challenge for Torabi was navigating Iran's intricate film permit process, which seems conceived to deter young filmmakers who are not yet established, or who are not affiliated with a recognized institution. The procedure entails several stages. First, the film script must be submitted to the Association of Young Filmmakers of Iran, along with supporting documentation such as a copy of the national ID card and a promissory note ranging from two to ten

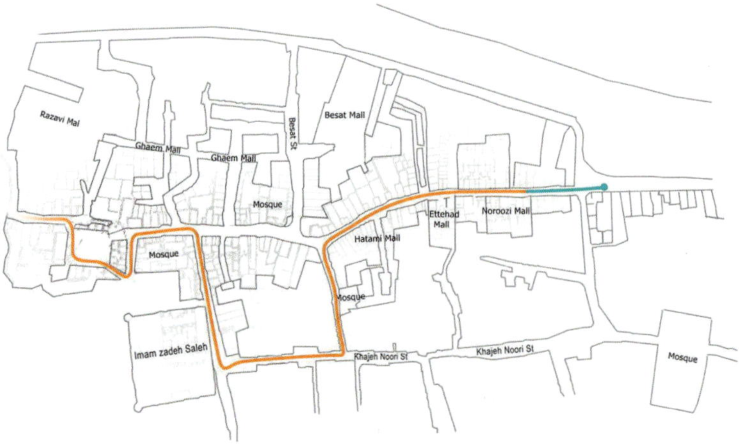

FIG. 66 The route through Tehran's Tajrish Bazaar navigated by performance artist Tanin Torabi, 2017. Courtesy of the artist.

million tomans (approximately $170 in 2024). It is wise to provide multiple copies in anticipation of changes in the rules. After review, the association provides a letter of introduction, which is presented, along with the script, to Naji Art (*naji-e honar*; literally, "savior of art"), an organization connecting art with law enforcement. If the documents are deemed to be satisfactory, a permit will be issued for city-level filming, mainly for ground-level scenes: filming in places like subways or state institutions requires additional permissions. Bearing this intricate process in mind, Torabi crafted a rather naïve storyline—revolving around a young Shirazi tourist's enchantment with Tehran's architecture, especially the bazaar—that helped her secure the necessary approvals. It is worth noting that, in Iran, and especially in interactions with the MCIG, it is common for artists to frame descriptions of their projects in subtle, apolitical, even unsophisticated terms that do not necessarily reflect the actual narrative.

Derive is a one-shot film lasting seven and a half minutes. Both Torabi's movements and the exaggerated motions attached to ordinary shopping actions are masterfully recorded by Sanaei using a DJI OSMO camera, renowned for its superior stabilization and blur-free action capture. The opening scene of the film unfolds in the vibrant core of the Tajrish bazaar, brimming with life and color: animated dolls, dashing male mannequins, vivid garments, shimmering gold trinkets, bright children's attire, sparkling traditional clothes, chic sunglasses, and an assortment of Persian nuts and sweets. The camera casually weaves through these wares before its gaze settles intently on a woman clad in a gray trench coat and scarf in the central artery of the bazaar. She stands with her back to the camera, poised and defiant, compelling the crowd to brush past her shoulders. Some onlookers glance toward the cameraman, quickly deducing that the solitary figure must be the focus of a commercial or television shoot, and they continue on their way, not sparing a second glance.

As Torabi's dance grows more expressive, escalating from a mere lifting of an arm or a stretch of the shoulder, the throng of people around her become visibly perplexed, but continue on their way without further interaction. In the tight confines of the bazaar, the camera lights on a shirt dangling above Torabi's moving body, emblazoned with a graceful calligraphic inscription of a verse from Ferdowsi: *Cho Iran nabashad tan-e man mabad* (If there is no Iran, let there be no existence for me). This marks the moment when her measured, rhythmic movements abruptly cease, giving way to a sprint—a rush of adrenaline propelling her faster, as though fleeing an unseen threat.

The lens then shifts, settling on the blooms of a florist before panning to the cerulean hues of Imamzadeh Saleh's dome, the bazaar's spiritual beacon, dedicated to a brother of Imam Reza. Pivoting again, the camera confronts Torabi directly—no longer a mysterious figure viewed from behind but now seen fully, her visage and movements crystal clear. After gazing into the camera, she begins to dance in the solemn shadow of the dome, amid the walls of the sacred Imamzadeh. She twirls once more, poised at the precipice of the shrine's female-only entrance, yet in the space of a breath she veers away, blending into the sea of faces. The continuous single shot draws to a close with all the elements of the film—Torabi's presence, her narrative, Fahimi's somber music—fading away into the labyrinthine alleys of the bazaar in unison FIG. 67.

The technique of a single shot is of course not exclusive to Torabi's *Derive* (and her subsequent films). A renowned example is *Russian Ark* (2003), with its unbroken eighty-seven-minute Steadicam sequence shot. With only one day available for filming, director Alexander Sokurov and cameraman Tilman Büttner turned a journey through the vast interior of the Hermitage Museum into an exploration of three hundred years of Russian history, involving thousands of actors and multiple orchestras. Unlike films such as

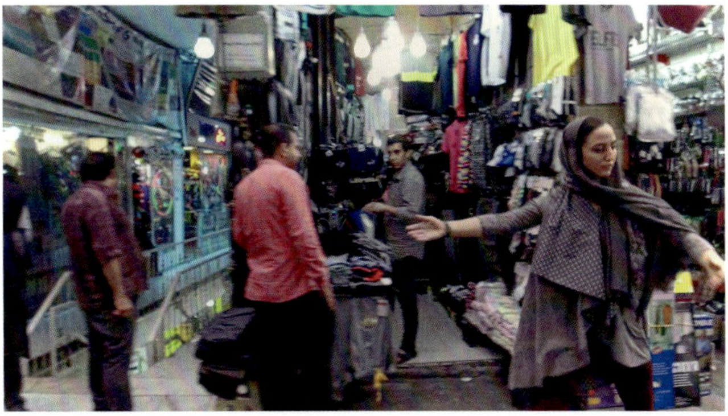

FIG. 67 Tanin Torabi performs at Tehran's Tajrish Bazaar, 2017. Courtesy of the artist.

Birdman, which simulate single shots through editing, *Russian Ark* and *Derive* deliver an experience akin to a live theater performance, with the added risk that any unforeseen interruption could compromise the singularity of the shot, necessitating a reshoot.[10]

In reenacting women's dance movements that can only happen in private, *Derive* explores the limits placed on the participation of women in the public realm. It captures the dynamic between the body and its surroundings, highlighting how one influences the other, reflecting Torabi's conviction that art mirrors life or truth. The idea of the derive—of leaving behind the usual paths and routines and drifting aimlessly through the city, guided only by random encounters—was championed by French philosopher and filmmaker Guy Debord. Far from being an innocent stroll, the derive was, for him, a politically subversive act that upturned established ways of looking at the urban landscape.[11] In a similar vein, Torabi's film, ostensibly a light-hearted journey through the bazaar, carries deep political undertones, offering her own subversive take on urban exploration. Like the derive in its original French context, Torabi's "dance-walk" engages and interacts with the city's conservative bazaar in a playful form of resistance and reimagining. More than just an unusual walk in the bazaar, Torabi's reenactment of the forbidden act of women's dance is part of a broader vision for social change.

While *Derive* disrupts the regular patterns of daily life and trade in a busy bazaar, Torabi's 2021 film, *In Plain Sight* (*Ayan* in Persian), takes place on the central pedestrian pathways of Keshavarz Boulevard, flanked by narrow green spaces and water channels, and set against a crowded backdrop of heavy traffic, commercial buildings, sidewalls, and parking zones. The entire setting provides visually striking, multidimensional shots, particularly when the camera is positioned at eye level and kept parallel to the ongoing scene. The one-shot film, which runs for ten and a half minutes, was coproduced with Sina Saberi and made its global debut at Cinedans in Amsterdam.[12] In a society rife with restrictions surrounding the notion of women's "bodily movement," it shows three young women—Torabi herself, Masoumeh Jalalieh, and Tina Beyk Abbasi—interacting with their surroundings as they attempt to define the boundaries of dance. Masoud Banafsheh was the cameraman and Mahsa Akbarabadi assistant to the director.

The preparation for this public display was honed in a "plateau," a term borrowed from French but uniquely adapted in Iran to denote private soundproof spaces free from distractions. Torabi chose a venue close to Keshavarz Boulevard that had long been a sanctuary for clandestine dance and movement classes, as well as theater rehearsals.

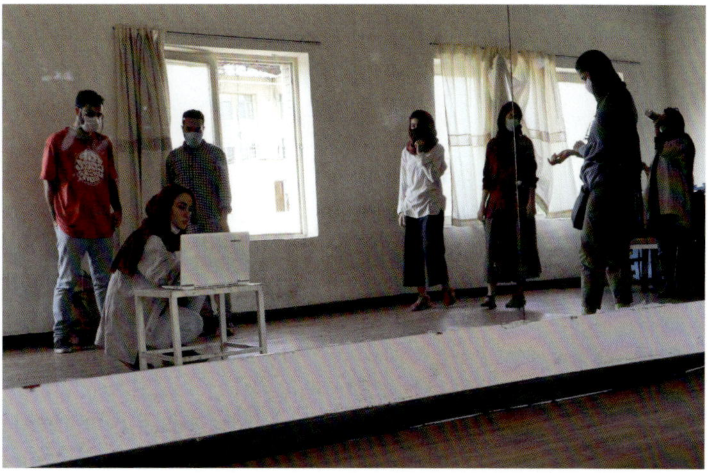

FIG. 68 Tanin Torabi and colleagues during rehearsals for *In Plain Sight* at Daroon plateau in Tehran, 2020. Courtesy of Tanin Torabi.

Daroon plateau (the name, "daroon," means "indoors" in Persian) had a certain patina of grime that came with age and overuse, but its brightly painted walls and windows gave it the feel of a traditional studio, a quality that endeared it to many.[13] The dancers had to find ways to adapt their choreography—rehearsed in private—to conform to the public decorum expected on Tehran's streets FIG. 68. For instance, Torabi described how, during a rehearsal, she instinctively corrected a performer who had posed with her back arched outward and her legs forward. Her reflex action made clear the profound internalization of societal norms: if it was challenging for her to even imagine a woman taking up this kind of pose within the safe walls of the plateau, it was impossible to conceive of it happening in a public space. This approach seems to distance Torabi from her earlier work, in which she pushed the boundaries of bodily movement to be nonnormative, but it was crucial to her vision for this film as a site-specific work, where the physical surroundings inherently shape both the choreography and the cinematography.

Captured during the golden hour, *In Plain Sight* avoids the starkness of noon and the obscurity of night FIG. 69. Natural city sounds form the initial soundscape, giving way to a subtle, melancholic melody as the performers make their entrance. They are clad in long, loose shirts and trousers and their faces are obscured by masks, in deference to COVID-19 protocols. Beginning with tentative, measured steps, their movements soon find a rhythm, harmonizing with the pulse of the city and the evocative music in the background. The camera captures every nuance of their movements without interruption, shifting perspectives from a panoramic view of the street to close-ups that reveal the texture beneath their feet and the contours of their forms, all set against the brooding canvas of the city.

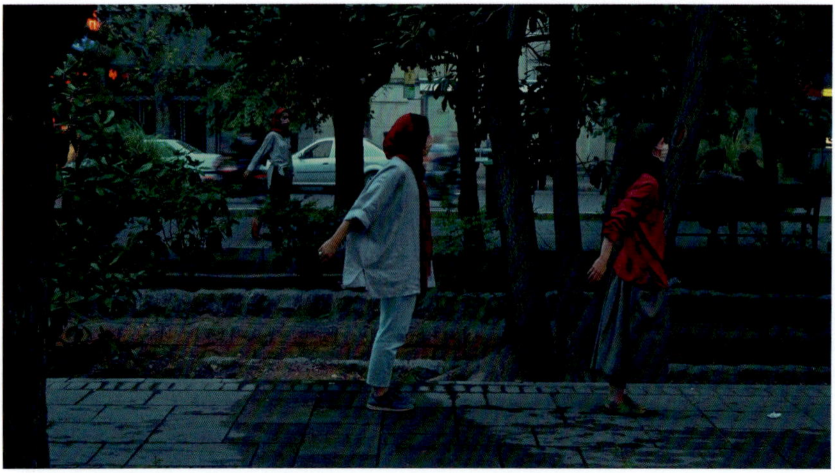

FIG. 69 Screenshot from Tanin Torabi's *In Plain Sight*, filmed on Keshavarz Boulevard, 2020, Tehran. Courtesy of the artist.

The casual movements become more choreographed, as the women come together in an ensemble reminiscent of Sandro Botticelli's *Primavera*. Graceful and harmonious, their motions seem to ripple with an infectious charm. Along the main promenade, a young girl—an onlooker, not a member of the production team—begins to swirl a container of smoldering esfand seeds above her head, a timeless tradition that took on renewed meaning at the height of the pandemic.[14] With each pop and crackle of the burning seeds, a performative act steeped in Zoroastrian heritage unfolds, symbolically safeguarding joy and dispelling negativity.

The dancers then converge on a green area, their path illuminated by glowing artificial trees, crafting a juxtaposition of the natural and the synthetic. They glide by a digital billboard featuring the then president-elect Ebrahim Raisi. With the last note of the fading music, Raisi's image dissolves and the performers move beyond his pixelated appearance, slipping quietly into the embrace of the park. The final frame captures another woman in a vibrant headscarf poised to cross the street, possibly to chase the echoes of the dancers' steps. The film leaves us there, at the precipice of continuation, with the implication that the dance, like the life of the city itself, goes on.

The serenity and understated elegance of the film stand in stark contrast to the challenges faced during its production. Keshavarz Boulevard is dotted with unmarked buildings linked to security agencies. During filming, the performance was stopped by an undercover agent (*lebas shakhsi*). In a tense exchange, the crew were forced to justify their intentions, and parts of the footage were forcibly deleted. Torabi, however, had had the foresight to secure "rented permission" through a reputable film company—a common workaround for young filmmakers navigating Iran's stringent regulatory landscape. After they had presented their official documentation and earnestly explained the film's focus on the everyday flow of pedestrians—not the surveillance of sensitive sites—the agent reluctantly allowed them to proceed. This incident underscores the unpredictability of making art in public spaces, which often pushes other, perhaps less courageous artists toward the relative sanctuary of private venues.

In *Derive*, Torabi challenged conventional perceptions of womanhood within the traditional setting of the bazaar. Similarly, *In Plain Sight* pushes the boundaries of accepted women's behavior on a tightly regulated Tehran street. By navigating the bazaar in an unconventional manner and performing dance live on the streets, Torabi and her fellow actors made a revolutionary statement, compelling themselves and onlookers to reconsider their view of the public space of the city. I regard both *Derive* and *In Plain Sight* as forerunners of Torabi's bold film *Until...*, which uses reenactment to represent the essence of Woman, Life, Freedom uprising—at great risk to the cast and crew themselves.

REENACTING PROTEST

Torabi's thirteen-minute film *Until...* (*Ta Roozi Keh* in Persian) made its debut at New York's e-flux on September 16, 2023, at an event commemorating the anniversary of Jina Mahsa Amini's death. It is a collaborative tour de force in which the performers capture the frenetic energy of the activity at the peak of the protests, using only the switch between the front and back camera of a smart phone.[15] Once again, the film unfolds in a seamless single take, eschewing any form of editing or montage for an uninterrupted cinematic flow. Wearing multiple hats as director, choreographer, and designer, Torabi orchestrates this cinematic symphony with daring creativity.[16]

The film begins with a powerful statement:

> Since September 2022, following the tragic death of Mahsa [Jina] Amini, a 22-year-old Kurdish Iranian woman who was in the custody of the 'hijab police,' a new wave of intense protests has erupted in Iran. Iranian women have courageously removed their hijab in both public and online spaces, rejecting compulsory hijab, while men have stood beside them in pursuit of a more just and unprejudiced society.[17]

This statement is followed by a quote from Bertolt Brecht: "In the dark times will there also be singing? Yes, there will also be singing about the dark times."[18]

In the opening scene of the film, we witness Ava Jalali, a performer without a veil, holding a camera as she navigatesa politically resonant area of Tehran. She weaves her way past a French café and pastry shop, a rare vestige of the shah's era that has resisted both gentrification and the Islamic regime's efforts to erase Pahlavi architectural influences. This café, at the corner of Enghelab and Vesal Shirazi Streets, is next to the spot where Vida Movahed stood on a utility box, waving her white scarf in defiant protest of the mandatory hijab FIG 108 B. In an attempt to thwart similar protests, authorities have since covered the box with a pitched roof, a detail *Until...* captures along with the façade of the pastry shop.

As the narrative unfolds, the performer looks around apprehensively, perhaps wary of being followed by the police, until she finds a temporary place of sanctuary and the tension is briefly lifted. A second figure then enters the scene—Torabi herself, her hair also uncovered—melding into the narrative without uttering a single word. Their silent camaraderie underscores the wordless yet potent resonance of their shared defiance. The connection between the two protagonists is revealed only through their intermittent glances at the camera, which passes from hand to hand, moving from the first woman to the second woman and then to a man. This exchange is marked by a close-up of their interlocked arms and the texture of their winter attire highlighted against the chilly, rain-misted backdrop. They progress with a guarded air, their movements suggesting a shared secret, an unspoken knowledge they shield from the surrounding world.

Next, the perspective shifts dramatically, plunging into the busy street, as if carried by the current of traffic. The scene pivots to capture the man and woman, now hand in hand, darting into an alleyway in search of refuge. A new female protagonist, her hair short and dyed yellow, then takes possession of the camera. She angles it down from her gaze to her feet, drawing attention to the boots of another young woman. This woman, in turn, becomes the next guardian of the camera, bringing it up to frame her own expression—one of uncertainty and apprehension. Her eyes dart swiftly, scanning the street for something unseen, as if searching for an anchor in the unpredictable flow of the city.

The camera is seamlessly handed from one person to the next, capturing a succession of unsettled individuals: no words are spoken, but their heavy breathing can be heard against the backdrop of muted car sounds. The lens follows as the young men and women sprint away, seeking refuge in another alley. Passed on to a woman with long, unveiled hair, the camera tracks her rapid movement until she encounters a friend with similarly dyed hair. In this brief meeting, the camera captures the two holding each other tightly, a momentary celebration of escape from an unseen threat.

The scene transitions to a back alley tucked away behind a construction site. Here, hidden from prying eyes, they pause, taking a moment to breathe before darting off again. The camera captures a sudden encounter with another pair—a young woman and a man who embrace tightly, finding momentary shelter in a recessed apartment. The presence of the authorities is unseen but the atmosphere is oppressive: walls that shortly before had been a canvas for vibrant Woman, Life, Freedom graffiti are now starkly whitewashed. In a moment of vulnerability, a woman stumbles and falls, but is swiftly aided by her companions.

The camera continues its raw and unrefined journey, passed from hand to hand, eschewing calculated zooms and pans for an authentic in-the-moment experience. In an alleyway, the actors once again encounter Torabi, who bursts into a dance, joined by a male counterpart. As they clasp hands and spin together, the movement blurs the line between childlike whimsy and the mystical rotations of dervishes, entrancing and vertigo inducing. Abruptly, the camera tumbles to the ground, only to be scooped up by another actor who captures the frantic dash of their companions ahead. As they spill into the throng of a busier street, a female passerby mistakes their

FIG. 70 Tanin Torabi et al., still from *Until…*, 2023, Tehran. Courtesy of Tanin Torabi and photographer Arya Khaksari.

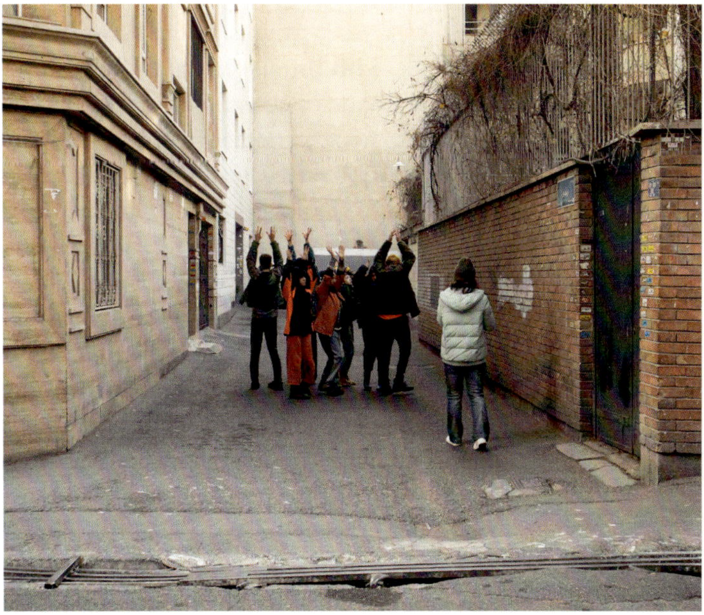

urgency for evasion and advises them to move faster, as the police are nearby. This interplay, which Torabi confesses was entirely serendipitous, lends an unintended layer of reality to the artistic endeavor, embodying Torabi's vision of art imitating life FIG. 70.

The camera shifts its gaze to the layers of graffiti—the scars that narrate the city's tale—being erased from a brick wall. The rhythmic tapping of feet, reminiscent of a military or revolutionary march, echoes against the asphalt, fluctuating between simple strides and hurried dashes, suggesting a flight from impending danger. The palpable breathlessness of these young people on the move dominates the film's soundscape, while the restless camera, with its frequent zooms, pans, and tremors, intentionally induces an unsettling sensation in the viewer. The scene transitions to five actors dancing like whirling dervishes, culminating in a zoom in on the sky, where the tips of home security fences point upward, like missiles. The camera then hops onto a motorcycle and we see the young women, all unveiled, navigating Tehran's frenetic traffic. Approaching an institution with murals depicting a blue sky and white birds, two girls pass the camera around a utility box, revealing its metal fabric, before focusing on another woman entering a glass bus shelter.

The film culminates in a poignant scene at the bus shelter, framed by its yellow metal structure. The words "Woman, Life, Freedom," inscribed in the center frame, are flanked by a to-the-point "fuck the system." An actor dances gracefully into the frame, her silhouette seen from behind the glass panels of the bus shelter. Moments later, we see another woman, initially just a bystander at the shelter, step out and join the other characters from the film. The camera then lowers its view to capture the walking feet on the rain-soaked sidewalk, with the ambient noise of cars moving through the rain recalling the sound of ocean waves. The film draws to a close on this uplifting, hopeful note, giving the impression that the population has risen in solidarity with the film's protagonists, sharing their yearning to reclaim the spaces of the city.

The mobility of bodies is central to all sequences of the film. As Talia Hatuka writes, street protests are marked by their inherent mobility, often taking the form of marches, which gives them both dynamism and symbolic power. This mobility, Hatuka argues, disrupts the regular rhythm of city life, intensifying the impact of the protest by drawing in onlookers as well as active participants. As the protest moves through the city, it broadcasts its message to a much broader spectrum of the public than it could reach from a single, centralized location such as a main square.[19] In reenacting and effectively replicating a mobile protest, *Until...* draws the viewer's attention to various corners, nooks, and crannies of the city ripe for political action. In this sense, *Until...* could be seen as an act of street protest in its own right.

Iranian cinema often adheres to efficient, linear storytelling, focusing on a protagonist's determined pursuit. In contrast, Torabi's film introduces a nonlinear narrative, blending elements of horror, escape, and heightened emotion. "We move forward, sprint, stumble, and reconnect with those dear to us, only to set off again. Together, we journey until the walls move," says the synopsis on the film's secure Vimeo page.[20] The idea that people might lift the pall of oppression if they join forces and move together is relayed through the tremors of the camera, which give life to the walls that are painted with revolutionary and dissenting messages. The entire city seems to vibrate beneath the feet of its restless young people.

This film exemplifies how real-life activism can be presented as art. The very act of participating in the film was risky: the performers could have faced arrest and interrogation for their unveiled hair and their unconventional behavior both on camera and under the watchful eye of the city around them. In the tense months following Jina Mahsa Amini's death, great care had to be taken to avoid any direct clashes with the authorities that might have jeopardized the project. For this reason, during rehearsals in the plateau, the female actors practiced their roles in full hijab. Torabi credits two male actors with securing the necessary permissions through their connections with well-established theater companies (unnamed here, for safety reasons).

Until... is dedicated to the memory of the "women, men, and children whose blood was shed on the path to 'Woman, Life, Freedom.'" That it was created during the winter of 2022, in a city filled with an atmosphere of fear, is a powerful reflection of the fusion of art and activism in Iran. While the film blurs the lines between activism and artistic expression, it also stands alongside more direct real-world challenges to the authorities from professionally trained artists. Indeed, Torabi's rigorous artistic training distinguishes her work from simple protest or overt artivism. In Syria, a tragic event occurred in November 2012, when four women staged a rare antiwar protest in Damascus's main souk, dressed as brides to symbolize the "Brides of Syria" opposing violence. Despite their peaceful intentions, they faced immediate arrest by security forces, revealing the risks of overt actions.[21] Conversely, artists like Torabi employ their training to subtly navigate systems without overt protest. This nuanced approach is crucial for their sustained "artivism," as it allows them to utilize extraordinary tactics without drawing unnecessary attention.

REENACTING EDGY POWER DYNAMICS

Persbook, established in 2010 by artist and curator Neda Darzi, stands out as one of the pioneering Iranian art collectives, known for its hosting of Persbook's Annual of Contemporary Art, which in 2023 was cocurated by Darzi and Reza Monjezi.[22] The twelfth annual event was postponed in a gesture of solidarity with the Woman, Life, Freedom movement, but when the event resumed in October–November 2023, it took as its theme *tan bafi* (body weaving), signifying the collective's deeper engagement with personal and physical expression in their artistic works. The projects on show included a striking performance where a woman and a man each wrapped their bodies in a long piece of cloth and pulled in opposite directions. The piece symbolized the struggle of Iranian women to assert their rights in the face of the limitations imposed by the male-dominated leadership and lawmakers in the ruling system. But more than just a straightforward representation of interaction between men and women, it was a reenactment of a collaborative piece performed six years earlier.

In September 2017, Nadia Sajjad and Neda Darzi led a group of artists who carried a long red cloth into Iran's central Khara Desert.[23] Their performance, *The Red Artery*, represented both the unity of male and female artists, working in solidarity, and the infusion of vitality into the desert. However, the 2023 iteration transcended a simple act of solidarity—whether with fellow artists or the victims of the Woman, Life, Freedom uprising—aiming to memorialize the tensions that suffused Iranian society even months after the peak of the uprising. The reenactment was staged in the Siahkal forest in Gilan in northern Iran, an area with a long history of opposition to the ruling authorities. In the early twentieth century, the forests of Gilan were the base of the revolutionary Jangal (Jungle) Movement led by Mirza Kuchik Khan, which called for land reform and an end to government corruption.[24] Later in the twentieth century, the Iranian People's Fedai Guerrillas (a communist faction) would attack a gendarmerie post near Siahkal to secure the release of two of their comrades. Three policemen were killed in the attack and thirteen men were later executed for their involvement in it. This incident, on February 8, 1971, marked the start of guerrilla operations against the Pahlavi government, which would continue unabated until the Iranian Revolution. (Interestingly, one of the leading members of the guerrillas, Bijan Jazani, was an artist by training.[25]) With its emblematic use of the color red, the performance not only captured the deep historical and political significance of the site as a battleground between the government and opposition forces but also served as a reminder of the struggles that Iranian women face daily within a

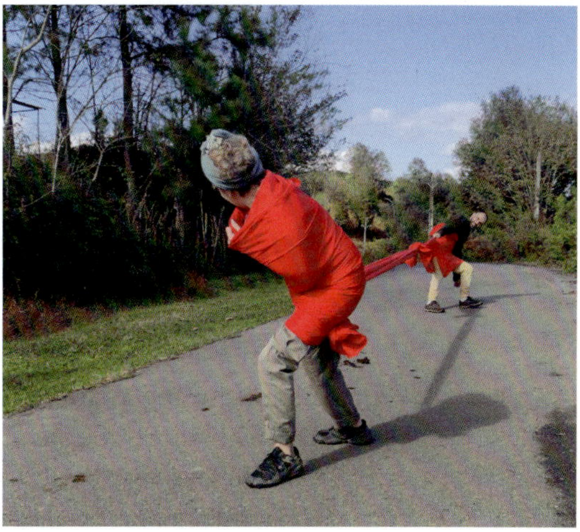

FIG. 71 Mahmoud Maktabi and Shadi Parand, *The Red Artery* performance at Siahkal forest in northern Iran, presented at Persbook's 12th Annual of Contemporary Art, November 2023. Photograph by Ensieh Saleh Nia. Courtesy of Neda Darzi.

male-dominated system. The act of pushing a strip of cloth between two people is a way to emphasize human relations, all mediated by something else—an object, a totem, a thought, or an ideology that might bring us together or drive us apart. Alternatively, this mediator can serve as a communication channel, where, instead of spoken or written words, one communicates via the tensions conveyed by the body of the person on the other side of the interaction.

Mahmoud Maktabi, who participated in this performance, stated, "When we pulled, we inadvertently entered into an intense form of communication, where we could sense the desires, intentions, and the aspirations of the other person on the opposite end of the 'communication spectrum.'"[26] This interaction can be seen as a microcosm of the broader tensions that exist between a male-dominated society and women. However, in the context of the recent uprising in Iran, it also encapsulates the dynamics between the state and the protesters FIG. 71.

REPRISING PUNISHMENT

Farzin Hedayat Zadeh, who transitioned from calligraphic arts to sculpture during his college years, is another artist whose work notably engages in reenactment. His project confronts the pressing issue of corporal punishment in Iran, a practice that has intensified since the Woman, Life, Freedom uprising. One of the regime's favored forms of punishment is lashing, meted out for infractions such as consuming alcohol, attending parties, or not wearing the hijab—activities deemed normal in many parts of the world, including other

Islamic countries. While the stigma attached to such punishments means they are often kept private, one particular case in January 2023 attracted significant media attention. A young woman, Roya Hashemi, was sentenced to seventy-four lashes—the precise number prescribed by Islamic Punishment Law—when she chose to defy the mandatory hijab. Brought into the courtroom, she continued to assert her right to resist the enforced dress code, boldly removing her headscarf in front of the judge, who, while expressing regret, insisted on the need to uphold the law.[27] After the ordeal, Hashemi detailed her harrowing experience on a widely shared post on social media, describing how she had quietly uttered words of defiance while enduring the punishment in a room akin to a medieval torture chamber.

Invited by Persbook to contribute to its 2023 event, Farzin Hedayat Zadeh decided to reenact a lashing in a piece titled *The Apocalypse* (*akhar-o-zamman*). For his performance, he donned an outfit that resembled a scarecrow (or a medieval samurai or even Darth Vader, depending on how you look at it). His initial intention was to lash the Azadi Tower—an emblematic structure, built to honor the shah, but now a hotspot for government-sponsored demonstrations. Due to security concerns, the performance was switched to a location outside the city where there are concrete slabs emblazoned with old ideological slogans, such as "I give my life for my leader" and "Salute! the Messiah" FIG. 72. The title of the piece, *The Apocalypse*, naturally relates to the concept of catastrophic destruction prevalent in Abrahamic religions. In Shiite Islam, the return of the awaited savior, Mahdi, signifies the end of time. Importantly, the postrevolutionary constitution in Iran endows this role with the nation's ultimate authority, which is believed to be under the guidance of the Hidden Imam, or Mahdi.[28] However, the term *apocalypse* is also used in colloquial Persian to denote deep-rooted communal anxieties about the instability of the country, socially, politically, and economically. Hedayat Zadeh's critical stance toward the regime's ideological slogans suggests the impending downfall of a system deeply entwined with religious beliefs about the apocalypse. He also brings a personal perspective to this concept, suggesting that each crisis, like the corporal punishment of political activists, represents a point of no return—the collapse of an individual's world.

In their studio projects, other artists draw direct inspiration from their challenging interactions with the morality police and other agencies regulating women's conduct in public spaces. These artworks, which at first appear somber, in fact embody a spirit of resilience against the government's oppressive measures. Badri Valian's art, in particular, delves into her encounters with the authorities, emphasizing the significance of preserving and narrating these stories

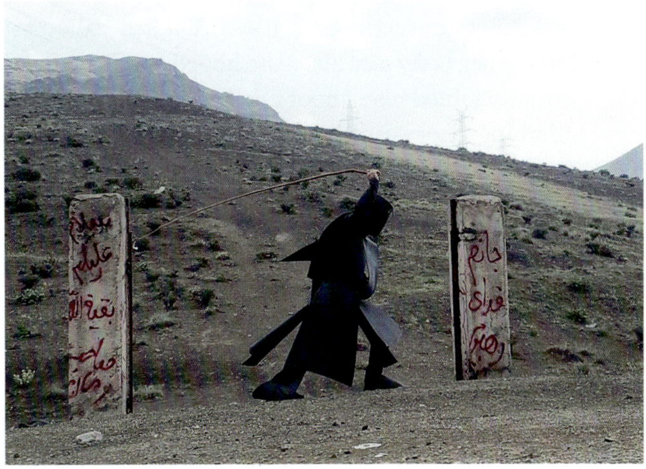

FIG. 72 Farzin Hedayat Zadeh, *The Apocalypse*, footage and photographs presented at Persbook's 12th Annual of Contemporary Art, 2023, Tehran. Courtesy of the artist.

through artistic expression. While Valian has relocated to Northern California, her art is directly linked to the everyday realities on the streets of Iran.

IRAN STREET ENCOUNTERS RECREATED IN DIASPORA

When she lived in Iran, Valian was a celebrated mountain climber and member of the women's national climbing team: "A Woman as Steadfast as the Damavand Peak," is how she was presented in a state-run women's magazine in 2009.[29] However, she was keenly aware that such praise was intended only for public show: in real life, no matter how celebrated, female athletes are still treated unequally, like all women in Iran.[30] While Valin's experience of discrimination is one that is shared by millions, her narrative gains additional resonance due to her dual role as an athlete and artist.

Born in 1977 in Shahroud, Semnan province, Valian comes from a modest family. As the second daughter in a family of six, she soon became conscious of the vulnerability of women in society. She describes growing up in the conservative city, with the ever-present morality police and the regime's propaganda blaring from loudspeakers and plastered across the walls of buildings. As a child, she witnessed brutal public punishments. She knew, too, that early morning calls to prayer, the *adhan*, sometimes signaled impending public hangings. Later, on her way to school, she would see authorities dismantling the gruesome instruments of execution while passersby looked on, some in shock and others in approval.

These unsettling realities propelled Valian toward sports, to fortify her body and also, she hoped, to find a brighter future. She initially joined her school's volleyball team, but took up mountain climbing after enrolling at Mashhad's Ferdowsi University's School of Art, one of Iran's premier institutions. While volleyball had submerged her in teamwork, mountain climbing provided solitude, forcing her to confront her reality both as a woman and a human. The challenges of scaling mountains like Alborz, which she conquered in record time, honed her resilience FIG. 73.

While Valian's athletic achievements soared as part of Iran's national climbing team, her personal life was tumultuous. After a short-lived relationship and marriage in Tehran, she focused on her dual passions: sports and art, the latter manifesting in her work as a high school teacher and private tutor. Her rigorous training and adventures transformed her physique, sculpting her into a beacon of strength and beauty. She learned survival skills on climbing expeditions in the Himalayas, using the warmth of her body to combat the bone-chilling temperatures at high altitudes. Yet, even under these extreme conditions, Valian confronted vulnerabilities: not only did she have to negotiate the dynamics of being in close quarters with male climbers, she also had to grapple with societal perceptions of women's roles and desires.

At the height of her athletic success, Valian was sexually assaulted in Tehran. The experience left deep scars. Though immensely strong, she chose not to fight back, fearing that if she injured her assailant she would face the same kind of fate as Reyhaneh Jabbari, an interior design student who had defended herself—with fatal consequences—when she was sexually assaulted by a potential client who took her to an empty apartment for a work-related matter. Jabbari was imprisoned for seven years and then executed, despite international appeals for clemency. The chilling tale, later the subject of the film *Seven Winters in Tehran* (2023), resonated with Valian back in 2007, long before it made global headlines. For Valian, Jabbari's ordeal is not an isolated occurrence, but representative of the many hidden stories of women's plight in Iran.[31] She believes the regime used Jabbari's prolonged incarceration and eventual execution to convey a chilling message: that women, irrespective of the circumstances, remain perpetually vulnerable, and should always submit rather than defend themselves against male aggressors. As she puts it: "This is a calculated subjugation of women and a tacit endorsement of all men, whether virtuous or vile."[32]

These traumas permeate Valian's art, which address themes of sexual harassment. Her work is further influenced by particularly disturbing encounter with the morality police during a public religious

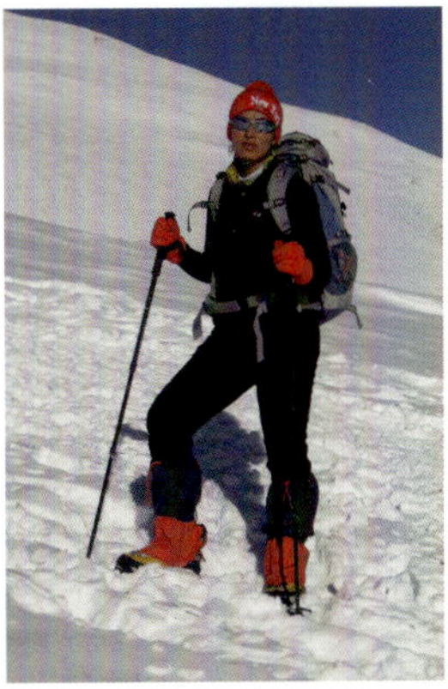

FIG. 73 Badri Valian during the peak of her career as a member of Iran's Women's National Mountain Climbing Team, October 2008. Photograph by Saeed Kafshgeeri.

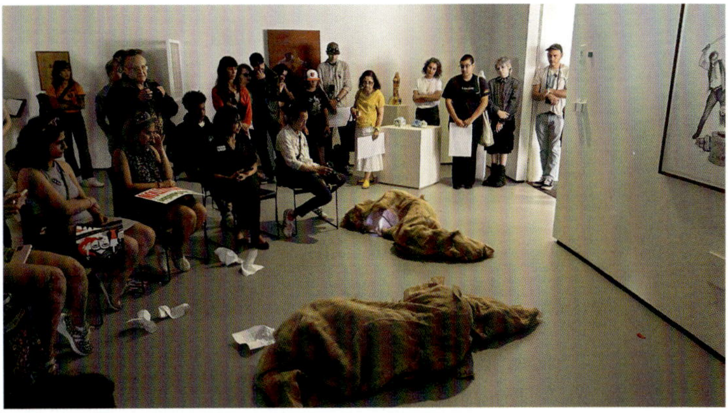

FIG. 74 Badri Valian and Sarah McCarthy Grimm, *Detained Imprints*, performance at the Yerba Buena Center for the Arts, San Francisco, California, 2023. Courtesy of Badri Valian.

procession on the Day of Ashura in 2006. After an exhausting practice, Valian was returning to her apartment without her required trench coat when she unintentionally neared the procession. There, she was confronted by an agent who spewed threats of violence—he thought she should be put in a sack and abandoned in the desert outside Tehran—because of her attire. Haunted by the experience, Valian collaborated with California-based artist Sarah McCarthy Grimm on a lengthy poem, which they performed at the Yerba Buena Center for the Arts in San Francisco while wrapped inside rice sacks. Valian's portion of the poem, set in italics, tells the story of a young girl, her secret mirror, the objects in her room, and her struggles with the brutality of the men in her life. The poem appreciates the objects in her room in these words: "Thanks objects; thanks objects for not being human; thanks objects for treating her humanely." McCarthy Grimm's part, in roman type, describes her experiences assisting victims of sexual violence in Argentina, Uganda, and Guatemala FIG. 74. Titled *Detained Imprints*, the performance reenacted women's experiences, reminding us that the life of a celebrated athlete can resonate with the struggles of everyday people.

If reenactment is essentially a performative replication of life's struggles and conflicts, then documenting these realities, especially during the height of the uprising, is a significant contribution that deserves recognition. While the documentation undertaken by Iranians in the diaspora is often rooted in academic, archival, or publishing backgrounds, and compiled retrospectively, the documentation by artists in Iran tends to be more immediate and spontaneous. I will explore the distinctive nature of these expressions, and the part they play in artistic activism, in the next "act" of this book. ■

Act Six

DOCUMENTING URBAN UNREST

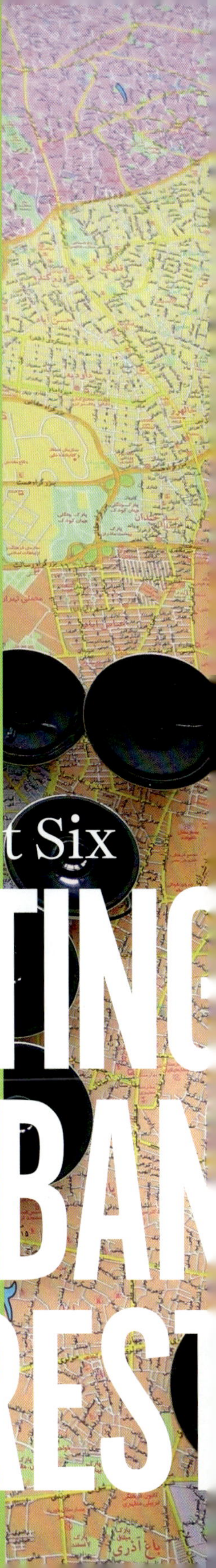

In *The People Are Not an Image: Vernacular Video after the Arab Spring*, filmmaker and researcher Peter Snowdon discusses the Arab revolutions of 2010 to 2012, emphasizing the unprecedented rise in the public using video to document the events for themselves. As Snowdon sees it, these videos were not just records of their experience, but spurs to collective action and political change. He stresses not only the political importance of these amateur videos but also their sensory qualities, underscoring their role in capturing the raw emotions and atmosphere of the revolutions. For Snowdon, these videos directly present reality, going beyond mere representation. In the same vein, Tunisian film critic Tahar Chikhaoui sees these videos shot on mobile phones as bringing a renewed, more intimate lens to visual storytelling, suggesting a potential evolution in cinema.[1]

Many of the photos and videos of the Woman, Life, Freedom protests are the work of untrained eyes and hands. In these images, there is no filter between the people who are protesting or being harassed by the authorities—high school or middle school students, for example—and those who are recording the event. The documentation is unfiltered and authentic. Similarly, the amateur archives that have been set up to preserve this material break with convention. Whereas official archives primarily house historical documents related to the state, these new archives are forward-looking, intended to serve as sources of inspiration for future generations.[2] While traditional archives are meticulously and systematically organized, these new archives exude spontaneity.

An exceptional description of such unfiltered footage that borders on art can be found in a moving editorial in the special

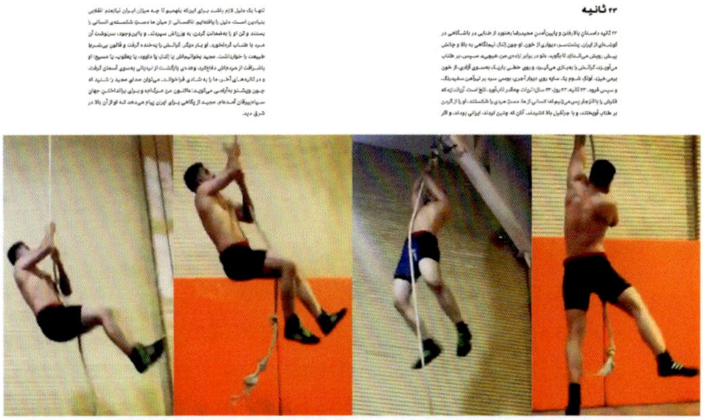

FIG. 75 Kaarnamaa editorial, Majidreza Rahnavard montage piece. Courtesy of *Karnameh: Journal of Art Criticism and History*.

issue of *Karnameh* dedicated to the Woman, Life, Freedom uprising (a project of the Kaarnamaa organization, discussed earlier in this book). The editorial focuses on a video of Majidreza Rahnavard, who was accused by the regime of fatally stabbing two Basij militia guards during a Jina Mahsa Amini protest. The charge was "emnity against God."[3] Rahnavard's trial was conducted in secrecy, but his pre-execution moments were widely broadcast. In a press interview shortly before his public hanging, the blindfolded Rahnavard spoke calmly and assertively, urging his family and compatriots not to mourn him with traditional religious chants but to celebrate his life with joyful music. After his execution, footage emerged of him during an athletic exercise. Defying gravity, he ascended a rope against the orange wall of his gym, completing the climb in twenty-three seconds. The number twenty-three became symbolic: Rahnavard was also twenty-three years old and imprisoned for twenty-three days before his execution. The *Karnameh* editorial related this footage to Rahnavard's life, expressively conveying how he rose above hardship, pushing against a backdrop symbolic of blood FIG. 75.

This interpretation acknowledges the value of documentary and candid footage taken by ordinary individuals. As eloquently detailed by the *Karnameh* editorial, the image of Rahnavard is transformed into a work of art, thanks to its poetic and art historical ekphrasis, reminiscent of an expert's detailed analysis of a masterwork of painting. My narrative below focuses on how artists drew inspiration from these forms and contributed to documenting the uprising as it unfolded. I will discuss how, in capturing revolutionary moments, seasoned artists have straddled the line between pure documentation and aesthetic appreciation.

A MEMORIAL WITHIN A MEMORIAL

In the category of artistic documentation, Parastou Forouhar's persistent record of the murder of her parents stands unparalleled among Iranian artists. Outspoken critics of the theocracy and of human rights abuses in Iran, Dariush Forouhar and Parvaneh Eskandari Forouhar were assassinated in their home on November 22, 1998. The case drew significant attention, bringing to light a series of politically motivated killings in Iran over the previous decade—the "chain murders"—which were widely believed to have been orchestrated by the Iranian Ministry of Intelligence.

Now living in Frankfurt, and known for her large-scale installations featuring (pseudo)calligraphic works and imagery of violence, Forouhar makes a pilgrimage to Iran every year to commemorate the anniversary of the assassination. The memorials are attended by numerous cultural and political figures, among them the human rights activist Nasrin Sotoudeh. Forouhar has turned her home into a quasi museum, preserving her parents' political activism through reproductions of original photographs that she has meticulously framed and curated herself. She has marked the exact spots of their murders, and kept most of their personal belongings intact—though some items have been stolen over the years in what she suspects is a systematic effort to erase her parents' memory FIG. 76.

Forouhar has described her complex emotions on returning to Iran on the twenty-fourth anniversary of her parents' death, which coincided with the peak of the Woman, Life, Freedom uprising:

> Ten days before the twenty-fourth anniversary of the political assassination of my parents, [...] I went to Tehran, as I do every year, for a justice-seeking action, which, over the years, has grown and developed into an integral part of my life [...] This trip, however, took place under entirely different circumstances, amidst a passionate and bold revolutionary uprising. The Woman, Life, Freedom movement signaled a new era opening up to justice, equality, and the coexistence of diversities. [The] agents of repression were wildly and ruthlessly attacking the people. Reports indicated an endless wickedness fueling anger, pain, and desperation. [...] However, upon arrival the unveiled women in the [...] airport terminal were the first signs of the revolution that I had admired from afar; the first clear indication of protest with one's body that I had pondered for years. [...] On the long journey from the airport to the house, signs of change were like sparks of hope on the city's body, slogans were scattered on the walls. [...] The next day [I saw] a young shopkeeper telling a

> woman complaining about the stuffy air in his shop, 'It's because of this ridiculous hijab you're wearing. First, we'll get rid of this, then the mullahs.' The woman agreed with an 'Amen.' [...] Early on Friday morning, on the way to Behesht Zahra, I saw municipal workers in two or three places covering up slogans with paint. [...] On Saturday morning, I published the call for the anniversary ceremony on social networks. Unlike previous years, I refrained from placing an obituary in the 'In Memoriam' column of the *Ettela'at* newspaper [...] I no longer wanted to print that veiled photo of my mother, which she despised.[4]

The bravery she saw on the streets inspired Forouhar to repurpose her parents' "museum" as a space to honor the youth involved in the uprising. Central to this commemoration was the dead magnolia tree in her parents' yard, planted by her mother Parvaneh nearly forty years before. Forouhar wrote:

> In addition to the usual preparations this year, we decorated the dried-up magnolia tree. On small, thin slips of paper, remnants from the desk drawer in the library room from my parents' time, we wrote 'Woman, Life, Freedom, Justice, Long live Iran, Jin Jiyan Azadi.' Each slip was tied to the dry branches of the tree. The wind was blowing, and the dead tree seemed to flutter and dance. In the afternoon, when images of this tree spread on social media, a friend wrote under one of the pictures: 'The tree that Parvaneh planted years ago, twenty-four years after her death, has borne the most beautiful fruits of our land.' [...] I thought that this gathering and this house, a place of remembrance and resistance, [had finally become] a united body.[5]

In this way, Forouhar turned the dead tree into a living monument that commemorated not just her parents' writings but the spirit of the movement itself. Forouhar's trip to Iran at the peak of the uprising, her candid documentation of what she saw and experienced, and her poignant recycling of her parents' belongings all epitomize the courage of an artist striving to archive and memorialize the uprising as it was unfolding on the ground. This effort is echoed in the varied documentations by other Iranian artists, each contributing to the idea of resistance through recording.

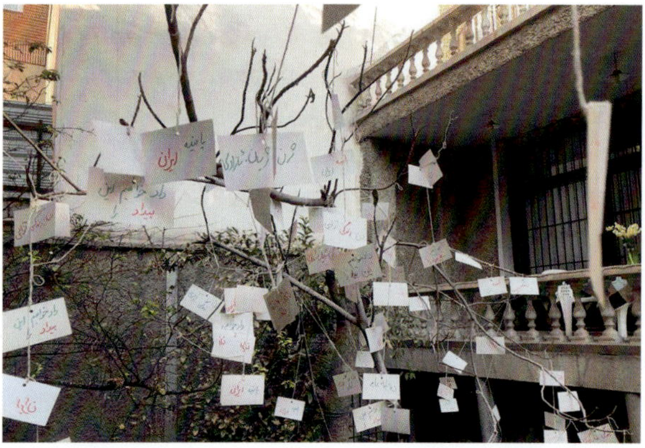

FIG. 76 Installation by Parastou Forouhar in the yard of her parental home, captured in November 2022. Courtesy of the artist.

SHOOTINGS AT THE PEAK OF THE UPRISING

Mona Sartoveh (b. 1982) is a gifted photographer who became an inadvertent chronicler of a pivotal moment in the revolution. Trained in Tehran under the tutelage of the celebrated photojournalist Bahman Jalali and photographer Niloofar Mo'taref, she was schooled in the art of truthful representation—of photographing reality in its purest form. Central to Sartoveh's visual storytelling is the juxtaposition of contrasting elements, a technique seen already in an image from 2008, which captures a moment at a bus stop. A young woman is seen gesturing toward a van, its side emblazoned with the ominous words "Morality Police" (Gasht-e Ershad). But the focus extends beyond the van, taking in the striking mural of Khamenei placed side by side with a billboard for a film. For Sartoveh, this composition served as a metaphor for the internal tensions that run through Iranian society FIG. 77.

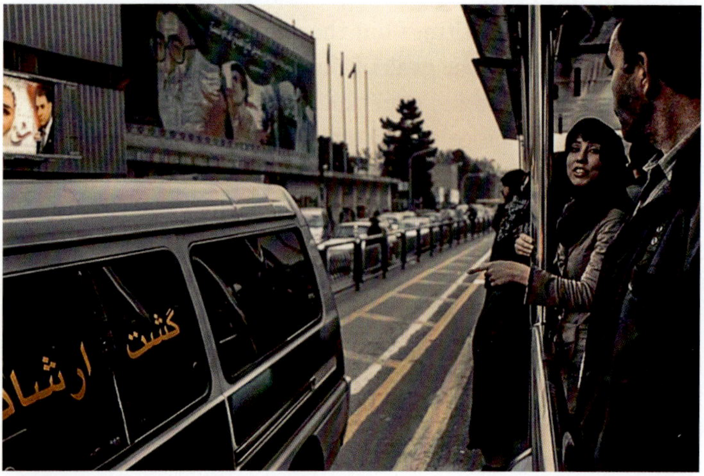

FIG. 77 Mona Sartoveh, documentation of the morality police van, 2011, Tehran. Courtesy of the artist.

In the tumultuous period of the uprising, both Sartoveh and her husband, a filmmaker and producer for state TV, found themselves under intense surveillance by the authorities. Targeted by suspicious phone calls and messages, they received an official warning about their protest images on Instagram. In the early days of the movement, Sartoveh's lens captured the defiant antiregime slogans scrawled across the walls of northern Tehran; although many were soon whitewashed or defaced, their persistent presence spoke volumes to her. However, as the weeks went on, and the protests were quelled with increasing brutality, Sartoveh was appalled by the wanton cruelty displayed by the police, who seemed to take pleasure in acts of violence.[6]

On February 2, 2023, the fortieth day after Jina Mahsa Amini's death—a significant day of mourning in Iranian culture—Sartoveh witnessed a disturbing scene on returning home after picking up her young son from daycare. On the street below, a group of policemen stood close enough for her to hear them talk about targeting unarmed citizens traveling in cars, and in particular aiming for the head or the eyes of women who were not adhering to hijab regulations. The casual nature of their murderous conversation was something Sartoveh found hard to absorb. Though she had never seen herself as

FIG. 78 Mona Sartoveh, documentation of random shooting in Tehran, November 2022. Courtesy of the artist.

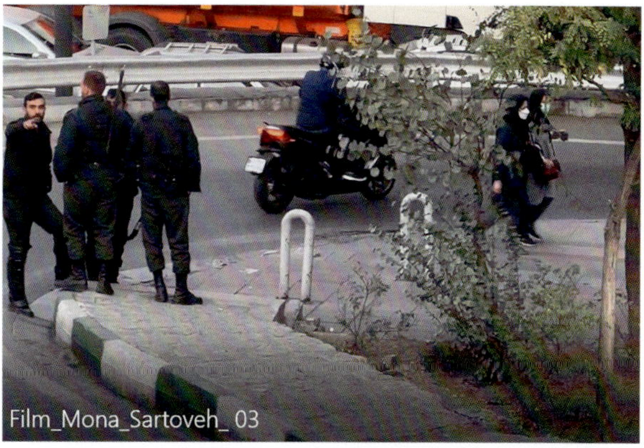

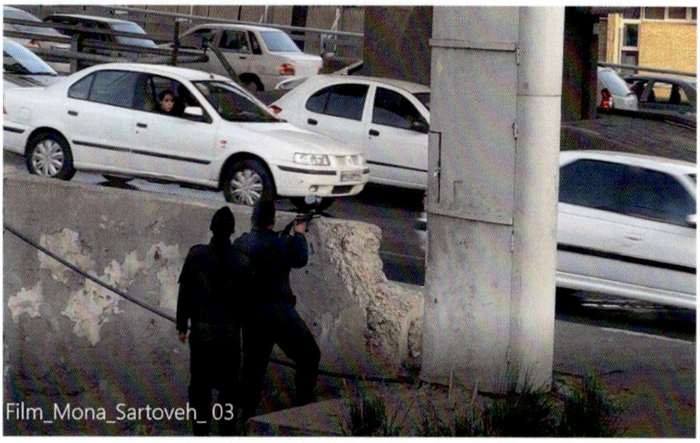

especially political, she felt duty bound to document the event. But as she began to film, she was spotted by an officer, who pointed in her direction. Immediately, she became afraid that the police might storm the apartment and harm her family. The tension increasingly ramped up when her husband arrived home and stepped onto the balcony to confront the officers about their invasive laser lights. The police responded that it was unlawful to record them, their shouted threats mingling with the cries of protesters further away FIG. 78.

After the incident, the couple pulled down the shutters of their apartment, but the sense of sanctuary ordinarily provided by the home had gone. That night, amid the chaos of laser lights and shouting, they decided to leave Iran. Over the next forty days, they liquidated their assets, sold their home and possessions, and departed for the US.

A DARING CHRONICLE OF PROTEST VICTIMS

Meysam Azarzad (b. 1985) began his artistic career as a teenager, working first with various publications in Tehran as a professional illustrator and then taking up roles that allowed him to pursue his passion for animation. Over fifteen years, he has built up a portfolio of over two hundred projects, his talents spanning across motion graphics, cinema (both medium length and short narrative films), documentaries, video art projects, music videos, and video advertisements. He has also shared his expertise in motion graphics through teaching in Tehran. Azarzad's creative projects have earned him numerous awards in caricature, graphic design, animation, and video art from both national and international festivals.

One notable aspect of Azarzad's art is his innovative use of Instagram as a platform for political expression. Since the early days of the uprising, he has shared images of what he calls "fighting girls" (*dokht-e jangi*), black-and-white silhouettes of unveiled young women in stances traditionally attributed to male heroes. These figures, significantly, are juxtaposed with rhyming couplets from the great epic poem *Shahnameh*, written in the early eleventh century by Ferdowsi. Once suppressed by the Islamic Republic because of their undercurrent of criticism toward Muslim invaders and their celebration of Iran's ancient past, Ferdowsi's writings resonate with contemporary struggles, especially in light of the restrictive laws imposed on women in Iran. Azarzad's adaptations of Ferdowsi's verses, occasionally blended with lines from other poets influenced by Ferdowsi, carry a revolutionary charge for Persian speakers. Through the fusion of visual art and national poetry, his work creates a compelling narrative that serves as a testament to the ongoing movement and its potential to effect lasting change.

Drawing inspiration from Ferdowsi's epic poem is not a new development in Iranian art. For example, *Kaveh's Uprising* (1946), by the modernist painter Jalil Ziapour, depicts a blacksmith from the *Shahnameh* in a style influenced by Soviet realism. The tale of Kaveh, of his hard work and his revolt against injustice and tyranny, resonated in particular with those affiliated with the Tudeh Party (Hezb-e Tudeh, or "Party of the Masses"), founded in 1941.[7] References to stories in the *Shahnameh* continued into the 1960s and 1970s, notably in the works of the Saqqakhaneh school, which were inspired by calligraphy and elements of vernacular and folk culture. More recently, artists like Siamak Filizadeh (in his series *Rostam 2*, from 2008) have used *Shahnameh* narratives as the basis for an oblique and humorous critique of Iran's kitsch culture and the regime's surveillance and punishment of people on the streets.[8]

Through his powerful appropriation of Iran's national epic, *Shahnameh*, Azarzad ensures that the heroes of the revolution will remain permanently etched in the memory of the nation, despite the digital age's risks of erasure. Since Jina Mahsa Amini's death in September 2022, Azarzad has meticulously compiled and presented portraits of nearly every individual killed in the uprising. His collection also highlights the significant events and people of the subsequent months, including the parents of the young people who died, as well as those who were injured or tortured and imprisoned for their participation in the protests. Many young women lost their lives at the hands of the regime during the initial stages of the Woman, Life, Freedom uprising. They had taken to the streets to protest against the mandatory hijab; they were seen twirling their headscarves in the air or setting them on fire—and for this, they ended up dead. The state denied any involvement in their deaths—claiming that the girls must have had heart problems or other existing medical conditions—but eyewitness accounts painted a starkly different picture of brutal confrontations with the police. In line with the focus of this book on street art, I will selectively discuss a few poignant examples from the series that tell the story of young women who displayed remarkable bravery on the street.[9] Although these illustrations differ significantly from other forms of art discussed in this book, they are nonetheless crucial. Shared publicly on Azarzad's Instagram account, they serve as a gateway to understanding the courage of these young women.

One of the early posters features an image of a young, unveiled woman with her fist raised in defiance. Ranks of soldiers are massed in front of her, but she remains fearless. Above the image we read: "This massive army is useless. Indeed, a single fighting girl is worth

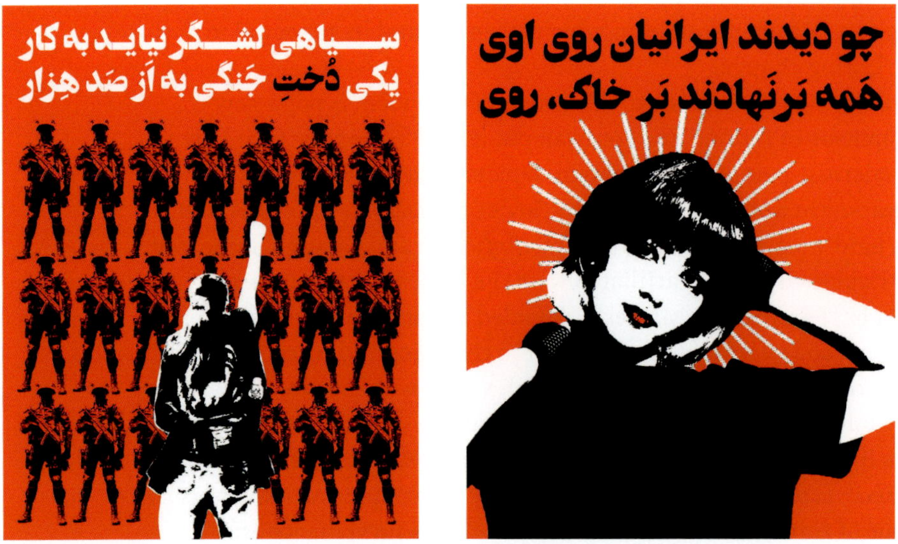

FIG. 79A–B: Meysam Azarzad. Left: An unveiled and unarmed young woman raises her fist at the ranks of soldiers, fall 2022, Tehran. Courtesy of the artist. Right: Portrait of Nika Shahkarami, a fallen heroine of the September 2022 protests.

hundreds of thousands of them"—a reworking of Ferdowsi's original couplet: "The increase of troops is of no use. For from Egypt and from the Hamaavaran [the lands beyond the Oxus] there are a hundred thousand." The message is one of empowerment, suggesting that the strength of a single determined woman can overcome a whole army FIG. 79A.[10]

While it is impossible to list here all the young women who lost their lives (Azarzad has captured most of them in his portrait series), I would like to mention by name Nika Shahkarami, a sixteen-year-old art student at a Tehran art high school, who went missing on September 20, 2022, in Tehran. Her family was informed of her death ten days later. Iranian authorities gave contradictory accounts about what had happened and allegedly coerced family members into supporting their narratives. The case received international attention, sparking further protests, and Shahkarami's burial was marred by an apparent attempt by the authorities to steal her body to prevent public mourning. Her face, along with those of Sarina Esmailzadeh and Hadis Najafi, who also died after their participation in protests, would become a symbol of the movement for change, appearing on posters throughout the country.[11] Azarzad's depiction of Nika is based on a photograph that was shared by relatives and subsequently went viral on social media platforms. Above the image, which was posted on his Instagram page on October 5, 2022, is a couplet by Ferdowsi: "When Iranians saw her face, they forced their own faces to the ground." FIG. 79B

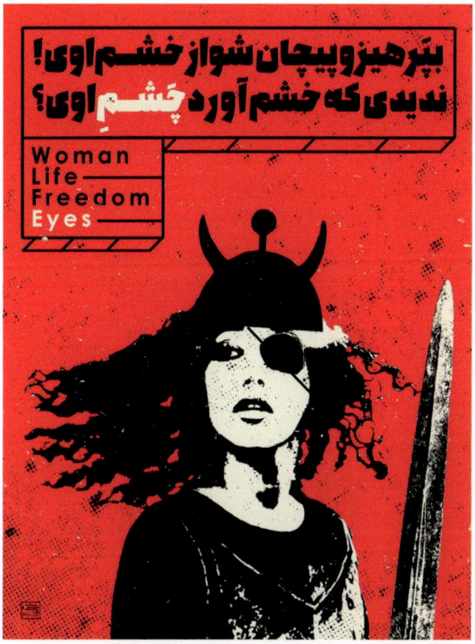

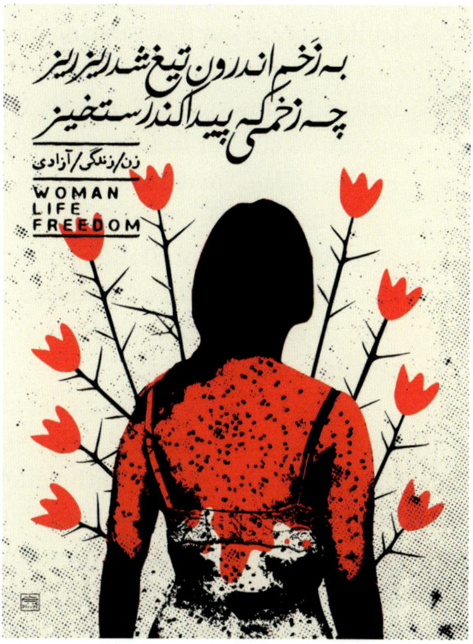

FIG. 80A–C. Meysam Azarzad. Top left: Portrait of Elahe Tavokolian, fall 2022, Tehran. Courtesy of the artist. Top right: Portrait of a girl in the Kurdish region of Saqqez whose body was punctured by more than five hundred shotgun pellets. Bottom: A young woman with distinctive green hair boldly confronts the police, causing them to appear visibly intimidated.

Other young women avoided death, but sustained injuries from paintballs fired by the security forces. Among them was Elahe Tavokolian, a graduate student who got caught in the crossfire during protests in Mashhad in September 2022 and lost sight in her left eye. Following the incident, she expressed her feelings through a post on Instagram: "Three months have passed and after three eye operations, I am still smiling. And for the last operation in the next few days, I will smile more, even if my eye no longer has light."[12] Azarzad depicts her in a medieval suit of armor, evoking images of the soldiers immortalized in Ferdowsi's *Shahnameh*. Numerous other peaceful protesters sustained similar injuries, apparently as a result of deliberate targeting by the police. "Avoid and turn away from [her] anger, Did you not see what [her] eyes brought forth in anger?" is the quote from Ferdowsi atop the portrait of Elaheh posted on Azarzad's Instagram page on May 12, 2023 FIG. 80A. Azarzad elaborates in his own words: "We have gotten used to your lies. These eyes that you have blinded have become more perceptive than before."[13]

The police also fired pellet shotguns at protesters, causing significant, but not fatal, injuries. Azarzad's artwork shows us the back of a girl peppered with pellets, but with tulip flowers sprouting from the wounds. "More than five hundred shotgun pellets have been fired at the body of a girl from Saqqez,"[14] he wrote on his Instagram page on October 22, 2022. The accompanying couplet from *Shahnameh* reads: "The wound inside has been torn apart, piece by piece. What a wound it is that finds resurrection." Its message: the wounds borne by a warrior can ignite a revolution FIG. 80B.

Azarzad also beautifully encapsulates a moment from a powerful piece of footage that gained widespread attention in October 2022. The scene of a young woman with distinctive green hair fearlessly shouting at the police, telling them to go away, and causing them visible unease, is skillfully captioned with a verse praising the valor of a warrior by 'Ayyuqi, a poet heavily influenced by Ferdowsi FIG. 80C. Also, on top of the artwork in Azarzad's Instagram post on October 17, 2022, is the modified verse that replaces the word *child* with *girl*: "A brave-hearted girl let out a scream that turned those who heard it into ashamed wanderers."

Iran's cyber police quickly identified Azarzad and subjected him to harassment and even threats of arrest. Having been incarcerated in Evin for his role in the 2009 Green Movement, Azarzad understood that imprisonment would silence his artistic voice and impact. To continue his activism, he initially opted for anonymity, using aliases for the Instagram account where he posted his illustrations. He still changes these pseudonyms periodically. But eventually he decided to grant permission to use his real name in exhibitions and publications featuring his art (including the ones featured here). The desire to share his impactful documentation with a broader audience outweighed his need for secrecy and personal safety.

THE EVIN WATCH: A DOCUMENTATION OF WAITING AND HOPE

In November 2022, *Iran International* published an article featuring a photograph of the elderly parents of Hossein Ronaghi, a human rights activist and journalist who was then detained.[15] The photo depicted them spending every night outside the walls of Evin Prison, hoping to feel emotionally close to him. This image of the parents, wrapped in blankets and sleeping by the roadside in harsh conditions, quickly went viral on social media platforms, vividly capturing the suffering of those left behind, waiting for their loved ones' release and pleading with the regime for their freedom. The story extends beyond Ronaghi's parents, as many others endure similar situations. One particularly striking example is that of a gallery curator who also waited outside Evin. Instead of relying on the press to convey her pain, she ingeniously documented her experience in her own way.

How would a mother react to finding out her two college-aged children had vanished from their apartments? What would she do when she discovered their homes had been raided and they had been carted off by the police to Tehran's most infamous political prison, Evin? This was the plight faced by the curator Lili "Ayda" Vakilian. Vakilian has an extraordinary knack for transforming Iran's societal challenges into art. In my previous work, I have discussed a project by her that ingeniously turns art censorship into a captivating curatorial display.[16] A pioneer of Iran's blogging sphere through the platform *Webloggestan*, she has chronicled events on a day-to-day basis over the years. Sometimes, these entries serve as a therapeutic outlet; other times, they emerge as art pieces.

What particularly drew my attention in her body of work were the accounts of her regular trips to Evin, which she posted simultaneously on her Facebook and Instagram platforms. Initially, I struggled to understand the visuals: daily snapshots of the dashboard and steering wheel of her car juxtaposed with the towering walls of the prison, random photo essays drawing on her travels along Tehran highways trying to locate important government facilities for the necessary paperwork, pictures of her children's shoes left at the entrance to their empty apartments, and posters by graphic designer friends calling for their release FIG. 81. Alongside her photos, Vakilian shared vivid tales. Once, her daughter called, her voice shaking, worried that they had been forgotten. Vakilian assured her, "Every morning, I'm right outside Evin, just behind the wall." She remembered when her son was a child, and he had "wandered off from a hotel called Azadi [freedom] near Evin Prison, triggering a panicked search."[17] Now

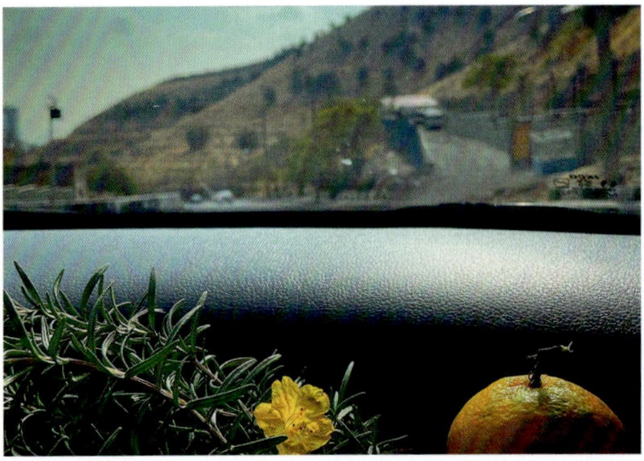

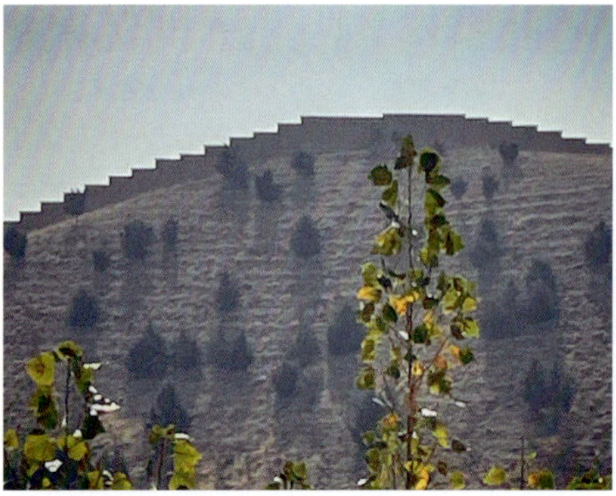

FIG. 81 Ayda Vakilian, two snapshots of wall of Evin Prison seen from her car, fall 2022, Tehran. Courtesy of the artist.

she awaited updates from her son at Evin Prison. She was allowed to see him, through the glass of a visitation booth, after twenty-three days of confinement. Instead of picking up the phone to speak, he removed his glasses, wiping away tears. The stories shared by Vakilian are not only deeply moving but also strikingly real.

Gradually, I came to realize that these social media posts were more than just impulsive or emotionally driven reactions. There is a deliberate consistency to the photos and accompanying narratives that turns them into a form of professional documentation of a life-altering tragedy as it unfolds in real time. Initially, I was perplexed. How did a mother under such pressure find the mental resources to record these harrowing moments? Why was she so methodical in her approach? What was her motive? The more I looked, the more it became apparent that this was an act of profound bravery, in defiance of a repressive regime that monitors not only the streets but also sensitive content on social media. In my conversation with her, Vakilian recalled the night her children were taken. Overwhelmed by the amount of information she suddenly had to process, she grabbed a purple notebook to record vital details. This notebook became her "prison notebook," accompanying her everywhere, always at hand in case of a crucial call. And it is from this notebook that some passages were selected for her social media posts.

Vakilian's children—like many others whose "crime" was as simple as being seen walking amid the protests or posting images paying tribute to the fallen heroes—were detained for nearly three months. Vakilian found it heartbreaking to stand in the queue of parents outside Evin's imposing walls, waiting to spend just minutes with her offspring. All interactions, whether over the phone or through the glass, were closely monitored, ruling out any talk of delicate matters or politics. "It's unbearable to see your child encased in glass, close enough to touch yet so out of reach," Vakilian told me.[18] Freeing the children seemed to be an impossible challenge. As it was for countless others, those months were one of the darkest periods in her life: "It feels as if someone has lodged a fork in my heart, and is constantly turning it," she wrote.[19]

Vakilian's story attracted widespread attention. Many of her followers on social media sympathized with her. After a while, not just online followers but even strangers on the street approached her to ask if she was the mother of the imprisoned art students. Once best known as a curator, she was now the mother of two heroes. While many marveled at her resilience, others begged her to stop, fearing that her posts might affect the fate of the children. But Valikian could not stop: "I always transform life into art; it's my craft. It eases my anxieties," she shared with me. Vakilian's account highlights the ability of art to expose the tensions that underpin an authoritative system. A source of personal comfort during a difficult time, her art was also a means of informing and inspiring her many followers. Finally, and not least, by providing a lasting record of details that may later be forgotten or forgiven, such documentation enables future generations to grasp the full scope of a movement.

There is a noticeable absence of documentation about the longer history of waiting outside the Evin Prison. But some artists are taking it upon themselves to fill this gap. In 2016, Bahar Majdzadeh initiated an innovative artistic campaign that aims to preserve the memories of activists who played a significant role in the 1979 revolution. The oral histories she gathers contain valuable details that have never been officially documented or included in any printed records or books. Some of these recollections revolve around the pivotal moment when the revolutionaries liberated Evin Prison, setting free the political activists who had been imprisoned under the shah's regime. The

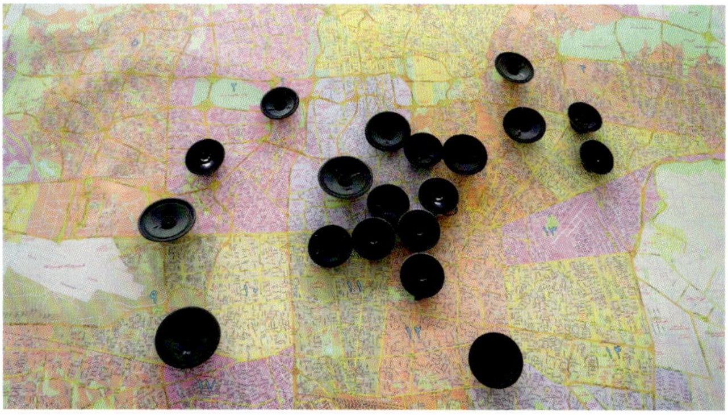

FIG. 82 Bahar Majdzadeh, *Map of the Absentees*, 2016, installation in France. Courtesy of the artist.

recorded voices present these truths exactly as they occurred, devoid of any ideological bias FIG. 82).

In essence, Majdzadeh (much like Vakilian) has created a counterarchive that challenges the conventional narratives of the anti-shah revolutionaries who prevailed—the religious fundamentalists, rather than the leftists. She calls this *Map of the Absentees* (*naghsheh-ye ghayebin*), taking the name from a concept or practice related to land ownership in the context of the Israel–Palestine conflict. Rather than a literal map, it refers to the Israeli government's policy of confiscating and redistributing land and property that belonged to Palestinian Arabs who were considered "absentees" after the creation of the State of Israel in 1948.

On the *Map of the Absentees* of Tehran made by Majdzadeh, we can locate the stories of those whose memories and voices have been confiscated by the current regime. Similar to Vakilian's efforts in archiving such details surrounding the Evin Prison, these audio records will help future generations envision the entirety of an uprising in relation to Iran's notorious political prison, encompassing all its successes and challenges. In both cases, the approach is artistic, engaging not just our intellectual understanding but also our emotional connection to political prisoners.[20]

THE DIARIES OF AN ARTIST BETWEEN HOME AND EXILE

Jinoos Taghizadeh's life as an artist has been shaped by tumultuous events. A child during the revolutionary years of 1979 to 1984, she has since witnessed a succession of uprisings and revolutions. As I noted earlier in this book, in the context of women's guerrilla interventions in street spaces, Taghizadeh's work has been a significant influence for many artists across generations. Beyond her individual creations, she has been involved in collaborative art projects that verge on outright activism. A notable example is her role as a prominent member of the art collective Nafas (breathe), formed in 2017, which focused on combating pollution in Tehran. Taghizadeh and her fellow artists performed rap songs, using rhythmic beats of their hands and feet to draw the attention of the public to environmental issues.[21] Next to them, along the walls of the sidewalk, were pasted large sheets of paper on which passersby were invited to pen their thoughts on the pollution blighting the capital. Taghizadeh's activism also extends beyond visual arts. She has authored manifestos, written political commentaries, and actively participated in various activist groups, all aimed at improving the lives of Iranians.

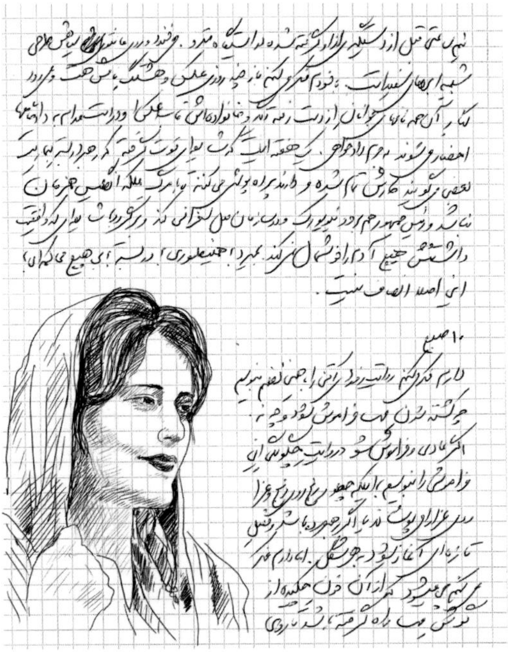

FIG. 83 Jinoos Taghizadeh, diary page pondering the death of Jina Mahsa Amini—how she might be forgotten, how she could be remembered, fall 2022, Tehran. Courtesy of the artist.

Taghizadeh's diary from the early days of the Woman, Life, Freedom uprising features portraits of the victims—akin to Azarzad's compilations—but it also incorporates her personal reflections FIG. 83. Rather than focusing solely on the victims' stories, she shares her own emotions and dialogues with friends and fellow artists. She also speaks of heroes who are less well known. For instance, her diary page for September 24 includes this story:

> In the morning, I went to the pharmacy for my mother's medicine. There's a young [...] beautiful girl named Shabnam who works there; my mother is very fond of her. I approached her to inquire [...] As she turned around, I noticed three circular scars on her forehead and eyebrow. They were from shotgun pellets that had been fired at her the day before. Her colleague commented [...] 'What if she had been hit in the eye? What then? She would have been blinded.' It reminded me of the poet Shahryar's words: 'If everything is ugly, then what are the eyes for?' [...] These [young women] want a more beautiful Iran.[22]

In another page from early October, she writes:

> My mother calls me every hour [...] to make sure I've stayed home. Finally, I tell her I have taken some pills because I have a headache and am going to bed early. After hanging up the phone, I head out to join the march.[23]

Taghizadeh also devotes sections of her work to contextualizing the movement historically. She does this by, for instance, drawing parallels between the current victims and those who were killed during the Green Movement, such as Neda Agha-Soltan, who was shot dead by a regime agent on a motorcycle. She also recounts, in words and stunning illustrations, the acts of Vida Movahed and the Girls of the Revolution. In this way, the diary rises above personal narrative to serve as a form of historical documentation.

Taghizadeh's participation in the protests, coupled with her candid social media posts, led to serious repercussions. Fearing imprisonment, she was forced to make the difficult decision to leave Iran. She moved to Toronto—Canada being the only country to offer her a long-term visa. Despite the challenges of settling in a new country, Taghizadeh remained actively involved in the movement from a distance. Initially, she grappled with how to convey to others outside Iran the many years of systematic oppression, the dictatorship that reached into every aspect of people's daily lives, and the extreme cruelty of religious despotism. The dark scenarios played out in dystopian fiction seemed to pale in comparison. Taghizadeh shared these reflections with other artists in Toronto, including Simin Keramati, who had experienced this oppression for herself before migrating to Canada around ten years earlier. They took part in demonstrations and marches, but the chanting of slogans was not enough to assuage their deep-seated feelings of helplessness—of anger and sorrow. Since words had proved inadequate, they had to find a way to channel their emotional turmoil through art. On December 6, 2022, Taghizadeh, Keramati, and a group of artists and activists organized a flash mob performance. Converging on the Ontario Parliament building at noon, they first subtly blended into the crowd in the adjacent park and then, one by one, they unleashed years of suppressed anger and grief through screams, turning their act into both a protest and a cathartic outpouring. Their hope was that this visceral demonstration might prompt Canadian politicians to sever diplomatic ties with Iran, exerting more pressure on the regime. The collective performance, titled *Anger Needs No Translation*, was conceived from a desire to give voice to their suppressed emotions, but they were also determined to ensure their cries were heard. In the final act of their performance, one participant solemnly placed a flag bearing the words "Woman, Life, Freedom" on the ground before they all quietly departed the area.

They would gather again soon after, following the execution of another young protester, Mohsen Shekari, on December 8, 2022. This time their collective scream echoed in front of the CBC Canada building, leaving the performers visibly shaken and emotionally drained. Similar performances were later held in New York and Montreal, attracting significant media attention. However, these subsequent adaptations, while valuable from an activist point of view, strayed from the original intent. While they were meant to be raw expressions of anger transcending language, they seemed to morph into theatrics, more akin to acting rehearsals than genuine outlets for deep-seated emotions.[24]

How should we interpret these acts of screaming and their repeated instances? Are they a form of documenting the uprising? I believe they are. It appears that Taghizadeh could effectively communicate her thoughts and activism through words, drawings, and direct involvement in street protests while she remained in her homeland. In exile, however, she found she was blocked from expressing her anguish through these conventional means. Her activism thus transformed into screaming—a wordless yet emotionally charged act that not only reflects Taghizadeh's personal experience but also resonates with many political refugees who often find it challenging to express themselves in the language of a new country, the language of exile. I view this screaming as a unique documentation of feelings and emotions.

Above all, the essence of the project was a sarcastic take on how feminism is often perceived by the laymen. Mirroring the perceived "disruptive" nature of feminism, it stirred excitement, captured attention but also discomfited passersby. By these means, as Sara Ahmed explains:

> We learn about the feminist cause by the *bother* feminism causes; by how feminism comes up in public culture as a *site of disturbance*. When you speak as a feminist, you have to deal with strong reactions. To be committed to a feminist life might require being willing to elicit those reactions. When you speak as a feminist, you are often identified as [...] overreacting, as if all you are doing is *sensationalizing the facts of the matter*; as if in giving your account of something you are *exaggerating*, on purpose or even with *malice*.[25]

While screaming, as a "site of disturbance" par excellence, evolved into a metaphor for the struggles of Iranian women in exile, other more cloaked expressions within Iran became means of voicing grievances, including a call to liberate women. The following "act" delves into these "camouflaged" forms of expression. ■

Act Seven

CAMOUFLAGING DEFIANT WORDS

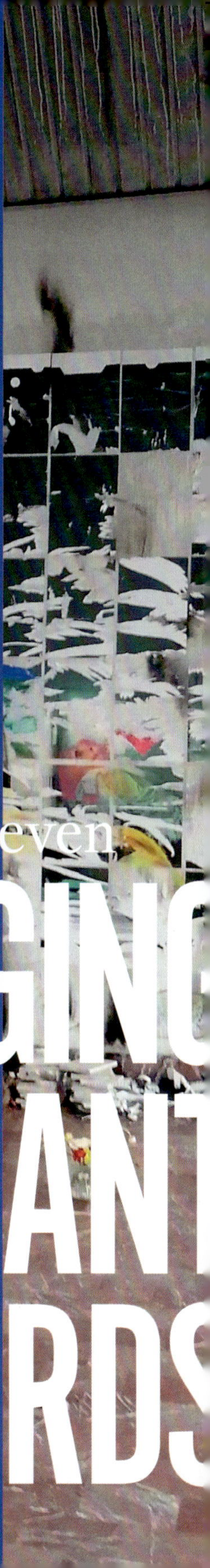

It is impossible to put into words the full extent of the Iranian people's suffering during the regime's brutal suppression of the uprising from September 2022 to March 2023. Young women and men risked imprisonment, torture, and even execution for their participation in peaceful protests. Many were shot or bludgeoned in the streets, victims of indiscriminate violence meted out by the police. Parents mourned the loss of their children. The nation was enveloped in collective grief as the cruelty persisted with no end in sight.

Even those who live by language, such as poet and literary scholar Fatemeh Shams, found it hard to articulate their feelings at the height of the unrest. Shams's response was to write a poem that asserts itself as something other than poetry, using visceral imagery to paint a graphic reflection on violence and the struggle against a system of oppression. The words stand in for the victims themselves—tortured and executed, their true meaning denied. Suggesting a reality too raw to be contained within the bounds of traditional poetry, it is titled, appropriately, *This Is Not a Poem*. It is reproduced below in its English translation by Armen Davoudian.

This Is Not a Poem
It's a fistful of blood, splattered
on mute papers on the capital's newsstands.

It's a kind of throwing
the sudden throwing of rebel girls from the roofs of the side-
streets of Revolution.

This is not a poem
it's the forced confession of an eyewitness
her tongue worn down by the narration of successive shots.

A fat worm crawls through this poem
and swallows the termites from the faces of the words
tortured words buried under a bloody heap.

This is not a poem
it's the guts of a ten-year-old who dreamt of inventing the
Rainbow God one day
it's a chain of tattered bodies throbbing in nameless graves
cut hairs
scratched cheeks.

When midnight strikes the words will begin to violate each other
they will draw guns on each other
tenses present and past will be taken hostage
bullets will mark the confusion of adverbs of time and space.

This is not a poem
it's the wounded body of a fifteen-year-old festering from
successive rapes
it's the severed head of a singing girl whose words were
crushed in her throat
it's the mauled chest of a captive laborer who laughed at his
torturer till the last blow

This is not a poem
it's the story of a murderer who brings home fresh bread every
night with the blood money of rebel poets

Before sunrise the corpse of these words will be on the hands of
these white pages
one by one they will fall into eternal sleep with fattened insects
in a mass grave

This is not a poem
for weeks words have been hung up by their feet
the hands of light and metaphor chained to iron fences
and water denied to the dry throat of song ... and
denied ... and denied
like us these words were unarmed
and their fists were full of stones

and their bodies naked as the day they were born from the
womb of the mother tongue

This is not a poem that runs in my mouth
it's the convulsions of a tortured order that runs wounded and
naked in the streets
and falls to the ground at the newsstands.[1]

In writing *This Is Not a Poem*, Shams came to understand the power of deconstructing her words. This realization would lead to a compelling art installation at Ohio State University in collaboration with media artist Ilya Mousavi. The exhibit grapples with the complexities of capturing violence through poetry FIG. 84. Central to it is the concept of fragmentation as a means of conveying the disjoined nature of traumatic experiences. The entire poem was inscribed onto wood, each character meticulously carved out and then stained a deep red. A segment of the work displays words suspended from the ceiling, mirroring a torture technique used on political detainees. On-site, a recital of the poem in its English translation underscored the visceral impact of the work. This powerful installation of fragmented poetry encapsulated Shams's feelings on the limitations of language during the uprising, yielding to visual art as a more potent means of conveying the unspeakable horrors the people endured.

Shams's presentation can be thought of as a stylistic evolution in a genre of poetry that has been developing in Iran for over a decade. In my exploration of the diverse ways Iranian poets have given voice to the Woman, Life, Freedom uprising, I discovered an intriguing alternative—or, better, camouflaged—scene in the northernmost part of Tehran that is the base for improvisational performative poetry (*she'r ejra*) or poetry jamming. As in a jam session in music, this genre emphasizes improvisation and interaction as poets develop and exchange their work. Often seen as arising with the prominent Iranian poet Reza Baraheni, the style acquired a distinct character within various alternative poetry circles, including Telefus and the School of Farsi Poetry, both linked to faculty of literature at the University of Tehran.[2] While many members or affiliated members of these two groups eventually merged into the mainstream,[3] a third, more anarchistic and informal poetry faction known as Matrood (meaning "rejected" or "refused") maintained its independence.

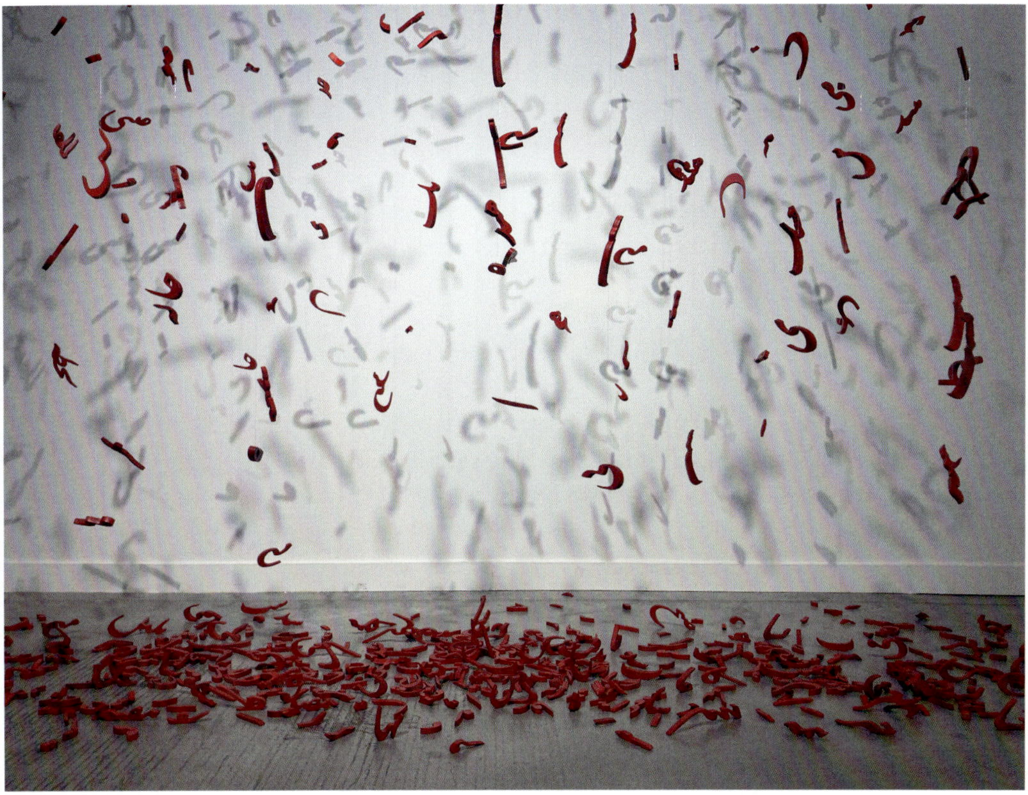

FIG. 84 *This Is Not a Poem* by Fatemeh Shams in collaboration with media artist Ilya Mousavi for the group exhibition *Iran: Deciphering Violence and Resistance*, curated by Ilya Mousavi, at Urban Arts Space, November–December 2023, Ohio State University, Columbus, Ohio. Courtesy of Fatemeh Shams.

Matrood was cofounded in 2005 by a group of young men, all born in the early 1980s: Yaavar Bazrafkan, Arash Allahverdi, Behnam Badri, and Ali Satvati Qale. It has since expanded to include other collaborators, including female poets. The group's formation was initially a reaction against the "aestheticization" of poetry by certain factions that positioned themselves as the opposition to the official poetry of the Islamic Republic of Iran. This aestheticization, pursued by notable poets like Shams Aghajani, Mehrdad Fallah, Rosa Jamali, and Ali Babashahi, also percolated into the realm of graphic design, with typography that transmuted Persian words into indecipherable phrases. A notable instance of this style, Matrood members told me, was for example the cover produced by renowned Iranian graphic designer Reza Abedini for the controversial book *Alijenab Sorkhpoosh and Alijenaban-e Khakestari* (The master with the red mantle and the gray masters), a 1998 critique of President Akbar Rafsanjani and his circle by Akbar Ganji FIG. 85.

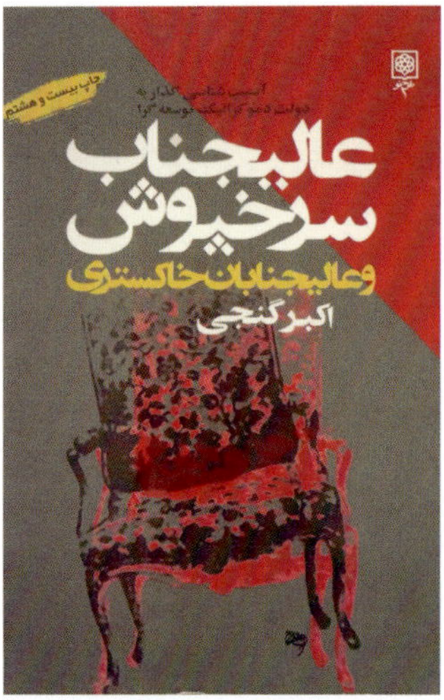

FIG. 85 Cover design by Reza Abedini, 1998. Courtesy of University of Heidelberg Libraries.

As Matrood saw it, these groups embraced a literary style that was abstract and "sublime" (in Persian, *mote'ali* or *fakher*) yet elitist, distancing itself not just from progovernment institutions but also from the everyday realities of Iranians. In contrast, the dynamics of Matrood were significantly influenced by the experiences of "street life" of its founding members, notably Ali Satvati Qale (b. 1983). Satvati Qale holds multiple university degrees in Persian literature and sociology, but he does not belong to the typical middle-class demographic of artistic groups from northern Tehran. Rather, he was born and raised in Javadiyyeh, a predominantly working-class district in southern Tehran that is home to many migrant families from the Turkic Azerbaijan region. Satvati Qale was the seventh child in one such family. He describes growing up in a densely populated neighborhood where the main public space—a one-way street lined with homes and shops—offered little scope for freedom of expression. The area had its own social dynamics and challenges, as it was controlled by macho figures who often intimidated the younger men. But Satvati Qale descibed how everything changed for him with the establishment of Farhangsara, or "houses of culture," around the capital—particularly in southern neighborhoods—after the Iran–Iraq War.[4] These new cultural centers had a significant impact on attracting young people from more conservative and southern neighborhoods to the arts. This trend was so profound that it drew criticism from hardliners, who accused Gholamhossein Karbastschi, the progressive mayor responsible for initiating the cultural centers, of diverting the youth's attention away from mosques and toward the arts.[5] Previously, poetry and literature—widely banned in schools in the 1980s—had been taught clandestinely in the underground. Now these cultural centers, and in particular the Bahman Cultural Center near his home, allowed Satvati Qale to find companionship and intellectual stimulation, engaging with others in discussing complex theoretical and philosophical texts.

Satvati Qale talked about the concept of the "geography of expression" (*joghrafiyay-e bayangari*), which relates to the capacity of poetry—and especially of the anarchic style originating from Matrood—to establish a meaningful dialogue with the specific physical spaces in which it is performed.[6] To illustrate how spatial and geographic contexts influence writing, he cited two of his favorite novels: *Zemestan 1362* (Winter of 1983) by Esmail Fasih and *Tehraniha* (Tehranis) by Amirhossein Khorshidfar. Both books capture the essence of a creative life that often remains hidden, operating underground, and unknown to the wider public. In our conversations, Satvati Qale demonstrated the profound impact of place on artistic creation by taking me on a walk through the landscape of these novels and the neighborhoods that had been instrumental in shaping his own expressions in poetry and prose.

He shared that he and like-minded friends (some of whom would later become members of Matrood) sometimes found themselves in a rough café in southern Tehran frequented by homosexuals and prostitutes. Against a backdrop of generally mundane conversation, Satvati Qale and his friends would engage in what he calls *haad bayangari* ("heated expressions") as they delved into the works of Jean-François Lyotard or Jacques Derrida. The intense form of discourse they developed in this space would eventually influence the poetry of Matrood members. Satvati Qale gave as an example Matrood member, Yaavar Bazrafkan's poems, in which calm and ordinary words suddenly yield to fiery lines like "They throw us out of the house." These "heated expressions" would surface during Matrood's practice of "collective poetry" or poetry jamming (*she'r-e daste jami*), where one person starts with a verse and the others take turns adding to it, improvising on the lines until everyone is satisfied with their work. Referring to the influence exerted by the different urban spaces or atmospheres in which the poetry was created, Satvati Qale noted that gatherings in central Tehran or the city's upper-class areas sometimes lacked the usual expressive charge, and, rather than leading to vibrant debate, they might degenerate into smoking sessions for some of the participants. Other settings, Satvati Qale explained, are able to accommodate an absence of words. At times, simply sitting in silence alongside others is enough: the silence communicates something profound—a shared experience or mood reflective of their lives. It is a quiet collective acknowledgment of their powerlessness in the face of authority.

Matrood's fervor was not limited to their discussions. In the early stages, their ardent opposition to any form of "aestheticization" in literature meant they were not afraid to clash with widely-celebrated figures, even if it meant being further marginalized themselves, sidelined by both the official poets of the regime and the oppositional poets. They memorably caused uproar and chaos when they intruded on poetry reading sessions by a prominent practitioner, in their eyes, of "sublime" (*mote'ali* or *fakher*) underground poetry. To make their presence felt, they also presented their poetry in eccentric formats, one example being the innovative poem/art installation created by Satvati Qale for the men's bathrooms at a major art institution, the House of the Artists. The announcement for this exhibit, as advertised on the House of the Artists and Matrood websites, stated:

> Location: House of the Artists, Men's Restroom, Last Cabin
> Visiting Hours: 12 noon to 8 pm
> Entry is free and open to the public.

The visual artist Hamed Jaberha (b. 1984) has collaborated with Matrood and other groups in the fields of literature on in-the-moment activist projects of this type. His own independent studio work, however, has a separate character. Rather than being defined by immediate action, it focuses on projects of political art that evolve over the long term. Jaberha's approach is exemplified by a piece that

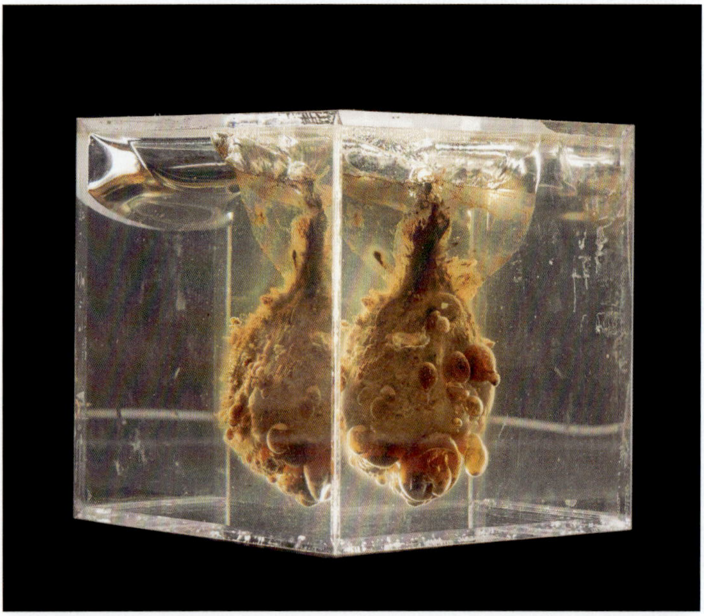

FIG. 86 Hamed Jaberha, *Tormentum Insomnia*, 2017–2023, Tehran. Courtesy of the artist.

reflects on the failure of regime changes and coups in Iran. In August 2017, Jaberha filled some translucent fiberglass cubes with organic tissue—sheep's hearts—floating in gelatin. Over twenty days, the tissue decomposed, producing blood clots and worms, symbolizing futility and decay. These cubes were then preserved in a sealed, oxygen-free environment for five years, until 2022, when Jaberha stacked them on top of each other like a tower and set fire to them in the mountains near Tehran. The act is captured in the one-hour-and-forty-five-minute video installation *Tormentum Insomnia*, from August 2023. The video shows us a once vibrant, pulsating heart that is repeatedly broken and ultimately ceases to function. The tale it narrates is of a nation in a state of perpetual conflict—battles against the state, clashes with authority, and internal strife—incapable of being reconciled with itself or with others FIG. 86).

As part of the other side to his work, his "activist" art projects, Jaberha produces booklets for Iranian poets whose politically charged works are often suppressed and not disseminated in any form. For Matrood, for example, Jaberha personally laid out and designed each page of poetry, and then found opportune spots in public places through the city to distribute these pages, posting them onto the walls of buildings, for example, or tucking them under windshield wipers. By these innovative means, the banned poetry was distributed to a diverse audience, bypassing traditional barriers to publishing.[7]

Taking this artistic activism further into the streets, Jaberha also inscribed verses from the poems on Tehran's walls, only to have them erased by authorities each morning. In collaboration with Matrood member Alireza Mohammadi, he preserved these fleeting messages by photographing them and later incorporating them into a booklet. This practice, of documenting Tehran's walls animated with poetic resistance, took on new relevance following the death of Jina Mahsa Amini. Jaberha recorded the Woman, Life, Freedom graffiti scrawled over the city, building up an extensive archive that he presented (under a pseudonym) in a photo essay for a US art journal.[8]

Satvati Qale admits to some initial skepticism about the potential of the Woman, Life, Freedom uprising, as he thought of the younger generation as being less engaged with politics than his own. However, he came to appreciate that their true strength lay in their use of their bodies, their postures, their songs, and their emotions, detached from any formal ideological or philosophical means of expression. The language that fueled the impassioned atmosphere of the uprising also seemed to chime with the anarchic behavior and language of Matrood, its unruliness and divergence from the "norm." Most strikingly, in Satvato Qale's view, was the way the movement brought together Iran's diverse ethnic groups, with a proud showcasing of traditional costumes, local dances, songs, and even languages. There was a flourishing of poetry and revolutionary songs in Turkish, Kurdish, Baluchi, and Arabic, among others. For example, Mehdi Ganjavi composed a multilingual elegy using both Kurdish and Persian words.[9] These manipulations of the Persian language, though potentially rendering the poetry unintelligible to many, evolved into a potent manifestation of personal identity. Individuals boldly and unapologetically proclaimed their desire for visibility and recognition, confidently embracing their distinct cultural heritage.

This diversity went beyond the issue of ethnicity; the protesters were not largely confined to the middle classes—the demographic of the 2009 Green Movement—but also included economically disadvantaged and less privileged communities, as well as religiously conservative neighborhoods. Abroad at the time, Satavti Qale found it astonishing to see footage of his densely populated working-class neighborhood rising up.

For Matrood, however, the Woman, Life, Freedom movement was not the catalyst that took them out of their private domain and into political activism. That had happened several years earlier, in 2019, when they took the decision to revamp their website and revise their "countermanifesto" in the wake of the "Bloody November" series of nationwide civil protests. The rewriting of the countermanifesto—a collective effort shaped primarily by founding member Yaavar Bazrafkan—reflects a renewed engagement with the changing societal and political landscape:

> Art and literature in themselves are oppressive, and there is no such thing as liberating art and literature.
>
> [...]
>
> Everything changed after 2019, but one thing remains constant: art and literature are the sublime manifestations of oppression, and any writer or artist who continues to perpetuate and institutionalize it will be part of the same machine of stupefaction and power [...] creation.
>
> [...]
>
> We emphasize that the only way out of this quagmire is reverse appropriation. One must step out of the funnel of art and

> literature, move to its back, and either forcefully or politely [...] play it. This is a total exit and entry, on both sides of production and presentation. A total exit means refusing to recognize and produce any text that follows categorical [...] patterns. It means refusing to commodify the text, especially in luxurious mediums like books, magazines, etc. And a total entry means planting bad seeds. It means producing a text that is evil, outcast, and rejected. It means starting the machine of anti-aesthetics, not as an antithesis in the fake dialectic of poetics, but as a desire. A strong, acute, self-organized, collective, and relentless desire. It means weakening and weak writing. It means wasting the Persian language's structure. It means destroying instead of composing. Wasting instead of offering. Spilling instead of giving out. Spreading on skin, on walls, on pedestrian bridges and billboards, on the glass of malls and cars, on asphalt, on shirts, on the forehead of the earth and the chest of reeds.
>
> We have written these things before. Fourteen years have passed since the start of Matrood's work, and today, after Aban 98 [November 2019], insisting on these positions is more vital than daily bread. Matrood does not stop because it is an inevitable existence within power structures, not a literary or artistic genre. There is no Matrood project that will end happily, or [...] become sterile [...]. Matrood does not stop and as long as it exists, it extends its hand for collaboration to all marginalized writers and artists: to wall-writers, graffiti artists, street artists, detournement artists, body-writers, LGBT artists, and all those who have been rejected and pushed aside by governmental apparatuses, society, or left and right-wing intellectuals. And finally, our answer to those gaping mouths that accuse us of attacking independent art and literature is the same as always: Buzz off![10]

Setting out the principle of what Matrood calls "reverse appropriation" (*mosadereh-gari-e ma'koos*), the countermanifesto encapsulates Matrood's distinctive perspective on the Woman, Life, Freedom movement. While aware of the ineffectiveness of traditional forms of poetry and literature during the uprising, Bazrafkan noted the emergence of a peculiar language (*kalam*) within the revolutionary lexicon. Often graffitied words like *azadi* (freedom) or *zan* (woman) were, surprisingly, not entirely whitewashed by the authorities but were instead deformed, possibly by progovernment individuals: for instance, the letter "A" in *azadi* might be elongated, or the "N" in

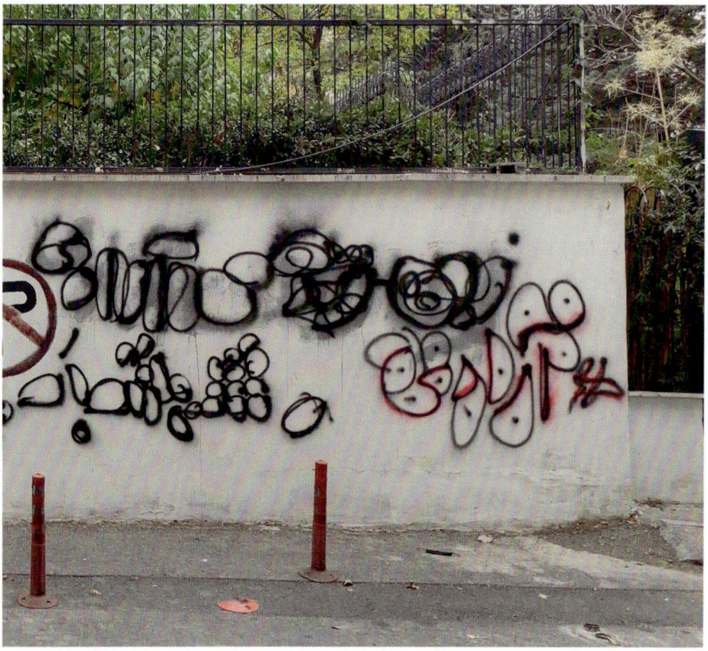

FIG. 87 Street graffiti. Photograph by Yaavar Bazrafkan.

zan exaggerated FIG. 87). As Bazrafkan put it, "it seemed as if even the censors found these words too precious to fully erase."[11]

Matrood found this visual battle of words on the walls particularly significant, linking literature and poetry with political activism. Unlike earlier forms of "sublime" underground literature, Bazrafkan explained, these new, Dadaist-like confrontations over words resonated deeply with the group. Despite their disdain for the progovernment actors tasked with defacing political graffiti, they were intrigued by the back-and-forth exchange. After all, Matrood's style of "weak poetry" (*she'r-e zaif*) plays with words in an often improvisational manner, aiming not to aestheticize or strengthen the language but rather to undermine it. This form of "escape from expression" (*bayan gorizi*), sometimes even bordering on meaninglessness, reflects the dark reality overshadowing Iranians who have grown up under the Islamic Republic, feeling the weight of an unchangeable atmosphere. While Matrood's approach might chime with the impulse of Dadaism, Bazrafkan insists they do not seek to emulate that nihilistic—but now canonized—early twentieth-century movement. Initially, he questioned my effort to document their activities, saying he would prefer Matrood to remain "rejected," outside mainstream art history, but was persuaded to participate when I pointed out that documenting a "rejected" group has its own merits, and that the view of postrevolutionary Iranian art should not be confined to "sublime" frameworks.

The most engaging aspect of the group's endeavors, especially in relation to this book, is their integration of various activities into their "atelier," a covert space on the northernmost edge of Tehran, where the city and the Alborz Mountains meet. The tale of atelier's inception was recounted to me by another member of the group, Alireza Mohammadi. Born just before the end of the Iran–Iraq War, Mohammadi majored in carpet weaving and textiles before shifting his focus to installation art and graffiti. A formative moment in his artistic development was witnessing the dynamic exchange of political graffiti on Tehran's walls during the Green Movement—a silent yet profound dialogue between artists and the regime. He remembers how simple symbols of resistance, like a painted V for victory, would be transformed by state authorities into innocuous images such as ice cream cones.

Mohammadi was away from Tehran at the time of Jina Mahsa Amini's death. Returning home a month later, he found the city transformed: walls filled with scribbles, reminiscent of a vast Cy Twombly canvas FIG. 88. This visual shift spoke to his fascination with art as a medium of dialogue with an adversary—a concept he admires in the works of the anarchist writer Hakim Bey (a.k.a. Peter Lamborn Wilson). Bey's writings, and in particular *Sacred Drift* (*Yaleh Gardi-e Moghaddas* in Persian), challenge monolithic perceptions of Islam, offering instead resistance, heresy, and esotericism from a viewpoint on the margins.[12] For Mohammadi, Bey's outcast figures—for example, Noble Drew Ali, the founder of "The Moorish Science Temple of America"—embody the role of artists in society. They are the silent yet persistent forces that can subtly shift the course of events, challenging and nourishing from the outside, rather than operating at the core of the system. In Iran, where direct dialogue is often impossible, wall art becomes a means of conversation with the forces of the state, manifested in the form of the continuously

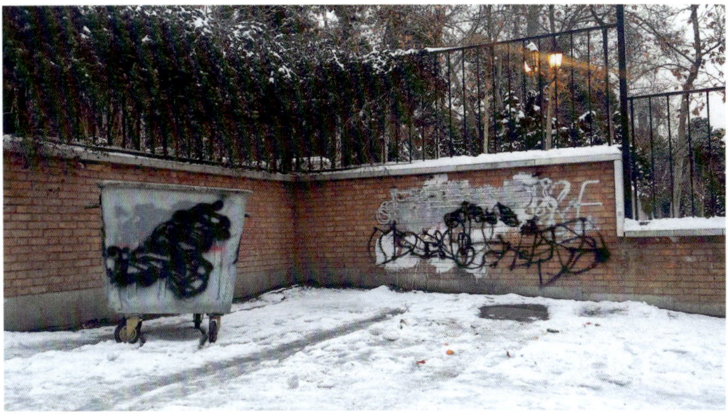

FIG. 88 Tehran wall graffiti. Photograph by Ali Mohammadi.

evolving drawings, scribbling, and whitewashing. For Mohammadi, this silent, ongoing battle on the walls represents both genuine art and political discourse. And the dialogue extends beyond the trope of people versus state ideology. Mohammadi's own artistic actions and motives are sometimes questioned, confrontationally, by passersby, and he sometimes finds himself explaining and defending his art to the public, often through supplementary artistic gestures rather than talking. This interaction with viewers becomes yet another layer in his continuous exploration of art as a means of communication and resistance.

As tensions escalated between authorities and students at Tehran's University of Art, Mohammadi felt compelled to act, but as someone disinclined to participate directly in demonstrations, he found an alternative way to contribute to the students' lives, which was to create a safe haven for art. On his regular walks in Jamshidiyyeh Park, near his home, he had noticed several deserted structures. Most of them had been bustling cafés and restaurants in less stringent economic times. But one of them in particular caught his attention: a simple, open building with dual entrances on the upper edge of the park. Unlike the other venues, it had no kitchen facilities. Mohammadi and his friends speculated that it dated to the late Pahlavi era, and had possibly been designed as a dance floor or as a small hall for music performances. A local Afghan construction worker later told them it was a postrevolutionary structure that originally served as a prayer hall for the park staff.

Seeing potential in this forgotten space, Mohammadi began inviting friends and fellow students from the University of Art to join him in transforming it into a creative refuge. This initiative was his way of providing support and continuity for the artistic community during a time of turmoil and uncertainty, when many art classes were canceled and the activities of most art galleries paused. Numerous videos showcasing the atelier are available on a password-protected website and *Aparat*, Iran's counterpart to Vimeo. Constructed of exposed concrete, the building blends seamlessly into the rocky landscape, making it difficult to spot from a distance. Inside, the stark (possibly mihrab) wall of the former prayer hall became, during the uprising, a canvas for a group of artists who transformed it with graffiti and other art forms, echoing the activism on Tehran's street walls within a private, secluded environment.

For Mohammadi, the atelier served a dual purpose. It was not just a hidden sanctuary, a place of refuge from the chaos of the city, but a rehearsal space—a creative crucible where the language of dissent could be honed before it was displayed in more public arenas. Video of one notable event shows an artist wearing a hoodie

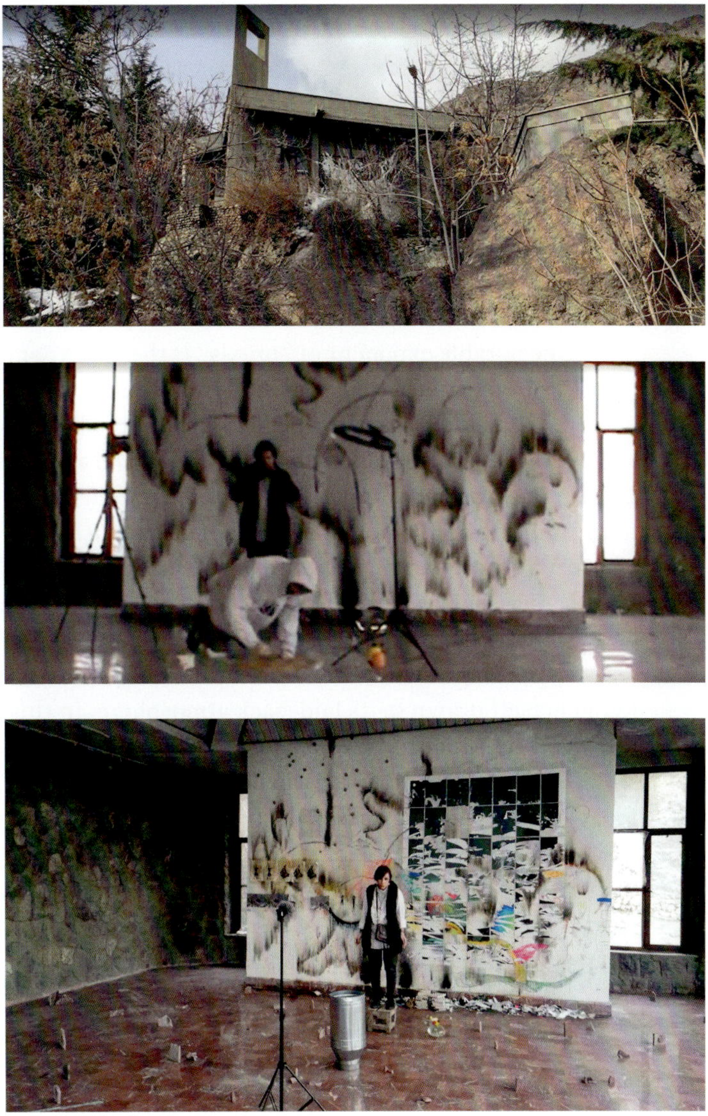

FIGS. 89A–C Composite image showing exterior and interior views of the Jamshidiyyeh Park Atelier, including artists performing, winter 2023. Courtesy of Alireza Mohammadi and Hamed Jaberha.

(Hamed Jaberha) enter the atelier carrying a large unprocessed block of pot-making clay. He steps in front of the white wall, now enlivened with the works of other artists, and first warms up his hands, preparing for the task ahead—a process that begins with kneading the clay, but quickly escalates. The artist's movements become increasingly forceful as he violently attacks the clay, breaking it into pieces, which he scatters around the room FIGS. 89A–C. As the video progresses, the focus shifts from the enraged artist to a serene outdoor scene. The camera pans to a mountain on the outskirts of Tehran, where a child and his father are seen exploring the snowy landscape at the foot of the slopes. The contrast between the artist's chaotic energy and the peacefulness of nature is stark, heralding an abrupt end to the video.

This casual, untheatrical approach to the action and its equally casual, even seemingly aimless, documentation were deliberate, as Bazrafkan explained to me. "It's not a performance," he said, "it's a praxis." For the Matrood collective, this is a form of engagement that has taken on an essential role in recent uprisings, beginning with Bloody November in 2019 and extending to the Woman, Life, Freedom movement.[13]

One notable exponent of "praxis" is the artist Samira Yahyaie (b. 1983), who has long collaborated with Matrood but does not consider herself a formal member of the group. She was quick to join Mohammadi, Bazrafkan, and Jaberha in the activities at the atelier in Jamshidiyyeh Park, motivated, she told me, by her belief in the importance of living in the moment, cherishing good times, and responding to friends' calls to gather for simple joys.[14] Yahyaie's perspective, inspired by the philosophy of Omar Khayyam, reveals a resignation to the present, with little expectation that the horizon will become brighter in the future. On visiting the atelier, Yahyaie found herself drawn to its laid-back atmosphere. In this rustic setting, a kettle whistled on an old burner, shards of broken window glass lay scattered on the floor, with no audience in sight. The space allowed for complete freedom; one could scream, show disregard—anything was possible, she said. Hamed Jaberha, for example, had been meticulously working on a painting, which he eventually affixed to the freestanding whitewashed wall. In a bold move, another female artist then covered the painting with pure mud gathered from the park, after which Yahyaie tore the entire creation apart. It was this freedom, and nothing more, that "embodied the essence of the atelier," Yahyaie explained. After nonchalantly sharing the story of this collaborative "antiart," she seemed ready to end the call. However, when I pressed for more details, a whole new world unfolded.

It turned out that Yahyaie has a vast knowledge of Persian literature, having studied under some of Iran's most valued poets and literary scholars. She spoke passionately about her fascination, bordering on obsession, with specific genres and concepts, transporting me back to the Middle Ages, reciting Rudaki with an ease as if the words were from a contemporary friend, but equally revealing how she drew inspiration from Forough Farrokhzad's "fiery and revolutionary" modernist poetry.[15] Yahyaie also noted parallels between Soviet and Iranian poetry, art, and literature, but observed that dissident artists during the Cold War appeared to still be hopeful, still driven to recover what they had lost, whereas artists in Iran seem to be navigating through the fog of impossibilities:

> There's no impulse to claim or reclaim anything. Things are taken from us, and we don't yearn to retrieve them or make them our own [...] That's why I have no interest in publishing with any institutionalized press. The thought of having to prove myself to a publishing house, only for my manuscript to be scrutinized by the MCIG, is deeply unsettling.[16]

For this reason, "I'd rather my poetry book stay underground. Let it exist in anonymity and obscurity, mirroring our life's mistiness, devoid of future, hope, or any aspiration to resurrect anything or anyone."[17]

At the atelier in Jamshidiyyeh Park, Yahyaie offered impromptu performances, standing on a stool to deliver improvised poetry that she often couldn't recall afterward. In one performance, she held a piece of broken glass found on the floor, adding a tactile element to her spontaneous expression. In other places, when performing, Yahyaie adopts a hunched, somewhat shy posture. However, in the relaxed atmosphere of the atelier, she became more audacious, presenting a different side to her character from her day-to-day persona as an editor for Ney Press, one of Tehran's most prestigious cultural publishing houses.

Similar to members of Matrood, Yahyaie expressed her general dissatisfaction with Iran's poetry scene, perceiving it as overly sentimental, and not just in official and formal circles but also among groups purporting to be unconventional or underground. Yahyaie proposed an alternative approach, suggesting that the diffusion of poetry in spaces like the atelier in Jamshidiyyeh Park would be a more fitting and effective means for it to become intertwined with the soul of society.

Yahyaie's unique approach to performative poetry has its roots in her family traditions. Her father was a custodian of a Ta'ziyeh, an ancient tradition involving the performance of handwritten scripts during the Muharram rituals. These scripts, passed down through families, are performed in designated places, and in Yahyaie's case her father directed these performances at their ancestral home in Atash Deh, a village near the city of Arak in central Iran that possibly has Zoroastrian origins (its name means "place of natural fires"). While Yahyaie's parents were deeply involved in these religious ceremonies and prayed regularly, they maintained a distinct stance, choosing not to align themselves with ideological orientations.

Indeed, Yahyaie's upbringing exposed her to a rich and diverse culture, with a unique blend of tradition and openness. The family library was a treasure trove of Persian literary classics, including works from renowned masters, as well as various religious texts.

Yahyaie was particularly drawn to *Ghesas Sour Abadi* by Abubakr Atigh Neyshabouri, a medieval work exploring narratives from Abrahamic faiths, such as the tale of Noah's ark, and creatively reimagined these stories in the context of twenty-first-century Iran, infusing them with a personal touch and relevance to her daily life.

Even though Yahyaie's poetry may be informed by traditional (even medieval) sources, it has features that speak to contemporary times. One example is the unique collaboration in which Alireza Mohammadi turned selected phrases from her poetry collection, *Abhay-e Sathi* (Surface waters), into graffiti art on Tehran's walls: the graffiti, photographed before it was erased by the authorities, was eventually documented in an underground book by Jaberha. One poignant line, "Indeed, we came back home in one piece," resonated deeply with many Tehran residents, reflecting the precariousness of life in the capital—the encounters with the morality police and the risk of getting arrested, or worse—and the sense of relief on reaching the comparative safety of the home.

Weeks after her atelier performances, Yahyaie showcased her "praxis" at Vayu Residency, located in the historic city of Kashan, a short drive from Tehran. The title of the piece, *We Were Searching before We Saw*, was inspired by a phrase from Michel de Montaigne's essay "On Friendship."[18] Much like the French Renaissance philosopher, Yahyaie emphasizes practical, lived experience over purely intellectual knowledge. The choice of title also references a moving personal experience on an island near the Persian Gulf, where she and a friend spent a night immersed in poetry, searching for words in the darkness until dawn broke.

We Were Searching before We Saw was set within an empty circular pool in the courtyard of an old house in Kashan. Yahyaie's improvised poetry initially revolved around a collection of simple figurative drawings prepared by an artist friend, Samira Zinati. Every drawing, every figure, was weighted down by a stone, to preserve it from the relentless wind. Yet the stones served as a profound metaphor, with Yahyaie asserting that she was herself "burdened by the weight of stones," like the figures in the drawings.[19] The mass of stones was a symbolic graveyard, representing the youth who had perished since September 2022 and the friends who had left Iran for good, fearful of being arrested. What started as seemingly abstract and playful poetry riffing on these drawings gradually acquired a political undercurrent. Standing in the center of the space, Yahyaie invited the audience members around the edge of the pool to join her, either by voicing their own thoughts or reciting poetry, creating a collaborative and immersive experience.

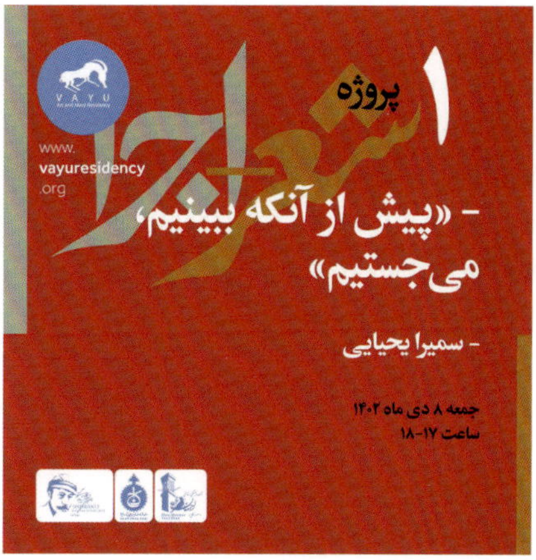

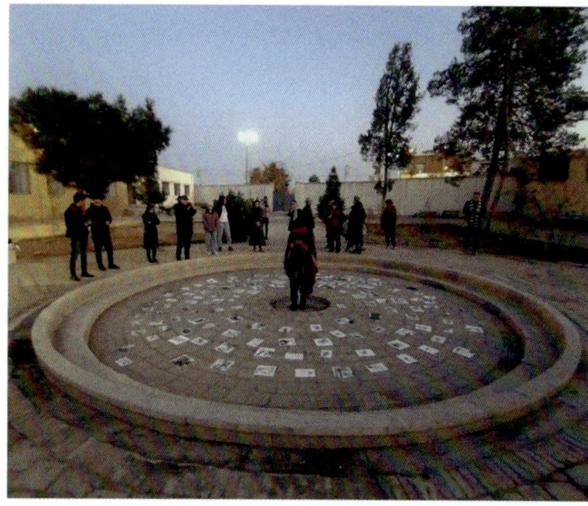

FIG. 90 Poster designed by Hamed Jaberha for Samira Yahyaie's poetry jam, *We Were Searching before We Saw*, at Vayu Residency. Courtesy of Hamed Jaberha.

FIG. 91 Samira Yahyaie during her performance at Vayu Residency in Kashan. Courtesy of Mahmoud Maktabi, director of Vayu Residency.

In her performance, Yahyaie boldly gave voice to the victims of the regime's violent suppression of the uprising, uttering names that are usually not spoken out loud in public spaces. "Give me your ... name, so I can remember who I am, who we are," Yahyaie began, as the call to prayer resounded loudly in the background. She would look for this name in "the land of stone and metal," she said. "Your presence is part blood and part body [...] I see you in the Aban of 1401 [referring to the height of the uprising in October], there is blood, and the blood encompasses everything."[20]

Yahyaie then continued: "I am strong. I stand beneath these stones, amid these faces, and among the line drawings and bodies." After a pause, she invited the audience to pick up her words, and a woman stepped forward, saying, "I am a woman, but I never stood by that kitchen stove with force." Yahyaie responded warmly, "You are beautiful; the day dawns because of you, and the night concludes for your sake."[21] The focus shifted again to the word "woman," reaching a crescendo that moved everyone to tears.[22] This improvised crafting of poems, giving rise to seemingly spontaneous political expression, reflects the essence of postuprising art in Iran. Though labeled "performative poetry" (*she'r ejra*), it is devoid of theatrical pretense and unassuming, authentic. As the performance unfolds, it naturally assumes a form that could best be described as political and activist. This mirrors the trajectory of the protests themselves, which evolved from joyful moments of dancing around fires to tragic events.

Mahmoud Maktabi, the director of Vayu Residency and a performance artist himself, was deeply impressed by the emotional intensity of Yahyaie's act, by the striking assertiveness of her physical presence and her spoken words. Alternative spaces like Vayu provide a safe haven for artists, allowing for the emotions unleashed during the uprising to be captured and reenacted. Whether intended to keep the movement alive or to serve as posttrauma therapy, these artistic endeavors are invaluable, offering solace in challenging times—a beacon of hope for society as a whole FIGS. 90–91.

While Matrood and Yahyaie have developed distinctive approaches toward integrating space and poetry jamming, there is a lineage of avant-garde poetic practices that extends long before the Woman, Life, Freedom uprising, as Farshad Sonboldel has detailed in his recent groundbreaking study *The Rebellion of Forms in Modern Persian Poetry: Politics of Poetic Experimentation*.[23] Having been involved with the events around Matrood and other poetic collectives such as Telefus and the School of Farsi poetry at the University of Tehran, Sonboldel has firsthand knowledge of the influence of these earlier practices, which is not always manifested in a direct or straightforward way.[24] His work not only sheds light on the evolution of these methods but also repositions them within the broader context of Persian political and anarchist literary traditions.[25]

Sonboldel traces the roots of these innovative approaches to the poetry that emerged during Iran's Constitutional Revolution.[26] In the period from 1905 to 1911, poetry performances served as a powerful vehicle for voicing societal aspirations and building solidarity. The language, characterized by memorable, melodic lyrics, was deeply influenced by traditional, colloquial poetry. Rather than being secluded in the realm of literature, the creations of leading political poets of the era were taken into public spaces, where they reached a large audience. Turned into a tool of resistance, poetry became deeply integrated in the dynamics of revolutionary movements and public dialogue.[27]

In 1939, the anarchist poet Abbas Shams al-din Kia (1910–1988), known as Tondar Kia, returned from his studies in France bearing the imprint of Dadaism. From his first manifesto in November 1939, he was on a mission to ignite a "literary revolution," aiming to carve out a path opposed not only to Persian literary traditions but also to the more conservative modernist movement spearheaded by Nima Yushij. Kia skillfully used sounds to capture emotions, as seen in his 1940 poem "Chizake-Sa'at" ("The small thing that is the clock"; hereafter, "The Clock"), with its onomatopoeic "hu hu" for the wind and "tik tak" for the ceaseless motion of the clock suggesting internal turmoil.[28] Crucially, Kia's "The Clock" also embraced visual elements, providing context for Yahyaie's contemporary contributions.[29]

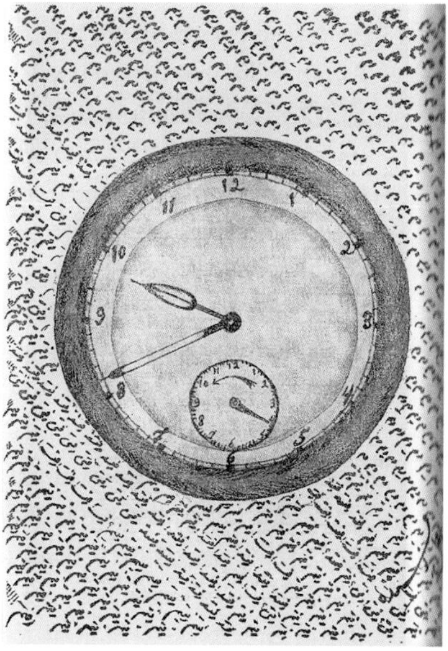

FIG. 92 "Chizak-e Sa'at" ("The Clock"). Image courtesy of Farshad Sonboldel. Originally published in Tondar Kia, *Nahib-e Jonbesh-e Adabi-e Shahin*. Reproduced in Sonboldel, *The Rebellion of Forms*, 179.

A drawing of a clock sits atop calligraphic script that is scattered across the page, with the words of the poem running into each other without a break—a strategy that defied not only the traditional standards of Persian poetry but also the aesthetics of classical calligraphic arts FIG. 92.

This practice might be seen as derived from "concrete poetry," a genre that gained prominence during the Dadaist and Surrealist movements. But whereas concrete poetry conventionally arranges the words to visually illustrate the theme—as shown by Guillaume Apollinaire's "Il pleut," (1918) for example, where the words resemble falling rain—Kia adopts a more abstract strategy in "The Clock," densely clustering words to metaphorically represent the concepts of the passage of time and aging.[30] In contrast to the visual emphasis of traditional concrete poetry, Kia prioritizes the rhythm of sounds, crafting an experience meant for performative reading. In particular, he invites readers to immerse themselves in the auditory dimensions of the poem, thereby marking a transition from visual to aural appreciation in his artistic expression.

Performative poetry not only persisted after the 1979 revolution but gained fresh impetus due to the prevailing political climate. From the early 1980s on, distinguished poets hosted gatherings that were instrumental in elevating straightforward poetry readings into dynamic performative acts. Taking place in the privacy of the poet's home, these performances incorporated rhythmic movements and, occasionally, gestures devoid of explicit meaning, that were impracticable in public settings.

The groundwork for these movements was laid by Reza Baraheni's innovative poetry, which deconstructs words to create rhythmic, poetic phrases. In his poem "Daf" (1989), for example, Baraheni artistically manipulates the word for the traditional Persian frame drum, mimicking the instrument's distinctive, scat-like rhythm through repetition and inventive variations in its spelling, e.g., *Dafdafdafast keh mikoobad* (*dafdafdaf* is that which is drumming).[31] This approach suggests that the poem is crafted primarily for performance, with a rhythmic quality that echoes the sounds of the *daf* itself. Intriguingly, Baraheni dedicates this poem to the painter Aydin Aghdashloo, underscoring the deep, symbolic connection between visual arts and poetry in his work. The renowned Iranian singer Mohsen Namjoo, who has vocalized Baraheni's poetry, explains that his own approach aligns with this "externalized" school of poets. Similar to Baraheni, Namjoo's method of singing makes use of the expressive qualities of vowels and words in the Persian language to impart feelings or meanings, focusing more on the acoustic and emotional impact of language than on the conventional lexical definitions of the words.[32]

The integration of poetry into performative acts and the visual arts was not limited to poetry gatherings and teachings alone. Visual artists actively sought to include creative poets in their circles. Artist Jinoos Taghizadeh notes that the fusion of spontaneous poetry with performance or visual art emerged out of necessity in the wake of the 2009 Green Movement.[33] Rather than following global art trends, it was born from the domestic political situation. Just as theater artists pivoted to a genre known as "home theatre,"[34] conducted in the security of their apartments, visual artists arranged "creative gatherings" (*dor-e hami khallagh*) in the comfort of their own homes.[35] Here, poets and visual artists collaborated, expressing creative ideas in rhythmic and artistic forms. A more formal instance of this kind of gathering was the collaboration of poet Ali Asadollahi and visual artists Farvah Famouri and Saleh Tasbihi at the Azad Gallery in 2015. Asadollahi recited a poem about human suffering, likened to meat being cooked and consumed, while the artists performed an act of cutting a large piece of raw lamb.[36] The audience observed in contemplative silence.

Rather than being a direct precedent for the work of Matrood, this cross-pollination of the arts occurred at the same time as members of Matrood and figures like Yahyaie were refining their artistic styles. To reiterate, the unique genre of the poetry jam, which blends elements of recitation, singing, and at times performance art, emerged as a response to the specific living conditions in Iran, even if the origins of the genre can be traced to Dadaist and "concrete" poetry and to the Surrealist practice of "Exquisite Corpse," in which a group collectively assembled a sequence of words or images. In this "parlor game," which took place in cafés or homes, each participant would add to a composition following a set rule, sometimes only seeing the end of the previous contribution.[37] One could also find similarities with rap music, or with the practices of recitation and singing prevalent among young people during the US Civil Rights Movement. In particular, Beat poetry had a significant influence on figures like Baraheni, who encountered it firsthand in the US. The term "beat" encapsulates a dual meaning: it signifies being marginalized or oppressed within mainstream culture, while simultaneously suggesting a beatific quest for spiritual elevation or higher consciousness. Baraheni's work embodies these dual aspects. Similarly, Beat poetry is noted for its free verse, open structure, and spontaneous, jazz-inspired cadences. Baraheni's creations, along with the works of those inspired by him (including Matrood, albeit indirectly), exhibit a sense of improvisation and spontaneity.

In my earlier analysis, I explored how artists engage with and reinterpret historical themes and ideas, often through subversive appropriation. However, Matrood and their associates use the term "reverse appropriation" (*mosadereh gari-e ma'koos*) to describe their method, which draws on past anarchist and anti-institutional artistic movements while at the same time maintaining a distance from them, crafting a narrative uniquely attuned to Iran's specific sociopolitical context. Yahyaie's performance in Kashan may echo the practices of Kia, but it deliberately avoids the aestheticization found in works like "The Clock," which plays on calligraphic traditions and Dadaist art. Unlike the orderly presentation in "The Clock," with its symmetry and refinement, Yahyaie's performance is dynamic, with the audience's physical intrusion into the installation of the artist challenging the conventional boundaries between performer and viewers. These acts of "reverse appropriation" by Matrood and Yahyaie might be seen as reinterpreting or repackaging the past, but, more than anything else, they point toward timelessness, perhaps a time in the future, reflecting a shift in the perception of progression of Iranian art, and by extension political and activist art.

Up to this point, I have emphasized artistic efforts that predominantly reveal connections to historical movements, albeit sometimes through the process of "reverse appropriation." However, a subtle yet persistent tension with traditional and historical contexts also infuses activist art. At first glance, these clashes might appear as abrupt breaks from the past, but a closer examination reveals that they, too, often sustain a dialogue with the past. The following "act" will unravel this intricate and multi-layered interplay. ■

Act Eight

CLASHING WITH FAITH IN BROAD DAYLIGHT

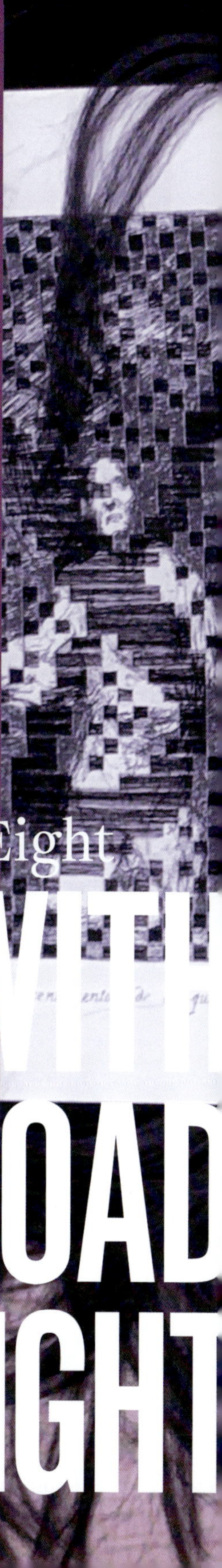

Many individuals, including academics and progressive thinkers outside Iran, find it hard to grapple with the art and images emerging from the Woman, Life, Freedom movement. How should they begin to discuss images that present a potential challenge to a Muslim believer's way of life—that show women setting fire to their veils, for example—when the principle of honoring traditions and religious beliefs is embedded in canonical frameworks such as postcolonial theory? This raises a broader question: what do values mean, and for whom? Do some values inevitably take precedence over others?[1]

The viewpoint of the women in Iran who are fighting for the right to freely choose whether to be bound by those same traditions and religious beliefs is forcefully articulated by Bahareh Hedayat, a journalist imprisoned in Evin, who takes aim at those who

> accuse us [...] of Islamophobia; meaning I, as a Middle Eastern woman, have no right to cry out against [...] [compulsory] hijab, because according to the "progressive" rules that have been issued by [...] the intellectual circles of the West, this act of lamenting under the pressure of historical oppression that hijab has enforced upon me signifies fear of Islam, and no one has a right to fear Islam. [...] [T]hey do not deem the Middle Eastern Muslim woman as having the right to lament so that the tensions and contradictions of their own intellectual apparatus would not be revealed![2]

The suppression of Iranian women was the focus of the first retrospective of Iranian American artist Taravat Talepasand, which opened on January 27, 2023 at Macalester College's Law Warschaw Gallery in

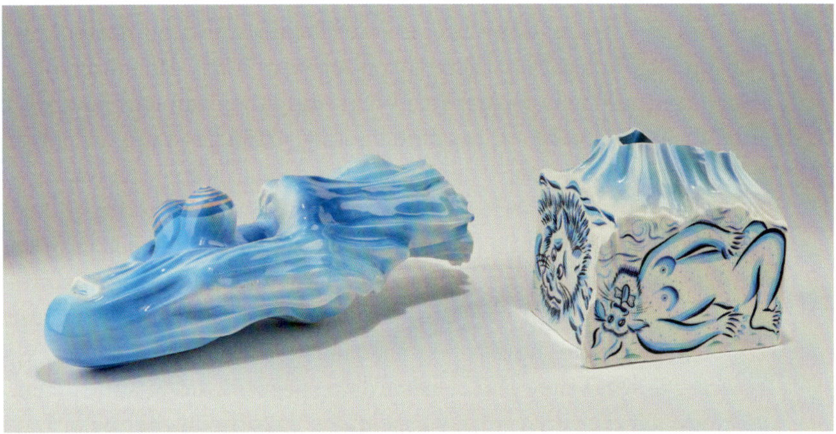

FIG. 93 Taravat Talepasand, artwork from the *Blasphemy* series, exhibited at Macalester's College, Minnesota, January 2023.

Minnesota. The fate of that exhibition is illustrative of some of the tensions and contradictions that infect campus conversations about what is happening in Iran. The show featured artworks honoring the Woman, Life, Freedom movement, but also a few provocative drawings and sculptures from her *Blasphemy* series, depicting conservatively veiled women in ironically salacious postures, inspired by Roxana Shirazi's memoir, *The Last Living Slut: Born in Iran, Bred Backstage* (2011), and created with the author's consent.[3] The book, as Shirazi communicated to Talepasand, is about "what it means to be a provocative woman from Iran."[4] At the age of ten, Shirazi was sent to England, where she left behind her traditional upbringing and became, eventually, a rock and roll groupie, following bands like Guns N' Roses and Motley Crue. Her book vividly recounts personal experiences, including her enjoyment of sex, and its illustrations include some photos of Shirazi in erotic poses with the traditional veil.[5] In a media interview, Shirazi made the point that these photos were not intended as a direct critique of Islam: rather, they sought to highlight how authoritative regimes (ab)use Islam as a tool to further their own ideological goals.[6] The pairing of sex and traditional veil is also rooted in Shirazi's experience of being sexually abused as a child in a Muslim household—a dimension often missed by those observing the works by Talepasand that are inspired by the memoir FIG. 93.[7]

What is the significance of Talepasand creating art that reflects on this particular life journey and the complex cultural and political forces that shaped it? Should this identity be viewed as positive or negative? Is Talepasand's artwork an adaptation of Shirazi's story—or a commentary on, or even possibly a parody of, her narrative?

It seems essential to delve deeper into the process that fostered the connection between these two creative women. What kind of discourse could this project spark regarding the contemporary art of Iranians in the diaspora, or contemporary art in general?

Talepasand's pieces depicting chador-clad women in pornographic poses are undeniably provocative, reconstructing the real-life experiences of a provocative individual. If taken at face value, without exploring their origin and meaning, they could be misinterpreted as a straightforward critique of devout Muslim women. From the moment of the show's opening, Macalester's Muslim students objected to what they perceived as disrespect toward hijabi women, voicing their concerns through social media, official channels, and the protest posters they affixed to the gallery's glass wall. To be clear, the (non-Iranian) Muslim students who criticized the exhibition openly supported the Iranian women's movement, but objected to elements of the work that appeared to mock veiled women.[8] It took just a few days for the administration to bow to the pressure and "pause" the exhibition.[9] "The pause," they wrote, "provide[d] space for members of [the] community who expressed pain caused by pieces in the exhibition."[10] The gallery's glass windows were covered with black curtains so that no one could look inside FIG. 94. Many commentators were opposed to the university's approach. Blogger Jill Filipovic wrote:

> [N]othing I can find suggests [the exhibition] depicts 'violence.' Most of what I see are boobs. If you can't handle seeing breasts—including breasts on a woman who wears a hijab or niqab—I would recommend not going to any art museum or exhibit. I might stay off of the internet, too, and perhaps reconsider leaving the house.[11]

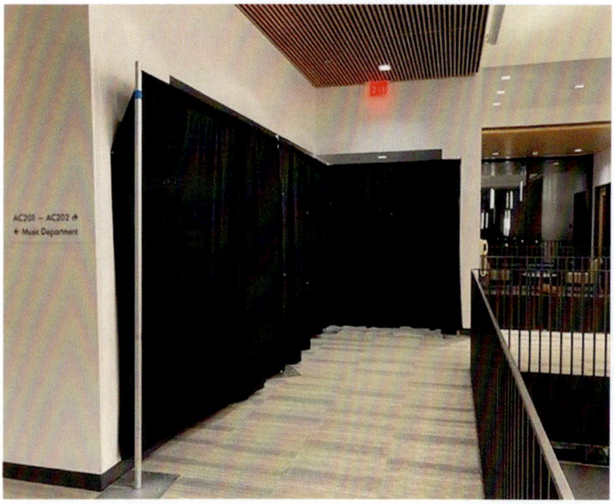

FIG. 94 Black curtains were draped over the glass walls of the Law Warschaw Gallery in an attempt to censor Talepasand's exhibition. Courtesy of Taravat Talepasand.

The 'pausing,' or rather cancellation, of Talepasand's show happened at a time when exhibitions and imagery in Iran were challenging aspects of Islam—not setting out to disprove religious beliefs but rather questioning the regime's interpretation of them. As the examples that follow show, negotiations around religious matters and freedom of expression take on diverse forms in Iran. Some of the artists who are questioning the Islamic Republic's restrictive ideologies—the mandatory hijab and the imposition of religious practices in everyday life—are themselves devout Muslims who pray, fast, and wear headscarves. This aspect of art making is a vital, but less discussed, part of the narrative around the Woman, Life, Freedom uprising. By extending our focus beyond secular-minded artists to include believer artists who have been part of the movement, we can see a more fluid landscape of resistance in Iran.

A BOLD JOURNALISTIC DECISION AT THE PEAK OF THE UPRISING

Nadastan (meaning "nonfiction") is a journal that features articles and narratives akin to documentaries, capturing the real lives and thoughts of individuals. It also includes translations of nonfiction works. Its 2022 winter edition, devoted to women, began with an excerpt from *Suvashun*—the title refers to mourning for an unjust killing—by Simin Daneshvar, the first Iranian woman to publish a modern novel under her own name:

> Don't cry, my sister. Trees will grow in your home, and trees in your city, and many trees in your land. The wind will carry the message of each tree to another, and the trees will ask the wind: 'Did you not see the dawn on your way?'[12]

The issue includes a concise translation of Rebecca Solnit's *Men Explain Things to Me*, as well as narratives about immigrant women. What garnered most attention, however, was its "taboo" cover design, showing a striking mane of long, shiny, brown hair FIG. 95. The cover photograph was the work of the journal's photography director, Mehri Rahimzadeh (b. 1981), who hails from a traditional family in Qazvin. Rahimzadeh wears the veil, observes prayers, and fasts, but maintains a distinct stance from the Islamic Republic, regarding its actions as incompatible with Muslim or basic humane values.

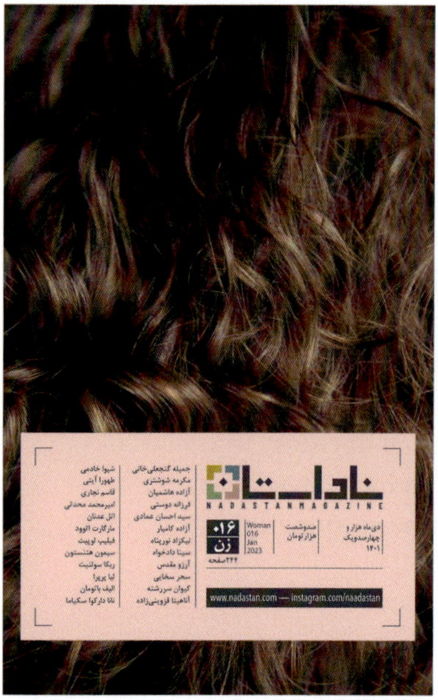

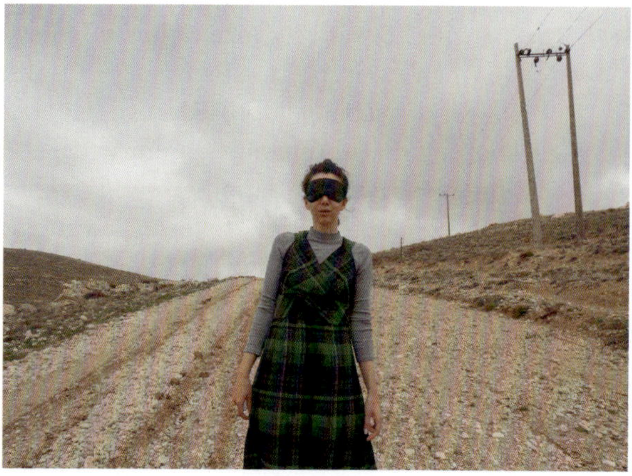

FIG. 95 Mehri Rahimzadeh, cover of *Nadastan*, no. 16 (January 2022). Courtesy of the artist.
FIG. 96 Mehri Rahimzadeh, artwork from the series *A Changing Dreamscape*, 2011, Iran.

"My Islam," she explains, "is different. It's for my own peace, not for others."[13] Most of Rahimzadeh's friends are nonbelievers who neither wear the veil nor fast and who wonder why she remains so steadfast in her practices. Rahimzadeh says her family has also encouraged her to relax certain aspects of her faith, like consistently wearing the veil, but she chooses to continue. For Rahimzadeh, her faith is a deeply personal matter, a source of solace and hope.[14]

Veiled herself, Rahimzadeh fully supports women who choose not to wear the hijab. At the height of the Woman, Life, Freedom uprising, she would often walk behind unveiled girls, a protective shield to ward any potential attacks. But despite her empathy and evident concern for the well-being of these young women, she found herself in some difficult situations—confronted by passersby who were opposed to her wearing of the hijab. In encounters of this kind, she remained composed and chose not to react.

This was the context in which she and the journal's editor in chief took the bold decision to feature hair on the cover of the winter issue. When they did so, they did not anticipate the widespread attention it would receive, including internationally. Both were summoned to the Office of Evaluation of the Press, where they were interrogated about their motives. In contrast to books, fiction, and art, press content does not require approval from the MCIG. However, those who cross editorial boundaries risk severe penalties, including the suspension of a publication.

Rahimzadeh was responsible not just for the cover of *Nadastan* but for a series of photographs that unfolds throughout the journal. Made in 2011, more than ten years before the Woman, Life, Freedom uprising, *Living with Blindfolded Eyes* (a.k.a. *A Changing Dreamscape*) aimed to portray the struggles faced by her generation, who grew up in the 1980s under the cloud of the Iran–Iraq War.[15] The subjects of the images—friends of Rahimzadeh—are blindfolded, symbolizing how their lives are dictated by external forces and systems of oppression. Their body language conveys hesitation, representing the challenges of navigating through life FIG. 96. Rahimzadeh chose secluded locations outside the city for these shoots. "It would have been impossible to shoot these on the streets of Tehran back in 2011," she confided.[16] The photograph I have selected for this book transforms a road into a desolate, desertlike setting, highlighting the plight of this earlier generation, who played a key role in laying the groundwork for the Woman, Life, Freedom movement.

When I inquired about the timing of these photographs, Rahimzadeh said they were not conceived for a particular purpose or event—artistic or political. Instead, as the photography editor for a number of publications, from the small-circulation *Nadastan* to the prominent *Hamshahri*, she has a practice of taking photos wherever she goes, "collecting" images for potential stories or covers, then methodically filing them away, awaiting the opportune moment to use them. This approach to photo archiving—capturing the essence of an era through the experiences of women—has become something of a passion for Rahimzadeh. She told me that the scenes once restricted to remote landscapes could now be openly staged on the bustling streets of Tehran. But there would be a key difference: the female subjects would no longer be blindfolded but would stand assertively, with bodies poised and eyes wide open, vigilant and aware.

Rahimzadeh's eye always finds intriguing subjects. She refers to how this new generation is distinct, with interests and aspirations far removed from those of earlier generations. They are connected to their peers. Rather than looking to their family for guidance, they work out the answer to their problems with their friends on social media.[17] The desire to live differently—to have the freedom to choose how to express themselves—is evident, for example, in the way some young women are immersing themselves in K-pop, adopting Korean fashion (without the addition of a veil), and even learning the language. Rahimzadeh's portrait of two teenagers at the Dizin ski resort outside Tehran reflects the spirit of this generation, the girls' unconventional hair color a match for their blue lollipops (to safeguard the privacy of the young women depicted, this image is not included in this book).

VEILED ARTISTS IN DEFENSE OF WOMAN, LIFE, FREEDOM

Hamideh Sobhani, an artist residing in Iran, embraces the veil as a choice rather than an imposition. Her art explores her personal belief in the principles of hijab and considers the societal constraints that have historically diminished women's roles. The video installation she created for Persbook's 12th Annual of Contemporary Art in fall 2023, *The Conversation of the Roots*, was born from this contemplation.

The installation is set against the backdrop of the gardens of Ghazvin, a city to the west of Tehran. Sobhani describes these gardens as magical spaces defined by a spirit of generosity. She found inspiration in the words of the renowned eleventh-century explorer Naser Khusraw: "I arrived in Qazvin on the ninth of Muharram. There were many orchards without walls or thorns, and nothing to obstruct the passage of the way."[18] For Sobhani, this historical depiction of the gardens as a haven open to everyone parallels her own use of them as a canvas for her artistic expression.

The Conversation of the Roots was conceived as an expansion of *The Red Artery* project, codirected by Neda Darzi, which used red organza to symbolize a life-sustaining artery and cooperation between artists (see Act Five for a full description of the work). To make her video, Sobhani collaborated with a group of professional artist friends known for pushing boundaries. Dressed uniformly in white, these women engaged in the symbolic act of wrapping twenty meters of intensely red fabric around the trees in an orchard. The process of winding the fabric drew the women closer together, physically and metaphorically, weaving a visual narrative of convergence and solidarity. The soundtrack intermixes the sound of labored breathing with the gentle patter of water droplets, at times echoing the acoustics of a steamy bathhouse, at other times evoking the distant, collective exhaling of a crowd in a demonstration. Filmed in slow motion, the visuals match the languid pace of the audio. As the video approaches its conclusion, the sounds give way to the tranquil chirping of birds—the soothing balm of nature.

The performance, Sobhani asserts, is an allegory for the unity of all women (veiled or unveiled) who support the Woman, Life, Freedom movement. Regardless of religious beliefs, she discerns a shared desire among Iranians for the freedom to navigate public spaces and a collective commitment to environmental stewardship. Sobhani's work as a whole is imbued with the colors of the Iranian flag—white, green, and red—each shade an emblematic thread in the context of Iranian women's voices, interwoven to symbolize their harmonious call for autonomy and the preservation of the environment FIG. 97.

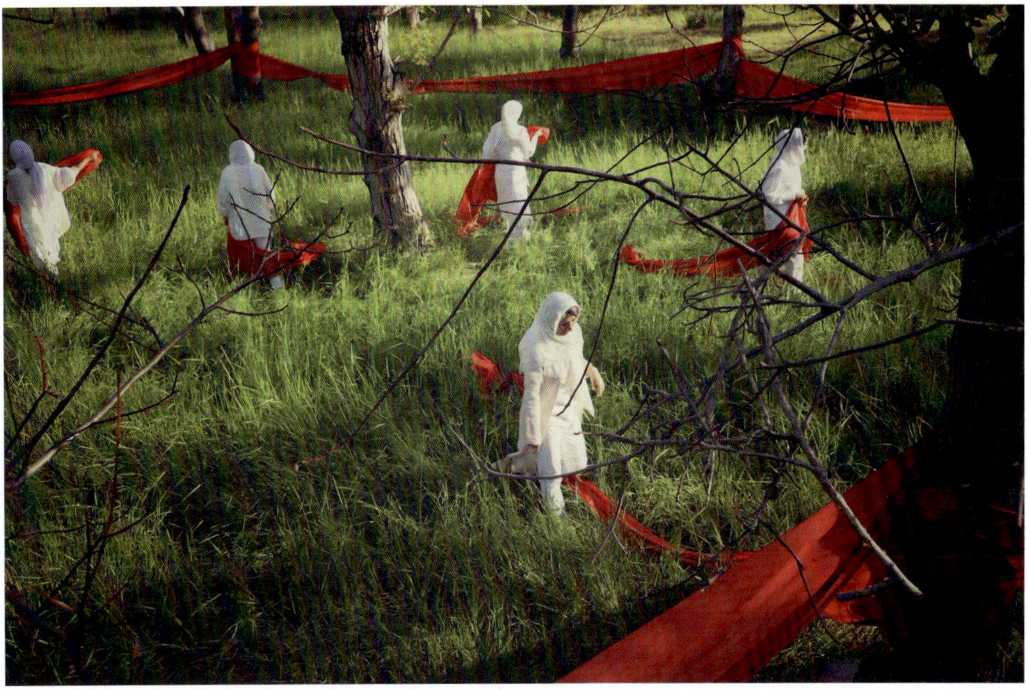

FIG. 97 Hamideh Sobhani, *The Conversation of Roots*, Performance (also made into video) presented at Persbook's 12th Annual of Contemporary Art, 2023. Courtesy of the artist.

"LET THERE BE NO COMPULSION IN RELIGION"

Masoumeh Mohtadi (b. 1983) grew up in a devout environment. She wore the hijab when she was younger and some of her extended family members continue to wear the chador, the most conservative form of women's dress in Iran. Like many others, her family has always taken pains to distinguish the version of Islam they practice from the regime's stringent, politicized interpretation of the religion. But, as Mohtadi pointed out, this strategy does not work anymore. On the streets of the city, women in conservative dress are frequently met with raised eyebrows or verbal and even physical harassment. While she understands these reactions to some extent, she also expressed a longing for a solution that preserves the essence of faith, allowing it to be a source of comfort and inner peace.[19]

Originally trained as a painter, Mohtadi felt a lack of interaction with her audience in this medium and shifted her focus to installation art, particularly origami and book art. A voracious reader, she is particularly drawn to political novels, with George Orwell's *Animal Farm* being a favorite. She also delves deeply into works by Soviet dissident authors like Fazil Iskander, seeing in them a reflection of the authoritarian system of Iran. Her faith in the written word was

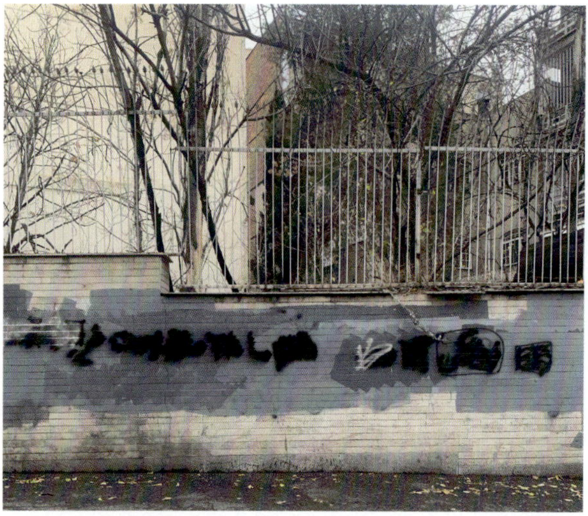

FIG. 98 Defaced graffiti. Photograph by Masoumeh Mohtadi.

instilled, above all, by her childhood experience of reading the Qur'an (in both Arabic and Persian). This belief profoundly influences her art, especially the body of work she has produced in response to the Woman, Life, Freedom uprising.

Forty days following the demise of Jina Mahsa Amini—a significant day of mourning—artists rallied at the House of the Artists (one of the more lenient state institutions), taking over both the interior of the central Tehran building and the space outside it. Initially, as Mohtadi explained, the slogans chanted by the artists were relatively generic and not explicitly aimed at the regime. However, as the day progressed, their chants took on a more political tone, with phrases like "Death to the Dictator" echoing through the air. But several undercover security guards were present among the crowd, and when the police learned that the gathering was not just a silent tribute to the deceased but a politically charged assembly, they moved in with ferocious speed, unleashing a tsunami of violence. Mohtadi described the sheer brutality as surreal, akin to a movie. The police opened fire indiscriminately. "All I could do was cover my eyes," Mohtadi recalled, "I could endure anything, but the thought of going blind was unbearable."[20] She miraculously avoided being shot, but suffered a brutal beating at the hands of undercover officers. Mohtadi went home, to the northern part of Tehran, only to find herself once again in the midst of violent clashes between the police and protesters FIG. 98.

The traumatic events of that day and night deeply unsettled Mohtadi. The fear and the injuries she sustained made her hesitant to participate in further street protests. For months, the most she could do was go for a walk and document the street slogans

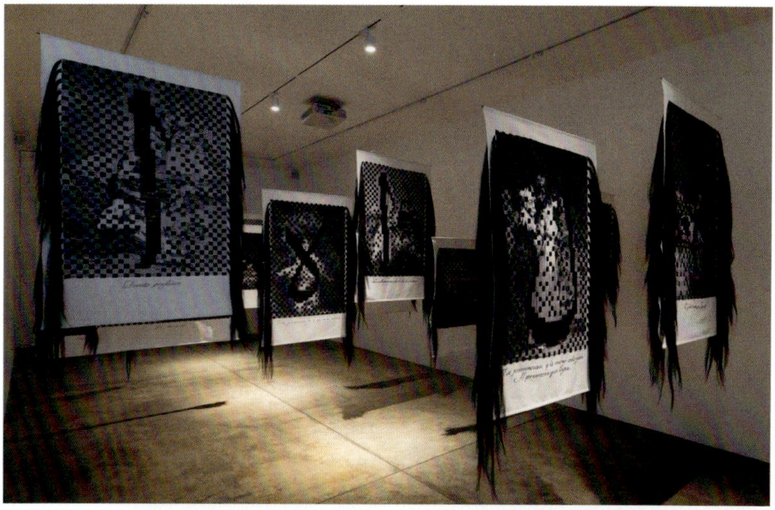

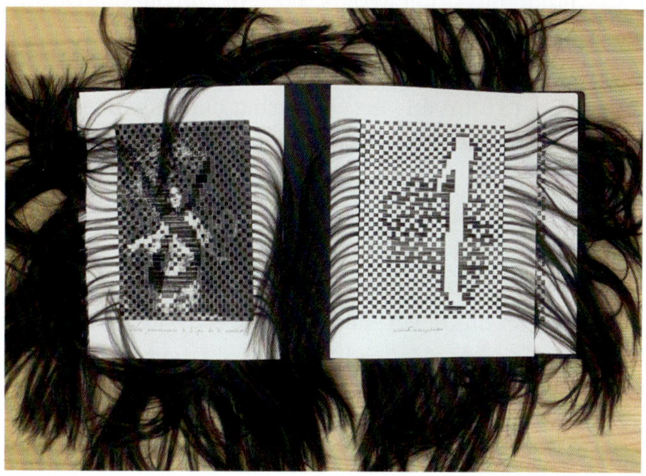

FIGS. 99A–B Masoumeh Mohtadi, *The Sleep of Reason*, featured at 009821 Gallery, 2023, Tehran. Courtesy of the artist.

meticulously and systematically deleted by the state authorities FIGS. 99A–B. However, this fear and pain also became a catalyst for her creativity, as she started channeling her emotions into her art. She began a significant art project that critically examines the regime's interpretation of the Qur'an, in particular verse 2:256: "Let there be no compulsion in religion, for the truth stands out clearly from falsehood." Mohtadi contrasts the teachings of the Qur'an with the harsh reality in the Islamic Republic, where people are not free to choose their level of religious observance, and deviation from the regime's strict regulations brings the risk of punishment, imprisonment, or even execution.

Mohtadi named her piece *The Sleep of Reason*, inspired by an etching from Francisco Goya's 1799 *Los Caprichos* series, "The Sleep of Reason Produces Monsters." Goya's pieces were a critique of the political, social, and religious abuses of his era, combining caricature—a popular technique at the time—with artistic innovation. Mohtadi's artistic expression echoes the critical spirit of Goya's work, signifying the senselessness that she perceives in contemporary Iran. The installation consists of pages, each representing a letter from the second surah of the Qur'an, emphasizing the verse relating to the absence of compulsion in religion. These pages are displayed in two formats: a larger version suspended from the ceiling, and a smaller book format placed on a stand reminiscent of the traditional wooden rehal. All the pages are intricately combined with replicas of Goya's political etchings. This setup creates a compelling blend of historical critique and contemporary struggle.

All pages—whether hung or placed on the wooden book rest—incorporate synthetic black hair as a medium, a choice made by numerous other artists, both in and outside of Iran, as a tribute to the Woman, Life, Freedom uprising. In Iran, however, this material has become highly politicized. Galleries risk losing their license if they exhibit any artworks that depict women's hair, regardless of form or style; on top of that, they face the threat of being shut down permanently if the works are perceived as challenging or critiquing Islam in any way. In this context, few artists have dared to use the Qur'an as a subject of their art (one artist, who wishes to remain anonymous, once experimented by pouring asphalt over a copy of the Qur'an but never mustered the courage to exhibit it). Faced with these constraints, Mohtadi and Iman Safaie, director of the 009821 Gallery (the numbers are the area code for Tehran), had to devise a strategy for displaying the work. They mutually agreed not to publicize the exhibit with an explicit statement: instead, Mohtadi committed to visiting the gallery daily, so she could personally explain the intentions behind her work to the curious visitors who inquired about the significance of the letters.

Returning to the title of the exhibition, Mohtadi explained that the regime's actions have not only stripped away all semblance of reason but also led to a widespread desensitization toward its ever-evolving rules and regulations. The omnipresent police, often in disguise, contribute to this atmosphere of subdued compliance. While Mohtadi holds on to the hope that more people will rise in support of the uprisings, she acknowledges there is a growing numbness in society as time moves on. The government has intensified its surveillance tactics, photographing women who choose not to wear veils and subsequently summoning them via text message to face punishment in court. The sight of women walking the streets unveiled, especially in Tehran's more conservative areas (and likely in other cities as well) is becoming increasingly rare. People now fear being reported even in places that seem safe and trustworthy. This "sleep of reason" is, indeed, reflected in Mohtadi's intricate art.

As demonstrated in the three case studies above, women engage with Islamic issues in diverse ways. Men also face these challenges, and the following example illustrates one of the ways men confront aspects of the faith.

A MALE ARTIST WEARS THE HIJAB

Painter Mohsen Jamalnik (b. 1979) has a deep interest in performance art. One particular issue he grapples with is the mandatory hijab for women in Iran and, more specifically, societal reactions to it. He poses a thought-provoking question: what if, as a form of protest against the Islamic Republic's hijab policy, everyone—men and women—chose to cover themselves completely from head to toe in their everyday lives?

Jamalnik had a vision of taking twenty visitors on a tour of the Tehran Museum of Contemporary Art and its famous Impressionist paintings, which include works by Claude Monet. The twist in his plan was to have all the participants—men and women—clad in black burkas akin to those worn in Afghanistan. With their faces covered by burka-like masks, the wearers would be able to see without being seen—or identified by the morality police's CCTV cameras. While Jamalnik was unable to realize his vision of guiding fully covered visitors through the museum, he ingeniously adapted this concept for a performance in his own car. Tehran's roads are surveilled by traffic enforcement cameras, which are used by the police to identify—and issue fines to—women not wearing the hijab in their vehicles. Jamalnik tested the capacity of the cameras by growing out his mustache, draping himself in a purple scarf, and driving around the city. He then captured this performance in a photograph that he shared on his Instagram account, where it received an overwhelmingly positive response. This act highlighted the absurdity of the situation and drew attention to the issue in a creative, impactful way.

The photograph could also be interpreted as a critique of the religious mandate that the headscarf is exclusively for women. Rather than focusing on this religious aspect, however, Jamalnik is concerned with the use of the hijab as a tool for surveillance and control of citizens and believes that men should actively oppose the mandatory hijab—and engage in protests alongside women—instead of simply looking on as women face detention and punishment. As Jamalnik sees it, artists have a responsibility to be the voice of society. Skilled

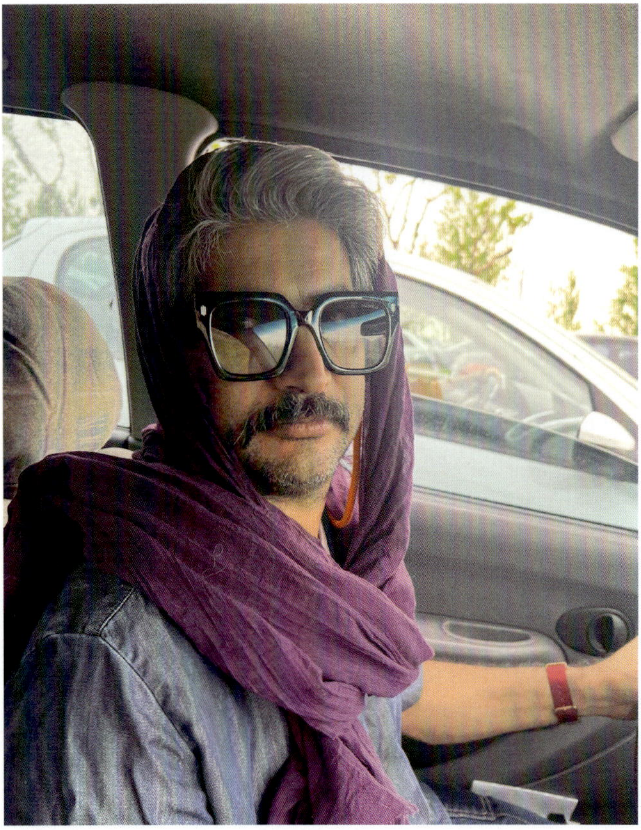

FIG. 100 Portrait of Mohsen Jamalnik during his activism/performance in his car, 2023. Courtesy of the artist.

in presentation, they can craft and execute protests in a thoughtful, meaningful way, increasing the impact of their message FIG. 100.

Men protesting in hijab is not a new phenomenon. During the 2009 Green Movement, Majid Tavakoli, a student at Tehran's Amir Kabir University of Technology, was arrested after delivering a speech opposing dictatorship. Proregime news agencies subsequently published a photograph of him wearing a full-length black chador, claiming he had tried to evade security forces by disguising himself in women's clothing. The image of Tavakoli was paired with a 1981 photo of Abolhasan Bani-Sadr, the first president of the Islamic Republic, who is said to have fled Iran in women's attire after being deposed—a pairing that implied a similar narrative of cowardice, as cultural historian Negar Mottahedeh has pointed out. Online, the hashtag #iranelection became a powerful platform for expressing opposition to the ridicule aimed at Majid Tavakoli by official channels. Thousands of Iranian men worldwide donned veils, took selfies, and uploaded them to the internet. The accompanying captions and comments denounced the human rights abuses of the Islamic Republic and called for Tavakoli's immediate release.[21]

Jamalnik's performance in his car is reminiscent of the actions taken by men during the 2009 Green Movement, but also diverges in that it integrates the protest into everyday life. In this act, the male artist incorporates wearing the scarf into his daily routine. The earlier protest was a response to the humiliation of protesting men, whereas Jamalnik's performance raises questions about the concept of the hijab itself.

Jamalnik's approach also illustrates the evolution in the perception and use of the veil in performative protest acts from the Green Movement to the Woman, Life, Freedom uprising. Rather than simply taking a selfie and posting it online with a low resolution that obscures personal identification, he boldly ventures onto the streets in women's scarves. His method demonstrates a more direct and tangible engagement with the issue of veiling, moving beyond virtual expressions to a physical manifestation of protest on the streets.

NAVIGATING GENDER AND RELIGION IN THE QUEST FOR FREEDOM

Does (mainstream) feminism conflict with the principles of Islam? The intersection of religion and gender in the Woman, Life, Freedom uprising requires a nuanced understanding of the complexities of the issue in relation to feminism, Islam, and the Middle East. Many scholars, including several from Iran, have elaborated on the ways the connotations of Muslim women's agency and freedom are different from those of women in Western societies.[22] In an earlier part of this book, I explored postrevolutionary Iran's concept of "Islamic feminism," a term introduced mainly by diaspora Iranian scholars to describe a women's rights movement that originated in the female ranks of the Islamic Republic's power structure.[23] While their perspectives on women's freedom were somewhat constrained, these "Islamic feminists" managed to bring about notable improvements in women's lives within an otherwise highly restrictive system. Moreover, the concept of Islamic feminism extends far beyond the geographical boundaries of Iran, encompassing a broader spectrum of ideas and movements that advocate for gender equality and women's rights within the framework of Islamic faith and culture across various regions of the world. Muslim women worldwide are increasingly rejecting patriarchal interpretations of Islam in favor of an egalitarian perspective. Also called Islamic feminism, this global movement combines the work of female scholars exploring gender equality in the

Qur'an with the efforts of activists advocating for progressive reforms in Muslim families, societies, and laws.[24] But this separate kind of feminism seems to be precisely what many women participating in the Woman, Life, Freedom movement are trying to undo. Through images, performances, and speech acts, the still evolving movement is giving the impression that Iranian women want the same things that white Euro-American feminists have always wanted. In particular, many Iranian women protesters have made it very clear that they do not wish to be seen as pious or devout Muslims. This approach may echo the white feminist agnostic position that descends from the European Enlightenment, with its critique of religious dogma and clerical authority.[25]

How to address the dilemma of reproducing a monotonic feminist discourse imported from the West? How to explore these topics in academic contexts and intellectual circles that have worked so hard to see, accept, embrace, and teach feminism in all its diversity, as manifested in the contributions of scholars like the late UC Berkeley professor Saba Mahmood? Or is Woman, Life, Freedom perhaps a very healthy development for the feminism discourse writ large, as it helps feminists "stay uncomfortable within feminism"?[26] This "discomfort," as Sara Ahmed aptly puts it, "means always questioning our own investments."[27]

To address this sense of unease with appropriate seriousness, we must delve deeper into the interpretation of feminism in Islamic contexts, as led by notable scholars in the field. My intention here is to demonstrate that Woman, Life, Freedom is not inherently in conflict with the "Islamic feminist" paradigm. When we reflect more deeply, and view the Iranian movement through the lens of "Islamic feminism," we can see that it is not merely a counterpart to Western frameworks but aligns in some respects with the Islamic model, as elucidated by Mahmood. In her widely cited study of women in Egypt, Mahmood problematizes Western feminism and its fixed formula of agency as subversion.[28] Drawing on her fieldwork with pious women participating in the mosque movement, Mahmood argues that—far from making these women eternal and absolute victims of false consciousness (as Western feminists would have it)—abiding by certain norms in their community gives them agency, enabling them to exercise their freedom and secure their independence. In other words, the pious woman "displaces the location of agency from the self to a nexus of social relations that permeate and shape the self."[29] It is this very "nexus of social relations" that Iranian women are critically examining, questioning, and even attacking. Rather than a struggle against the core tenets of Islam, the Iranian Woman, Life, Freedom movement is predominantly a challenge to the way social and political structures interpret and enforce Islam in the everyday lives of citizens. The global community may have overlooked this crucial aspect, possibly because the protests in Iran were intensely emotional.

In Spring 2023, Iranian religious scholar Sedigheh Vasmaghi criticized the Islamic Republic's interpretation of the hijab as an obligatory religious law, asserting that the government's approach is politically motivated rather than religiously based.[30] She warned Supreme Leader Ayatollah Ali Khamenei about the mandatory hijab law, an audacious act that led to her imprisonment.[31] However, the focus at the peak of the uprising was not on legal aspects of women's rights or the thoughts of religious authorities, political parties and organized groups; but rather on fervent, physical demonstrations of opposition to the veil and other Islamic-related issues. Were these emotionally charged tactics an error? I would argue not, especially since feminist scholars have enlightened us on the significance and impact of emotional responses in such circumstances.

Rage, despair, hope, but also disobedience, resentment, fury—all are emotions that Iranian women of all ages have used, and still use, to shape a bold feminist message that sometimes resonates with other waves of feminism, and at other times departs from them.[32] In using the term "emotion," I do not mean it as some "psychological disposition" but, rather, following Sara Ahmed, I consider how it "work[s], in concrete and particular ways, to mediate the relationship between the psychic and the social, and between the individual and the collective."[33] Can emotions and the ways they are performed, endorsed, or policed be a productive site to observe, analyze, and interrogate the feminist dimensions of Woman, Life, Freedom? Do these emotions contribute to coalition building or, conversely, do they prevent alliance and intersectional work across the various Middle Eastern communities or those with an Islamic background?

As Ahmed writes, *angry expressions* are sometimes one of the "conditions of possibility for feminist anger to get a just hearing."[34] Similarly, feminist scholar Léa Védie has described how extreme emotional expression can be framed as something that helps, rather than backfires. She uses the reception of Valerie Solanas's *SCUM Manifesto* in 1970s France to argue that the statement of hatred can have empowering effects. For Védie, Solanas's text helped subvert the norm of feminine respectability and also made feminist rage palpable.[35] She notes that some French feminists saw it as a vehicle for expressing "fantasies, fictitious representations that are not intended

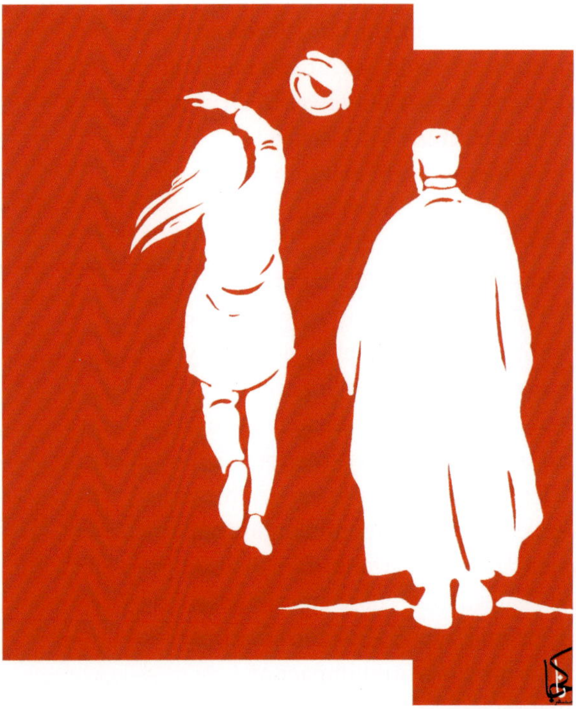

FIG. 101 Stylized version of a viral *Turban Throwing* photograph, a creative adaptation by Hassan Nozadian following similar renditions that gained popularity online.

to come true (as they are not actual political projects) but rather to foster the political imagery of the movement."[36] When men read *SCUM*, feminist and lesbian activist Cathy Bernheim wrote, they "will ask us [...] is it true that you want a world where we would not exist? We will answer them [...] that we do not desire such a world: we are plotting it."[37] This world without men is purely a "collective fantasy," as she puts it. It is something that belongs only to the realm of imagination and spectacle.[38]

Iranian women setting fire to their veils, offending their veiled counterparts, or flipping and tossing clergymen's turbans may suggest a desire for alternative possibilities FIG. 101. While these actions may be extreme and fueled by transitory emotional rage, they can also be seen as empowering—a means of challenging male-dominated power structures. It is important to acknowledge the political risks attached to these actions, which are perceived to be Islamophobic. However, rather than mocking devout Muslims, the repetition of such acts over the long term could open up the possibility of envisioning a different way of life.

Despite all the positive and hopeful reflections I have described in this "act", I would also like to emphasize the specific hardship that the feminist engagement with art creates for those who come from more conservative milieus. While artists like Sobhani and Rahimzadeh have navigated the realm of resistance without forsaking their religious beliefs, secular artists from religious families face a dual struggle, in conflict not only with the authoritarian ideology but also with their own circles of family and friends. Zohreh Solati (an artist featured in Act One) conveyed to me the challenges she has to overcome to pursue her art. Referring to her body of work where she presents contrasting images of herself—one a "free" woman, the other bound by societal norms—she writes:

> I am still afraid. I have changed the statement of this body of art several times because I don't know how to write it in a way that those close to me will not be hurt by reading and seeing the photos, and I am even worried about the judgment of society at large. [...] Surely, after publishing and exhibiting my photos and the statement related to the collection, I will face many problems. [...] These fears cause me to always face two issues when I want to write, photograph, or talk about [anything] related to me and my lived experiences, which are distressing for me: self-censorship and hiding part of my femininity, which is defined by patriarchal laws in society, and numerous social prohibitions that not only do not tolerate me and my feminine presence in the public sphere, but also consider living with these norms and prohibitions a virtue. However, my representation of my lived experiences is never in the form of a victimized and humiliated woman without agency, but rather a reflection of the intertwining of defiance in everyday life, persistence in reclaiming rights and human dignity amid a multitude of imposed pains and deaths, questioning and reevaluating the norms governing private and public matters, and exposing this 'me' desire to create, and all that I yearn for in my mind. A 'me' that, in the most despairing and uncertain conditions, desires to live alongside others.[39]

I would like to conclude this act with this statement by Solati, which clearly underscores the complex challenges that the religious perspective poses for artists, particularly female artists. It is never just about addressing one issue or another; rather, there is a multitude of intricate terrains that artists must traverse in relation to religion. ■

Act Nine

OPPOSING ART WITH ART IN CITYSCAPES

One of the most captivating aspects of art is its ability to communicate without relying on words. Art can embody a form of agency, serving as a powerful instrument for artists to respond to various situations. This means artists are not confined to making public statements, engaging in legal disputes, or articulating their concerns through written text. Instead, they can create art as a form of reaction to works they disagree with or wish to critique. This approach has been a staple of countercultural movements for years, which is often described as "culture jamming." Originating from the tactics of the Situationist International in 1960s France, particularly those advocated by notable leftist figure Debord, culture jamming is a form of artistic disturbance.[1] It challenges the passivity and alienation brought on by the spectacle of modern life. By employing tactics such as "détournement," culture jamming twists messages to forge new meanings, often through parodies that undermine the original messages' purposes. Because of its Marxist origins, the goal of culture jamming is predominantly to prompt critical reflection on the effects of consumer culture on society. In his manifesto on culture jamming, Kalle Lasn, the founder of the activist media foundation Adbusters, draws inspiration from Situationist philosophy to champion the disruption of consumer culture's narratives. Lasn writes that culture jamming serves as a metaphor for pausing the relentless stream of spectacle, allowing us the opportunity to recalibrate our perspective.[2] Culture jamming encompasses a wide array of practices aimed at subverting the messages propagated by consumer culture, not always limited to visual satire but extending to textual interventions, like bold and sarcastic messages written over McDonald's advertisements. In the ensuing discussion, while I address artist manifestos and declarations, my focus will remain on how Iranian artists use art as a form of resistance against official art or prescribed artistic visions, creating works that not only speak back but actively contest and challenge.

ARTFUL REACTIONS TO OFFICIAL ART

Under the presidency of Hassan Rouhani (2013–2021), the Islamic regime adopted a strategy of soft control of the arts. On state TV, viewers could tune in to *Asr-e Jadid* (New age)—Iran's version of *America's Got Talent*. More than simple entertainment, the show was part of a "plan to prevent the youth from going underground, and an effective way to encourage them to bring their artistic talent above ground, under the supervision of the authorities," in the words of a former MCIG staff member.[3] At the same time, the government's all-encompassing flagship Fajr Festivals, held annually to commemorate the 1979 Iranian Revolution, became a little more flexible, attracting younger artists who needed a platform for their work. Not everyone, however, responded to this new direction. More established artists, curators, filmmakers, and directors refused to contribute or participated in limited ways. Some created alternative festivals to accommodate the needs of young and emerging art professionals.[4] Others went as far as "hacking" the official celebrations. The 2018 Fajr Festival—which was particularly significant as it marked the fortieth anniversary of the Iranian Revolution—was "gate-crashed" by multimedia artist Homayoun Sirizi. Exasperated at the failure of fellow artists to condemn the events, Sirizi handed out four hundred airplane-issue sick bags—one side read "for vomit," the other "for reconciliation"—urging the participants in the festival to seek forgiveness and reconcile with the opposition. The accompanying "safety cards" had instructions on how to deal with the nauseating atmosphere of the arts scene in Tehran and the repugnant appropriation of quotations from political prisoners who had been confined in Qasr. More specifically, they offered advice on how to shake off motion sickness after looking at the artworks and how to exit the space in case of "emotional emergency."[5]

Despite clever tactical interventions of this kind,[6] the debate around engaging with the regime remained relatively muted until the 2021 elections which installed hard-liner Ebrahim Raisi as the Islamic Republic's eighth president. The elections were boycotted by many, as they were widely seen as rigged. Two months later, in August 2021, the new minister of culture and Islamic guidance, Mohammad

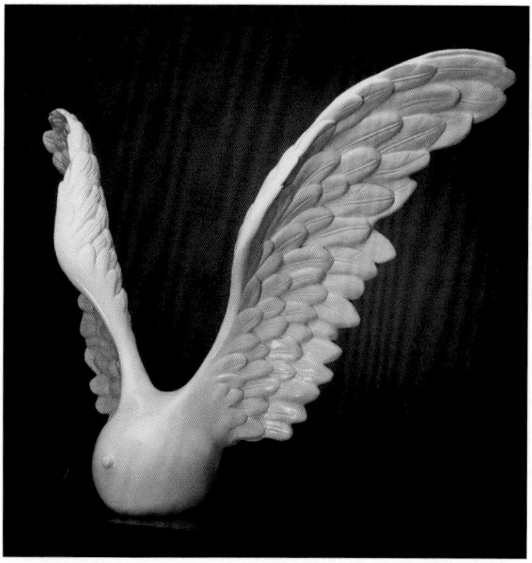

FIG. 102 Nastaran Safaie, *Flying*, 2012. Displayed for the first time in Tehran's Afra Gallery in 2024. Courtesy of the artist.

Mehdi Esmaili, set out a "program" (*barnameh*) to further "Islamicize" the arts on the MCIG website. The seventy-nine-page PDF document (since removed from the website) was structured into different sections—visual arts, film, painting, music, theater, etc.—each critiquing the current state of that art and outlining reforms to deal with the identified issues. For example, in the visual arts section, art galleries were condemned as hotbeds of antirevolutionary sentiment, found guilty of promoting an antiveiling movement and eroding revolutionary values. The proposed remedy was to shift the focus from conceptual art toward handicrafts and traditional arts, and to increase support for artists whose work aligned with the values of the Islamic Republic.[7]

Every sector of the arts community, from filmmakers and theater experts to graphic designers and painters, published open letters to the newly appointed minister, objecting to almost every single phrase of the new "program." On their Instagram pages, some prominent artists wrote that they would no longer engage in any art project or publication that required permission from the MCIG. Numerous galleries similarly chose to forgo the formalities of obtaining permission from the MCIG, showing a new readiness to display controversial works, even at the risk of being shut down by the authorities. This form of resistance was in many instances unprecedented. Pieces that had previously only been displayed at international venues were now shown in Iran. One notable example, albeit from a later period, is Nastaran Safaie's *Flying*, a sculpture depicting a large breast with wings, created in 2012, but only making its Iranian debut in the Afra Gallery in Tehran in January 2024 FIG. 102.

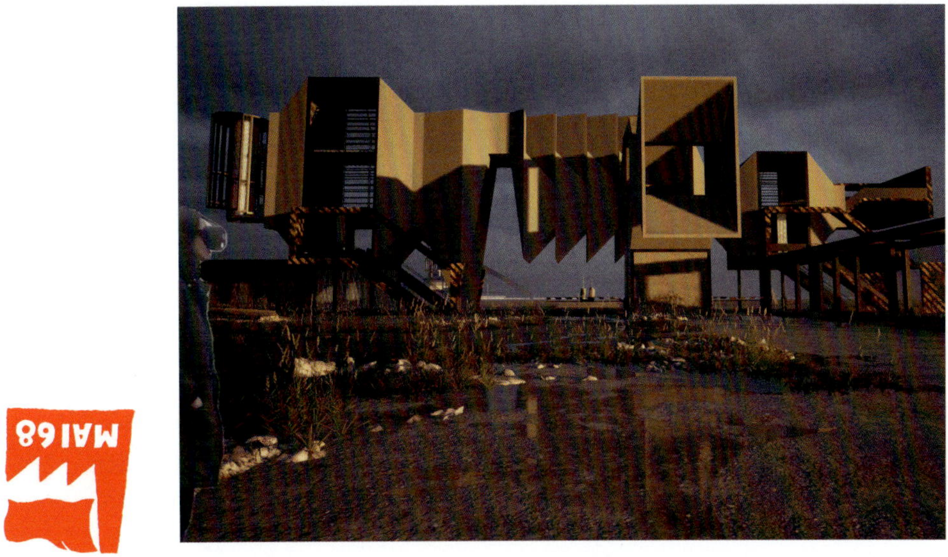

FIG. 103 Left: Reversed logo of the May 1968 *évènements*. Right: Snapshot from Afrooz Partovi's VR protest design for the entrance of the Sabzevar Pars Steel Company, inspired by the red factory logo that was significant during the May 1968 civil unrest in France. Courtesy of the artist.

The year 2021 was also marked by prolonged industrial unrest, as Iranian workers went on strike in protest against low wages, poor working conditions, and the lack of affordable housing and healthcare.[8] Against this backdrop, the Sabzevar Pars Steel Company teamed up with the Association of Architects at the University of Tehran to organize a competition for the design of a monumental entrance to its steel plant. Many architects called for the cancellation of the competition, pointing out the contrast between the company's readiness to lavish money on a monument and their reluctance to pay their workers a living wage. Among them was female architect and media artist Afrooz Partovi, who created, in lieu of a competition entry, a virtual reality experience in which the immersant has an opportunity to interact with a monument whose shape evokes an upside-down version of the red factory logo that animated the May 1968 civil unrest in France FIG. 103.

As the Woman, Life, Freedom uprising unfolded, the usual activities of the Iranian arts scene ground to a halt. For a whole host of reasons—rage, a desire to honor the protesters and fallen activists, an urge to assert opposition to the regime, or a need for security—artists canceled their shows, gallerists closed their businesses, and many new initiatives were placed on hold. Meanwhile, the state authorities sought to use arts and culture to give the false impression that life in Iran was continuing as normal. Incongruously, their efforts to encourage artists to resume their activities were accompanied by "a spree of arresting musicians, filmmakers, actors, authors, visual artists, and any prominent public figure who ventured to raise their voice in support of the protest movement, one that has been crushed violently."[9] While the population was tormented by grief, the government pressed ahead with the Fajr Festivals. This time around, however, artists did not just casually ignore the celebrations; nor did they organize alternative festivals, as they had done previously. Instead, many celebrated artists chose to stand by the protesters and publicly boycott the state-sponsored extravaganza. Among them was Iran-based actor and film director Mani Haghighi, whose passport had been seized in October 2022 to prevent him from attending the London Film Festival for the screening of his film *Subtraction*.[10] In December, two months before the Fajr Celebrations, he published footage on his personal Instagram platform in which he stated:

> Last week Mr. Mohammad Mehdi Esmaili, the current Minister of Guidance [*sic*] invited all artists to participate in this year's Fajr. He then added that this year's festival will go on as usual. Mr. Esmaili, you are that same person who had earlier spoke of making compulsory hijab more conservative across the film industry. You are the same person who threatened Iranian artists. [...] We have already paid a big price on the demands for more conservative compulsory hijab. How dare you invite us to collaborate now? You represent a belief system that treated us like criminals when my generation was young. You would arrest and chastise us for carrying music cassettes [...] You are the representative of a faction who does not even allow music instruments to appear on TV for fear of popularizing it. Now under the current circumstances, when the best of our [...] directors and rappers are in prison, you expect us to come and take part in the Fajr Festival? I confess that there was a time when we naively assumed that our participation in the Fajr Film Festival would protect Iran's art and culture from a wave that intended to destroy it. We were wrong. The Fajr Festival does not belong to us. It's yours. Now I wonder who will participate in the Fajr events. Which artist or cultural figure will join your celebrations? What citizen will buy tickets to attend your festivity? You cannot hold people's head under water and order them not to kick and gasp for air; when they resist and lash out, you call them troublemakers? Now you expect that same group of underwater people to come out and attend your festivals and even entertain? No. We are too busy; we don't have time for that.

> We are busy going to prisons to visit our detained colleagues; we are dropping in on those girls who have lost their eyes with your bullets; we are burying the fallen protesters in all corners of this country. We are mourning. No. We don't have time to dance for you.[11]

THE BATTLE OF THE ARTS AT TEHRAN'S UNIVERSITY OF ART

In an article published in January 2024, music historian Siamdoust explores how students from the music department at Tehran's University of Art pioneered what she calls a new "university music genre" at the height of the Woman, Life, Freedom uprising.[12] Videos of the students' performances of revolutionary songs, which adapted existing, often censored music and poetry, were widely shared on social media platforms, broadcasting a message of defiance and resilience. However, the creation of this new genre of art making was not an overnight achievement, but the result of a prolonged process of development and refinement. If we consider the stories of a professor and a student at the university—one dismissed for supporting students during the uprising, the other central to escalating tensions with the school's administration before it—we can appreciate the evolution that led to the University of Art becoming the source of some of the most iconic artistic expressions of the time.

On February 6, 2023, Kourosh Golnari, a leading Iranian sculptor and director of the university's sculpture department, received a letter out of the blue from the university president. Referring to his public statement of support for the student protests, the letter informed him that he had been suspended with immediate effect. Moreover, his contract would not be extended into the next semester and his tenured position would be reviewed by a university expert committee. The suspension of Golnari and other faculty members stunned art circles in Iran and beyond. Soon, major outlets like *BBC Persian* picked up the story, urging the university's leadership to reconsider their decision, emphasizing the invaluable knowledge and expertise these esteemed professors brought to the countless students who relied on them. Their pleas were in vain: to this day, Golnari and a colleague, Amir Maziar, who specializes in art theory and philosophy, remain in academic limbo, their status unresolved.

Discussing these developments with me, Golnari said his sole intention in issuing the public statement of support had been to shield his students from potential police aggression.[13] The performances—which I detailed in Act Four of this book—were nonviolent,

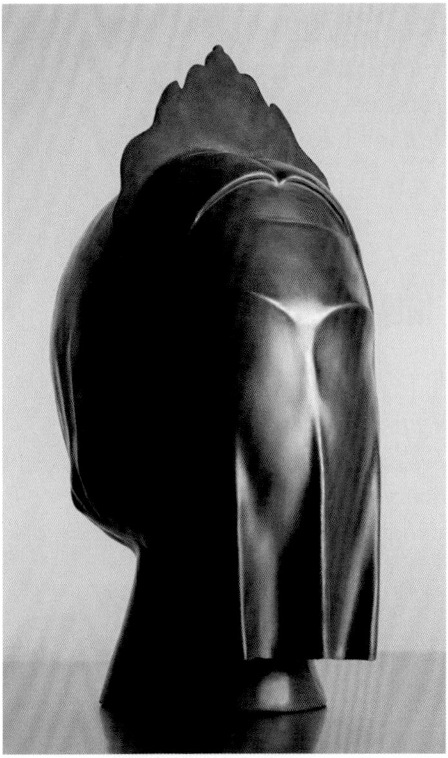 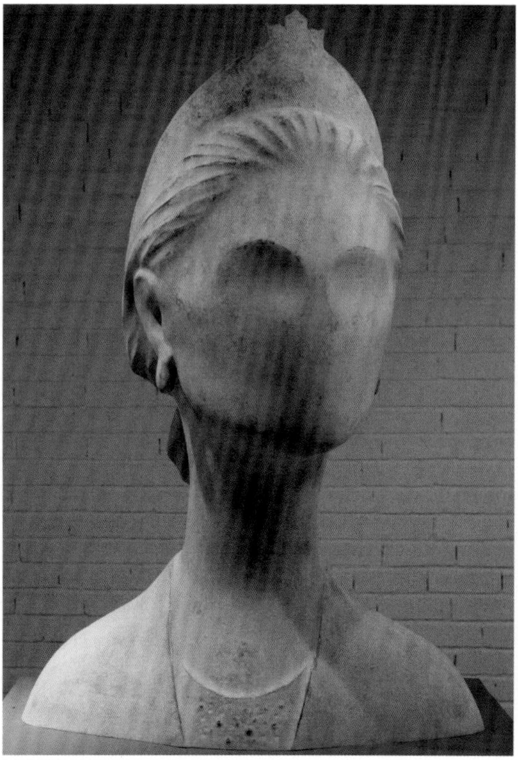

FIGS. 104A–B Kourosh Golnari, left: *Goddess of Centuries*, bronze, 50 × 25 × 28 cm., 2011. Right: *Wisdom*, bronze with white patina, 100 × 68 × 55 cm., 2018. Courtesy of the artist.

marked by peace and inventive expression. During his tenure, Golnari consistently championed the well-being of his students, both intellectually—ensuring they received a modern and unparalleled education—and in terms of their physical and mental health. Sometimes, he said, he would get calls from parents worried that their children had fallen in with the wrong crowd while studying away from home. To address this, Golnari implemented measures on campus to deter harmful behaviors like substance abuse. More significantly, he revitalized the curriculum, aiming to channel the students' energy and focus entirely into art creation and learning. Golnari introduced social practice art and encouraged students to initiate collaborative art projects on the campus grounds. He also challenged the university's traditionally rigid and restrictive knowledge framework by welcoming critics from outside. His approach shifted the perception of sculpture: no longer an abstract object on a pedestal, it became a living art, integrated into the daily realities of Iran.

The ethos of the Woman, Life, Freedom uprising struck a profound chord with Golnari, who is renowned for a series of female busts he has crafted over the years, reflecting on the pivotal role women have played in shaping the art and culture of Iran. At first glance, these sculptures have ambiguous facial features, but a closer look reveals resemblances to prominent women from modern Iranian history. Their veiled faces allude to the fact that they have often remained in the shadows, despite the importance of their contribution FIG. 104 A-B. As an example of these largely forgotten women, Golnari referred to the mother of Amir Kabir, the nineteenth-century statesman and reformer who founded the first center for higher education in Iran and was assassinated allegedly on the orders of his former master, Naser Al-Din Shah. In the twentieth century, Farah Diba, the wife of the last shah, introduced avant-garde artistic talent from around the globe in Iran and simultaneously propelled Iranian artists to prominence through initiatives like the Shiraz Arts Festivals. Yet, as with other women in the circles of the ruling elites, her monumental contribution to the vibrant arts scene of that pre-revolutionary era has been mostly overlooked.

The initial impetus for the sculptures were family tales of Golnari's great-grandmother, a self-taught herbal healer who ventured into the mountains to gather plants for remedies. A valued figure in her community, she was often referred to as the local doctor. Golnari wondered why stories like hers remained shrouded in mystery, passed down quietly, from one generation of women to the next. His enigmatic sculptures of women not only highlight this cultural pattern but also underscore the broader issue of women's marginalization in Iran's historical narrative.

When I asked Golnari why he thought the University of Art had taken on a more proactive role in the uprising than other educational institutions, he directed me to the work of one of his former students, Mohsen Rafei. The debate around Rafei's revolutionary art had sparked a dispute between students and administrators in the weeks before the death of Jina Mahsa Amini. Delving deeper into the story, we find a narrative of art anticipating, paving the way for, future revolutionary endeavors.

Rafei, born in Mashhad shortly after the 1979 revolution, was drawn to illustration and graphic design before his passion evolved toward three-dimensional art forms. After taking various art classes in his hometown, he enrolled at Tehran's University of Art, where he majored in sculpture during his undergraduate years. Later, for his MFA at the same institution, Rafei shifted his focus to the theory and philosophy of art. This amalgamation of disciplines deepened his reflection on art's potential to reshape societal norms. He became especially intrigued by themes of reuse, waste control, and the societal frameworks related to gender dynamics within the Islamic Republic.

What makes Rafei's work distinct from that of his peers in Iran, and particularly those specializing in sculpture, conceptual art, or installations, is his profound fascination—bordering on obsession—with the dynamism of *movement*.[14] For Rafei, the depiction of motion is an opportunity to explore and articulate novel perspectives on how we live. By stripping away familiar comforts and confronting the viewer with an environment that provokes and disorients, even if momentarily, he forces them to reconsider their corporal movements and behavior—to think differently about how they operate in the world.

This concept was materialized in the form of a giant sculpture, *Dome*, made for the Seventh Tehran National Sculpture Biennale in 2016. More reminiscent of a water tank than a traditional dome, the structure—two and a half meters high, and four and a half meters in diameter—rested atop a hemispherical base. On entering the installation, visitors were plunged into a dark, spiraling interior that challenged their perception of space and their equilibrium. As they navigated a forty-meter path, their bodies felt unstable, and the solitude within the structure intensified the sense of disorientation—unless, by planned or fortuitous timing, another visitor entered and restored a sense of balance FIG. 105.

To realize his artistic vision, Rafei collaborated with an engineering professor from Sharif University and a team of industrial design students. The intricate two-and-a-half-ton structure was fabricated in a workshop in the industrial heartland of Chahar Dangeh, south of Tehran, by skilled craftsmen more typically employed in making gas containers. Transporting *Dome* to its installation site on the grounds of the Tehran Museum of Contemporary Art required a crane, a sizable flatbed truck, and meticulous planning—the move was scheduled for after midnight, to avoid the most congested hours on the thoroughfares of Tehran.

The artwork generated palpable excitement among visitors, but also presented them with a kind of endurance test—a sensory experience of extremes: by day, the black metal dome absorbed the scorching heat; at night, it got uncomfortably cold. In a North American context, such an installation might be considered an invitation to litigation, due to the risk of burns from the overheated metal or the possibility of inducing claustrophobia, perhaps even nausea among the visitors. However, in Iran, the biennale's organizers gave their consent, under the condition that Rafei himself was responsible for the logistics of the sculpture's creation, funding, and transportation.

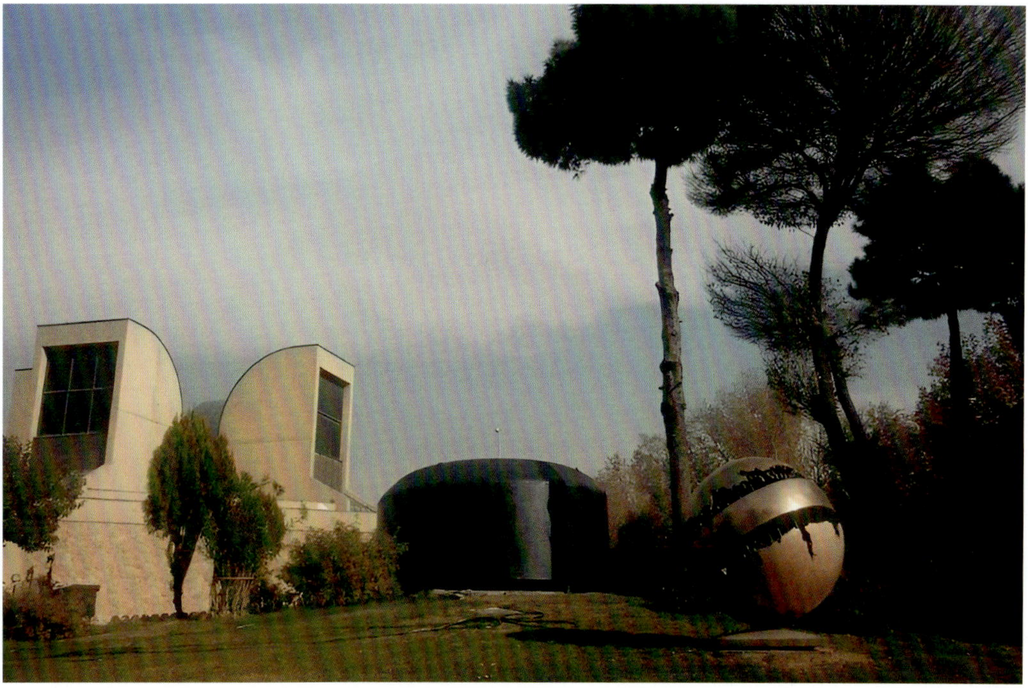

FIG. 105 Mohsen Rafei, *Dome* at the Museum of Contemporary Art for the 7th Sculpture Biennale in 2016. Courtesy of the artist.

Among the many visitors who were impressed by the *Dome* was Noriyuki Haraguchi, the Japanese artist famed for his 1,190-gallon *Oil Pool* (1977) installation at the Tehran Museum of Contemporary Art, who had returned to assist in the restoration of the work. Rafei recalled how Haraguchi had vanished for a long time into the spiral interior—so long that he became concerned for his well-being. When the Japanese artist reappeared, he was momentarily lost for words, but then expressed astonishment that the work had been created by an artist as young as Rafei: for him, the space suggested a lifetime of experience of the world.

Rafei's engagement with disconcerting experiences breathes life into all his works. The unanticipated movements he crafts prompt visitors to engage in deep introspection and to enter into an enigmatic exchange not only with themselves but also with the environment, the people, the objects, and the architectural spaces they encounter.

The University of Art has expanded beyond its original 1960s home near the busy Valiasr intersection (formerly Chahar Rah Pahlavi) to encompass multiple campuses in central and southern Tehran and the neighboring city of Karaj. The sculpture department is located in the

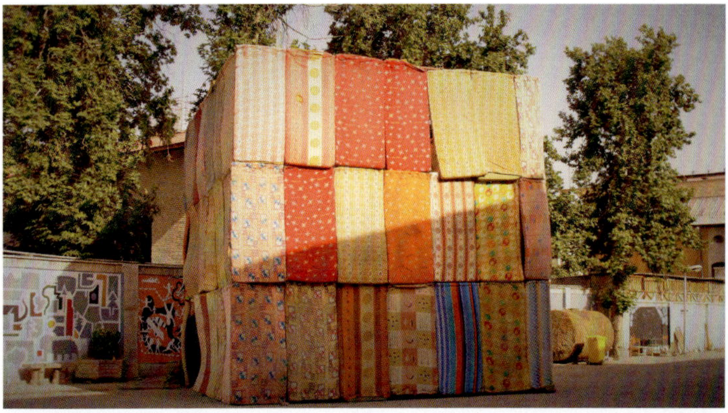

FIG. 106 Mohsen Rafei, *Dream House*, 2015–2017, Tehran's University of Art. Courtesy of the artist.

southern part of the capital, in a nineteenth-century building that was commissioned during Naser al-Din Shah's rule and served as the headquarters for the Cossack-style unit led by Reza Shah Pahlavi. An aura of discipline and structure, reminiscent of the military personnel the building once housed, still adheres to the complex. Set around a vacant courtyard, the campus quad lacks vitality, offering no inviting spaces for students to congregate, lounge, or interact. Seeing this void, Rafei envisioned a structure to foster better social interaction.

In 2015, Rafei spotted a pile of old mattresses with vibrant covers that had been removed during the refurbishment of the university dorms and were awaiting disposal at a landfill outside the capital. Seizing the opportunity, he stepped in and offered to transport them to the campus quad at his own expense. He used the colorful mattresses to construct a sizable cube, which was entered through a dim corridor. Walking into the piece—aptly called *Dream House*—brought a shift in perception. The flooring was soft, made unstable by a water mattress, meaning viewers often fell on their backs, gaining an unexpected prospect of the Tehran sky. Adding to its allure, *Dream House* was built around a majestic maple tree. Rather than being overshadowed by the imposing buildings, students could lie on the water mattress and gaze up at the towering tree, a living beacon pointing to the beauty of nature FIG. 106.

Dream House stood as a world in itself, but the school administration grew increasingly wary, believing it facilitated "inappropriate" interaction between male and female students. In 2017, the house was burned down and the majestic tree was reduced to charred remains. The circumstances surrounding the fire remain a mystery, but some blamed Rafei for the loss of the treasured tree. In Tehran, and Iran as a whole, ancient trees hold immense value. Given their scarcity and the years they take to mature, they are cherished, especially for the shade they offer during the blistering summer months.

Overwhelmed by the loss of the tree, Rafei channeled his energy into incorporating its burned trunk into another intervention on the same campus quad. By 2019, the tree—its trunk thirteen meters long, and weighing two and a half tons—had been reincarnated as the centerpiece of a massive metal bench. The transformation was funded jointly by Ali Tavasoli, director of the Deedee Gallery in Mahmood Abad (a city by the Caspian), and Rafei's own resources. Called *Ja beh Ja* (which loosely translates as "from place to place" or "shifting bench" or "Metamorphosis"), the bench responded when the students seated on either side of the trunk shifted their weight, creating an interactive and dynamic experience as it swayed with their movements.

But the completion of the bench coincided with a conservative shift in the administration of the university. The new leadership was displeased with the piece, and urged Rafei to move it somewhere else FIG. 107. Rafei attempted to reason with them, presenting all the relevant paperwork and approvals from the previous leadership. He also made it clear that the art was designed specifically for that location. Both the tree trunk and the metal framework were extremely heavy, and moving them would be a major challenge, both logistically and financially.

The school authorities remained adamant. Without consulting Rafei, they removed the bench from the campus under cover of darkness one night. Days later, an acquaintance of the artist discovered it in a new location near Tehran's Milad

FIG. 107 Mohsen Rafei's artwork *Ja beh Ja* or Shifting Bench (also known as *Cradle* or *Seesaw*), a site-specific installation crafted for the campus quad at Tehran's University of Art in 2019. Courtesy of the artist.

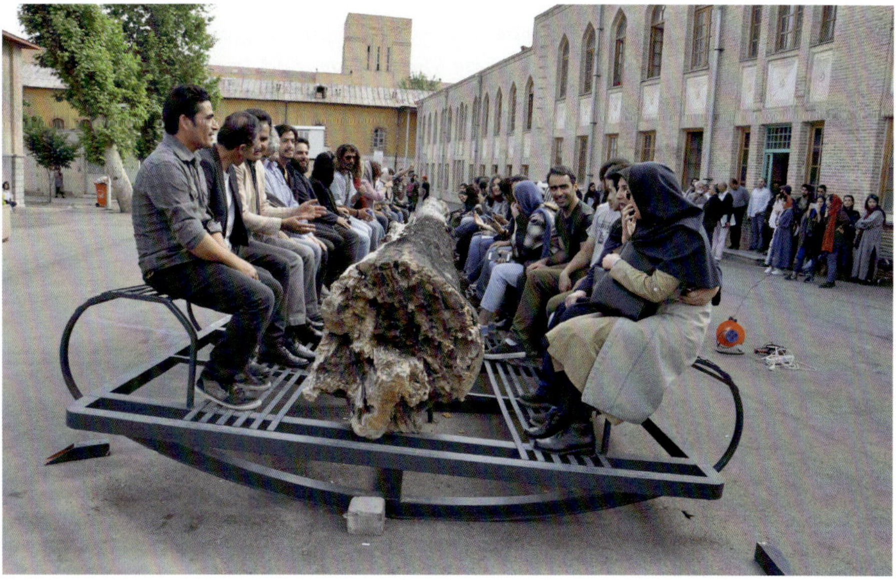

telecommunications tower. Rafei launched a legal battle with the institution, and when operators of the Milad Tower understood the disputed nature of the bench, they asked the school's administration to remove it. The artwork would be taken to an undisclosed disposal site, hidden from Rafei.

That was not the end of the matter. The dispute between Rafei and the school intensified, drawing many students into the fray. The situation caught the attention of leading news platforms, including Iran-based *Etemad Newspaper*, which conducted an in-depth interview with Rafei.[15] The interview aimed not only to elucidate the original artistic intentions behind the work but also to uncover the legal boundaries breached by the university authorities.[16] The news was also picked up by international Persian news agencies. "Shared Student Laughter Now Silenced in Iran" was the compelling headline of the article *The Independent Persian* ran on August 30, 2022:

> With Ebrahim Raisi coming to power in Iran, social and personal restrictions in universities [have] intensified. [...] This 13-meter seesaw, which was installed in the University of Art in May 2019, was called 'Place to Place' and was a single tree trunk placed in the middle of a metal cradle where students could sit and swing on it. [...] This work [...] comes alive and gains meaning with the presence of people in its heart [...]; however, the officials of the university interpreted this interaction differently, telling Mohsen Rafei, the creator of this work, that since girls and boys gather around this seesaw and 'laugh outlawed and make noise', it should be removed.[17]

Expanding on the narrative of *Ja beh Ja* (the Shifting Bench)—referred to as the "cradle" and "seesaw" by *The Indipendent Persian* —in relation to the increased enforcement of regulations under the new president, the article continued:

> The situation [...] is [now] reminiscent of the era [of] Mahmoud Ahmadinejad [...]. [Recall] increased social restrictions, forced retirement of professors, gender segregation, attempts to establish single-gender universities, and changing the curriculum of humanities courses [...].[18]

A connection was also made between the ongoing dispute and the clashes between students and authorities during the 1997 student uprising at the University of Tehran dormitories,

> where very harsh slogans against the leader of the Islamic Republic were shouted [...] These protests, which met with violent suppression, gradually turned into a basis for confronting students [...] expulsion or deprivation of education—a policy that is still on the agenda.[19]

Finally, the article used the story of the artwork as a way to paint the picture of universities one year into Raisi's term of office:

> In a year since the establishment of the thirteenth government, social and personal restrictions in universities [...] have significantly increased. From limiting and preventing female students from watching male students' competitions to barring women from entering university campuses due to their type of dress, and intensifying scrutiny of students' personal relationships, all are manifestations of [stricter] policies in the current government. Mohammad Hosseini, the Parliamentary Deputy of the thirteenth government, who was also the Minister of Culture and Islamic Guidance during Ahmadinejad's tenure, recently confirmed [...] that the established government supports single-sex universities.[20]

The dispute over Rafei's artwork arose just twenty days prior to Jina Mahsa Amini's death. While it might be a stretch to draw a direct line between the two events and the subsequent large-scale demonstration at the University of Art's campus quad, one could argue that the tussle between students and authorities over the *Shifting Bench* ignited an artistic uprising. Importantly, Rafei contends that the stringent codes of public conduct in Iran prevent people, and particularly women, from exploring alternative life experiences. In making work that elicits dynamic engagement, he is indicating that life should not be constricted to a uniform mode of existence and bodily movement, as dictated by the Islamic Republic, and asserting his unwavering belief in the capacity of art to transform human behavior.

In November 2023, Rafei collaborated with fellow artist Ali Seyed Alikhani on an exhibition at Tehran's Bostan Gallery dedicated to the memory of those who perished in the Woman, Life, Freedom uprising. Titled *In-between*, the exhibition was presented as an exploration of diverse ways of existing in the world. The abstract theme was carefully chosen to smooth the approval process with both the MCIG and the municipal authorities. Those who issued permission appear to have been unaware of the deeper implications and true purpose of the exhibit. Among the elements designed by Rafei were two dynamic structures. One of these, *Hejleh*, was positioned at the entrance to the gallery, serving as a threshold to the main space FIG. 108 C. In form, it resembled a traditional *hejleh* or *tabaq*—a temporary, portable canopy often adorned with mirrors, lamps, and flowers; a memorial structure often seen in religious ceremonies and used to honor the deceased, especially young individuals. Such structures were a common sight in the city in the 1980s, commemorating young men who had lost their lives in the Iran–Iraq War. They were rented, installed, and deinstalled, moving from one family to another FIG. 108 A.

Here, however, the act of entering the *hejleh* was ingeniously integrated with the experience of ascending a set of stairs encased within the structure. As visitors climbed, the stairs moved, creating a feeling of unease. This sensation was not meant to annoy; the design of the trembling structure conveyed a fluidity and motion that enriched the immersive experience of the exhibit.

Rafei's second installation, *Jaygah* (pedestal), was positioned atop a utility box on the sidewalk adjacent to the gallery FIG. 108 C. As previously discussed, utility boxes took on a significant political dimension in Iran in 2017, with the Women of Revolution Street movement, which started when Vida Movahed took off her headscarf and waved it in defiance from her vantage point atop a utility box on the Revolution Street FIG. 108 B. Rafei's design subtly intertwines a political movement with the physical movement and sound of the installations, creating a poignant reminder of the recent historical events and the punishment these women endured. The utility box next to the Bostan Gallery was supplemented with three interlocked arches constructed from scaffolding. The arches were designed to move, producing distinct noises as they rubbed against each other. In combination with the trembling *hejleh* structure, the installation formed a cohesive auditory experience. Sometimes, their sounds harmonized with the bells of a nearby church, creating a chorus of urban resonance.

Visually and sonically, the two interconnected installations in Rafei's exhibition served as public monuments to those who suffered—who died, were injured, interrogated, tortured—in two significant prowomen movements in Iran spanning a five-year period. The temporary nature of the installations stood in stark contrast to the monumental structures erected by the regime to honor the "legitimate" heroes of the revolution and war. But while they were impermanent, they possessed the qualities of resilience and continuity. Like the traditional *hejleh*, they can be dismantled and relocated, possibly finding a new home in another gallery. As Rafei puts it, their capacity

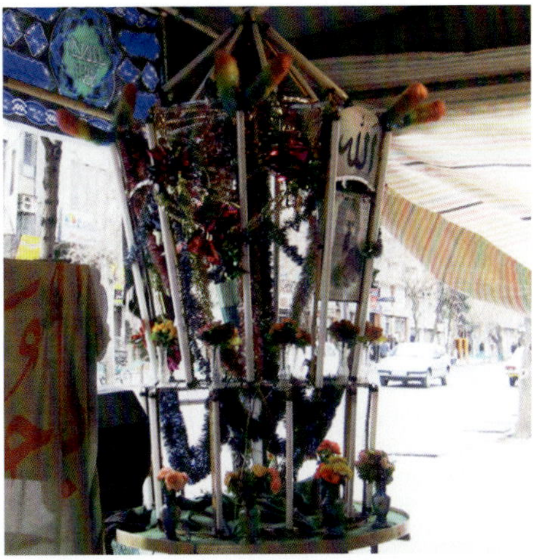

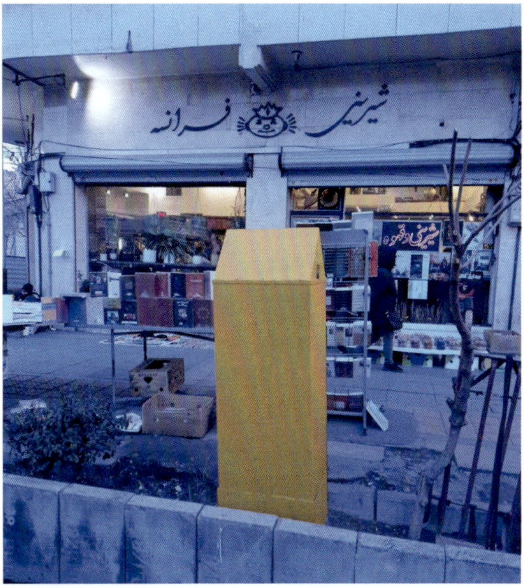

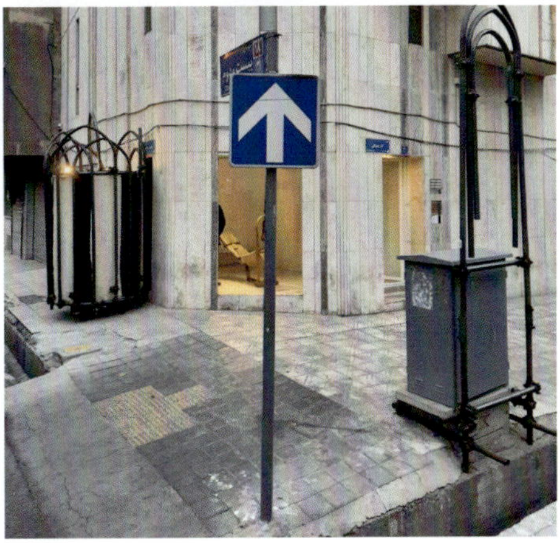

FIGS. 108 A-C Top left (A): A *tabaq* or *hejleh* installed during the Ashura ceremonies, in honor of Imam Hussein who was martyred in the Battle of Karbala in 680 CE. Photograph by the author. Top right (B): The platform on Revolution Street where Iranian anti-compulsory-hijab protester, Vida Movahed, took her stand is now roofed to deter future protest attempts. Photograph by anonymous artist. Bottom left (C): Mohsen Rafei, installations, *Jaygah* (pedestal) and *Hejleh*, at Bostan Gallery, Tehran, 2023. Courtesy of the artist.

to endure against the odds symbolically perpetuates the memory and the spirit of the women they honor[21] FIG. 108 C.

Rafei's sculptural pieces commemorating the Woman, Life, Freedom uprising use movement, sound, and touch to actively engage visitors. However, other artists interpret this memorialization as a bridge between past and future. Instead of viewing the uprising as a historical event akin to previous, mostly unsuccessful attempts to effect change in Iran, these artists see it as a catalyst for shaping Iran's future. Their art, in both meaning and form, suggests a desire for the movement to evolve, adopting new strategies while maintaining the ultimate goal of a more democratic and just atmosphere for women and the rest of the population. The projects I will discuss in the following "act" embody this dual focus on past and future. While they might seem complex to external viewers, they resonate with local audiences in Iran, sparking hope even amid their ambiguity. ■

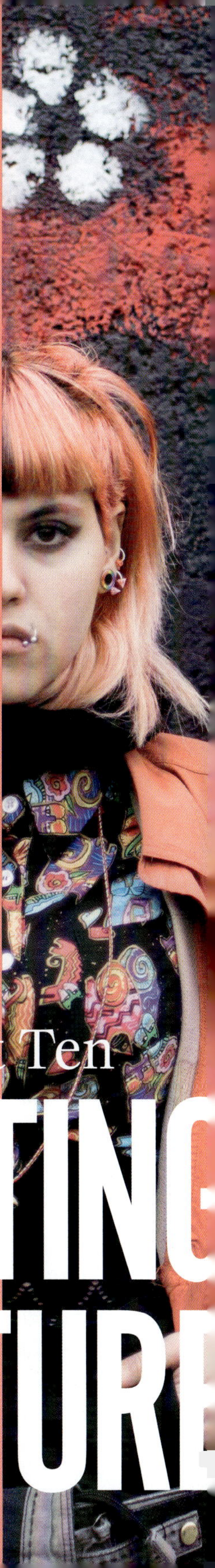

Act Ten

FORECASTING THE FUTURE

In January 2024, Mojtaba Amini (b. 1979) held an exhibition at Tehran's O Gallery titled *Not Everyone Will Be Taken into the Future*.[1] The title was taken from a 1983 essay by the conceptual artist Ilya Kabakov, which imagines Kazimir Malevich as a headmaster choosing students for a Soviet summer camp, drawing a line between those artists who would be carried into the future and those who would not.[2] Amini republished Kabakov's text in both English and Persian, using it as his own exhibition statement. This was not just a deliberate nod to Kabakov but a means to discreetly mask the true purpose of the exhibition. Although less frequent after the uprising, such tactics are still commonly used by artists to avoid confrontations with the MCIG.

The focus of Amini's exhibition was on the young people who had lost their lives in the uprising, and so would not be taken physically into the future, but would weigh forever on the collective memory of the nation. Alongside casts of young bodies stained with blood-red and black tar, depicted as tortured and burned, were canvases showing young women, awkwardly positioned at the very bottom of a green landscape, giving the viewer a questioning look, as if to ask: "Now what? What are you going to do?" This unsettling arrangement challenged viewers, urging them not just to mourn the lives lost but to think about the future of the movement FIGS. 109A–B.

Kabakov's original story was a satirical critique of how Soviet utopian dreams and visions of world salvation were often shaped by a select, self-appointed few. While probing deeper questions about the future of the Woman, Life, Freedom movement, Amini's work also subtly addresses the role of artists during tumultuous times. It raises important issues: should artists go on with business as usual, or succumb to despair? Is their role to become activists and engage directly in societal issues, or should they use their art as a political tool? Amini deliberately refrains from providing answers, instead offering questions that provoke thought.[3]

These questions prompted me to consider the ways art can predict, envision, and even shape the future, especially in contexts where legal and political avenues for change are closed off. Amini's exhibition is a reflection on the potential of art to influence societal structures. Above all, his work—in particular the casts of the fallen men and women—can be interpreted as a vision for constructing a more meaningful future. This viewpoint is consistent with scholars' perspectives on how images of murdered African Americans such as Emmett Till served as a catalyst for the Civil Rights Movement. Art historian Sampada Aranke, in her book *Death's Futurity: The Visual Life of Black Power*, highlights that these representations were not just depictions of death but strategic tools that helped transform the concept of death into a driving force for liberation—for imagining a future free from the constraints of white supremacy.[4]

In the same spirit, my intention in this "act" is to present a series of case studies that offer a more hopeful outlook on the future. Taking the concept of the future in its many different denotative and connotative associations, the artworks featured below delve into the tactical construction and reconstruction of time while challenging us to think about the relationship between past, present, and future. Within a system rife with constraints against alternative ways of living and thinking, they show different possibilities of envisioning and disseminating the idea of an alternate future.

FIGS. 109A–B Mojtaba Amini, *Not Everyone Will Be Taken into the Future*, January 2024, O Gallery, Tehran. Courtesy of the artist.

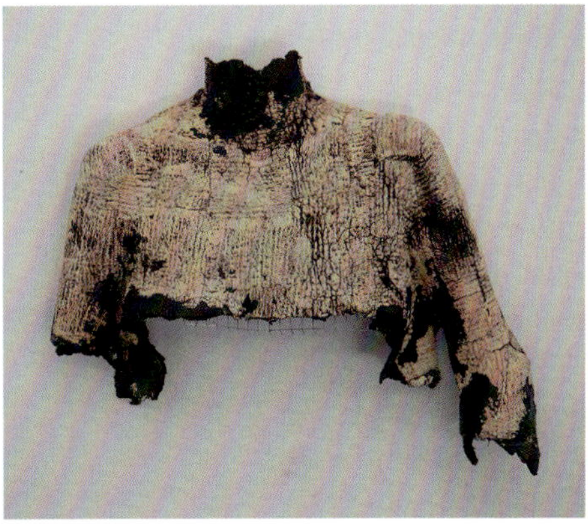

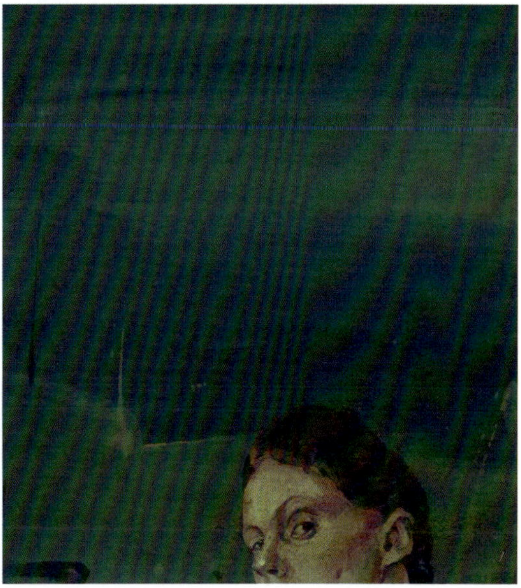

TO DEFER IS FUTURAL

Psychosocial scholar Lisa Baraitser asserts that "[t]o defer or postpone is *futural*; the possibility of deferral is precisely premised on the yet-to-come."[5] She augments this statement by linking it to Jacques Derrida's idea of democracy as a perpetual state of becoming, suggesting that politics—including the fight for emancipation—is fundamentally a temporal act.[6] From this vantage point, deferral is not only future focused but a significant political act—an active opportunity for renewal and initiation, rather than a passive waiting for an uncertain future.

However, how exactly does deferral in art production or art exposition function as a political act? Can deferred art presage future conditions, emerging first as performance before crystallizing into reality? To explore these questions, I will look at how certain performative acts pre-dating Woman, Life, Freedom were not only first revealed during the uprising but also perceived as art made for the uprising. I argue that these deferred artworks demonstrate the power of *delay* as a form of *political action.*

The photographer Shiva Khademi (b. 1989) grew up in the religious city of Mashhad, which she describes as a perpetually dark and somber place. Most women in her hometown wear black chadors in public. On moving to Tehran in 2018, she was struck by the relative vibrancy of the city, but most of all by the unconventional young women—art students, theater actors, and others—who dyed their hair bold colors and went unveiled. She would see them sitting cross-legged on metro floors or on the sidewalks, indifferent to the astonished stares of passersby. Feeling homesick—Khademi perceives Tehran as unwelcoming to immigrants and outsiders—she initiated a conversation with one of the self-assured girls at a metro station. She began to spend time with more of them, going on long walks where she familiarized herself with their stories, and together they discovered suitable walls to serve as the backdrop for their portraits, for which they all willingly posed. One of Khademi's subjects is Marzieh, an art student from the southern city of Bandar Abbas, who confided that before going home to her family—which she did only every six months, to avoid conflict—she would dye her colorful hair back to brown FIG. 110 A. In another instance, Khademi photographed a tall skinny girl with short yellow hair dressed in a large leather coat, who once told the police she was transgender to avoid scrutiny about her veil—a relatively safe excuse in Iran, where legal and medical frameworks exist for gender transition.[7]

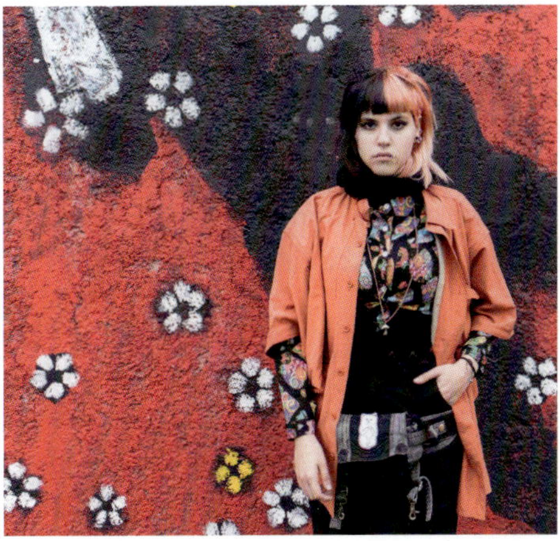

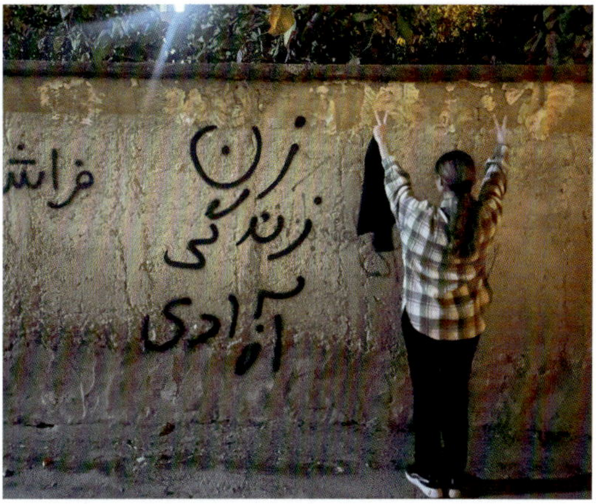

FIGS. 110A–B Left (A): Shiva Khademi, "Marzieh" from the *Smarties* series, 2019, Tehran. Courtesy of the artist; right (B): Shiva Khademi, woman gesturing victory in front of a wall animated with the slogan Woman, Art, Freedom, October 2022. Courtesy of the artist.

The photographic series, *Smarties*—the title evokes both the street-smart attitude of the girls and the name of Iran's favorite (brightly colored, M&M-like) sweet—was mainly shot between 2018 and 2019. Its imagery now appears strikingly prescient. During the uprising, Khademi took a new series of portraits. Now the girls (like many others) were dressed inconspicuously to blend in with the crowd and avoid attracting the attention of the police. This time, their backs were to the camera to prevent them from being identified. In contrast to the earlier vibrant and dreamlike backdrops, the new photos were set against walls animated with the slogan "Woman, Life, Freedom," with the girls gesturing V for victory, looking to the time they would remove their veils for good FIG. 110 B.

My intention here is not to suggest that the work of the artist who captured the extraordinary unveiled girls before the Woman, Life, Freedom uprising was more significant than the girls' own actions. Rather, I want to point out Khademi's dedication to properly document this phenomenon played a crucial role in preserving images and ideas and projecting them into the future. By embracing and amplifying the girls' fearless behavior, Khademi elevated their everyday life to the realm of art—to something that endures over time, possesses surplus value, and lives on into the future.

The mere act of documenting these figures, along with the grassroots engagement and direct interaction between the artist and her subjects, not only denotes an inventive art process but also connotes a form of daily resistance. This practice is not unique to Khademi, but is a common thread among numerous artists who have documented acts of resistance over many decades. What is different about Khademi's *Smarties* series is that the images were not circulated at the time of its conception, but only garnered significant attention following the death of Jina Mahsa Amini, when they were featured in a photo essay in a collection on the uprising published in London.[8] Images from the past appear to have found relevance in a delayed manner, almost as if they were ahead of their time, too futuristic for the moment when they were created.

The widely shared GIF of a young woman fervently shouting "Fuck you!" while standing through the sunroof of a car speeding along a Tehran highway, her hair tossed wildly by the wind, is another prime example of a previously overlooked or "hushed" image that gained traction during the uprising FIG. 111. Initially, many perceived this as an impromptu recording from the streets of Tehran during the peak of the protests. It was, in fact, a carefully crafted scene from the "underground" film *Critical Zone*, directed by Ali Ahmadzadeh. Though the film was shot entirely in Tehran over the course of 2019, its postproduction was not completed until 2023. Ahmadzadeh posted the powerful clip on his public Instagram account in anticipation of its release (incurring the wrath of the state authorities). Though not directly related to the uprising, the scene in question mirrored its core sentiments—the strong desire to openly challenge the oppressive rules imposed by the Islamic regime and the broader struggle for women's rights and freedom.

Faced with a lack of expert collaborators and a tight budget, Ahmadzadeh took on a multitude of roles in *Critical Zone*, his fourth

FIG. 111 Ali Ahmadzadeh, screenshot from *Critical Zone*. Courtesy of Ali Ahmadzadeh.

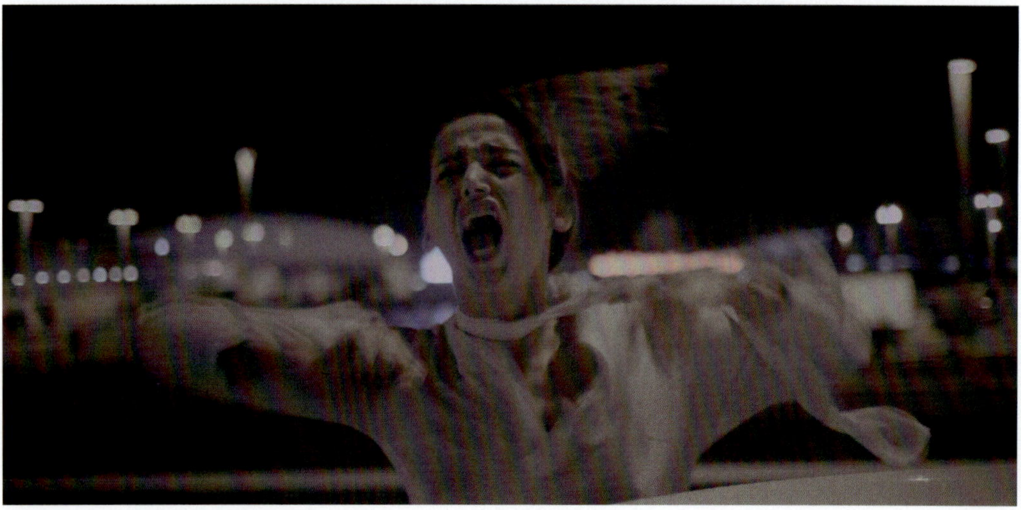

underground production.[9] Not only did he direct the film, he also handled most of the sound effects, montage, and editing. He even stepped in front of the camera, playing roles in scenes featuring anonymous gangs in pursuit of the drug dealer protagonist. Aside from the actors, all nonprofessionals who participated out of friendship with the director, the crew was minimal, consisting of a cameraman who was also a close friend of Ahmadzadeh, and a sound recorder. This close-knit team played a crucial role in the shooting of the film in Iran. For the final stages of production, they collaborated with colleagues in Portugal and Germany, drawing on international expertise to complete the project.

Ahmadzadeh, who is officially banned from filmmaking in Iran, described the challenges of making the film. His own apartment had to serve not only as a film set—the base for the intrepid protagonist—but as a makeshift production studio. Here, he dedicated countless days and nights to refining the film, aiming to achieve a production quality that could stand shoulder to shoulder with entries in international film festivals. Notably, *Critical Zone* utilized hidden cameras for shooting, reflecting its guerrilla filmmaking approach—and the fact that it lacked a filming permit. *Critical Zone* made its debut at the 76th Locarno Film Festival on August 10, 2023. Ahmadzadeh was unable to attend—prevented by the authorities from leaving Iran—but the film took the Gold Leopard in the main international competition.

The narrative unfolds around Amir, a drug dealer adept at traversing Tehran's intricate underworld and the different levels of its society. Amir's odyssey through the city is underscored by the voice of his GPS, guiding him through the mazelike streets and alerting him to potential dangers. The film's spatial dynamics and soundtrack reflect Ahmadzadeh's background in architecture and music. Given the obstacles to engaging a large cast and filming in crowded settings, architecture becomes a defining characteristic of his storytelling, offering a unique lens through which viewers experience the narrative.[10]

In the opening scene of *Critical Zone*, a camera glides through a long tunnel, following an ambulance as it descends underground. Ahmadzadeh explained that this journey serves as a metaphor for burrowing into the hidden layers of the city, probing its prevalent middle-class lifestyle and psyche.[11] The camera rests on a discreet door along the side of the tunnel, suggesting a clandestine space, perhaps a drug distribution hub, apparently operating with the complicity of the police. This shift in perspective is further heightened when the cargo of the ambulance is revealed: rather than a medic and a patient, we see two men surrounded by packages of drugs. This powerful imagery not only advances the storyline but accentuates the film's exploration of the unseen and unspoken elements of city life.

The film continues to track Amir as he navigates the city's diverse landscape to serve his eclectic clientele. The array of characters paints a vivid portrait of the complexity of Tehran's society. They include a solitary female traveler on a final journey out of the country, male sex workers in the shadow of the Karimkhan Bridge, a female dancer, residents of a senior living facility, and a psychologically troubled man. The subject of the clip that went viral is a flight attendant just off an international flight, who stands up, intoxicated, and yells out of the sunroof of Amir's taxi FIG. 111.

Each transaction in the film is not just an exchange of goods but a deeply emotional encounter between Amir and his buyers. The film's soundtrack plays a pivotal role in amplifying the emotional depth of these scenes. Ambient sounds capture the essence of the neighborhood—the mournful meowing of stray cats, the distant clamor of city residents arguing and cursing. The auditory backdrop takes us to the senior home, contrasting their peevish complaints with a scene where the dealer, assisted by an attractive young nurse, provides them with hash brownies. Ahmadzadeh recorded real-life sounds—including the groans and mutterings of his friends, both men and women—to add authenticity to the film's melancholic soundscape. The edited soundtracks were then repurposed for different segments of the film.

For Ahmadzadeh, this melancholic portrayal of the city at night, coupled with the depiction of a predominantly young cast of characters who rely on drugs to navigate their existence, reflects a broader commentary on life in Iran. He described a society scarred by unrealized dreams, and talked about the highly educated and talented young men and women he knows who spend endless days lying on their sofas, feeling they have no future. The stagnant reality of life for many of Iran's youth—the lack of opportunities—remains largely unseen in the news and even in films about Iran. In this respect we can say that *Critical Zone*, while possibly overstating drug use in Iran, brings to light the unfulfilled desires and overlooked creative energies of its people.

For Ahmadzadeh, the Woman, Life, Freedom movement is essentially the story of the marginalized and unheard voices in society, much like those depicted in his film. Rather than a sudden eruption, he sees the uprising as a development that had been brewing over many years: "Women have been engaged in this struggle for a significant duration, often persisting where men have faltered."[12] Ahmadzadeh confidently declares himself a feminist, acknowledging women's strength and resilience in the face of oppression. Like many others in Iran, he emphasizes the importance of an inclusive approach to feminism that acknowledges and addresses the complexities of gender roles and identities, championing the rights of all those who are marginalized by a rigid, binary system.[13] Despite the perception that men enjoy more rights and freedoms under Islamic rules and regulations, they too experience a sense of marginalization. The regime's "idealized image of a man is one who embodies a tough, macho persona—the primary provider for the family, seemingly indifferent to sensitive matters."[14] *Critical Zone* gives us a more multifaceted view of masculinity. The protagonist, Amir, is portrayed as an asexual man, mistakenly thought to be gay by many of his acquaintances. The film portrays his kindness toward transgender sex workers under the Karimkhan Bridge, where he offers them small bags of marijuana free of charge and they show their gratitude by kissing his hand. These sexual and social dynamics allow us a glimpse into the complex layers of societal challenges and transformation in Iran.

Amir is shown driving his taxi for much of the film. The driving scenes indicate going through a troubled, endlessly looping journey, but they also bring to mind other Iranian films in which the main actor combines the role of a taxi driver with that of a therapist, a listener—or a "prophet" or "messenger," to borrow from Ahmadzadeh himself. Those familiar with Abbas Kiarostami's *Ten* (2002) and Jafar Panahi's *Taxi* (2015) will recognize that in Tehran a taxi is often more than a simple means of transportation. It may be a sanctuary where passengers indulge in the luxury of listening to banned music; more frequently, it is a safe space for the open expression of disappointment, cynicism, or even conspiracy theories.

While the *Critical Zone*'s protagonist may not engage in extensive conversations with his passengers or "drug customers," he is portrayed as a deeply empathetic listener, attuned to their struggles and concerns. This silent, attentive demeanor adds a layer of authenticity to his character. Coupled with the film's unique soundscape, these nuanced interactions say much about the darker aspects of life in Iran—elements often censored in other films. Ahmadzadeh explains that, for various reasons, with censorship being the most significant, the previous generation of filmmakers often omitted from their portrayals of everyday life in Iran the struggles of the younger generation with issues such as sex, addiction, loneliness, and depression. Thus, instead of connecting the driving scenes to past films, Ahmadzadeh highlights the difference.

Returning to where we started the discussion of this film—the image of the shouting girl that became a symbol of the Woman, Life, Freedom movement even before the film's release—it is important to underscore the foresight of art that was already created before the uprising took place, but its dissemination was delayed. In line with

Baraitser's argument, introduced at the beginning of this section, I see these *deferred* artworks as *political actions* precisely because of their particular modes of temporal engagement; they signify calls for the emancipation of women that were in the process of becoming for some time. The act of exposing previously unseen images and footage from the past and integrating them into the present, making them look as if they belong to the here and now, blurring the lines between before and after, takes me to my next case study. Here, past, present, and future converge in a single exhibit: a monument erected in honor of women in the open and closed spaces of a gallery in northern Tehran.

PROJECTING HER NAME ONTO THE FUTURE

Call Me by My Name was shown between December 2023 and April 2024 at Risheh 29, a gallery in the upscale Elahiyyeh district of northern Tehran directed by entrepreneur Houman Deyhimi. Its focal point was a massive installation, thirteen by thirteen meters, and eight meters high, prominently positioned in the gallery's expansive 3,000-square-meter grounds. The gardens are a rare vestige of the former character of the neighborhood, which is now dominated by monotonous skyscrapers—a consequence of Tehran Municipality's environmentally destructive policies, combined with corruption, over the past three decades. The installation consisted of a series of large moving screens supported on a grid-like structure of scaffolding that mirrored the grid pattern of the residential tower blocks. Moreover, it seemed to be perfectly timed to coincide with the construction of yet more towers in the background. Many videos and photos from the exhibition (including the one that appears on the cover of this book) strikingly reflect this synchronicity, making a visual link between the scaffolding of the installation and the evolving urban landscape, with the cranes and scaffolding of the buildings under construction.

At first sight, the installation serves as a miniature representation of Tehran and a pointed critique of the city's misguided urban policies, but it is about more than that. Appearing in three phases (Memory, Remembering, Forgetting), it is a monument to the Woman, Life, Freedom uprising, created by artist and filmmaker Mohammad Parvizi (b. 1972) in collaboration with architect and set designer Mahsa Masoudi (b. 1989), actress Pantea Mehdinia (b. 1981), and visual media designer Pejman Zahab, along with other artists, photographers, musicians, and craftspeople. The moving screens display the silent expressions of Mehdinia as she responds to behind-the-scenes prompts from the director, Parvizi. In one segment, she reflects on her dreams

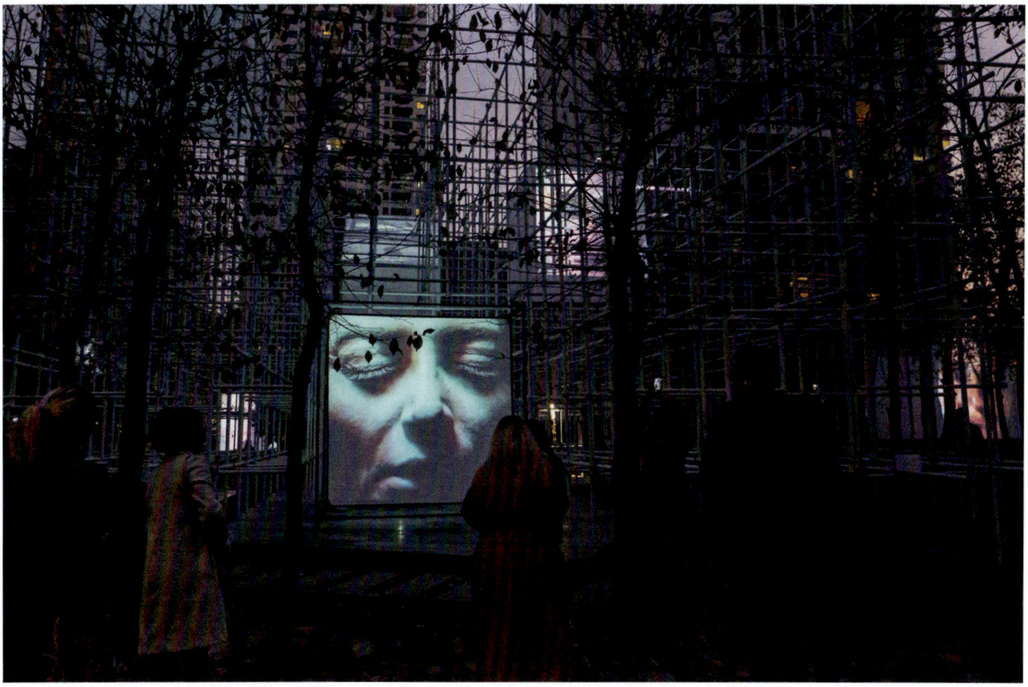

FIG. 112 Mohammad Parvizi et al, *Call Me by My Name*, December 2023–April 2024, Risheh 29 Gallery, Tehran. Courtesy of Mohammad Parvizi and the Deyhim Foundation. Photograph by Vida Mousavian.

for the future. In others, she conveys reactions to specific memories, such as her attempts to express herself or her love for someone, only to be stifled by the "regimes of suppression" prevalent in Iranian society. The expression of emotion is heightened by the meticulous application of makeup FIG. 112.

According to the official exhibition statement, "*Call Me by My Name* [...] deals with [re]claiming repressed names. It is the story of one of us wanting to recall oneself [amid] these ruins so that, if not obtaining one's life, one will at least find reason to hope."[15] In direct terms, the narrative centers on the way an authoritarian society strips women of their true identity, supplanting it with artificial one imposed from above. The woman's true identity—symbolized here by her name—gradually fades from memory. As it recedes, it takes with it the hope of change, of living life to the fullest. This concept is also relevant in the context of political movements. To truly honor these movements—and to perpetuate their potential—it is crucial to recall and celebrate their names.

The MCIG granted permission for the project on the condition that the actor's hair would not be visible on screen. To comply with this restriction, Parvizi mainly opted for shots focused only on the actor's facial expressions. However, there are also scenes where she is exposed to a strong wind, so her hair covers her entire face and the screen (see cover image of this book).

The actual movement of the screens produces an effect akin to the dolly zoom technique in filmmaking, where the zoom lens is adjusted while the camera moves toward or away from the subject so that the subject remains the same size within the frame. This technique leads to a continuous distortion of perspective where the background appears to change in dimensions relative to the subject, either growing in size and becoming dominant, or shrinking and giving way to the foreground. This undermining of normal visual perception often elicits strong emotional reactions.

The dolly zoom technique can also be seen as a tangible representation of the psychological process of recollection—an act of mentally zooming in and out to recapture past events through association. As the actor journeys through her memories, her facial expression transforms. When fully immersed in the past, her face turns pale, as if drained of life, consumed by the horror of the recalled event. Heightening the dramatic effect, the actor's portraits are occasionally disrupted by glitches, alluding to the numerous interruptions in women's personal and even collective memories of suppression and oppression under the authoritarian regime. These glitches also represent the moments of forgetfulness and forgiveness that have enabled the system to persist at the expense of the hopes and desires of the general population. As such, it is also possible to think of these memories as shared histories. Dominick LaCapra argues that memory does not stand in opposition to history, nor is it synonymous with it. He emphasizes that memory, despite its occasional unreliability, carries substantial importance as a source for historical understanding. Conversely, history provides a framework for the critical examination and validation of memory. These two components, history and memory, are interrelated; they complement one another.[16]

In the climactic moment of the exhibition, the actor's face is projected onto the floor beneath the installation. As she applies makeup, a trio consisting of one male and two female performance artists, donned in full black attire reminiscent of the attire worn by the female members of the morality police, ceaselessly try to erase her projected image. But no matter how persistent their washing and scrubbing, the woman's portrait endures, persistent and ineradicable. At this point in the exhibition, visitors have the opportunity to ascend the scaffolding via staircases integrated into its structure, allowing them to view the enormous images laid out on the floor below. A projector positioned atop the scaffolding casts stencil-like portraits of actress Pantea Mehdinia onto the ground. Simultaneously, a roller reminiscent of those used in traditional printing presses syncs with the projector, creating the illusion that the image is being printed onto the surface. As workers (or censors) continue to mop the floor, the projector intermittently projects whitewashed surface that represent the erased portions, only to reintroduce the actress's image, which seems to resurrect repeatedly. This effect, coupled with the movement of a large roller across the floor, suggests that the printing process is continuously re-creating the actress's face FIG. 113.

This printing technique echoes the practice of stenciling portraits of heroes on walls for their rapid execution and the striking, bold emphasis they bring to facial features. Across Tehran, such stenciled

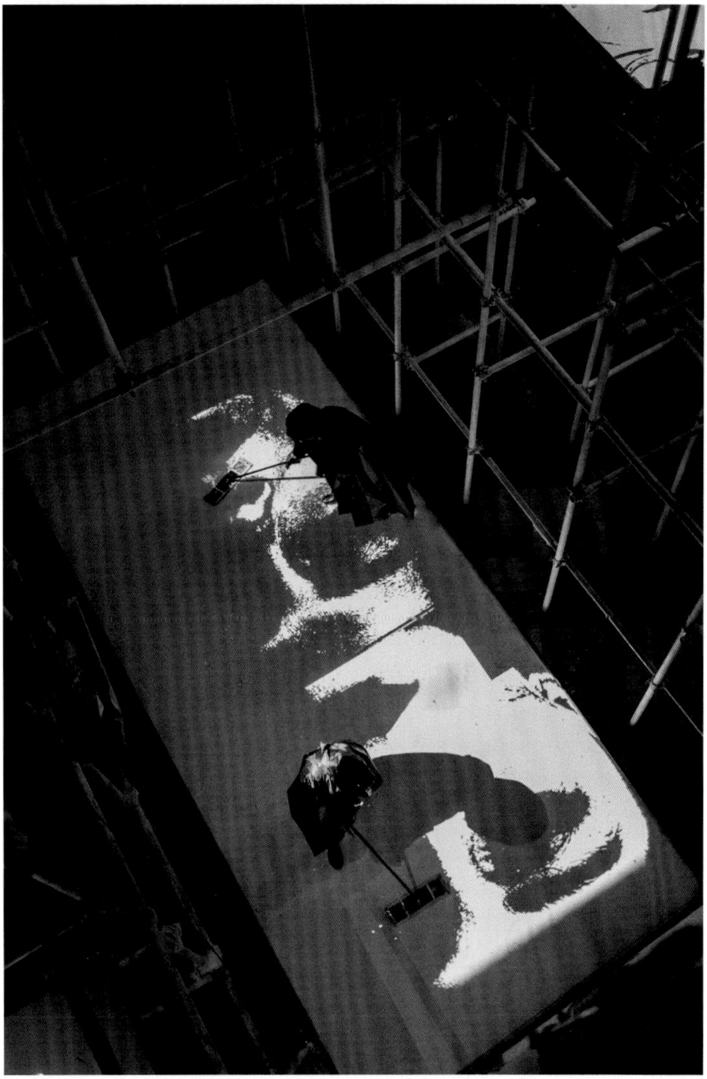

FIG. 113 Mohammad Parvizi et al., *Call Me by My Name*, April 2024, Risheh 29 Gallery, Tehran. Courtesy of Mohammad Parvizi and the Deyhim Foundation. Photograph by Vida Mousavian.

images of female revolutionaries (as opposed to older male ones) are now ubiquitous, including depictions of Vida Movahed on utility boxes, as depicted in Act One. Thus, the repeated appearance and disappearance of the actress's portrait closely align with the tradition of creating revolutionary imagery. However, in a transformative shift, the image that emerges and reemerges is now that of a woman, marking a departure from the traditionally male-dominated icons of martyrs and heroes. Despite being erased, the female portrait resiliently returns time and again, symbolizing a new form of revolutionary representation.

The suppression of the Woman, Life, Freedom uprising left behind a pervasive sense of emptiness: it felt as if all the sacrifices had been in vain. At the same time, the regime's monitoring of women's veiling became increasingly harsh—and less visible to the casual observer, as more covert CCTV cameras took over from the traditional morality police vans. The severity of punishments—fines, threats of imprisonment, or even lashings—was also ramped up. In this atmosphere of aggression, it was a fine response to create a monument that not only commemorates but also encapsulates a dystopian shared reality. The shared history and collective memory of the people is symbolized by the subtitle of the open exhibition *Rhizome*. The term was initially suggested by Mohammad Parvizi to delineate the garden, an environment suited for the scaffolding installation. However, Risheh 29 Gallery has permanently adopted the name Rhizome for this open space, embracing the concept fully.

"Rhizome" is a term used in philosophy to describe the interconnectedness and relationships among entities. Gilles Deleuze and Felix Guattari employ it to denote a network akin to dispersed root systems, characterized by their spreading underground without a specific direction, beginning, or end.[17] In *A Thousand Plateaus*, they contrast rhizomatic thinking with hierarchical thinking: the former involves planar thinking, while the latter depends on vertical, linear connections. Similarly, they view history and culture as an intertwined map with no distinct beginning or end, challenging traditional linear narratives in favor of a fluid, nomadic pattern of growth and dissemination.

This concept is exemplified by the *Call Me by My Name* installation. Even the initial sketches (made by architect Mahsa Masoudi) have a rhizomatic character FIG. 114. The exhibition celebrates a woman entangled in a complex web, addressing not just the present but also the past and the future. It challenges the linear perception of time and space, adopting a cyclical approach to contemplate various themes:

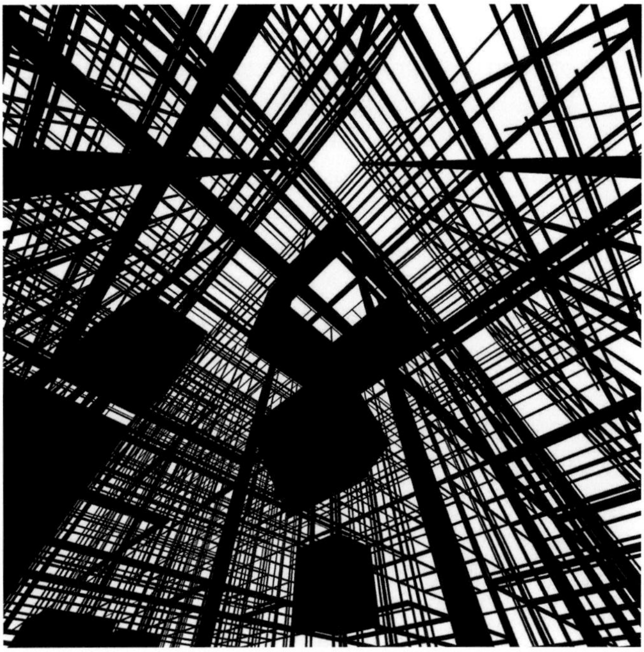

FIG. 114 Rendering by Mahsa Masoudi for the outdoor segment of the exhibition *Call Me by My Name*. Courtesy of Mahsa Masoudi.

women; the Woman, Life, Freedom movement; the physicality of the city; and the politics of public spaces. The rhizomatic approach allows for a more comprehensive and interconnected understanding of these subjects.

The idea that we are all interconnected—that one person's actions are linked to all others, and that one structure represents a microcosm of the city—embodies the concept of a rhizome as defined by Deleuze and Guattari. So, too, does the integration, within the entire ensemble, of various media platforms—film, video art, architecture, and music (with saxophone played as visitors entered on Thursdays and Fridays). The installation was itself a powerful philosophical representation of connection and interrelation, but the experience was further enhanced by the two-dimensional grids that viewers were invited to explore inside the gallery, and by the miniature versions of the exhibit that could be seen through a series of holes around the perimeter of the garden. This intimate viewing method was designed to bridge the personal and the collective.

Looking up at the gridded scaffolding of the garden installation FIG. 114, viewers saw screens displaying the actor's face, silently crying or shouting. Simultaneously, they became aware of the gridded backdrop of the tall buildings that overshadow the garden. Set against the lush greenery of the gallery's garden, these repetitive patterns, a metaphor for a system within a system, served as poignant reminders of Tehran's current state—a city in mourning of its losses, its trees, its dreams, its women—all, unfortunately, ground down by the weight of oppressive prisonlike systems (the scaffolding evoking the regime's preferred means of capital punishment).

This unique spatial experience was devised by the architect Mahsa Masoudi, whose earlier involvement with Iran's avant-garde experimental theatre group Av extended from set design to acting.[18] For Masoudi, the project encapsulated the entire Woman, Life, Freedom movement. As an architect, she views everything through the lens of the city, a place where dreams and disappointments play out at both personal and collective levels.[19] Masoudi further articulated how the exhibition invited visitors into a unique spatial experience "akin to the awe and discovery felt when wandering through historical sites like the Shah or the Sheikh Lotfollah mosques in Isfahan."[20] In this exhibition, Masoudi added,

> visitors are presented with the opportunity to explore the artwork from various vantage points, even climbing the scaffolding to gain an elevated perspective. They are encouraged to look in all directions, uncovering unexpected spaces and perspectives, much like the comprehensive exploration required to fully appreciate historic architectural wonders of Iran.[21]

Parvizi's expertise as a filmmaker enriched this spatial experience, introducing cinematic dynamics where the viewer at times becomes part of the scene, akin to a camera being acknowledged by its subject. This interaction is highlighted by instances "where the gaze of Pantea Mehdinia, the main protagonist of the exhibition, follows the viewer, inverting the conventional dynamics of surveillance."[22] Masoudi further reflected on this unsettling yet profound reversal, where, "instead of being the objects of surveillance, Mehdinia surveils the viewers and passersby, challenging traditional power dynamics and inviting a contemplation on visibility and control."[23] This multifaceted approach to viewing, with its layers of engagement and perspective shifts, is the exhibition's core message, highlighting the omnipresence and observant role of women in this space.

But past and current conditions are not what this exhibition emphasized. What captivated me most about it was its focus on the future, hinting at a cityscape where women, depicted larger than life, will play a central role. However, this woman still lacks a voice and is portrayed in a state of limbo, caught between being and nonbeing. The glitches on the screen cause her image to blur and appear jagged, almost artificial, conjuring images akin to those found in *Blade*

Runner (1982), in which Ridley Scott masterfully blended the visual style of film noir with a futuristic backdrop to make the iconic sci-fi detective story. In *Blade Runner*, women are depicted in larger-than-life forms on the sides of buildings, with a technologically advanced city unfolding in the background. There is also a notable parallel between Parvizi's behind-the-scenes questioning of Mehdinia and the celebrated close-up shot of Rachael (Mary Sean Young) as she is interrogated by Deckard (Harrison Ford) to determine whether she is a replicant. In both scenes, the camera consistently zooms in on their facial expressions, capturing their efforts to remember. This raises the question whether their memories are artificially implanted or derived from real experience. The glitches that sporadically distort Mehdinia's face further suggest the possibility that she might not be a real person, but rather a representative, state-created figure—a compliant woman whose past is merely a fabricated narrative shaped by an authoritarian "Big Brother." These scenes come to mind when viewing Parvizi's installation in northern Tehran. Indeed, while a temporary installation, Parvizi's work evokes the dynamism of a futuristic film.[24] Perhaps we can think of this installation as a scene in the far future, depicting an artificially made woman who tries to process the memories implanted in her brain from a time previous to the Woman, Life, Freedom uprising—an era when the state molded women as artificial proxies embodying a specific ideology. This interpretation might seem a bit of a stretch, yet it is somewhat fitting. When contemplating the future of the movement, it is crucial to imagine scenarios where state ideology has diminished to the point where it is nothing more than a distant "implanted" memory. This reading, facilitated by artwork, transcends the imaginary realms of science fiction. It offers a means to overcome both internal and external oppression, highlighting the vital role of women (or the oppressed, more generally) in shaping the future and the importance of recovering their often-overlooked pasts.[25] Above all, the installation prompts us to contemplate ethical questions regarding our authentic selves. It makes us wonder: are we living as our genuine selves, or are our identities shaped and dictated by the state? (*Blade Runner*, too, questions the authenticity of the human self, challenging the binaries between human and nonhuman, and illustrating that the "other" is essential for defining the "self.")[26]

A number of artists in Iran have been critical of the cinematic flair and grand scale of *Call Me by My Name*, seeing this kind of aesthetic enhancement as catering primarily to the upper-class art lovers rather than speaking to the sacrifices made by the defenseless young women who were brutalized by the police. Offering a different outlook,

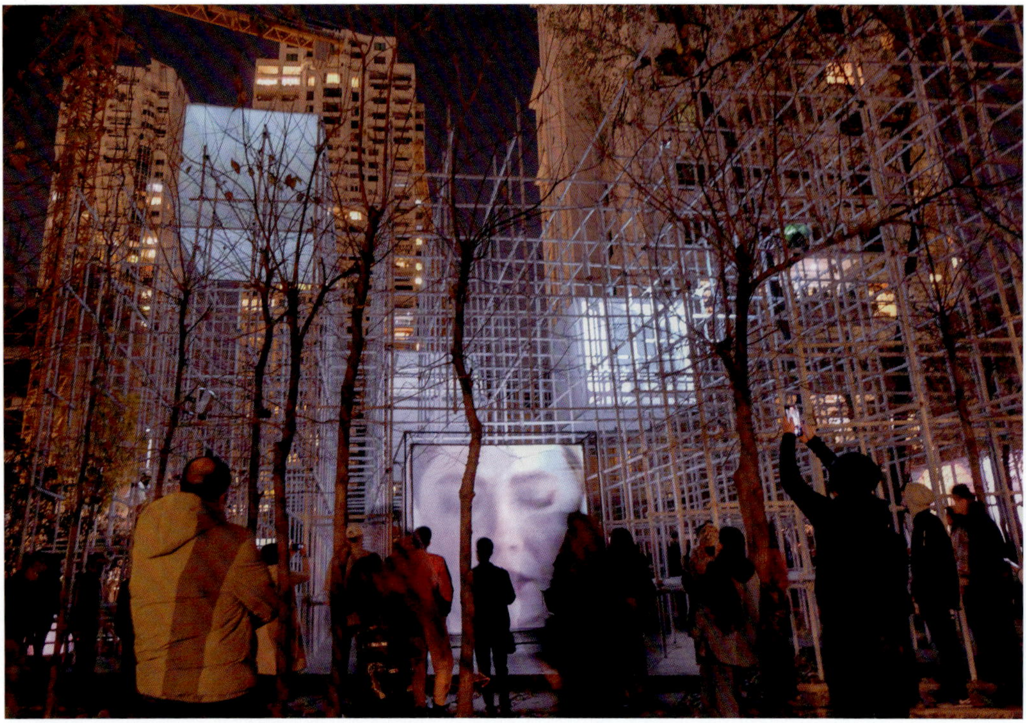

FIGS. 115A–B. Left: *Call Me by My Name* as viewed by visitors. Right: *Call Me by My Name* as seen from the street. Note the defaced slogans from the Woman, Life, Freedom uprising. Photograph courtesy of Mahsa Masoudi.

Masoudi highlighted how the exhibition seamlessly integrated into the urban environment, providing a sanctuary amid the bustling cityscape.

> Since its inauguration, the space has welcomed those seeking refuge, including dog owners navigating the complexities of local regulations. The exhibition area has evolved into a liberated zone, free from surveillance, dress codes, and entry fees, recalling the unregulated spaces of Tehran before its massive reconstruction and regulation by the government in the 1990s, and serving as a haven from the scrutinizing gaze of authority. This unique public space, maintained through an understanding with the municipality, operates beyond the reach of conventional oversight, embodying a rare oasis of freedom in the urban landscape. Moreover, the towering scaffoldings, some reaching heights of up to eight meters, are not only visible within the Risheh 29 complex but also from the surrounding streets, integrating the exhibit into the cityscape.[27] FIGS. 115A–B

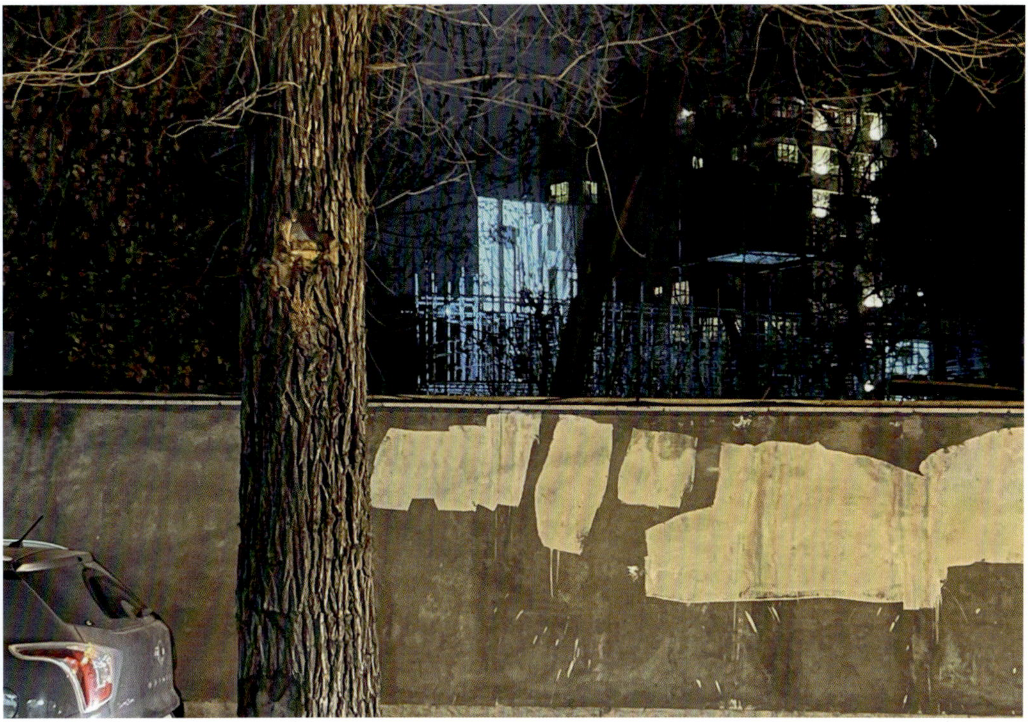

Some argue that the installation is too chic for a movement that unfolded on the gritty streets. However, Parvizi holds a different perspective, seeing in the movement an elegance, beauty, and all-encompassing nature that needs to be commemorated. While fundamentally feminist, this movement also stands for the rights of men and women (from all social classes), ethnic minorities, and different shades of gender and sexuality in Iran. For Parvizi, the demonstrations—which he also engaged with—are the most direct means to express raw emotions: in other words, to protest. While acknowledging that the collective spirit of the uprising was captured by the spontaneous street art that surfaced during the uprising, such as dyeing fountains red or covering the CCTV cameras on trains with sanitary pads, he believes that the artist must play a different role now that the phase of street protests is over. To ensure that the essence of the movement does not fade, but continues to thrive in collective memory, it is necessary to create art that is monumental, even if shrouded in opaqueness to secure permission from the MCIG. Art, he says, requires space and time for reflection to make works that are thoughtful and skillful, as opposed to hastily crafted responses. Parvizi's viewpoint may differ from the de-aestheticized approaches of some of the artists discussed in this text or in other reports on the art of the Woman, Life, Freedom uprising. Nevertheless, I see merit in it.

In fact, one reason I selected an image from this exhibition for the book cover was the intriguing tensions surrounding the artwork. I believe that *Call Me by My Name*, with its rich layers of meaning and varied interpretations, aptly encapsulates the complex facets of the Woman, Life, Freedom movement, which remain deeply resonant. In my view, *Call Me by My Name* is a Gesamtkunstwerk of activist art. Additionally, drawing inspiration from Boris Groys, I consider this work as one that both aesthetically enhances Tehran and actively and critically engages with it. To borrow from Groys:

> One can aestheticize the world—and at the same time act within it. In fact, total aestheticization does not block political action; it enhances it. Total aestheticization means that we see the current status quo as already dead, already abolished. [...] [T]otal aestheticization [...] does not preclude political action; it creates an ultimate horizon for successful political action [...].[28]

Seeing the exhibition as an opportunity to address a "historical wound" (*zakhm-e tarikhi*), Parvizi and his colleagues devoted considerable time and energy to perfecting the installation, working outdoors in often cold weather over a period of several months.[29] Their dedication was motivated by their belief, as Parvizi puts it, that "our ethical obligation extends beyond merely remembering important events by erecting monuments; we should create interactive memorials that not only engage the audience intellectually but also serve as tools for collective therapy and healing."[30] The exhibition was accompanied by a program of eight lectures by distinguished art historians and critics, each of whom delved into facets of memory and history, connecting these themes to diverse elements of culture and the lived experiences of Iranians. Over its five-month duration, *Call Me by My Name* attracted over four thousand visitors, many of whom were deeply moved by it, responding with both tears and dance. At an event in early January 2023, for example, one visitor stood before a screen for a long time, thoughtfully brushing her hair while seeming to connect with the portrait of the emotionally expressive actor in front of her. Meanwhile, another unveiled attendee performed a series of bodily movements that resonated with the emotions conveyed by the actor's face on the screen. The reactions of audiences were intuitive; they didn't feel the need to read the exhibition text or to seek explanations from the artists. The silent expressions of the actor conveyed everything without words. One of the speakers in the lecture series drew attention to the way the exhibition mirrored the state of limbo, or "purgatory," that Iranians find themselves in following the uprising: "Here, everything is in a constant state of change, with the visitors' bodies moving around the installations in ways that are ritualistic, as if they are going through a rite of passage."[31]

WOMAN, LIFE, FREEDOM AS HYPERSTITION

While numerous artworks and films have presented the Woman, Life, Freedom uprising as a contemporary phenomenon, others have explicitly envisioned it as an audacious expression of ambition for the future. Among them is Erfan Ghiasi (b. 1989), a multimedia artist and curator whose *Asymmetrical Warfare* is featured earlier in this book (see Act Three). At the height of the protests, Ghiasi was struck by the realization that, in stark contrast to previous uprisings such as the Green Movement, Woman, Life, Freedom sought not merely to reform the system but to start anew. In response, Ghiasi embarked on a unique project for his solo exhibition at Tehran's O Gallery, a futuristic artwork that explores the innovative concept of "hyperstition," blending elements of reality and fantasy.

The core idea behind hyperstition is that if a fictional narrative or concept becomes deeply embedded in the collective consciousness—if enough people believe in or engage with it—then it can start to bring about actual change, shaping real-world events and behaviors in tangible ways. Hyperstition is not just about the power of belief; it also deals with the feedback loop between fiction and reality. Fictional concepts can generate real-world effects, which in turn can feed back into the narrative, evolving and reinforcing it FIG. 116. Drawing from the concept of hyperstition, Ghiasi's project encourages audiences to contemplate Iran's present sociopolitical state and imagine its future,

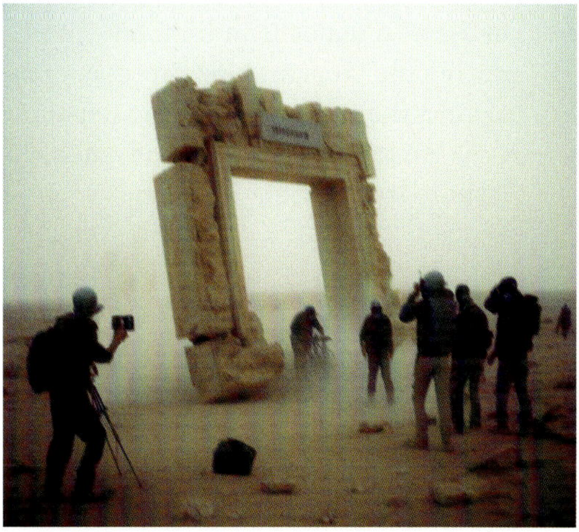

FIG. 116 Erfan Ghiasi, *A Deep, Big, and Weird Research on the Historical Objects of Future Civilizations*, 2023, O Gallery, Tehran. Courtesy of the artist.

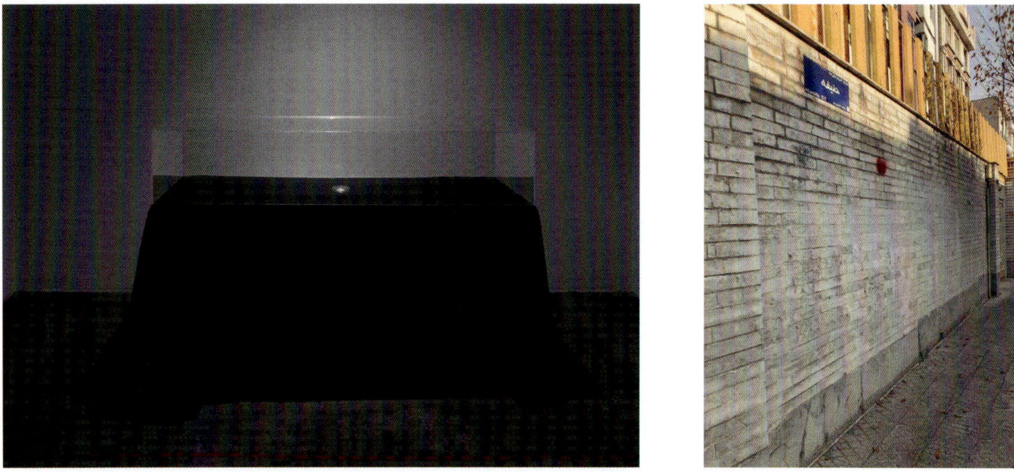

FIGS. 117A–B. Left (A): Erfan Ghiasi, a portion of *A Deep, Big, and Weird Research on the Historical Objects of Future Civilizations*, 2023, O Gallery, Tehran. Courtesy of the artist. Right (B): The wall of Erfan Ghiasi's home, where the Woman, Life, Freedom graffiti was erased by authorities.

but through a journey into the past—and specifically into the ancient Persian city of Susa, where a team of Iranian archaeologists discover a hitherto unknown teleportal gate. The team is led by one Dr. Faramarz Keyhani (the name translates as "Dr. Beyond the Boundaries of the Cosmos"), a cyborg-like character synthesizing Ghiasi's persona with AI technology. The absurdist title of the project, *A Deep, Big, and Weird Research on the Historical Objects of Future Civilizations, 2023*, is a nod to the avant-garde, prerevolutionary work of the esteemed Iranian playwright Abbas Nalbandian.[32]

Far from an artistic jest, this is a thought-provoking mind game that aims to stretch the boundaries of the viewer's imagination as well as their capacity to engage with deeply sensitive subjects. The glory of the ancient Persian Empire is a long-standing foundation of the nationalist dialogue in Iran. But it has also been invoked—notably, during the Woman, Life, Freedom protests—as a form of resistance against the rule of the Islamic Republic.

An invented article about the surprising discovery of another layer to Iran's history tells us:

> In late 2022, an ensemble of archaeologists, guided by the fictional Dr. Faramarz Keyhani, made an extraordinary discovery in Susa: a mysterious teleportal gate, suggesting a link to a future Iranian civilization. This gate, defying conventional notions of time and space, was unearthed during nocturnal explorations. [...] Using carbon-14 dating, it was determined to originate from a future civilization. This pivotal finding led to a wider search

> across Iran, unveiling similar gates in locations such as Qom, the Caspian Sea, and the Persian Gulf. Each discovery alludes to a future civilization. [...] Dr. Keyhani, as imagined by Ghiasi, expresses excitement, stating, 'We've encountered gates that offer insights into different eras and dimensions, leading us to confront an unknown future. These artifacts from the future invite us to ponder the world we aspire to shape.'[33]

In the gallery, each stone portal was artfully conjured using AI software. The images of the gateways—printed in a style that echoes the look of C-type prints from the predigital era—were carefully positioned next to their respective locations on a map of Iran. When visitors scanned a QR code alongside the image, they heard audio tracks narrating the story of Dr. Keyhani, as if told by the character himself. A professional voice actor delivered the lines with meticulous precision, reading from texts composed by the artist after a thorough study of the standard descriptive style used by UNESCO to document its designated World Heritage Sites. The artist's attention to detail lent an air of authenticity and scholarly depth to the fictional narrative, and the innovative blend of visual and auditory elements enriched the viewer's experience, immersing them in the imagined history of these AI-generated gateways.

One striking exhibit purported to show the remnants of a portal that had undergone carbon-14 dating analysis, indicating, intriguingly, that these objects did not belong to the past but had originated from a point 50,000 years into the future. The carefully arranged display focused on a transparent container of powdered material, which was placed on a pedestal and preserved under a glass case, giving it a sense of primary importance. FIG. 117 A Naturally, the powdered substance had no connection whatsoever to the material of the gateways. Instead, it had a personal origin, coming from the walls of the artist's own home, where an anonymous graffiti artist had inscribed the Woman, Life, Freedom motto in red paint. The house is located in the historic neighborhood of Tehran Pars, and its external walls are made of durable white granite, so the motto proved difficult for the police to erase in the normal way. Their solution was to use a stone carving machine to erase the words. When they were done with their destruction, Ghiasi gathered the stone powder that had dropped onto the sidewalk below FIG. 117. The incorporation of this element into the show symbolically bridged past actions with future aspirations.

While the exhibition highlighted the deep sense of pride in the country's cultural heritage, emphasizing the unique role this phenomenon plays in the Iranian collective consciousness, it did not simply glorify the past. What was captivating about it was the way it challenged the audience, seeming to present the Woman, Life, Freedom movement as a portal that could either lead them to a better future or cause them to regress into a petrified past, depending on how they chose to channel their emotions. I borrow this notion of petrification in the sense that Franz Fanon used it when he implied that in a colonial world the colonized people are rendered ontologically akin to inanimate objects, stripped of their dynamism and trapped, like stones, in a state of enforced stagnation and "zone of nonbeing."[34] Acknowledging this potential for stasis, the exhibition does not cast the movement in a purely optimistic light, but provokes a deeper contemplation of the attachments and values Iranians hold dear when envisioning their future via certain events.

In a personal conversation, Ghiasi talked about how he views the Woman, Life, Freedom movement as an invitation to explore a different time and space, transcending the current moment. During the uprising, he saw how people were envisioning their future through countless self-created thresholds. It was as if beams of light, symbolizing these thresholds, were emanating from every city and region, each with its distinct culture, language, and traditions. The various ethnic groups in Iran—among them, Kurds, Fars, Lurs, and Baluchis—were all embracing the possibility for change, and together contributing to diverse and hopeful futures. In the same spirit, the portals in the exhibition invite people to look through them and to speculate on what lies ahead, on the other side of the threshold FIG. 116. They challenge Iranians' perception of the future, and at the same time mirror the diverse and forward-looking aspirations of the Iranian people. They invite reflection: what does it mean for a nation to strive to transcend its current time and space? How significant is the desire to imagine a collective future, one that is ideal and inclusive for everyone?

ENVISIONING THE FUTURE OF EVIN PRISON

Erfan Ghiasi was also behind an urban art project that extended from Tehran to Ahvaz in the south of the country in the spring of 2023. Among the participants was artist Bahar Sabet (b. 1988), who chose as the site of her installation a spot very close to her home: the mountains on the edge of Tehran that offer a commanding view of the notorious Evin Prison, the regime's main site for holding political prisoners—human rights defenders, journalists, activists, and dual nationals. Sabet and her family see the prison every day from the window of their apartment. At any time, it is a hateful sight, but it began to weigh even more heavily on the artist's mind in October 2022, following a series of

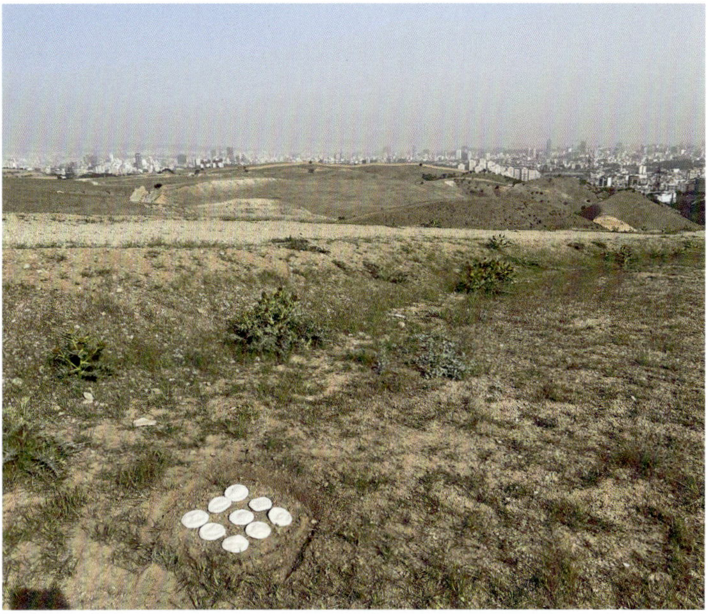

FIG. 118 Bahar Sabet, installation outside Evin Prison, 2023. Courtesy of the artist.

deadly incidents—a massive fire, explosions, and unlawful assaults by the security forces—over a period of just forty-eight hours. Eight were killed and sixty-one injured in the fire, which the government's media center claimed was started by clashes among prisoners. Its actual cause remains obscure to this day.[35]

Sabet dreams of a day when Evin prison is transformed from a place of suffering into a joyful gathering spot where people come together in freedom. She wants to be able to open the window of her apartment and see something beautiful. To symbolize this hope for the future, her project aims to capture and preserve the ephemeral beauty of the Mediterranean redbuds that flower for just a few weeks in April in the dry mountains around the prison. Sabet adapts an age-old technique known as *kangineh*, where fruits like grapes are stored in sealed boxes made from adobe to keep them fresh into the winter months. The purple flowers, stored in containers made of straw and mud, form the center of her installation, which is located in a place frequented by serious hikers, but rarely visited by casual passersby, partly due to its proximity to Evin. This secluded setting adds a layer of solitude and contemplation to her artistic expression FIG. 118.

Sabet's decision to create this ephemeral installation reflects her longing to envision Iran in a new light. It symbolizes her hope for a future where happiness is not criminalized, and where "a piece of cloth" (hijab) no longer dictates the moral standing of women.[36] This hope is kept fresh along with the redbuds in the sealed containers made of straw and mud—deferred until the day it becomes reality.

Coda

On December 23, 2023, *Vice News* released a video report by journalist Isobel Yeung, who had traveled to Iran with permission from the authorities—though that did not prevent her and her crew from being surveilled and intimidated from the moment they entered the country. The report, which asks "What happened to Iran's women-led uprising?," makes for dispiriting viewing. Yeung secured an interview with Ensieh Khazali, vice president for women and family affairs in the Raisi government, who denied flat out that women have no freedom of choice in public: mandatory hijab was not an ideology, she maintained, just a law. Khazali also refuted the fact that Jina Mahsa Amini was killed by beating. In the report, Yeung described the constant struggle against oppression, referring to Yalda Moaiery, a photographer who has been documenting the arrest and interrogation of girls by the morality police for sixteen years now, and has repeatedly been arrested for her activism. But she also looked at how the regime is perpetuating this oppression by indoctrinating young children with its ideology. All in all, the report painted a bleak picture of the despairing atmosphere of everyday life in Iran.[1]

However, an essay published a few weeks later in *Radio Zamaneh*, an Amsterdam-based Persian-language news outlet, offered a different perspective.[2] Somayyeh Dibajizadegan described how art galleries in Tehran have emerged as sanctuaries for women who choose not to wear the hijab. The women themselves express the sense of freedom they feel inside the galleries, in stark contrast to the constant surveillance outside. These galleries, which are often situated in areas heavily policed for hijab compliance, have emerged as spaces for open dialogue and community building. They can be seen as emblematic of the brighter side of life in Tehran and other cities, offering hope and a platform for resistance and strategic action against the forces of oppression.

From January 19 to February 13, 2024, Tehran's prominent Etemad Gallery showcased a new collection of paintings by Shohreh Mehran. Born in 1957, Mehran grew up during the shah's rule and reached adulthood just as the regime change was unfolding. Her generation witnessed the immediate aftereffects of the Iranian Revolution—the curtailing of personal freedoms, the devastation of the Iran–Iraq War from 1980 to 1988, and the social and political turmoil that followed. Particularly for women like Mehran, the early 1980s were a time of shrinking educational and career opportunities, as universities closed for ideological restructuring under the Islamic Republic's own version of a cultural revolution.

Mehran's art has consistently sought to capture the essence of Tehran and its inhabitants. Her early projects portrayed the monumental murals of those martyred or wounded in the revolution alongside the towering architecture of the capital. Later paintings capture schoolgirls clad in the traditional uniform of manteaus (trench coats) and *maghnaehs*, head coverings designed to encase the head, forehead, chin, and chest in a display of propriety. The girls are shown strolling through quintessential streets of Tehran, sometimes against a backdrop of walls emblazoned with revolutionary slogans. The comprehensive coverage provided by the head coverings and trench coats, among other obligatory garments designed to conceal the body, sparked Mehran's imagination. In her works about the schoolgirls, their faces "are generally out of frame; when they are shown, they are covered or shy away."[3] Their *maghnaehs* appear to flutter in the breeze, momentarily veiling their faces. "The presence of fabric has always been palpable, overwhelming, in the bustling streets of Tehran," Mehran told me.[4] In her latest work, however, the depiction of girls has evolved. Their heavy traditional attire has given way to the more relaxed, post–Woman, Life, Freedom uprising fashion, featuring loose pants and white shirts. These young figures are no longer framed against the backdrop of Tehran's streets, but are set on stark white canvases. "The streets have disappeared," Mehran explained. "What's important now are the girls who fill these spaces every day. When you step outside, you see their presence, their courage—it's all about these fearless young women now; nothing else compares."[5]

The new series, featured at Etemad Gallery, captures the girls in various poses that mirror the imagery prevalent on social media during the uprising: girls tying their hair back, preparing to join the protests; girls caught in midair, possibly at the moment they encounter paintballs or police batons FIG. 119; girls knocked down but preparing to get up again, adjusting their bodies on the sidewalk and using one arm for support as they rise to their feet. Everything seems suspended, as if time has frozen at the climax of the revolution. Mehran added,

> the essence of the uprising is captured in these bodies and their defiant stances; I generally prefer not to surround my paintings with too many words. This sentiment resonates with all of us; the feeling that the uprising persists, never diminishing, and these artworks strive to encapsulate that.[6]

The exhibition catalog, under the rubric *Why Hast Thou Suddenly Cast Away Thy Veil?*, tells us that Mehran

> used to veil and hide the corners of Tehran, so that we would imagine what we could not see, and thus see it, through the prism of imagination, more sharply. This time, however, the shrouds are lifted. The subject, slipping yet assertive, is now everything in the frame. It is the city that has vanished. What has our city done to us to deserve this erasure?[7]

Like many catalog essays in Iran, this one raises more questions than it answers. However, its underlying message is unmistakable.

Indeed, as Mehran explained to me, the staging of the exhibition at Etemad Gallery reflects Tehran's spirit of defiance. Despite the risk that the authorities might shut the gallery down, given the sensitive nature of the subjects, the decision was made to remove only one painting that depicted a revolutionary girl tying her dyed hair, preparing to join a demonstration—an image closely associated with Hadis Najafi, who was shot dead by the police while protesting.

The contribution of the visual arts to a new wave of societal transformation in Iran was also addressed by artist and former professor Shahnaz Zahtab in a January 2024 podcast with the Tehran-based editorial staff of the journal *Nahib*.[8] Zahtab recounted her history of engagement with the evolving art scenes during President Khatami's reformist era, but emphasized there had been an even more profound shift following the Woman, Life, Freedom uprising. "It's as if I am in a different country," she said, reflecting on her visits to recent exhibition openings (see FIG. 102 for another relevant example of bold and brave art displayed after the uprising).

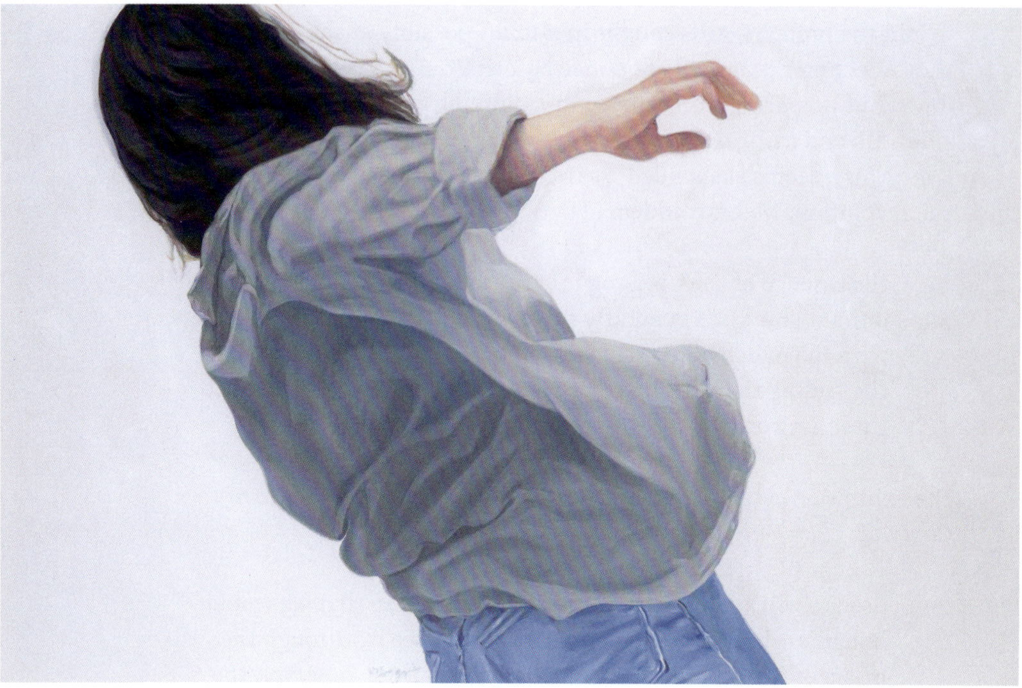

FIG. 119 Shohreh Mehran, *Untitled #3*, oil on canvas, 150 × 100 cm, 2023. Courtesy of the artist.

This enthusiasm is mirrored across various creative industries. Faezeh Bakhti (b. 1981) gained widespread attention after designing the dress actor Lily Farhadpour wore for the awards ceremony at the 74th Berlin International Film Festival in February 2024. Farhadpour, the star of *My Favourite Cake*, was representing the film's cowriters and codirectors, Maryam Moghadam and Behtash Sanaeeha, who had been banned from traveling and faced legal threats for their groundbreaking work—the story of an older woman's quest for freedom under a regime that severely restricts women's rights. Among the first cinematic instances of this kind in the Islamic Republic, the film shows women without hijabs. Much like the film, the dress Bakhti designed for Farhadpour eschews the veil and other restrictive elements that the regime prescribes for film crews attending international festivals.

Bakhti herself has a deep understanding of the struggle for personal freedom: coming from a religious family, she had to battle for her right to choose how she dressed in her teenage years.[9] At the height of the uprising, she channeled this understanding into creativity, reimagining a newly designed collection of headscarves as flowing, comfortable dresses.[10] In some photographs showing this restyling, the scarves are swept away from the model Sogand's head, symbolizing freedom FIG. 120. In tandem, Bakhti crafted a Woman, Life, Freedom–themed jewelry line, which was sold across Tehran until the authorities threatened the shops with closure if they persisted in stocking Bakhti's expressive creations FIG. 121.

Women, like Bakhti, who choose to forgo the veil in public become targets of the morality police. They may be tackled directly on the street, but even more disturbing, in Bakhti's view—as an indication of the all-pervasive nature of the intrusion of the state into private lives—are the citations mailed to individuals' homes after they have been caught on CCTV driving without a veil. The fines for this infraction are exorbitant, equivalent to a significant portion of the average monthly earnings. "What should we do?" is a question Bakhti frequently ponders.[11] She sees herself as an activist designer, and believes that those involved in women's fashion have the responsibility to devise counterstrategies that will enable women to navigate their daily lives without a veil, challenging the constraints imposed by the morality police, but without incurring punishment. Among her ideas for "resistance clothing" is a white hood (perhaps inspired by those worn in *The Handmaid's Tale*), which could be discreetly integrated into the car seat or the collar of a dress or shirt, ready to swiftly unfold and cover the head in sensitive

FIGS. 120–121 Designs by Faezeh Bakhti. Left: Transforming scarves into elegant dresses. Right: Necklace in a pseudo-silver finish featuring the map of Iran, adorned with the inscription "Woman, Life, Freedom." Images provided by the designer.

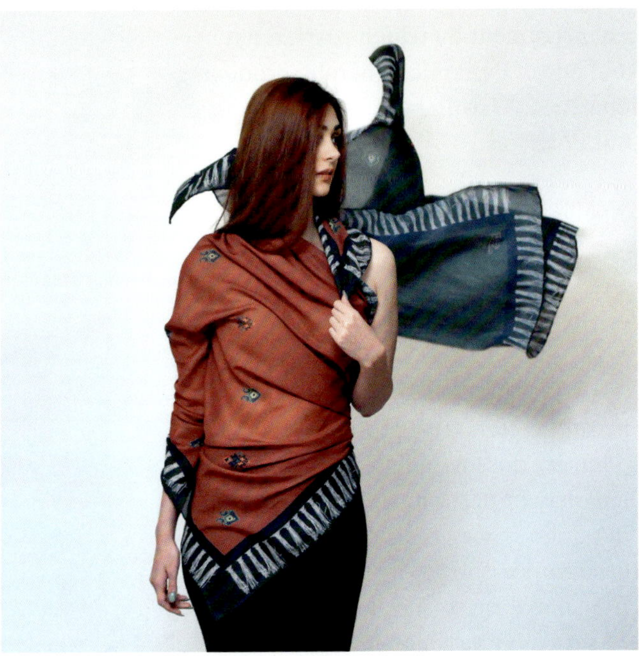

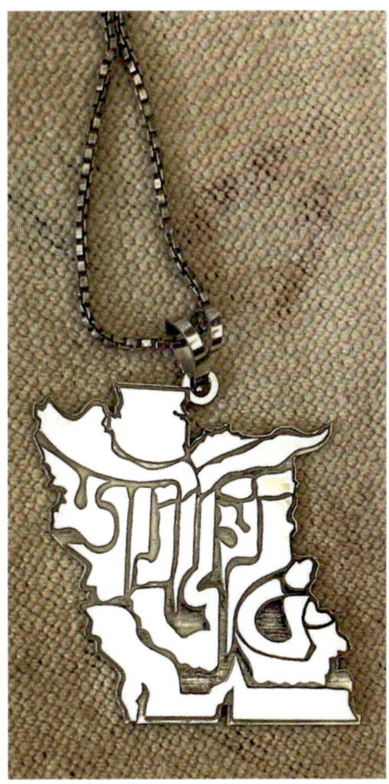

situations (such as driving on busy roads or walking near police stations or any public space bristling with CCTV cameras). A form of headgear that covered the hair, but did not in any way resemble the traditional veil, scarf, or shawl, would, Bakhti explained, stand as a symbol of defiance against the state authorities while also ensuring women's safety. Such innovative acts of resistance through art and design, whether they are ongoing projects or still in the conceptual phase, signal that Woman, Life, Freedom is far from over. For Iranian artists like Bakhti, this is merely the beginning of a broader movement.

On April 13, 2024, coinciding with Iran's first direct strike on Israel, state authorities launched the "Noor" (Light) campaign. While morality police enforce "proper hijab," Noor specifically targets businesses defying hijab laws and women who refuse to wear the hijab.[12] Despite the continued violent suppression of the Woman, Life, Freedom movement—with hundreds of reported executions and thousands of arrests—the Iranian people bravely persist in their demands for freedom.[13] What I have set out to show with this book is how creative agents are at the forefront of this movement for change. On the one hand, galleries and other art spaces are creating opportunities for resistance; on the other, political and activist art is constantly repositioning and reinventing itself to fight the system. Judith Butler has argued that norms of gender are discursively constructed and reinforced through repeated performance. This repetition acts as the main instrument by which patriarchal systems naturalize heterosexual power dynamics, thereby producing the illusion of static gender identities. Warning that repetition never fully accomplishes identity, Butler writes,

> If heterosexuality is compelled to repeat itself in order to establish the illusion of its own [...] identity, then this is an identity permanently at risk, for what if it fails to repeat, or if the very exercise of repetition is deployed for a very different performative purpose?[14]

In Iran, the repeated occurrence of performative protests against the regime's definition of gender identity does not align with the type that Butler discusses here. There may be certain parallels between contemporary interventions in public spaces and streets and earlier artworks, but the nature of these works is in a perpetual state of motion, constantly evolving from one form to another, finding new ways to challenge the regime. Asef Bayat has characterized the

Woman, Life, Freedom protests as an ongoing process rather than a single event—a "revolutionary course" rather than a "revolutionary situation."[15] He argues that, despite the lull in protest activity, the movement is far from over. As Bayat sees it, Iran has already undergone a significant paradigm shift, with a growing drive for dignity and a rejection of subjugation, paving the way for a new era of openness and possibility. In this context, the intermittent periods of calm could continue to build toward radical political reform.

As Iran's political system does not tolerate official opposition, artists have taken on the responsibility of constructing an alternative vision of the country's future. Their creative and ever-evolving interventions clearly resist the system. Have they also effected a measure of change? Artist Nastaran Safaie (profiled in Act Three and Nine) has long been concerned with the challenges faced by women when walking in Tehran, both from men who feel entitled to pass comment, and from women who look disapprovingly at outfits that fail to conform to Islamic dress codes. For a 2017 video titled *High Heels*, Safaie walked the entire length of Vali Asr in her favorite high heels. The video, captured on a hidden GoPro camera, brings home the misogynistic response to her action: the staring, puzzled looks, verbal harassment, and sexually explicit pickup lines.[16] But Safaie has noted that the catcalling and disapproving looks have fallen off sharply since the uprising. The "man on the street" now appears to regard unveiled women with greater respect, a testament to the impact of women's acts of resistance as they continue to go out unveiled, despite the risks.[17]

The ten acts in this book reveal some of the most intriguing characteristics of art inside Iran since the start of the Woman, Life, Freedom uprising. It is difficult to predict what direction the art of the uprising might take in the months and years to come, but four decades of determined dissident art in the Islamic Republic have shown that artists will persevere under the hardest of circumstances. Turning back from where Iranian art stands today seems unlikely. A note written from prison by Amir-Hussein Barimani, a theater director who brought Kafka's *Metamorphosis* to a Tehran stage shortly before his arrest in 2019, captures it all: "Let me say it plainly, I have not one iota of regret."[18] Driven by curiosity, I asked artists who have been punished by the regime for their actions—imprisoned, summoned by the Ministry of Intelligence, lashed, or fined for not wearing the hijab—whether they rued what they had done. Their responses consistently echoed Barimani's assertion: "I have not one iota of regret." ■

270 — 271

Notes

Introduction

1 For the completion of this book, I am grateful to the artists who engaged in discussions and permitted me to feature their works here. I extend special thanks to Jinoos Taghizadeh and Neda Darzi, whose assistance in identifying contributing artists was indispensable. Heartfelt gratitude to the Persian Heritage Foundation for funding this publication.

2 Amini's name appears variably as Jina Mahsa Amini, Mahsa Amini, or Mahsa Jina Amini. Here I have adopted the version provided by *Encyclopedia Britannica*. See *Encyclopedia Britannica* editorial, "Death of Jina Mahsa Amini, Iranian citizen," *Encyclopedia Britannica*, April 25, 2024, https://www.britannica.com/biography/death-of-Jina-Mahsa-Amini, accessed April 28, 2024.

3 See Youhanna Najdi et al., "Jina Mahsa Amini: The Face of Iran's Protests," *DW*, December 6, 2022, dw.com/en/jina-mahsa-amini-the-face-of-irans-protests/a-64007550, accessed May 2023.

4 Öcalan's words, more fully: "The woman comes by as a slave; she is weak; extremely incapacitated and dangerous. [...] I mean, she uses her fallen state to cause the society to fall. These are the things that we need to be alert to during the national liberation process. [...] Do you have any idea that a relation to woman for which we are prepared and in which we are situated is a trap? And the enemy uses this skillfully." S. Erdem, ed., *Kadın ve Aile Sorunu* (Istanbul: Melsa Yayınları, 1992), 106, cited in Handan Çağlayan, *Women in the Kurdish Movement: Mothers, Comrades, Goddesses*, trans. Simten Coşar (London: Palgrave McMillan, 2019), 69 and 85.

5 Ibid, 194–197.

6 Negar Mottahedeh, *Hashtag Solidarity and the Transformation of Online Life* (Stanford: Stanford University Press, 2015).

7 *Karnameh* 6, no. 3 (Fall 2022), https://www.kaarnamaa.com/zza, accessed March 2023.

8 Ibid. My translation.

9 Other notable women photographers include Hengameh Golestan (known for her documentation of the 1979 million women march against the compulsory veiling) and Rana Javadi (who documented the events of the Iranian Revolution, particularly in and around the campus of University of Tehran). See further: Anahita Ghabaian Etehadieh, *Breathing Space: Iranian Women Photographers* (London: Thames and Hudson, 2024). There were also foreign photographers like Michel Setboun who documented the seizure of the Niavaran Palace, among other events. See the collection on Setboun's personal website: www.setboun-photo.com/gallery/RN024-murals/G0000LhZNB4AxkDc/C0000EcHmKbQlQqI, accessed January 20, 2024.

10 *Karnameh* 6, no. 3 (Fall 2022), https://www.kaarnamaa.com/zza, accessed March 2023. My translation.

11 Coleman, Rebecca. "Social Media and the Materialization of the Affective Present," in *Affect and Social Media: Emotions, Mediation, Anxiety, and Contagion*, eds., Tony D. Sampson, Stephen Madison, and Darren Ellis (London and New York: Rowman & Littlefield International, 2018), 67–75.

12 Ibid.

13 Jacques Rancière, *Dissensus: On Politics and Aesthetics*, trans. Steven Corcoran (London: Continuum, 2010).

14 "Official Art, Culture, Action Website," *Art, Culture, Action*, https://www.artcultureaction.com/, accessed September 2023.

15 For an example of their statement in support of art students, see https://statementiranianartists.wordpress.com/, accessed January 2024.

16 "Notebooks before the Fall," *Naakojaaketab*, https://www.naakojaaketab.com/daftarhayepishassoghout, accessed January 2024.

17 See further, Rudabeh Tajik and Farzan Khorramdin, "The Chronology of the Revolution of 2022: 13 September–28 November," in "Notebooks before the Fall," special issue, *Journal of Thought and Literature*, no. 1–2 (November–December 2022): 1–28.

18 Frontline Defenders editorial, "Sepideh Rashnu," *Frontline Defenders*, https://www.frontlinedefenders.org/en/profile/sepideh-rashnu, accessed March 2024. Titled *Derakht Nam-e Oost* (The tree is her name), Sepideh Rashnu's book of poetry was published in 2021 by Sarzamin-e Ahooraie Publishing. This book contains poems on various themes such as love, nature, life, death, God, and humanity.

19 For a full history of compulsory hijab law, see Nasrin Sotoudeh, *Women, Life, Freedom: Our Fight for Human Rights and Equality in Iran*, trans. Parisa Saranj (Ithaca and London: Cornell University Press, 2023), 13–23.

20 United States Commission on International Religious Freedom, "Sepideh Rashnu," December 2023, https://www.uscirf.gov/religious-prisoners-conscience/forb-victims-database/sepideh-rashnu, accessed January 2024.

21 Interview with Hassan Nozadian, December 2024.

22 Official website of Woman, Life, Freedom: An Archive of Defiance, https://archiveofdefiance.com/, accessed January 10, 2024.

23 Roghayeh Rezaei, "Archive of Defiance: A Compilation of Iranian Protest Art," *Iran Wire*, May 26, 2023, https://iranwire.com/en/society/116930-archive-of-defiance-a-compilation-of-iranian-protest-art/#google_vignette, accessed June 2023.

24 Modakheleh, *Telegram*, https://t.me/mpdakhelehh, accessed December 10, 2024, or search Instagram/@modakhelehcontact

25 I want to emphasize that my primary interest lies in platforms dedicated to presenting revolutionary art, sharing firsthand artistic experiences, exploring architectural spaces, and engaging with street politics. While there is a wealth of material covering the movement's broader dimensions, such as women's issues and the wider sociopolitical landscape, my focus here is more specialized. An illustrative example of the broader dimensions of the movement is the podcast *Woman, Life, Freedom: All In on Iran*: https://podcasts.la.utexas.edu/woman-life-freedom-podcast/podcast/discussing-what-iranians-want-women-life-freedom-with-arash-azizi/?fbclid=IwAR12fZk5zDUefHOQTRDyZn8XbdpZruoK-oB7HluVe20aPlIR1OaOO6v7gb8, accessed January 2023.

26 Malu Halasa, *Woman, Life, Freedom*: *Voices and Art from the Women's Protests in Iran* (London: Saqi Press, 2023), 103.

27 Interview with anonymous members of *Khiaban Tribune*, February 2024.

28 Ibid.

29 Ibid.

30 Lucy Lippard, "Trojan Horses: Activist Art and Power," in *Art After Modernism*, ed., Brian Wallis (New York: New Museum, 1984).

31 Mojtaba Amini in conversation with the author, January 2024. Also see Katayoun Vaziri, "How Anonymous Artists Built a Visual Language of Resistance during Iran's Woman Life Freedom Uprising," *AJAMMC*, September 19, 2023, https://ajammc.com/2023/09/19/iranian-art-resistance-uprising/, accessed May 2023.

32 Participants in this collective endeavor were Serminaz Barseghian, Raoof Dashti, Aylar Dastgiri, Armin Ebrahimi, Setareh Fatehi, Sepehr Hajiabadi, Shahrooz Karbalaei, Raha Khosroshahi, Farzad Majidi, Hanie Mirali, Kimia Mirzaei, Nickrouz O'johni, Elnaz Salehi, Mehdi Shiri, Mahoor Toosi, Sarah Yazdanirad, and Sepideh Zamani.

33 Interview with a participating artist who wishes to remain anonymous, December 2023.

34 Kaveh Fouladi Nasab, ed., *Khiaban-e Vali Asr: Revayathay-e Gheyr-e Dastani* [The Vali Asr Street: Nonfiction stories from Tehran] (Tehran: Sales Press, 2022), 29.

35 Maryam Kohansal Nowdehi, "In Khiaban Hamisheh Sabz Ast" [This street is always green], in Nasab, *Khiaban-e Vali Asr*, 45–51.

36 Navid Pourmohammadreza, "Vali to Bavar Nakon" [But you must not believe], in Nasab, *Khiaban-e Vali Asr*, 63–72.

37 Eshrat Rahmanpour, "Dar Jostejooy-e Khiaban-e Az Dast Rafteh" [In search of a lost street], in Nasab, *Khiaban-e Vali Asr*, 83–89.

38 Asef Bayat, *Street Politics: Poor People's Movement in Iran* (New York: Columbia University Press, 1999).

39 Michel de Certeau, *The Practice of Everyday Life*, trans. Steven Rendall (Berkeley: University of California Press, 1984), 34.

40 See, for example, Shahram Khosravi, *Precarious Lives: Waiting and Hope in Iran* (Philadelphia: University of Pennsylvania Press, 2017); Narges Bajoghli, *Iran Reframed: Anxieties of Power in the Islamic Republic* (Stanford: Stanford University Press, 2019); Blake Atwood, *Undergrounds: The Secret Lives of Videocasettes in Iran* (Cambridge, MA: MIT Press, 2021).

41 For details of the history of the mandatory hijab, see Edalat Baray-e Iran Group, *Sio Panj Saal Hejab Dar Iran: Naghs-e Gostardeh Hoghugh-e Zanan* [Thirty-five years of hijab in Iran: the massive rejection of women's rights], 2013, *Justice for Iran*, www.justiceforiran.org, accessed December 2023.

42 Adam Zeidan, "Morality Police Law Enforcement Body in Iran," *Encyclopedia Britannica*, https://www.britannica.com/topic/morality-police, accessed December 2024.

43 Kian Tajbakhsh, *Creating Local Democracy in Iran: State Building and the Politics of Decentralization* (Cambridge: Cambridge University Press, 2022).

44 Nazanin Shahrokni, *Women in Place: The Politics of Gender Segregation in Iran* (Berkeley: University of California Press, 2019).

45 Numerous observers, both in Iran and internationally, have remarked on the gradual changes in the state of women's rights and freedoms in the country over the years. Today's protestors leverage this historical backdrop to contend that

the Islamic Republic is beyond reform and must be supplanted. This viewpoint is deeply influenced by the experiences of the postwar reform era and the events leading up to the 1979 revolution. For more information, see, for example, Matin Ghaffarian, "Chera ghafelgir shodim?" [Why are we surprised?], *Ettemad*, December 28, 2022, https://www.magiran.com/article/4371602, accessed December 2022.

46 I have previously highlighted this in a short online article: Pamela Karimi, "Woman, Art, Freedom," Society for Cultural Anthropology, June 29, 2023, https://culanth.org/fieldsights/woman-art-freedom. For more information about the Av theater group, see Pamela Karimi, *Alternative Iran: Contemporary Art and Critical Spatial Practice* (Stanford: Stanford University Press, 2022), 82–87.

47 Fereshteh Daftari, "Apolitical Formalism," in *Persia Reframed: Iranian Visions of Modern and Contemporary Art* (London and New York: I. B. Tauris, 2019), 91.

48 Ulrich Linse, "Johannes Itten and Mazdaznan at the Bauhaus," *Bauhaus Imaginista*, https://www.bauhaus-imaginista.org/articles/4787/johannes-itten-and-mazdaznan-at-the-bauhaus, accessed December 2023.

49 Rainer K. Wick, "Three Preliminary Courses: Itten, Moholy-Nagy, Albers," *Bauhaus Imaginista*, https://www.bauhaus-imaginista.org/articles, accessed December 2023.

50 Linda Komaroff, "A Conversation with Shirin Neshat and Shoja Azari," in *Treasures of Modern and Contemporary Art from the Farjam Collection*, eds., Sarah Rogers, Nada Shabout, Linda Komaroff, and Venetia Porter (New Haven: Yale University Press, 2024), 467.

51 Jinoos Taghizadeh, "Unpublished Manifesto," December 2022. Delivered at a couple of panels in North America. Partially published with permission. Shared with the author by Taghizadeh. My translation.

52 Consider, for example, the instances where women's fiber arts from North Africa were excluded from the mainstream tapestry biennales under the assumption that they were merely craftwork, lacking the avant-garde qualities necessary to be classified as art. See further Jessica Gerschultz, "Mutable Form and Materiality: Toward a Critical History of New Tapestry Networks," *ArtMargines*, vol. 5, no. 1 (2016): 3–29.

53 See, for example, Leila Ahmed, *A Quiet Revolution: The Veil's Resurgence, from the Middle East to America* (New Haven and London: Yale University Press, 2012), specifically chapters 10 and 11.

54 *Radio Zamaneh* editorial, "Slavoj Žižek Sends a Message of Solidarity to the Iranians Protesting Mahsa Amini's Murder," *Radio Zamaneh*, September 30, 2022, https://en.radiozamaneh.com/32762/, accessed September 2022.

55 Amelia Jones, "1970/2007: The Return of Feminist Art," *X-TRA*, vol. 10, no. 4 (Summer 2008): https://www.x-traonline.org/article/19702007-the-return-of-feminist-art#refmark-26, accessed May 2022.

56 Victoria Horne and Amy Tobin, "An Unfinished Revolution in Art Historiography, or How to Write a Feminist Art History," in *Feminist Art History Now, Radical Critique of Theory and Practice* (London: I. B. Tauris, 2017), 33.

57 See, for example, Griselda Pollock, *Generations and Geographies in the Visual Arts: Feminism Readings* (London and New York: Routledge, 1996), 17, cited in Horne and Tobin, "An Unfinished Revolution," 33–34.

58 See, for example, Macarena Gómez Cortés, *The Extractive Zone: Social Ecologies and Decolonial Perspectives* (Durham, NC: Duke University Press, 2017), 9–11.

59 Kimberlé Crenshaw, "Whose Story Is It Anyway? Feminist and Antiracist Appropriations of AnitaHill," in *Racing Justice, En-gendering Power: Essays on Anita Hill, Clarence Thomas, and the Construction of Social Reality*, ed., Toni Morrison (New York: Pantheon, 1992), 402–440.

60 In crafting these thoughts, I am indebted to Éléonore Lépinard, *Feminists Trouble: Intersectional Politics in Post Secular Times* (Oxford: Oxford Academic, 2021).

61 Sara Ahmed, *Living a Feminist Life* (Durham, NC: Duke University Press, 2017), 11.

62 Ibid.

63 Ibid.

64 Noushin Ahmadi Khorasani and *Enkar Magazine* editorial, "Naghsh-e pedar va pedar salari dar badilhay-e nazm-e syasi [The role of fatherhood and patriarchy in the transformations of political order]," *Enkar Magazine*. April 29, 2024, https://enkarmag.com/articles/bf678427-6203-4d29-8c47-4f0d0fb8791f/,accessed April 2024. My translation.

65 Ibid.

Act One – Parading the Body on Sidewalks

1 Here I am drawing on social media posts from bookstores in Tehran, such as Afrabooks and Behjat Book Store.

2 Hannah Arendt, *The Human Condition* (Chicago: University of Chicago Press, 1958), 199.

3 Individuals also sought insights from Vaclav Havel's *The Power of the Powerless: Citizens Against the State in Central Eastern Europe*, which explores the idea that people's everyday choices—particularly, the choice of whether to conform to or resist state propaganda—play a significant role in determining their destiny under authoritarian governments. It is also noteworthy that a new translation, by Zahra Shams, of Hannah Arendt's *Eichmann in Jerusalem: A Report on the Banality of Evil* became a bestseller in major bookstores in Tehran. Showing evil not as a monstrous aberration but as an everyday phenomenon—the work of ordinary individuals participating in state systems without overt hostility or ideology—the book struck a chord with street protesters seeking to understand the brutality of the police.

4 Judith Butler, "Bodies in Alliance and the Politics of the Street," in *Sensible Politics: The Visual Culture of Nongovernmental Activism*, eds., Meg McLagan and Yates McKee (New York: Zone Books, 2012), 117–137.

5 Ibid., 121.

6 Asef Bayat, "Is Iran on the Verge of Another Revolution?," *The Journal of Democracy*, March 1, 2023, https://www.journalofdemocracy.org/is-iran-on-the-verge-of-another-revolution/, accessed March 2023.

7 Ibid.

8 Janet Afary, *Sexual Politics in Modern Iran* (Cambridge: Cambridge University Press, 2014), 310.

9 Ibid.

10 Valentine Moghadam, "Islamic Feminism and Its Discontents: Towards Resolution of the Debate," *Signs: Journal of Women in Culture and Society*, vol. 27, no. 4 (2002): 1140.

11 Ziba Mirhosseini, *Islam and Gender: The Religious Debate in Contemporary Iran* (Princeton: Princeton University Press, 1999); Shahrzad Mojab, "Theorizing the Politics of 'Islamic Feminism,'" *Feminist Review*, vol. 69, no. 1 (2001): 124–146; Moghadam, "Islamic Feminism and Its Discontents." The timing of when the term "Islamic feminism" was coined to refer to Islam and women in general is debated. Shahrzad Mojab suggests that the term emerged in the 1990s within the expanding Western discourse on "women and Islam." However, she explains, intellectual engagements between Islam and feminism can be traced to the early twentieth century.

12 Saeed Zeydabadi-Nejad, *The Politics of Iranian Cinema: Film and Society in the Islamic Republic* (London: Routledge, 2010), 122.

13 Michelle Langford, *Allegory in Iranian Cinema: The Aesthetics of Poetry and Resistance* (London: Bloomsbury Academic, 2019), 118–119.

14 Moghadam, "Islamic Feminism and Its Discontents," 1135–1136.

15 For further details on these topics see, Janet Afary and Kevin B. Anderson, "Woman, Life, Freedom: The Origins of the Uprising in Iran," *Dissent Magazine*, December 2, 2022, https://www.dissentmagazine.org/online_articles/women-life-freedom-iran-uprising-origins/, accessed January 2023.

16 Moghadam, "Islamic Feminism and Its Discontents," 1143; Afary, *Sexual Politics in Modern Iran*, 316.

17 I have referred to this in my previous work. See Karimi, *Alternative Iran*, 59–69.

18 Antonia Carver, "Dead Dogs: A Decade of Public Art Experiments in Tehran," *Bidoun: Art and Culture from the Middle East*, no. 1 (Summer 2004): https://www.bidoun.org/articles/dead-dogs, accessed August 2018.

19 Karimi, *Alternative Iran*, 188.

20 Ibid., 164–167.

21 Ibid., *Alternative Iran*, 74–76.

22 Sotoudeh, *Women, Life, Freedom*, 7.

23 Mehraneh Atashi has adopted the artistic pseudonym Chupan. Honoring their preference, I will refer to them by this name throughout.

24 The "chain murders," a series of killings and disappearances occurring between 1988 and 1998, are believed to have been conducted by Iranian government agents targeting dissident intellectuals critical of the Islamic Republic.

25 Interview with Chupan, March 2023.

26 See further, Collier Schorr, "Wrestlers Love America," *ART21*, https://art21.org/read/collier-schorr-wrestlers-love-america/, accessed May 20, 2023.

27 Ibid.

28 Interview with Chupan.

29 Ibid.

30 Pedram Dibazar, *Urban and Visual Culture in Contemporary Iran: Nonvisibility and the Politics of Everyday Presence* (London: Bloomsbury Press, 2020), 30.

31 Ibid.

32 Benjamin Genocchio, "Revolution's Long Shadow Over the Tehran Art Scene," *New York Times*, March 30, 2011, https://www.nytimes.com/2011/03/31/world/middleeast/31iht-m31-iran-art.html, accessed March 2023.

33 Karimi, *Alternative Iran*, 195–199.

34 Ibid., 191–195.

35 Butler, "Bodies in Alliance and the Politics of the Street," 121.

36 See the official website of "My Stealthy Freedom." https://www.mystealthyfreedom.org/, accessed March 1, 2024.

37 Importantly, in the spring of 2019, Nasrin Sotoudeh, a lawyer imprisoned at the time, expressed in a letter to the governing council of the Paris Bar Association and lawyers of France that "[a]s long as the right to dress freely is not secured, other rights will not be respected. [...] I hope [...] that, through peaceful means, we shall put an end to the deprivation of women's rights in all the countries in which half of the population is deprived of its human rights in the name of an ideology, a religion, or an ethic." This letter was translated by Hirbod Dehghani-Azar and cited in Lucas Schmitz, "Women of Revolution Street," *Platform*, December 2, 2023, https://www.platformspace.net/translations/women-of-revolution-street, accessed March 2024.

38 Karimi, *Alternative Iran*, 182–184.

39 Ibid.

40 I borrow these terms from Laura Mulvey. See Laura Mulvey, "Visual Pleasure and Narrative Cinema," *Screen* 16, no. 3 (October 1975): 6–18.

41 Hilary Robson, "Witness It: Activism, Art, and the Feminist Performative Subject," in *A Companion to Feminist Art*, eds., Hilary Robinson and Maria Elena Buszek (London: John Wiley & Sons, Inc, 2019), 245–260.

42 Tehran Bureau, "The Chinese Companies Building Iran's Surveillance State," Tehran Bureau, September 30, 2022, https://tehranbureau.com/the-chinese-companies-building-irans-surveillance-state/, accessed April 2024.

43 On the popularity of Margaret Atwood's dystopian *The Handmaid's Tale in Iran*, see, for example, Azar Nafisi, "On Iranian Women and Atwood's *Republic of Gilead*," *Iran Wire*, February 21, 2023, https://iranwire.com/en/society/114012-interview-iranian-women-and-atwoods-republic-of-gilead/, accessed May 2023.

44 Linda Hutcheon, *A Theory of Adaptation* (London: Routledge, 2006), 174. Emphasis added.

45 Interview with Zohreh Solati, October 2023.

46 Critique exists around referring to Amini's passing as "martyrdom," a term some feel echoes the regime's ideology. However, in colloquial language, the term frequently serves to honor those who have lost their lives in protests, suggesting that their sacrifices were meaningful.
47 Interview with Nasrin Shahbeigy, November 2023.
48 Ibid.
49 Ibid.
50 Jonathan Littell, *Carnets de Homs* (Paris: Gallimard, 2012), 26, cited in Peter Snowdon, *The People Are Not an Image: Vernacular Video after the Arab Spring* (London and New York: Zone Books, 2020), 23. Also see Caroline Rooney, "Sufi Springs: Air on an Oud String," *CounterText*, vol. 1, no. 1 (2015): 52–54.
51 Interview with Shahbeigy.
52 Griselda Pollock, "Feminism and Language," in *Blackwell Companion to Art History*, eds., Elena Marina Buszeck and Helena Robinson (London: John Wiley and Sons, 2019), here 278.

Act Two – Hiding in Plain Sight

1 Statement sourced from the social media account of a renowned musician, whose identity remains confidential for safety reasons.
2 In early February 2023, multiple professors at the University of Art in Tehran released letters that resulted in ending or putting their contracts on hold.
3 *Kurdistan au féminin* editorial, "L'histoire d'un 'Homo Sacer' baloutche au pays des mollahs sanguinaires," *Kurdistan au féminin*, November 8, 2022, https://kurdistan-au-feminin.fr/, accessed May 2023.
4 Amnesty International, "Iran: At Least 82 Baluchi Protesters and Bystanders Killed in Bloody Crackdown," Amnesty International, October 6, 2022, https://www.amnesty.org/en/latest/news/2022/10/iran-at-least-82-baluchi-protesters-and-bystanders-killed-in-bloody-crackdown/, accessed November 2022.
5 I have made references to these examples in a former paper. See Pamela Karimi, "Art of Protest in Five Acts," *Roundtable on the "Woman, Life, Freedom" Revolution in Iran*: *Iranian Studies*, vol. 56, no. 3 (July 2023): 585–595.
6 Akhtar Safi, "Prison Sentence of Iranian Comedian Zeinab Mousavi Upheld," *Iranwire*, February 6, 2023, iranwire.com/en/news/113489-prison-sentence-of-iranian-comedian-zeinab-mousavi-upheld.
7 Elaine Velie, "Iranian Artists Criticize Berlin Museum's Display of Shirin Neshat Banner: Some Have Questioned Whether Neshat's Famous Images of Women Wearing the Hijab Represent the Struggles of Iranian Women Today," *Hyperallergic*, November 17, 2022, https://hyperallergic.com/780221/iranian-artists-criticize-berlin-museums-display-of-shirin-neshat-banner/, accessed April 2024.
8 Walter Benjamin, "Theories of German Fascism: On the Collection of Essays War and the Warrior," *New German Critique*, no. 17 (1979): 120–128.
9 Parts of the above sections and case studies were published in Karimi, "Art of Protest in Five Acts."
10 Interview with Meysam All-of-The, October 2023.
11 Ibid.
12 Ibid.
13 Rabih Mroué, *Image(s), mon amour: Fabrications* (Madrid: CA2M, 2013), 378–393, cited in Snowdon, *The People Are Not an Image*, 18.
14 Interview with Parviz Bina, August 2023.
15 Amy Malek, "On Unity & Fragmentation in the Iranian Diaspora," *Cultural Anthropology*, June 29, 2023, https://culanth.org/fieldsights/on-unity-fragmentation-in-the-iranian-diaspora, accessed February 2024.
16 "Art Behind Bars: Prison Art of Soudabeh Ardavan," *Actipedia*, https://actipedia.org/project/art-behind-bars-prison-art-soudabeh-ardavan, accessed January 2024. Also see Soudabeh Ardavan, *Yadnegarehhaye Zendan* [Prison drawings] (Laholm: Tydells Tyckeri AB, 2004).
17 Interview with Soudabeh Ardavan, January 2024.
18 Ibid.
19 Interview with Monireh Baradaran, January 2024.
20 Ibid.
21 Ibid.
22 Monireh Bradaran, *Haghighat-e Sadeh: Khaterati Az Zendanhay-e Zanan-e Jomhuri-e Eslami-e Iran* [A simple truth: memories from the political prisons of the Islamic Republic] (Cologne: Forough Publishing, 2012), 362.
23 Ibid.
24 See further "Omid Hoffnung," http://www.omid-hoffnung.de/, accessed January 2024.
25 Indeed, individuals who have recently been incarcerated attest that some guards are willing to cooperate with political prisoners.
26 Interview with Baradaran.
27 Interview with Shiva Nazarahari, January 2024.
28 Ibid.
29 *Reuters* editorial, "Jailed Iranian students start hunger strike" *Reuters*, December 21, 2010. https://www.reuters.com/article/uk-iran-prisoners-hungerstrike/jailed-iranian-students-start-hunger-strike-idUKTRE6BK30H20101221/?edition-redirect=uk, accessed May 10, 2023.
30 The adaptation of Dorfman's play at Evin featured three more cast members, who are featured on an invitation card that reads "Evin Theater Group Presents"; it was designed by the play's director, Deyhimi.

31 Sourced from the online archives of the Iranian Women Movement Museum. Iranwomenmuseum, "Baray-e cheshmhaie keh cheshmhayam ra miboosid [For Eyes that Kissed My Eyes]," November 11, 2023, https://www.instagram.com/p/Czg3CNdtwfc/?igsh=MTNhOGRiNHlubHVqeA==, Instagram/ @iranwomenmuseum, accessed January 16, 2024.

32 Amnesty International, "Iran: Security Forces Used Rape and Other Sexual Violence to Crush Woman Life Freedom Uprising with Impunity," Amnesty International, December 6, 2023, https://www.amnesty.org/en/latest/news/2023/12/iran-security-forces-used-rape-and-other-sexual-violence-to-crush-woman-life-freedom-uprising-with-impunity/, accessed February 2024.

33 *Radio Zamaneh* editorial, Parastou Forouhar, and Jinoos Taghizadeh, "Chaleshhay-e Sharayet-e Enghelabi baray-e Jame'eh Honari" [The challenges of a revolutionary situation for the art community], *Radio Zamaneh*, January 31, 2023, https://www.radiozamaneh.com/751659/?tg_rhash=0ceb6994783a68, accessed January 2023.

34 The Art, Culture, Action group has compiled a document listing all the artists who have faced imprisonment and punishment, available here: https://docs.google.com/spreadsheets/d/1Uz-i-QofhLsbjvQ1FBAkw3cfU-MMLiHUXQ6p2BbUP9E/edit#gid=0, accessed January 2024.

35 Interview with Homayoun Sirizi, December 2023.

36 Ibid.

37 Interview with Sara Sasani, November 2023.

38 On these issues, see, for example, Kelly Oliver, "Julia Kristeva's Feminist Revolutions," *Hypatia*, vol. 8, no. 3 (Summer 1993): 94–114.

39 Interview with Sasani.

40 Ibid.

41 Ibid.

42 Ibid.

43 Ibid.

44 On the role of poetry in the ideological lexicon of the Islamic Republic regime, see Fatemeh Shams, *A Revolution in Rhyme: Poetic Co-option under the Islamic Republic* (Oxford: Oxford University Press, 2021).

45 Interview with Shaya Shahrestani, July 2023.

46 Ibid.

Act Three – Staging Citywide Protest Props

1 Movahed's imprisonment began with one month in custody following her initial protest. However, after her second protest involving balloons, she was sentenced to one year for "promoting corruption and depravity through the act of removing the hijab." *Iran Prison Atlas* editorial, "Vida Movahed," *Iran Prison Atlas*, https://ipa.united4iran.org/en/prisoner/3977/, accessed March 2024.

2 Interview with Nastaran Safaie, January 2024.

3 Interview with an activist who wishes to remain anonymous.

4 Statement from the personal portfolio of the artist.

5 Interview with Mansooreh Bagharaee, January 2024.

6 Ibid.

7 Ibid.

8 See the Pussyhat Project Official Website: https://www.pussyhatproject.com/, accessed January 2024.

9 The term "Umbrella Revolution" originated from a tweet by Adam Cotton on September 26, 2014, but it rapidly gained popularity following its mention in an article in *The Independent*: Antonia Molloy, "Hong Kong Protests in Pictures: The 'Umbrella Revolution,'" *The Independent*, September 30, 2014, https://www.independent.co.uk/news/world/asia/hong-kong-protests-in-pictures-the-umbrella-revolution-9761617.html, accessed January 2024.

10 Quoted from artist's website: https://www.erfanghiasi.com, accessed January 2023.

11 Interview with Shaghayegh Kamyar, November 2023.

12 Philip Auslander, "The Performativity of Performance Documentation," *Perform, Repeat, Record: Live Art in History*, ed. Amelia Jones and Adrian Heathfield (New York: Intellect Press, 2008), 47–58.

13 Additionally, her interdisciplinary academic background, with degrees in photography, stage design, and art history and theory have culminated in interdisciplinary and historically rooted art.

14 Interview with Shaghayegh Kamyar.

15 Ibid.

16 *Iran International* editorial, "Iranian Activist Condemns Her 'Absurd' Prison Sentence Over Hijab," *Iran International*, December 06, 2023. https://www.iranintl.com/en/202312069773, accessed January 2024.

17 Ibid.

18 Amnesty International, "Iran 2023," https://www.amnesty.org/en/location/middle-east-and-north-africa/iran/report-iran/#:~:text=Hundreds%20were%20blinded%20or%20sustained,due%20to%20fear%20of%20arrest, accessed January 2024.

19 See, for example, Maryam Haghi and Fereshte Mahjoub, "The Magic of the Knot in the Iranian Folklore," *Culture and Folklore Literature*, vol. 39, no. 9 (August–September 2021): 283–325.

20 Interview with Hamed Safaie, December 2023.

21 Ibid.

22 Ibid.

23 Ibid.

24 Ibid.
25 Ronald Taylor et al., "Theodor Adorno: Reconciliation under Duress (Adorno on Lukács)," *Aesthetics and Politics* (London: New Left Review Books, 1977), 168.
26 Bayat, *Street Politics*, 137–138.

Act Four – Reclaiming Old Themes for New Protest Arts

1 Kristin Ross, *Communal Luxury: The Political Imaginary of the Paris Commune* (New York: Verso, 2015), 29, cited in Snowdon, *The People Are Not an Image*, 23.
2 Ibid.
3 Mohammed A. Bamyeh, *Anarchy as Order: The History and Future of Civic Humanity* (Lanham, MD: Rowman & Littlefield), 2009.
4 Ayman El-Desouky, *The Intellectual and the People in Egyptian Literature and Culture: Amara and the 2011 Revolution* (London: Palgrave Macmillan, 2014), ix–x.
5 Toronto Book Club, in conversation with Abbas Amanat, "Jonbesh-e zan, zendegi, azadi va darshay-e az enghelab mashrouteh [The Woman, Life, Freedom uprising and lessons from the Constitutional Revolution]," February 21, 2023, YouTube video, 1:59:09, https://www.youtube.com/watch?v=Z3YkVr1N4uI, accessed February 2023.
6 Negar Mottahedeh, *Whisper Tapes: Kate Millett in Iran* (Stanford: Stanford University Press, 2019), 1.
7 Often these poems too gain momentum by being turned into popular songs. See further Esfandyar Koosheh in conversation with Fatemeh Shams, "She'r-e Enghelab-e Novin dar Iran" [The poetry of the new revolution in Iran], *Radio Zamaneh*, December 23, 2022, https://www.radiozamaneh.com/742605/, accessed December 2023.
8 "Three Narratives of the Birth of the Song of Equality," *The Feminist School*; see also Esfandyar Koosheh in conversation with Fatemeh Shams, "She'r-e Enghelab-e Novin dar Iran."
9 Nahid Siamdoust, "The Birth of a University Music Genre in Iran's Woman, Life, Freedom Uprising," *International Journal of Middle East Studies*, vol. 55, no. 4 (2024): 1–9, https://www.cambridge.org/core/journals/international-journal-of-middle-east-studies/article/birth-of-a-university-music-genre-in-irans-woman-life-freedom-uprising/01BDC823C6A2F6FE6F64BF285A100363, accessed January 2024.
10 John Tagg, *The Burden of Representation: On Photographies and Histories* (New York: Palgrave McMillan, 1988), 4.
11 Julie Sanders, *Adaptation and Appropriation: A New Critical Idiom* (New York: Routledge, 2006), 26.
12 Robert Nelson, "Appropriation," *Critical Terms in Art History* (Chicago: University of Chicago Press, 1996), 162; Michael Baxandall, *Patterns of Intention: On the Historical Explanation of Pictures* (New Haven: Yale University Press, 1985), 58–92.
13 Susan Babaie and Talinn Grigor, eds., *Persian Kingship and Architecture: Strategies of Power in Iran from the Achaemenids to the Pahlavis* (London: I. B. Tauris, 2015).
14 David J. Roxburgh, *The Persian Album, 1400–1600: From Dispersal to Collection* (New Haven: Yale University Press, 2005).
15 Fereshteh Daftari, *Persia Reframed: Iranian Visins of Modern and Contemporary Art* (London and New York: I. B. Tauris, 2019), 148.
16 Ibid., 102.
17 Ibid., 102–103. See the full video at Leila Heller gallery's website: http://www.leilaheller.com/viewing-room/selected-works-by-farideh-lashai2, accessed May 10, 2023. I am gratefull to Leila Heller Gallery and Maneli Keykavousi for assisting with locating this artwork.
18 Some of the content about appropriation in the work of Lashai and the Saqqakhaneh movement have been addressed in a different context and in my contribution to another volume. See, Pamela Karimi, "Appropriation in Contemporary Iranian Art," in *Masterpieces of Modern and Contemporary Art from the Farjam Collection, eds.*, Venetia Porter, Linda Komaroff, Nada Shabout, and Sarah Rogers (New Haven: Yale University Press, 2024), 107-113.
19 Chupan coedited it with curator Sohrab Mohebbi.
20 Following Hafez's wisdom, the publication invites readers to ponder the insights of another medieval Persian poet, Sa'di, renowned for his sagacious prose and guidance for future generations. The book begins with a narrative from Sa'di's thirteenth-century work "Golestan" (Flower garden). Here, Sa'di reflects on the transient beauty of physical flowers and aspires to create an anthology of essays—a metaphorical "flower garden"—aimed at providing lasting comfort and companionship to its readers.
21 Mehraneh Atashi et al., *Only the Morning Bird Treasures the Flower Garden* (Los Angeles: RedCat Press in collaboration with CalArt's Downtown Center for Contemporary Art, 2019).
22 Daftari, *Persia Reframed*, 148.
23 Interview with Mojtaba Amini, January 2024.
24 Pamela Karimi, "The Many Shades of Iran's Protest Art," *Hyperallergic*, October 11, 2022. https://hyperallergic.com/768539/the-many-shades-of-iran-protest-art/, accessed April 2024.
25 Elizabeth Rauh, *The Graphics of Revolution and War: Iranian Poster Arts*, exhibition at the Hanna Holborn Gray Special Collections Research Center, University of Chicago, 2011. See: https://www.lib.uchicago.edu/collex/exhibits/graphics-revolution-and-war-iranian-poster-arts/visualizing-revolution/, accessed May 2023.
26 Other posters of this style were created by the major leftist communist party of Iran, Tudeh.
27 See, for example, "Russian Posters Collection, 1919–1989 and undated," Duke University Libraries, https://repository.duke.edu/dc/russianposters, accessed October 2023.
28 Maryam Zandi, *Hokumat-e 58* [*The Government of the 80s*] (Tehran: Nazar Press, 2019).

29 Craig Owens, *Beyond Recognition: Representation, Power, and Culture*, eds., Scott Bryson, Barbra Kruger, Lynn Tillman, and Jane Weinstock (Berkeley and Los Angeles: University of California Press, 1992).

30 Personal statement by Homayoun Sirizi. I am grateful to Sirizi for sharing this statement with me.

31 1500 Tasvir, "Students at Tehran University of Art participate in the coreography of the word blood, while shouting Woman, Life, Freedom," Instagram/ @1500tasvir, October 11, 2022, https://www.instagram.com/1500tasvir/?hl=en, accessed November 2023.

32 Black Fish Voice Group, @blackfishvoice1, "Received from the Faculty of Applied Arts, Tehran University of Art, October 30th," Instagram post, October 30, 2022,https://www.instagram.com/p/CkWE74JM1L2/?img_index=1, accessed November 2022.

33 Black Fish Voice Group, "Received from the Faculty of Fine Arts, Tehran University, November 12, 2022," Instagram/ @blackfishvoice1, November 12, 2022. https://www.instagram.com/p/Ck29KgNt1gs/?img_index=1, accessed January 2023.

34 For more information on these practices, see Karimi, *Alternative Iran*.

35 Varasteh also recognizes the connection between Iran's environmental concerns and political power dynamics. In one artwork, *Lonesome Tree*, he used road-marking paint to depict an elongated shadow of a tree on a highway, symbolizing the government's neglect of environmental issues. Despite attempts to remove it, this piece remains a poignant reminder of nature's importance in Iran's urban areas. In 2019, as a response to Iran's minister of the environment's proposal to divert water from the Caspian Sea to Iranian deserts, which would harm the Hyrcanian Forests, Varasteh placed a massive seven-meter-long straw on a Caspian beach, calling it *For Isa Kalantari*. This act demonstrated Varasteh's willingness to engage in critical dialogue with influential figures in the Islamic Republic, highlighting his commitment to environmental advocacy.

36 Sarah Schulman first coined the term in 2011 in reference to Israeli government PR strategies. It is closely associated with homonationalism, which allegedly involves exploiting issues related to sexual minorities to rationalize racism and xenophobia.

37 *France24* editorial, "Tehran Protests against Khamenei Cartoons in *Charlie Hebdo*'s Iran Special Issue," *France24.com*, January 4, 2023, https://www.france24.com/en/middle-east/20230104-tehran-protests-against-khamenei-cartoons-in-charlie-hebdo-s-iran-special-issue, accessed August 2023.

38 Comment by anonymous Iran-based user on the footage related to this activist performance on Masih Alinejad's personal Instagram page. Translation with slight modification is mine. Anonymous commentator, "Just How Dare..." Instagram/ @Masih.alinejad January 08, 2023. https://www.instagram.com/reel/CnJb20_DLJJ/?igsh=MWhreXc1dHhkODd6bQ%3D%3D, accessed January 09, 2023.

39 As, for example, in the works of Mana Neyestani, an Iranian cartoonist, illustrator and graphic novelist.

Act Five – Reenacting Street Battles

1 Vaziri, "How Anonymous Artists Built a Visual Language of Resistance During Iran's Woman Life Freedom Uprising."

2 Black Fish Voice Group, "The magnificent performance of Kurdistan University students in memory of Khodanur Lojei and in solidarity with Baluchistan," Instagram/@blackfishvoice1, November 15, 2022, https://www.instagram.com/p/Ck-68aTtMml/?img_index=1, accessed March 2024.

3 Elaine Velie, "Iran Massacre Prompts Poignant Protest at LACMA," *Hyperallergic*, November 10, 2022, https://hyperallergic.com/779080/iran-massacre-prompts-poignant-protest-at-lacma/, accessed December 2022.

4 On this topic and for further examples of reenactment, see Ellen Mueller, *Walking as Artistic Practice* (New York: SUNY Press, 2023); see also Sven Lütticken, "An Arena in Which to Reenact," in *Life, Once More: Forms of Reenactment in Contemporary Art*, ed. Sven Lütticken and Jennifer Allen, exh. cat. (Rotterdam: Witte de With, 2005), 17–60.

5 Jeremy Deller, "The Battle of Orgreave, 2001" artist's official website, https://www.jeremydeller.org/TheBattleOfOrgreave/TheBattleOfOrgreave.php, accessed March 2024.

6 See further "The Official Website of Koocheh Magazine," *Koocheh Magazine*, https://koochemag.ir/, accessed October 10, 2023.

7 The Bahá'í Institute for Higher Education (BIHE) was established in 1987 in response to the Iranian government's ongoing campaign to suppress Iranian Bahá'ís and their access to higher education. The BIHE offers many university-level programs across five faculties and continues to enhance and deliver academic programs in the sciences, engineering, business and management, humanities, music, and social sciences. See http:// bihe.org/, accessed June 10, 2019. More recently, with the aid of technology and professors teaching from exile, this clandestine education has expanded online, serving students within the country.

8 For the politics of dance in Iran, see Ida Meftahi, *Gender and Dance in Iran: Bio Politics on Stage* (London: Routledge, 2017).

9 Arang Keshavarzian, *Bazaar and State in Iran: The Politics of the Tehran Marketplace* (Cambridge: Cambridge University Press, 2007), 25.

10 *Film School Rejects* editorial, "'How They Shot 'Russian Ark' in One Take with No Hidden Cuts," *Film School Rejects*, November 16, 2020, https://filmschoolrejects.com/russian-ark-long-take/, accessed May 2023.

11 See further, Tom McDonough, ed., *Guy Debord and the Situationist International: Texts and Documents* (Cambridge: MIT Press, 2004); Guy Debord, "Théorie de la Dérive," *Les Lèvres Nues*, no. 9 (November 1956), reprinted in *Internationale Situationniste #2* (December 1958).

12 It was also showcased at the AVIF Cannes Art Film Festival and the Pool Movement Art Film Festival in Berlin.

13 Unfortunately, Daroon plateau was forced to close during the pandemic, after repeated investigations by the state authorities.

14 These seeds, from the plant *Peganum harmala*, native to the Middle East, are invested with both mythical and healing properties.
15 Interview with Torabi, November 2023. Also see https://calfilmfestival.com/2024/02/05/until/, accessed March 2024.
16 Delaram Mohammadi joined Torabi in producing the film, with a cast that included Torabi, Ava Jalali, Hamed Raad, Hannaneh Heydari, Sina Sheynbani, Zahra Fazl Allah, Farsa Hasanpour, and M. Erfan Jafarinejad, each delivering enthralling performances. Hamed Raad's guidance was instrumental in the film's direction, supported by the talents of Hannaneh Heydari and Sina Saberi. The visual quality was fine-tuned by color proofer Milad Sanaei, while Arya Khaksari captured the essence of the film through his photography. It is also worth mentioning that Sahar Maktabi lent her expertise to costume design, ensuring the actors' outfits were fitting for their roles, and logistical support for transportation was provided by Taleb Fatemi and Amir Hamidi Zadeh, ensuring smooth operations.
17 Tanin Torabi, "Until...," Vimeo Video, https://vimeo.com/user15273829, accessed November 2023.
18 Ibid.
19 Tali Hatuka, *The Design of Protest: Choreographing Political Demonstrations in Public Space* (Austin: University of Texas Press, 2018), 37–38.
20 Tanin Torabi, "Until...," Vimeo Video.
21 Erica Chenoweth, *Civil Resistance: What Everyone Needs to Know* (Oxford: Oxford University Press, 2021), 42.
22 The name Persbook cleverly merges *pers* (short, in Persian) with "book," echoing the social media platform Facebook, which rose to prominence during and after Iran's 2009 Green Movement.
23 Pamela Karimi, *Alternative Iran*, 119–120.
24 Pezhmann Dailami, "Jangali Movement," *Encyclopædia Iranica*, December 15, 2008, www.iranicaonline.org/articles/jangali-movement, accessed May 2023.
25 Ervand Abrahamian, "The Guerrilla Movement in Iran, 1963–77," in *Iran: A Revolution in Turmoil*, ed., Haleh Afshar (Albany: SUNY Press, 1985), 71–98.
26 Interview with Mahmoud Maktabi, February 2024.
27 See, for example, *Euronews* editorial, "Outrage in Iran after Woman Whipped for Refusing to Wear Hijab," *Euronews*, January 8, 2024, https://www.euronews.com/2024/01/08/outrage-in-iran-after-woman-whipped-for-refusing-to-wear-hijab, accessed March 2024.
28 Jean-Pierre Filiu, *Apocalypse in Islam*, trans. M. B. De Bevoise (Berkeley: University of California Press, 2011), 72–73.
29 *Behdasht-e Zanan* editorial, "Zani ba Eradeh-ie Beh Bolanday-e Gholleh Damavand" [A woman as steadfast as the Damavand peak], interview with Badri Valian, *Behdasht-e Zanan*, no. 8, Azar 1388 (January 2009): 6–7.
30 Parvaneh Kazemi, one of the few Iranian women to have scaled Mt. Everest, at the outsent of the Woman, Life, Freedom uprising stated that "the name and image of us women are only used [by the Islamic Republic of Iran] for abuse." See further Jordan Amirkhani, "Introduction," in *Taravat*, ed., Minnesota's Macalester College's Law Warschaw Gallery staff (Catalogue for the solo exhibition of Taravat Talepasand at Minnesota's Macalester College's Law Warschaw Gallery, January 27, 2023-March 10, 2023). December 20, 2022, 2.
31 Interview with Badri Valian, October 2023.
32 Ibid.

Act Six – Documenting Urban Unrest

1 Tahar Chikhaoui, "La rampe s'est déplacée," 2012, Africine.org, cited in Snowdon, *The People Are Not an Image*, 29.
2 In making this assertion, I draw upon the arguments presented in Paula Amad's book, *Counter-Archive: Film, the Everyday, and Albert Kahn's Archives de la Planète* (New York: Columbia University Press, 2010).
3 Farnaz Fassihi, "Iran Turns to Public Executions, Enraging an Already Protesting Public" *The New York Times*, December 12, 2022, https://www.nytimes.com/2022/12/12/world/middleeast/iran-protests-execution.html, accessed March 2023.
4 Parastou Forouhar, "The Intertwining of Everyday Life and Revolution: Fall 1401 Travel Report," January 21, 2023, *Asoo Journal*, www.aasoo.org/fa/articles/4184, accessed May 2023.
5 Ibid.
6 Interview with Mona Sartoveh, June 2023.
7 Daftari, *Persia Reframed*, 12. Some Iranian artists of the period were affiliated with the Tudeh Party or sympathized with their goals.
8 Ibid., 157. Also see, Mazyar Lotfalian, *What People Do with Images: Aesthetics, Politics and the Production of Iranian Visual Culture in Transnational Circuits* (London: Sean Kingston Publishing, 2022).
9 While not the central theme of this research, it is worth noting that several Iranian poets, including those in the diaspora, have also paid tribute to these fallen heroes in their poems. An outstanding example is the poet Geranaz Moussavi, based in Australia.
10 Pamela Karimi in conversation with Malu Halasa, "A Revolution Made by Art," in *Women, Life, Freedom*, ed., Malu Halasa (London: Saqi Press), 84–99.
11 For an in-depth exploration of the aspirations of young Iranian women, the work by Arash Azizi provides comprehensive insights. His book, *What Iranians Want: Woman, Life, Freedom*, particularly Chapter 9, offers a detailed profile of Sarina Esmaeilzadeh—a notable YouTuber who openly discussed the desires of her generation. Arash Azizi, *What Iranians Want: Women, Life, Freedom* (London: Oneworld Publications, 2024).

12 The NCRI Women's Committee Promotes Gender Equality editorial, "Brave Iranian Women Lose Their Eyes, but Their Hearts Still Beat for Iran," *The NCRI Women's Committee Promotes Gender Equality*, January 17, 2023, https://women.ncr-iran.org/2023/01/17/brave-iranian-women-lose-eyes/.

13 Meysam Azarzad, "Instagram post about Elaheh Tavakolian," Instagram/ @azzargoshasp, May 12, 2023, https://www.instagram.com/p/CsJZ4hbt4Cr/?igsh=MWlneHJ4dnNwaDZkYw==, accessed May 2023.

14 Ibid.

15 *Iran International* editorial, "Health Condition of Political Prisoners Deteriorating in Iran," *Iran International*, November 18, 2022, https://www.iranintl.com/en/202211184124, accessed November 2023.

16 See, Karimi, *Alternative Iran*, 236–240.

17 Lili Vakilian (Ayda), personal Facebook page post, September 2022. https://www.facebook.com/ayda.carpediem, accessed November 2022.

18 Interview with Ayda Vakilian, October 2023.

19 Lili Vakilian (Ayda), personal Facebook page post, October 2022. https://www.facebook.com/ayda.carpediem, accessed November 2022.

20 Interview with Bahar Majdzadeh, January 2024. Also see the documentation of Majdzadeh's project on *Asoo* website. Mehdi Shabani and Bahar Majdzadeh, "A Map with Memories, Sounds, and Images of the Streets of Tehran in the Sixties, Narrated by the Political Activists of that Era," *Asoo Journal*, October 11, 2022, https://www.aasoo.org/fa/multimedia/videos/4060, accessed November 2023.

21 Interview with Jinoos Taghizadeh, September 2023.

22 Jinoos Taghizadeh, "unpublished artwork." Courtesy of the artist. My translation.

23 Ibid.

24 Interview with Jinoos Taghizadeh, November 2023.

25 Ahmed, *Living a Feminist Life*, 21. Emphasis added.

Act Seven – Camouflaging Defiant Words

1 Fatemeh Shams, "*In She'r Nist*" [This is not a poem], Baang.news, November 27, 2022. https://baangnews.net/11670.

2 Interview with Farshad Sonboldel, February 2024.

3 For example, Solmaz Naraghi's career began with eccentric performances that later evolved into popular poetry recitation sessions for children, which have gained considerable popularity on YouTube and social media platforms.

4 After the revolution, the first cultural center to be established was the Bahman Cultural Center, which was founded in 1992 by repurposing the Tehran slaughterhouse, located between the areas of Javadieh and Naziyabad, in the current Bahman Square. This cultural center had a significant impact both at the neighborhood level and across the metropolis of Tehran. Masserat Amirebrahimi, "Naghsh-e Farhang Saraha Dar Democrasion Honar Dar Daheh Haftad" [The role of cultural centers in democratization of the arts in the 1990s], *Herfeh Honarmand* 82 (2024 [1403]): 32–39.

5 *Mashregh News* editorial, "Nagoftehay-e Salahshoor darbareh zarbeh-yi keh Karbaschi beh masjed zad" [Unspoken words of salhashoor about the negative impact Karbaschi's plans had on mosques], *Mashregh News*, March 2, 2016 [1394], cited in Ibid, 37.

6 Interview with Ali Satvati Qale, December 2023.

7 See further Alireza Mohammadi, "In Public Space: No. 6/1," Summer 2018, Aparat Video, 40: 45: 59, https://www.aparat.com/v/zGhtk?playlist=7226470, accessed March 2023.

8 The piece was published in Marjorie Barrick Museum of Art's Journal, *Dry Heat*. See further, Ain/Amal, Nima Abkenar, trans., "Walls: Melancholy within the Heart of a Confined Society," *Dry Heat*, no. 002 (Spring 2023): 6-9.

9 Esfandyar Koosheh in conversation with Fatemeh Shams, "She'r-e Enghelab-e Novin dar Iran."

10 "Manifesto," Matrood, 2019, http://Matrod.org, accessed May 2023. My translation which is a slightly paraphrased version of the original in multiple parts. Note that the link employs an alternative spelling of Matrood.

11 Interview with Yaavar Bazrafkan, November 2023.

12 Peter Lamborn Wilson, known as the American anarchist, lived in Iran in the 1970s and contributed to Iran's Imperial Iranian Academy of Philosophy. See further Raymond Foye, "A Tribute to Peter Lamborn Wilson (1945–2022)," *Brooklyn Rail*, October 2022, https://brooklynrail.org/2022/10/in-memoriam/A-Tribute-to-Peter-Lamborn-Wilson, accessed May 2023.

13 Interview with Bazrafkan.

14 Interview with Samira Yahyaie, December 2023.

15 Aspects of Farrokhzad's poems were recycled during the peak of the uprising by more conventional poets. See further Fatemeh Shams and Nahid Siamdoust, "Poetry & Protest with Fatemeh Shams," podcast episode, *Woman, Life, Freedom: All in On Iran*, March 3, 2023, https://podcasts.la.utexas.edu/woman-life-freedom-podcast/podcast/poetry-protest-with-fatemeh-shams/, accessed March 2024.

16 Interview with Samira Yahyaie.

17 Ibid.

18 The original French is "Nous nous cherchions avant que de nous être vus."

19 Drawing from the event's recording, kindly provided to me by Hamed Jaberha. My translation.

20 Ibid.

21 Ibid.

22 Interview with Mahmoud Maktabi, January 2024.

23 Farshad Sonboldel, *The Rebellion of Forms in Modern Persian Poetry: Politics of Poetic Experimentation* (London: Bloomsbury Academic, 2024).
24 Interview with Sonboldel.
25 Ibid.
26 Farshad Sonboldel, *The Rebellion of Forms*, 39–51.
27 Ibid, 162–173.
28 Tondar Kiā, *Nahib-e Jonbesh-e Adabi-e Shahin* (1940): 17. Cited in Sonboldel, *The Rebellion of Forms*, 180.
29 Tondar Kiā, *Nahib-e Jonbesh-e Adabi-e Shahin* (1970): 579. According to Sonboldel Kia reprinted some of his older poems (in this case along with an image) in later editions of *Nahib-e Jonbesh-e Adabi-e Shahin.* Interview with Farshad Sonboldel, February 2024.
30 Sonboldel, *The Rebellion of Forms*, 178.
31 For the full poem, see Reza Baraheni, *Khatab beh parvaneh-ha va chera digar man shae'r-e Nimayie nistam* [To Butterflies and why I am no longer following Nima's style of poetry] (Tehran: Markaz Press, 1995), 9–15; "Nima's style of poetry" in the title refers to the work of modernist Iranian poet Nima Yooshij (1895–1960).
32 Mentioned in Saman Salour's 2003 documentary *Aramesh ba Diazpam-e 10*, cited in Nahid Siamdoust, *Soundtrack of the Revolution: The Politics of Music in Iran* (Stanford: Stanford University Press), 197.
33 Interview with Jinoos Taghizadeh, January 2024.
34 See, Karimi, *Alternative Iran*, 56 and 79–80.
35 Interview with Taghizadeh. The 2009 film *My Tehran for Sale*, directed by poet Granaz Moussavi, presents a compelling portrayal of a poetry gathering in a residential context. Filmed in an Ekbatan apartment, it features a vibrant party scene populated by young attendees, where Moussavi, doubling as an invited poet, delivers a poetry reading in this specific segment of the movie. While the scene does not show any unusual performative elements, the ambiance—characterized by a coed gathering, the presence of alcoholic beverages, and smoking—subtly exudes the clandestine or underground essence of the event.
36 For the full poem see Ali Asadollahi, *Bon bast-e Fereshteh* [Fereshteh cul-de-sac] (Tehran: Manjanigh Press, 2017), 19–26.
37 Kanta Kochhar-Lindgren, ed., *The Exquisite Corpse: Chance and Collaboration in Surrealism's Parlor Game* (Lincoln: University of Nebraska Press), 2009.

Act Eight – Clashing with Faith in Broad Daylight

1 For further discussions on these challenges faced by scholars, particularly feminists, see Lépinard, *Feminist Trouble*.
2 Bahareh Hedayat, "'Revolution Is Inevitable': Bahareh Hedayat's Letter from Evin Prison in Tehran, Iran (December 2022)," *Jadaliyya*, January 4, 2023, https://www.jadaliyya.com/Details/44720, accessed April 2023.
3 Taravat Talepand, "Sculpture," Taravet Talepasand Official Website, https://www.taravattalepasand.com/sculpture, accessed January 2024.
4 Interview with Taravat Talepasand, January 2024.
5 For an example of an image, see Emerson Dameron, "On the Job: Confessions of an Iranian-Expat Hair-Metal Groupie," *Newcity Lit*, August 3, 2010, https://lit.newcity.com/2010/08/03/on-the-job-confessions-of-an-iranian-expat-hair-metal-groupie/, accessed May 2023.
6 Roxana Shirazi interviewed by Fox News about her memoir, *The Last Living Slut: Born in Iran, bred Backstage*, February 22, 2011, YouTube video, 10:08:26, https://youtube.com/watch?v=k3qhSv14agM, accessed November 2023.
7 Kristin Farr, "Bold Blasphemy," interview with Taravat Talepasand. *Juxtapoz: Art and Culture*, Fall 2023, https://www.juxtapoz.com/news/magazine/features/taravat-talepasand-bold-blasphemy/, accessed March 2024.
8 Racket staff, "Macalester Students Protest Feminist Iranian Art Show," *Racket Magazine*, February 9, 2023, https://racketmn.com/another-campus-art-vs-religion-fight-this-time-at-macalester/, accessed May 2023.
9 Ibid.
10 Len Gutkin, "The Blasphemer: Is Taravat Talepasand's Art Too Radical for Today's Campus?," The Chronicle of Higher Education, February 8, 2023, https://www.chronicle.com/article/the-blasphemer, accessed March 2023.
11 Jill Filipovic, "Fear of a Female Body Controlling Women's Bodies Is a Hallmark of Religious Fundamentalism. Why Are Liberal Institutions Getting on Board?," February 9, 2023, https://jill.substack.com/p/fear-of-a-female-body, accessed April 2024.
12 Simin Daneshvar, "Don't Cry...," *Nadastan Magazine*, no. 16 (Day 1401 [January 2023]): n.p. I am grateful to Malu Halasa for providing a copy of the magazine.
13 Interview with Mehri Rahimzadeh, December 2023.
14 Ibid.
15 Malu Halasa, "A Changing Dreamscape: The Photographs of Mehri Rahimzadeh," in Halasa, *Woman, Life, Freedom*, 218–227.
16 Interview with Rahimzadeh.
17 Angelique Chrisafis, "'The Little Girl in Persepolis Has Grown Up': Marjane Satrapi on Life After Her Hit Graphic Novel—and Her Radical New Work," *The Guardian*, March 16, 2024, https://www.theguardian.com/books/2024/mar/16/marjane-satrapi-interview-persepolis-woman-life-freedom, accessed March 2024.
18 Interview with Hamideh Sobhani, October 2023.
19 Interview with Masoumeh Mohtadi, December 2023.
20 Ibid.
21 Mottahedeh, *Hashtag Solidarity and the Transformation of Online Life*, 75–77.

22 See, for example, Jakeet Singh, "Religious Agency and the Limits of Intersectionality," *Hypatia*, vol. 30, no. 4 (2015): 657–674; Uma Narayan, "Essence of Culture and a Sense of History: A Feminist Critique of Cultural Essentialism," in *Decentering the Center: Philosophy for a Multicultural, Postcolonial, and Feminist World*, eds., Sandra Harding and Uma Narayan (Bloomington: Indiana University Press, 2000), 80–100; Sarah Bracke, "Conjugating the Modern/Religious, Conceptualizing Female Religious Agency: Contours of a Post-secular Conjuncture," *Theory, Culture & Society*, vol. 25, no. 6 (2008): 51– 67. For an example from Iran, see Azam Torab, *Performing Islam: Gender and Ritual in Iran* (Leiden: Brill, 2006).

23 See Act One.

24 Margot Badran, "Islam's Other Half," *The Guardian*, November 9, 2008, https://www.theguardian.com/commentisfree/belief/2008/nov/09/islam-women, accessed March 2023.

25 Rosi Braidotti, "In Spite of the Times: The Postsecular Turn in Feminism," *Theory, Culture & Society*, vol. 25, no. 6 (2008): 3, 6, 8, and 9.

26 Ahmed, *Cultural Politics of Emotion*, 178.

27 Ibid.

28 Saba Mahmood, *Politics of Piety: The Islamic Revival and the Feminist Subject* (Princeton, NJ: Princeton University Press, 2005).

29 Lépinard, *Feminist Trouble*, 6.

30 RFE/RL's *Radio Farda*, "Iranian Religious Scholar Challenges Khamenei Over Hijab Law," *Radio Farda*, April 14, 2023, https://www.rferl.org/a/iran-religious-scholar-challenges-khamenei-hijab/32363972.html, accessed April 2024.

31 Ibid. Vasmaghi, a former *Fiqh* (Islamic law) professor at the University of Tehran, was banned from teaching due to her political views. She was imprisoned in Evin for criticizing the hijab law, refusing to recognize the Revolutionary Court's legitimacy and denouncing the regime as oppressive. See further Maryam Sinaiee, "Prominent Female Islamic Scholar Challenges Khamenei's Hijab Edict," *Iran International*, April 13, 2023, https://www.iranintl.com/en/202304131002, accessed March 2024.

32 Sara Ahmed, *The Cultural Politics of Emotion* (Edinburgh: Edinburgh University Press, 2014).

33 Sara Ahmed, "Affective Economies," *Social Text*, vol. 79/22, no. 2 (Summer 2004): 119.

34 Ahmed, *The Cultural Politics of Emotion*, 177.

35 Léa Védie, "Hating Men Will Free You? Valerie Solanas in Paris or the Discursive Politics of Misandry," *European Journal of Women's Studies*, vol. 28, no. 3 (2021): 305–319.

36 Ibid., 312.

37 C. Bernheim, "SCUM ou l'écume inconnue" (1971), in *Mouvement de libération des femmes: textes premiers*, eds., C. Bernheim, L. Kandel, F. Picq et al. (Paris: Stock, 2009), 257–258, cited in Védie, "Hating Men Will Free You?"

38 Ibid.

39 Interview with Zohreh Solati, January 2024.

Act Nine – Opposing Art with Art in Cityscapes

1 McDonough, ed., *Guy Debord and the Situationist International.*

2 Kalle Lasn, *Culture Jam: The Uncooling of America* (New York: Quill, 1999), 107. Also see Marita Sturken and Lisa Cartwright, *Practices of Looking: An Introduction to Visual Culture* (New York: Oxford University Press, 2017), 281–282.

3 Interview with a former member of MCIG, June 2020. Also cited in Karimi, *Alternative Iran*, 102.

4 Karimi, *Alternative Iran*, 102–103.

5 Ibid., 161–164.

6 Ibid.

7 Document formerly available on the official website of MCIG, https://www.farhang.gov.ir/, accessed August 2021. PDF document titled, "Barnameh Vezarat-e Farhang va Ershad-e Eslami, Dolat-e Sizdahom" [The program of the ministry of culture and Islamic guidance, the thirteenth government], 44–45.

8 *IndustriALL* editorial, "Iranian Auto Workers Strike Against Non-Payment of Wages," *IndustriALL*, February 11, 2021, https://www.industriall-union.org/iranian-auto-workers-strike-against-non-payment-of-wages, accessed February 2024, accessed March 2023. The strike was also known known as Campaign 1400, referring to the year 2021 in the Iranian solar calendar.

9 Kourosh Ziabari, "Iranian Artists Reluctant to Get Back to Business as Usual," *Asia Times*, February 13, 2023, https://asiatimes.com/2023/02/iranian-artists-reluctant-to-get-back-to-business-as-usual/, accessed December 2023.

10 RFE/RL's *Radio Farda*, "Iran Prevents Filmmaker from Traveling to London Film Festival," *Radio Farda*, October 15, 2022, https://www.rferl.org/a/iran-filmmaker-london-film-festival-haghighi/32084516.html, accessed November 2022.

11 Mani Haghighi, "Instagram post about the Fajr Film Festival," Instagram/@mani_haghighi_, December 22, 2022, https://www.instagram.com/reel/CmWP80_Az9H/?igsh=MTJjeGRhOTVtYnQ3NQ==, accessed January 2023.

12 Siamdoust, "The Birth of a University Music Genre in Iran's Woman, Life, Freedom Uprising," 1–9.

13 Interview with Kourosh Golnari, October 2023.

14 Interview with Mohsen Rafei, October 2023.

15 Maryam Amoosa, "Enteghal-e asar bedoon ettela', naghz-e hoghoogh-e honarmand ast [Transferring the work without notification is a violation of the artist's rights]," *Etemad Newspaper*, vol. 20, no. 5292 (August 31, 2022): 7.

16 Ibid.

17 *Independent Persian* editorial. "*Khandeh Taamoli daneshjooyan ham dar Iran mamnoo shod* [Shared Student Laughter Now Silenced in Iran]." Wednesday, 8 Shahrivar 1401 [August 30, 2022], https://www.independentpersian.com/node/264766, accessed November 2023. My translation. Quotations within the article are paraphrased.

18 Ibid.
19 Ibid.
20 Ibid.
21 Interview with Rafei.

Act Ten – Forecasting the Future

1 Interview with Mojtaba Amini, January 2024.
2 Ilya Kabakov, *On Art*, ed., Matthew Jesse Jackson, trans. Antonina W. Bouis and Cynthia Martin, with Matthew Jesse Jackson (Chicago: University of Chicago Press, 2018), 57–59. Kabakov's essay, first published in the 1983 edition of the underground magazine *A-YA*, is reproduced in English in the same publication.
3 The soul-searching was particularly poignant as the exhibition coincided with the anniversary of the attack on O Gallery, when it was vandalized with crimson red paint, presumably by an art community advocating for galleries to abandon business in favor of revolution. See Introduction for more details.
4 Sampada Aranke, *Death's Futurity: The Visual Life of Black Power* (Durham, NC: Duke University Press, 2023).
5 Lisa Baraitser, *Enduring Time* (London: Bloomsbury Academic, 2017), 93.
6 Ibid.
7 Interview with Shiva Khademi, January 2024. Also see Malu Halasa, "The Smarties Hair Colour as Protest," in Halasa, *Woman, Life, Freedom*, 10–23.
8 Ibid.
9 Interview with Ali Ahmadzadeh, November 2023.
10 Ibid.
11 Ibid.
12 Ibid.
13 Ibid.
14 Ibid.
15 Official statement of the exhibition paraphrased from the translation by Parisa Hakim Javadi. Courtesy of Mohammad Parvizi.
16 Dominick LaCapra, *History and Memory after Auschwitz* (Ithaca, New York, and London: Cornell University Press, 1998), 17–23.
17 Gilles Deleuze and Felix Guattari, *A Thousand Plateaus: Capitalism and Schizophrenia*, trans. Brian Massumi (Minneapolis and London: University of Minnesota Press, 2005).
18 Masoudi currently operates her own office in Tehran. Previously, she gained experience working with Richard Meier and Partners in New York City and Shirdel and Associate Architects in Tehran, among other firms.
19 Interview with Mahsa Masoudi, January 2024.
20 Ibid.
21 Ibid.
22 Ibid.
23 Ibid.
24 Ben Sherlock, "Like Tears in Rain: 10 Behind-The-Scenes Facts About Blade Runner," *Screen Rant*, March 18, 2020, https://screenrant.com/blade-runner-behind-scenes-facts-ridley-scott-harrison-ford-sci-fi-movie/#deckard-and-batty-s-final-confrontation-was-originally-a-fight-in-an-old-gym, accessed May 2023.
25 This assertion draws inspiration from the contributors to a significant edited volume exploring the Futurist genre within non-Western contexts. See further Taryne Jade Taylor, Isiah Lavender III, Grace L. Dillon, and Bodhisattva Chattopadhyay, eds., *The Routledge Handbook of CoFuturisms* (New York: Routledge, 2024).
26 Tihana Bertek, "The Authenticity of the Replica: A Post-Human Reading of Blade Runner," *Literary Refractions*, vol. 5, no. 1 (2014): 1–12.
27 Interview with Masoudi.
28 Boris Groys, "On Art Activism," *e-flux*, issue 56 (June 2014), https://www.e-flux.com/journal/56/60343/on-art-activism/, accessed November 2023.
29 Interview with Mohammad Parvizi, January 2024.
30 Ibid.
31 Conversation based on a panel discussion featuring Pouria Jahanshad and Mohammad Parvizi held at Risheh 29 Gallery on Friday, December 29, 2023. I extend my gratitude to Parvizi for supplying a recording of this and other discussions and debates associated with the exhibition *Call Me by My Name*.
32 Nalbandian's first play, from 1966, was titled *A Deep, Big and New Research about Fossils of 25th Genealogy Period, or 20th, or Any Other Period, There is No Difference* (1966).
33 Taken from Erfan Ghiasi's personal website: https://www.erfanghiasi.com/a-deep-research/, accessed December 2023.
34 Frantz Fanon, *Black Skin, White Masks*, trans., Charles Lam Markmann (New York: Pluto Press, 1986), 10; Frantz Fanon, *The Wretched of the Earth*, preface by Jean-Paul Sartre, trans. Constance Farrington (New York: Grove Press, 1963), 93.
35 Tara Sepehri Far, "Fire, Explosions Erupt at Evin Prison in Tehran," Human Rights Watch, October 17, 2022, https://www.hrw.org/news/2022/10/17/fire-explosions-erupt-evin-prison-tehran, accessed November 2023.
36 Interview with Bahar Sabet, January 2024.

Coda

1 *Vice News*, "Inside Iran: What Happened to Iran's Women-led Uprising?" *Vice News*, December 23, 2023, YouTube video, 10:01:20, https://www.youtube.com/watch?v=VAQRCCWsi-s, accessed December 2023.

2 Somayyeh Dibajizadegan, "Jensiyyat dar fazahay-e shahri: Galerihay-e Tehran" [Gender in Iran's Urban Space: The Galleries], *Radio Zamaneh*, January 5, 2024, https://www.radiozamaneh.com/796769, accessed January 2024.

3 Orkideh Behrouzan, *Prozak Diaries: Psychiatry and Generational Memory in Iran* (Stanford: Stanford University Press, 2016), 145.

4 Interview with Shohreh Mehran, February 2024.

5 Ibid.

6 Ibid.

7 Etemad Gallery editorial, *Shohreh Mehran: January–February 13, 2024* (Tehran: Etemad Gallery, 2024), 1.

8 *Nahib* editorial, "Conversation with Shahnaz Zahtab," podcast episode, *New Wave: Oral History of Contemporary Visual Arts*, January 31, 2024, https://castbox.fm/episode/%D8%B4%D9%85%D8%A7%D8%B1%D9%87%E2%80%8C%DB%8C-%D8%A7%D9%88%D9%84%3A-%D8%B4%D9%87%D9%86%D8%A7%D8%B2-%D8%B2%D9%87%D8%AA%D8%A7%D8%A8-%F0%9F%94%B8-id5800515-id669018576?country=us, accessed February 2024.

9 Interview with Faezeh Bakhti, February 2024.

10 Ibid.

11 Ibid.

12 Parisa Hafezi, "Iran's Israel Strike Coincided with Crackdown on Dissent at Home," *Reuters*, April 23, 2024, https://www.reuters.com/world/middle-east/irans-israel-strike-coincided-with-crackdown-dissent-home-activists-say-2024-04-23/, accessed April 2024.

13 *UN News* editorial, "Record Executions, Large Scale Arrests and Detentions: New Iran Human Rights Reports," *UN News*, January 21, 2023, https://news.un.org/en/story/2023/06/1137987, accessed March 2024.

14 Judith Butler, "Imitation and Gender Insubordination," in *Literary Theory: An Anthology*, eds., Julie Rivkin and Michael Ryan (London: Blackwell: 1998), 722-730. Also see, idem, "Against Proper Objects," in *Feminism Meets Queer Theory*, eds., Elizabeth Weed and Naomi Schor (Indianapolis: Indiana University Press, 1997), 1–8; Tirza True Latimer, "Improper Objects: Performing Queer/Feminist Art/History," in *Otherwise: Imagining Queer Feminist Art Histories*, eds., Amelia Jones and Erin Silver (Manchester: Manchester University Press, 2016), 99.

15 Bayat, "Is Iran on the Verge of Another Revolution?"

16 Karimi, *Alternative Iran*, 179–181.

17 Interview with Safaie.

18 Official Instagram account of *Khaneh Cinema* (The House of Cinema) @khnecinema. For further information on the demands of politically active artists for the future, see *Radio Zamaneh* editorial, Parastou Forouhar, and Jinoos Taghizadeh, "Chaleshhay-e Sharayet-e Enghelabi baray-e Jame'eh Honari [The challenges of a revolutionary situation for the art community]."

Select Bibliography

A

Abrahamian, Ervand. "The Guerrilla Movement in Iran, 1963–77." *Iran: A Revolution in Turmoil*, edited by Haleh Afshar. Albany: SUNY Press, 1985, 71–98.

Afary, Janet, and Kevin B. Anderson. "Woman, Life, Freedom: The Origins of the Uprising in Iran." *Dissent Magazine*, December 2, 2022, www.dissentmagazine.org/online_articles/women-life-freedom-iran-uprising-origins/.

— *Sexual Politics in Modern Iran*. Cambridge: Cambridge University Press, 2014.

Ahmed, Leila. *A Quiet Revolution: The Veil's Resurgence, from the Middle East to America*. New Haven: Yale University Press, 2012.

Ahmadi Khorasani, Noushin and *Enkar Magazine* editorial, "Naghsh-e pedar va pedar salari dar badilhay-e nazm-e syasi [The role of fatherhood and patriarchy in the transformations of political order]," *Enkar Magazine*. April 29, 2024, https://enkarmag.com/articles/bf678427-6203-4d29-8c47-4f0d0fb8791f/.

Ahmed, Sara. "Affective Economies." *Social Text*, vol. 22, no. 2 (2004): 117–139.

— *Cultural Politics of Emotion*. Edinburgh: Edinburgh University Press, 2014.

— *Living a Feminist Life*. Durham: Duke University Press, 2017.

Amad, Paula. *Counter-Archive: Film, the Everyday, and Albert Kahn's Archives de la Planète*. New York: Columbia University Press, 2010.

Amirebrahimi, Masserat. "Naghsh-e Farhang Saraha Dar Democrasion Honar Dar Daheh Haftad" [The role of cultural centers in democratization of the arts in the 1990s]. *Herfeh Honarmand*, vol. 82 (2024): 32–39.

Aranke, Sampada. *Death's Futurity: The Visual Life of Black Power*. Durham: Duke University Press, 2023.

Ardavan, Soudabeh. *Yadnegarehhaye Zendan* [Prison drawings]. Halmstad, Sweden: Tydells Tyckeri AB, 2004.

Arendt, Hannah. *The Human Condition*. Chicago: University of Chicago Press, 1958.

Asadollahi, Ali. *Bon bast-e Fereshteh* [Fereshteh cul-de-sac]. Tehran: Manjanigh Press, 2017.

Atashi, Mehraneh et al. *Only the Morning Bird Treasures the Flower Garden*. Los Angeles: RedCat Press in collaboration with CalArt's Downtown Center for Contemporary Art, 2019.

Auslander, Philip. "The Performativity of Performance Documentation." *Perform, Repeat, Record: Live Art in History*, edited by Amelia Jones and Adrian Heathfield. Bristol, UK: Intellect Press, 2008, 47–58.

Azizi, Arash. *What Iranians Want: Women, Life, Freedom*. London: Oneworld Publications, 2024.

B

Babaie, Susan, and Talinn Grigor, editors. *Persian Kingship and Architecture Strategies of Power in Iran from the Achaemenids to the Pahlavis*. London: I. B. Tauris, 2015.

Bajoghli, Narges. *Iran Reframed: Anxieties of Power in the Islamic Republic*. Stanford: Stanford University Press, 2019.

Bamyeh, Mohammed A. *Anarchy as Order: The History and Future of Civic Humanity*. London: Rowman & Littlefield, 2009.

Baraheni, Reza. *Khatab beh parvaneh-ha va chera digar man shae'r-e Nmiyie nistam* [To butterflies and why I am no longer following Nima's style of poetry]. Tehran: Markaz Press, 1995.

Baraitser, Lisa. *Enduring Time*. London: Bloomsbury Academic, 2017.

Bayat, Asef. *Street Politics: Poor People's Movement in Iran*. New York: Columbia University Press, 1999.

— "Is Iran on the Verge of Another Revolution?" *The Journal of Democracy*, March 1, 2023, www.journalofdemocracy.org/is-iran-on-the-verge-of-another-revolution/.

Behrouzan, Orkideh. *Prozak Diaries: Psychiatry and Generational Memory in Iran*. Stanford: Stanford University Press, 2016.

Benjamin, Walter. "Theories of German Fascism: On the Collection of Essays War and the Warrior." *New German Critique*, no. 17 (1979): 120–128.

Bertek, Tihana. "The Authenticity of the Replica: A Post-Human Reading of Blade Runner." *Literary Refractions*, vol. 5, no. 1 (2014): 1–12.

Bracke, Sarah. "Conjugating the Modern/ Religious, Conceptualizing Female Religious Agency: Contours of a Post-secular Conjuncture." *Theory, Culture & Society*, vol. 25, no. 6 (2008): 51–67.

Bradaran, Monireh. *Haghighat-e Sadeh: Khaterati Az Zendanhay-e Zanan-e Jomhuri-e Eslami-e Iran* [A simple truth: memories from the political prisons of the Islamic Republic]. Köln, Germany: Forough Publishing, 2012.

Braidotti, Rosi. "In Spite of the Times: The Postsecular Turn in Feminism." *Theory, Culture & Society*, vol. 25, no. 6 (2008): 1–24.

Bryson, Scott et al., editors. *Beyond Recognition: Representation, Power, and Culture*. Berkeley: University of California Press, 1992.

Butler, Judith. "Imitation and Gender Insubordination." *Literary Theory: An Anthology*, edited by Julie Rivkin and Michael Ryan. London: Blackwell: 1998, 722-730.

— "Bodies in Alliance and the Politics of the Street." *Sensible Politics: The Visual Culture of Nongovernmental Activism*, edited by Meg McLagan and Yates McKee. New York: Zone Books, 2012, 117–137.

C

Chrisafis, Angelique. "'The Little Girl in Persepolis Has Grown Up': Marjane Satrapi on Life After Her Hit Graphic Novel—and Her Radical New Work." *The Guardian*, March 16, 2024, www.theguardian.com/books/2024/mar/16/marjane-satrapi-interview-persepolis-woman-life-freedom.

Coleman, Rebecca. "Social Media and the Materialization of the Affective Present." *Affect and Social Media: Emotions, Mediation, Anxiety, and Contagion*, edited by Tony D. Sampson et al. London: Rowman & Littlefield International, 2018, 67–75.

Cortés, Macarena Gómez. *The Extractive Zone: Social Ecologies and Decolonial Perspectives*. Durham: Duke University Press, 2017.

Crenshaw, Kimberlé. "Whose Story Is It Anyway? Feminist and Antiracist Appropriations of AnitaHill." *Racing Justice, En-gendering Power: Essays on Anita Hill, Clarence Thomas, and the Construction of Social Reality*, edited by Toni Morrison. New York: Pantheon, 1992, 402–440.

Çağlayan, Handan. *Women in the Kurdish Movement: Mothers, Comrades, Goddesses*. Translated by Simten Coşar. London: Palgrave McMillan, 2019.

Chenoweth, Erica. *Civil Resistance: What Everyone Needs to Know*. Oxford: Oxford University Press, 2021.

D

Daftari, Fereshteh. *Persia Reframed: Iranian Visions of Modern and Contemporary Art*. London: I. B. Tauris, 2019.

De Certeau, Michel. *The Practice of Everyday Life*. Translated by Steven Rendall. Berkeley: University of California Press, 1984.

Deleuze, Gilles, and Felix Guattari. *A Thousand Plateaus: Capitalism and Schizophrenia*. Trans and foreword by Brian Massumi. Minneapolis: University of Minnesota Press, 2005.

Dibazar, Pedram. *Urban and Visual Culture in Contemporary Iran: Nonvisibility and the Politics of Everyday Presence*. London: Bloomsbury Press, 2020.

E

El-Desouky, Ayman. *The Intellectual and the People in Egyptian Literature and Culture: Amāra and the 2011 Revolution*. London: Palgrave Macmillan, 2014.

F

Filiu, Jean-Pierre. *Apocalypse in Islam*. Translated by M. B. De Bevoise. Berkeley: University of California Press, 2011.

Forouhar, Parastou. "The Intertwining of Everyday Life and Revolution: Fall 1401 Travel Report." *Asoo Journal*, January 21, 2023, www.aasoo.org/fa/articles/4184.

Fouladi Nasab, Kaveh, editor. *Khiaban-e Vali Asr: Revayathay-e Gheyr-e Dastani* [The Vali Asr Street: Nonfiction stories from Tehran]. Tehran: Sales Press, 2022.

G

Genocchio, Benjamin. "Revolution's Long Shadow Over the Tehran Art Scene." *The New York Times*, March 30, 2011, www.nytimes.com/2011/03/31/world/middleeast/31iht-m31-iran-art.html.

Gerschultz, Jessica. "Mutable Form and Materiality: Toward a Critical History of New Tapestry Networks." *ArtMargines*, vol. 5, no. 1 (2016): 3–29

Ghabaian Etehadieh, Anahita. *Breathing Space: Iranian Women Photographers*. London: Thames and Hudson, 2024.

Ghaffarian, Matin. "Chera ghafelgir shodim?" [Why are we surprised?]. *Ettemad*, Decmber 28, 2022, www.magiran.com/article/4371602.

Gutkin, Len. "The Blasphemer Is Taravat Talepasand's Art Too Radical for Today's Campus?" *The Chronicle of Higher Education*, February 8 2023, www.chronicle.com/article/the-blasphemer.

H

Halasa, Malu. *Woman, Life, Freedom: Voices and Art from the Women's Protests in Iran*. London: Saqi Press, 2023.

Hatuka, Tali. *The Design of Protest: Choreographing Political Demonstrations in Public Space*. Austin: University of Texas Press, 2018.

Hedayat, Bahareh. "'Revolution Is Inevitable': Bahareh Hedayat's Letter from Evin Prison in Tehran, Iran." *Jadaliyya*, January 4 2023, www.jadaliyya.com/Details/44720.

Horne, Victoria, and Amy Tobin. "An Unfinished Revolution in Art Historiography, or How to Write a Feminist Art History." *Feminist Art History Now, Radical Critique of Theory and Practice*, edited by Victoria Horne and Amy Tobin. London: I. B. Tauris, 2017, 31–40.

Hutcheon, Linda. *A Theory of Adaptation*. New York and London: Routledge, 2006.

J

Jones, Amelia. "1970/2007: The Return of Feminist Art." *X-TRA*, vol. 10, no. 4 (Summer 2008), www.x-traonline.org/article/19702007-the-return-of-feminist-art#refmark-26.

K

Kabakov, Ilya. *On Art*, edited and introduced by Matthew Jesse Jackson, translated by Antonina W. Bouis et al. Berkeley: University of Chicago Press, 2018.

Karimi, Pamela. "Appropriation in Contemporary Iranian Art." *Treasures of Modern and Contemporary Art from the Farjam Collection*, edited by by Venetia Porter, Linda Komaroff, Nada Shabout, and Sarah Rogers. New Haven: Yale University Press, 2024, 107–113.

— "Art of Protest in Five Acts." *Roundtable on the "Woman, Life, Freedom" Revolution in Iran. Iranian Studies*, vol. 56, no. 3 (July 2023): 585–595.

— "The Many Shades of Iran's Protest Art." *Hyperallergic*, October 11, 2022, hyperallergic.com/768539/the-many-shades-of-iran-protest-art/.

— *Alternative Iran: Contemporary Art and Critical Spatial Practice*. Stanford: Stanford University Press, 2022.

Keshavarzian, Arang. *Bazaar and State in Iran: The Politics of the Tehran Marketplace*. Cambridge: Cambridge University Press, 2007.

Khosravi, Shahram. *Precarious Lives: Waiting and Hope in Iran*. Philadelphia: University of Pennsylvania Press, 2017.

Komaroff, Linda. "A Conversation with Shirin Neshat and Shoja Azari." *Treasures of Modern and Contemporary Art from the Farjam Collection*, edited by Venetia Porter, Linda Komaroff, Nada Shabout, and Sarah Rogers. New Haven: Yale University Press, 2024, 467-471.

Kochhar-Lindgren, Kanta, editor. *The Exquisite Corpse: Chance and Collaboration in Surrealism's Parlor Game*. Lincoln: University of Nebraska Press, 2009.

L

LaCapra, Dominick. *History and Memory after Auschwitz*. Ithaca: Cornell University Press, 1998.

Langford, Michelle. *Allegory in Iranian Cinema: The Aesthetics of Poetry and Resistance*. London: Bloomsbury Academic, 2019.

Lasn, Kalle. *Culture Jam: The Uncooling of America*. New York: Quill/HarperCollins Publishers, 1999.

Latimer, Tirza True. "Improper Objects: Performing Queer/Feminist Art/History." *Otherwise: Imagining Queer Feminist Art Histories*, edited by Amelia Jones and Erin Silver. Manchester: Manchester University Press, 2016.

Lépinard, Éléonore. *Feminists Trouble: Intersectional Politics in Post Secular Times*. Oxford: Oxford Academic, 2021.

Lippard, Lucy. "Trojan Horses: Activist Art and Power." *Art After Modernism*, edited by Brian Wallis. New York: The New Museum, 1984.

Littell, Jonathan. *Carnets de Homs*. Paris: Gallimard, 2012.

Lotfalian, Mazyar. *What People Do with Images: Aesthetics, Politics and the Production of Iranian Visual Culture in Transnational Circuits*. London: Sean Kingston Publishing, 2022.

Lütticken, Sven. "An Arena in Which to Reenact." *Life, Once More: Forms of Reenactment in Contemporary Art*, exhibition catalog. Witte de With, 2005, 17–60.

M

Mahmood, Saba. *Politics of Piety: The Islamic Revival and the Feminist Subject*. Princeton: Princeton University Press, 2005.

Malek, Amy. "On Unity & Fragmentation in the Iranian Diaspora." *Cultural Anthropology*, June 29, 2023, culanth.org/fieldsights/on-unity-fragmentation-in-the-iranian-diaspora.

McDonough, Tom, editor. *Guy Debord and the Situationist International: Texts and Documents*. London: October Press, 2004.

McLagan, Meg, and Yates McKee, editors. *Sensible Politics: The Visual Culture of Nongovernmental Activism*. New York: Zone Books, 2012.

Meftahi, Ida. *Gender and Dance in Iran: Bio Politics on Stage*. London and New York: Routledge, 2017.

Mirhosseini, Ziba. *Islam and Gender: The Religious Debate in Contemporary Iran*. Princeton: Princeton University Press, 1999.

Moghadam, Valentine. "Islamic Feminism and its Discontents: Towards Resolution of the Debate." *Signs: Journal of Women in Culture and Society*, vol. 27, no. 4 (2002): 1135–1171.

Mojab, Shahrzad, "Theorizing the Politics of 'Islamic Feminism,'" *Feminist Review* vol. 69, no. 1 (2001): 124–146.

Mottahedeh, Negar. *Hashtag Solidarity and the Transformation of Online Life*. Stanford: Stanford University Press, 2015.

— *Whisper Tapes: Kate Millett in Iran*. Stanford: Stanford University Press, 2019.

Mueller, Ellen. *Walking as Artistic Practice*. Albany: SUNY Press, 2023.

Mulvey, Laura. "Visual Pleasure and Narrative Cinema." *Screen*, vol. 16, no. 3 (1975): 6–18.

N

Nafisi, Azar. "On Iranian Women and Atwood's *Republic of Gilead*." *Iran Wire*, February 21, 2023, https://iranwire.com/en/society/114012-interview-iranian-women-and-atwoods-republic-of-gilead/.

Najmabadi, Afsaneh. *The Story of the Daughters of Quchan*. Syracuse: Syracuse University Press, 1998.

Narayan, Uma. "Essence of Culture and a Sense of History: A Feminist Critique of Cultural Essentialism." *Decentering the Center: Philosophy for a Multicultural, Postcolonial, and Feminist World*, edited by Sandra Harding and Uma Narayan. Bloomington: Indiana University Press, 2000, 80–100.

Nelson, Robert. "Appropriation." *Critical Terms in Art History*, edited by Robert S. Nelson and Richard Shiff. Chicago: University of Chicago Press, 1996, 160–173.

O

Oliver, Kelly. "Julia Kristeva's Feminist Revolutions." *Hypatia*, vol. 8, no. 3 (1993): 94–114.

Owens, Craig. *Beyond Recognition: Representation, Power, and Culture*. Edited by Scott Bryson et al. Berkeley: University of California Press, 1992.

P

Pollock, Griselda. "Feminism and Language." *Blackwell Companion to Art History*, edited by Elena Marina Buszeck and Hellena Robinson. Hoboken, NJ: John Wiley and Sons, 2019, 261–281.

— *Generations and Geographies in the Visual Arts: Feminism Readings*. London: Routledge, 1996.

R

Mroué, Rabih. *Image(s), mon amour: Fabrications*. CA2M, 2013.

Rancière, Jacques. *Dissensus: On Politics and Aesthetics*. Translated by Steven Corcoran. London: Continuum, 2010.

Robson, Hilary. "Witness It: Activism, Art, and the Feminist Performative Subject." *A Companion to Feminist Art*, edited by Hilary Robinson and Maria Elena Buszek. Hoboken, NJ: John Wiley & Sons, Inc, 2019, 245–260.

Rooney, Caroline. "Sufi Springs: Air on an Oud String." *CounterText*, vol. 1, no. 1 (2015): 52–54.

Ross, Kristin. *Communal Luxury: The Political Imaginary of the Paris Commune*. New York: Verso, 2015.

Roxburgh, David J. *The Persian Album, 1400–1600: From Dispersal to Collection*. New Haven: Yale University Press, 2005.

S

Sanders, Julie. *Adaptation and Appropriation: A New Critical Idiom*. Routledge, 2006.

Schorr, Collier. "Wrestlers Love America." *ART21*, art21.org/read/collier-schorr-wrestlers-love-america/.

Shahrokni, Nazanin. *Women in Place: The Politics of Gender Segregation in Iran*. Berkeley: University of California Press, 2019.

Shams, Fatemeh. *A Revolution in Rhyme: Poetic Co-option under the Islamic Republic*. Oxford: Oxford University Press, 2021.

— and Nahid Siamdoust. "Poetry & Protest with Fatemeh Shams." *Woman, Life, Freedom: All in On Iran*, March 3, 2023, podcasts.la.utexas.edu/woman-life-freedom-podcast/podcast/poetry-protest-with-fatemeh-shams/.

— *Soundtrack of the Revolution: The Politics of Music in Iran*. Stanford: Stanford University Press, 2017.

Siamdoust, Nahid. "The Birth of a University Music Genre in Iran's Woman, Life, Freedom Uprising." *International Journal of Middle East Studies*, vol. 55, no. 4 (2024): 1–9.

Singh, Jakeet. "Religious Agency and the Limits of Intersectionality." *Hypatia*, vol. 30, no. 4 (2015): 657–674.

Snowden, Peter. *The People is Not an Image*. New York: Zone Books, 2020.

Sotoudeh, Nasrin. *Women, Life, Freedom: Our Fight for Human Rights and Equality in Iran*. Translated by Parisa Saranj. Ithaca and London: Cornell University Press, 2023.

T

Tagg, John. *The Burden of Representation: On Photographies and Histories*. London: Palgrave McMillan, 1988.

Tajbakhsh, Kian. *Creating Local Democracy in Iran: State Building and the Politics of Decentralization*. Cambridge: Cambridge University Press, 2022.

Tajik, Rudabeh, and Farzan Khorramdin. "The Chronology of the Revolution of 2022: 13 September–28 November." *Journal of Thought and Literature*, no. 1–2 (November–December 2022): 1–28.

Taylor, Ronald, et al. "Theodor Adorno: Reconciliation under Duress (Adorno on Lukács)." *Aesthetics and Politics*. New Left Review Books, 1977, 151–176.

Taylor, Taryne Jade, et al., editors. *The Routledge Handbook of CoFuturisms*. London and New York: Routledge, 2024.

Torab, Azam. *Performing Islam: Gender and Ritual in Iran*. Leiden: Brill, 2006.

V

Védie, Léa. "Hating Men Will Free you? Valerie Solanas in Paris or the Discursive Politics of Misandry." *European Journal of Women's Studies*, vol. 28, no. 3 (2021): 305–319.

Velie, Elaine. "Iran Massacre Prompts Poignant Protest at LACMA." *Hyperallergic*, November 10, 2022, https://hyperallergic.com/779080/iran-massacre-prompts-poignant-protest-at-lacma/.

Z

Zandi, Maryam. *Hokumat-e 58* [The Government of the 1980s]. Tehran: Nazar Press, 2019.

Zeydabadi-Nejad, Saeed. *The Politics of Iranian Cinema: Film and Society in the Islamic Republic*. London and New York: Routledge, 2010.

Zeidan, Adam. "Morality Police Law Enforcement Body in Iran." *The Encyclopedia Britannica*, www.britannica.com/topic/morality-police.

Index

Page numbers in **bold** refer to illustrations